SIBERIA

SIBERIA

A HISTORY OF THE PEOPLE

JANET M. HARTLEY

YALE UNIVERSITY PRESS
NEW HAVEN AND LONDON

For information about this and other Yale University Press publications, please contact:

U.S. Office: sales.press@yale.edu   www.yalebooks.com
Europe Office: sales@yaleup.co.uk   www.yalebooks.co.uk

Typeset in Arno Pro by IDSUK (DataConnection) Ltd
Printed in Great Britain by TJ International Ltd, Padstow, Cornwall.

Library of Congress Cataloging-in-Publication Data
Hartley, Janet M.
    Siberia:a history of the people/Janet M. Hartley.
    pages cm
    Includes bibliographical references and index.
    ISBN 978-0-300-16794-8 (hardback)
1. Siberia (Russia)—History. 2. Siberia (Russia)—Social life and customs. 3. Siberia
(Russia)—Social conditions. 4. Siberia (Russia)—Biography. I. Title.
    DK761.H37 2014
    957—dc23

                                                                        2014007175

A catalogue record for this book is available from the British Library.

10 9 8 7 6 5 4 3 2 1

For my mother, Lilian Hartley

Contents

Illustrations and Maps

Maps

Editorial Note

Transliteration of Russian in the footnotes and the bibliography is according to the Library of Congress system. The transliteration has been amended in the main text: 'soft signs' have been omitted; surnames ending in 'ii' and 'yi' have been standardised to 'y'.

Russian names – forenames, patronymics and surnames – have been given in this system (e.g. Aleksandr, Nikolai Ivanovich, Ekaterina Mikhailovna, Mikhail Speransky), except in the case of tsars where the anglicised form of the name is more familiar (e.g. Peter I, Catherine II, Alexander II).

Footnotes to archives in Russia use Russian descriptors: fond (abbreviated to f.), opis' (op.) delo (d.), listy (l. or ll.).

Distances are given in both miles and kilometres. Historical terms for Russian weights and measures are explained in the text.

From January 1700 to February 1918, Russia used the Julian calendar, which was behind the Gregorian calendar used in the West by 11 days in the eighteenth century, 12 days in the nineteenth century and 13 days in the twentieth century up to 1918. Dates in the text before February 1918 are given according to the Julian calendar (e.g. February and October Revolutions in 1917, not March and November Revolutions). Dates after 1918 follow the Gregorian calendar.

Timeline

Rulers of Russia
Ivan IV (1547–84)
Fedor I (1584–98)
Boris Godunov (1598–1605)
Time of Troubles (1605–12)
Michael (1613–45)
Aleksei Mikhailovich (1645–76)
Fedor II (1676–82)
Sophia (regent) (1682–9)
Ivan V (ruled with Peter I) (1682–96)
Peter I (1682–1725)
Catherine I (1725–7)
Peter II (1727–30)
Anna (1730–40)
Ivan VI (1740–1)
Elizabeth (1741–61)
Peter III (1761–2)
Catherine II (1762–96)
Paul I (1796–1801)
Alexander I (1801–25)
Nicholas I (1825–55)
Alexander II (1855–81)
Alexander III (1881–94)
Nicholas II (1894–1917)

Leaders of the Soviet Union
Vladimir Lenin (1922–4)
Joseph Stalin (1924–53)
Georgii Malenkov (1953–5)
Nikita Khrushchev (1955–64)
Leonid Brezhnev (1964–82)
Iurii Andropov (1982–4)
Konstantin Chernenko (1984–5)
Mikhail Gorbachev (1985–91)

Presidents of Russia
Boris Yeltsin (1991–9)
Vladimir Putin (1999–2008)
Dmitrii Medvedev (2008–12)
Vladimir Putin (2012–)

Introduction

Why write a history of Siberia?

O NE REASON is to address popular preconceptions about Siberia. The first of these is the belief that Siberia is all ice and snow and that the temperature never rises above freezing. There is indeed a lot of ice and snow in the winter, and the village of Oimiako (in the far north-east) has the honour of being officially the coldest permanently inhabited settlement on earth, with an officially recorded temperature of minus 71 degrees Celsius. The harsh climate has undoubtedly had a significant impact on Siberian development: on patterns of settlement; on population density; on lifestyle; on agriculture and other occupations; on communications. Summers can be hot in southern Siberia, however, and the plains are fertile. Peasants migrated voluntarily to Siberia from European Russia and Ukraine from the seventeenth to the twentieth century to improve their quality of life by acquiring larger and more productive farms. Siberian peasants were thought to live better than their counterparts in European Russia. Indeed, it was the perceived wealth of Siberian peasants that led them to be particularly targeted as kulaks in the 1930s.

A second popular perception is that Siberia is inhabited by bears, wolves and tigers. That is true, although I have only seen stuffed animals in museums in Siberian cities, and there are more concerns nowadays – both in Siberia and in Western countries – about the sharp decline in the number of Siberian tigers than about their threat to humans and to livestock. It was in fact the enormous wealth that could be acquired by the sale of pelts, and in particular sable and fox fur, that attracted hunters and Cossacks to Siberia in the first place, and persuaded Tsar Ivan IV to claim ownership of these lands. That is a crucial part of the Siberian story.

A third perception, based very much on reality, is that Siberia is a vast empty land. Siberia is certainly vast: it comprises 77 per cent of the Russian state's territory and encompasses eight time zones. I have defined Siberia in this book in the broadest sense, including all the lands stretching from the Ural mountains to the Pacific Ocean. The size of Siberia and its low population density posed particular challenges in establishing communications and in governing over vast distances, and gave rise to concerns about security on the southern borders. There has always been a problem about the inaccessibility of Siberia's natural resources – from gold mines in the eighteenth century to the oil and gas reserves today – and that has been only partly relieved by the coming of railways and aeroplanes. Settlers were always, however, lured to Siberia. The population grew from some 270,000 indigenous people and settlers at the end of the seventeenth century to over a million by 1795 and over 2 million by 1830. The migration to Siberia in the late nineteenth and early twentieth centuries, when about 3 million peasants crossed the Urals, paralleled the mass migration from Europe to the United States in the same period. The population reached over 10 million by 1914. Further mass migration to new industrial bases and cities in the Soviet period saw the population double to over 20 million by the 1960s. Today the population of Siberia is some 30 million people.[1]

A further perception of Siberia is that it is a place of terror and exile, where Dostoevsky and other political figures were tormented and millions perished in the Gulag system. This was true from the very beginning of the Russian penetration of Siberia, and I discuss the exile system in the tsarist period and the Gulags in the twentieth century. The tsarist exile system helped to shape the distinctiveness of the social composition of Siberia, not least because almost all the exiles remained in the area. Millions of prisoners passed through Siberia to the Soviet prison camps, and some of those who survived remained in Siberian cities after their release. But not all Russian and Soviet prisons were, or are, in Siberia. When the Pussy Rioters were sent to prison in 2012 the headlines in some sections of the British press were 'Pussy Rioters Sent to Siberia', although in fact they were all sent to prisons in European Russia. Furthermore, some of the exiles in the tsarist period made a significant contribution to the cultural and economic development of Siberia.

I do not, however, want simply to address popular preconceptions; rather, I wish to offer a rather different type of history from the ones currently available.[2] When I was writing my last book on the impact of war on state and society in Russia (*Russia 1762–1825: Military Power, the State and the People*, 2008), I looked at garrison records in the Military Historical Archive and in the Archive of Ancient Acts, both in Moscow. The richest records I found were those of the garrison in Gizhiga, a desolate spot in the far northeast of Siberia on the northern shores of the Sea of Okhotsk. I looked at the establishment and development of the garrison in the mid-eighteenth century, the numbers of soldiers who were posted there, the cost of maintaining the garrison, and the difficulties of communication between the garrison and the military and civil administration in eastern Siberia. As a result, I was able to see the more human side of the garrison – how the soldiers lived and what happened, for instance, when the fishing suddenly deteriorated. I was also able to acquire some sense of the relations between the soldiers and the local population. There was often violent conflict but at the same time the garrison could intervene when there were disputes between local tribes. Moreover, soldiers hired local people to work for them and, not surprisingly, formed relationships with local women.[3]

It was the human side of life in Gizhiga that interested me most and made me curious about how other settlers fared in Siberia, from the first formal Russian presence in the late sixteenth century to the present. I have concentrated in this book on 'how people lived'. That covers different social groups in different periods. I have looked at how peasants lived – what crops they grew, what they ate, how they built their houses – and at urban life from the seventeenth to the twentieth century, as well as at the life of soldiers in a remote garrison. I have tried to understand the experiences of explorers, missionaries, priests, traders, officials, teachers, exiles and convicts in tsarist Russia. I have also looked in the twentieth century at what it was like to live in Omsk during the Civil War in 1918–21, at the experience of Siberian villagers during forced collectivisation in the 1930s, at living conditions in new Siberian cities in the 1950s and 1960s, and at life in Siberia after the collapse of the Soviet Union.

My approach has been broadly chronological, starting with the penetration of Siberia at the end of the sixteenth century (in Chapter 1). In the following chapter I look at the lands and the indigenous peoples who were conquered and discuss the difficulties of communication over such vast distances and inhospitable lands. Chapters 3 and 4 cover Siberia in the seven-teenth century: I concentrate in particular on who came to Siberia – Cossacks, soldiers, hunters, traders, officials, peasant settlers and exiles – and on the relationship between the new inhabitants and non-Russians in Siberia, including traders from Central Asia and indigenous peoples. Chapters 5 to 10 look at the way Siberia developed over the eighteenth and first three quarters of the nineteenth century. I give a picture of life in Siberian villages, towns and garrisons, and of the contact between people and the state, and of the experience of exiles and convicts in Siberia. I also try to understand what people believed in spiritually, and the relationship between Christianity, paganism and magic. The frontiers of Siberia expanded in the eighteenth and nineteenth centuries (Chapter 11): I look at the men who made this possible and the consequences of this expansion. Siberia lagged behind European Russia economically in the eighteenth and early nineteenth centuries but this changed dramatically in the late nineteenth century with the construction of the Trans-Siberian railway which transformed economic, social and intellec-tual life (Chapter 12). Siberia was then shattered by the experiences of the First World War, the Revolutions and the Civil War (Chapter 13) and the trauma of Stalin's policies (Chapter 14). The Soviet society in Siberia that emerged from this period is discussed in Chapter 15. In the last chapter I look at the issues and opportunities for people in Siberia today.

In this study of 'how people lived' I have inevitably been interested in the ways in which Siberia was different from European Russia. Siberia looks in many ways like European Russia: Siberian forts looked like northern Russian forts in the seventeenth century; peasant huts were constructed and villages laid out in much the same way as in European Russia; eighteenth- and nineteenth-century urban architecture was similar throughout the country; Siberian Soviet towns did not look very different from European Russian towns. The population of Siberia became predominantly Russian, and is even more so today (some 84 per cent) than in the seventeenth and eighteenth centuries. The main language of Siberia is Russian – even if some present-day nationalists are trying to construct a 'Siberian' language from old north Russian dialects. The majority of the population of Siberia identify themselves – now as in the past – as Russians and as Orthodox Christians. Culture and social habits spread from European Russia to Siberia. The schools, and then the universities, in Siberia were modelled on those of European Russia in the eighteenth and nineteenth centuries. The 'Sovietisation' of cultural and social life took place in Siberia in much the same way as in European Russia. Russian, and then Soviet, law applied in Siberia as well as in European Russia. The central government was in Moscow or St Petersburg in the imperial and Soviet period and in the present day.

Nevertheless, Siberia is different, and in many ways special, and this is what I hope to demonstrate in this book.

First, I look at the people who came from Russia/Ukraine to Siberia and settled there. The first men to open up Siberia to settlement were independent hunters and freebooting Cossacks. They were followed by peasant settlers and by dissident religious communities who sought a better life and somewhere to practise their beliefs freely. Many of Siberia's settlers were 'involuntary', that is, convicts and political exiles. This to me is one of the key features of Siberia – the mixture of the free and the unfree elements in its population – and is a constant from the seventeenth to the twentieth century. The settlers were always predominantly male, not only in the seventeenth century but also in the Soviet period and this posed particular problems for the gender balance in Siberia. In addition, there were few nobles and almost no serfdom in Siberia. This had an impact on both peasant and urban life. Did this also make Siberia freer than European Russia, despite also being seen as a place of punishment? It is a difficult question to answer but one that I examine in different environments and at different times in this book. I certainly think that people in Siberia *believed* that they were freer, whether they were Cossack adventurers in the seventeenth century, peasants who had escaped across the Ural mountains in the eighteenth or the nineteenth century, or scientists in the special academic city set up in Novosibirsk in the 1950s.

Second, I explore the role played by the indigenous peoples of Siberia and by Siberia's Asiatic neighbours in shaping Siberia, and their contact with settlers. Siberia was not, of course, empty when the Cossacks arrived. The relationship between settlers and indigenous people can be characterised as one of conflict and coexistence. That included military conflict, violence between indigenous people and settlers in villages and towns, disputes over land, and a continuing Russian fear of Asiatic migration into Siberia. There was also, however, an important trade with Central Asia and the East from the seventeenth century onwards, and some influence on the part of indigenous peoples on lifestyle and belief. In addition, social intercourse and marriages took place between Russians and non-Russians. Much of this contact was unwelcome and painful for indigenous peoples: the seizure of their land by Russian peasants; the disruption to their way of life through 'progress' in the form of the construction of roads and railways; the cost to the environment of the exploitation of the natural resources on their land; forced conversion to Orthodoxy; the imposition of Russian or Western ideologies, from Russian laws in tsarist Russia to forced collectivisation in the Soviet period. Although this book is primarily a study of what Russians and other colonists did in Siberia and how they lived, the story of Siberia is also the story of their contacts with the indigenous peoples.

Third, the vastness of Siberia posed special problems of administration. This is not a study of the relationship between centre and periphery, or the extent to which Siberia can be characterised as an internal 'colony' within the Russian/Soviet state. That would require a separate, and different, book. The central government in St Petersburg and Moscow did, however, develop policies that had a significant impact on the development of Siberia and on the lives of the people who lived there, and these are discussed in the book.

The Russian government certainly tried to control settlement, exile, administration, trade and economic development. It was not an easy task, and that was true from the seventeenth century to the second half of the nineteenth century, because Siberia was undergoverned and, indeed, often seemed ungovernable. It was less true once communications improved from the late nineteenth century with the construction of the Trans-Siberian railway. Siberia was one of the main centres of resistance to Bolshevik rule and then to forced collectivisation. The regionalist and separatist movements in Siberia in the late nineteenth century, and today, assert the difference of Siberia, and of Siberians. These movements were driven by a resentment of Moscow/St Petersburg, by a conviction that the central government exploited and then neglected Siberia, and a sense that Siberians were different, perhaps purer, than their fellow subjects and citizens in European Russia.

Fourth, Siberia is special in the richness – actual, potential and sometimes imagined – of its lands. It was the richness of the fur trade that attracted hunters and Cossacks in the sixteenth century, the abundance of its land that attracted peasants from European Russia to Siberia from the eighteenth to the early twentieth century, and the wealth of its oil and gas resources that led to the creation of mass cities in the twentieth century and that underpins

Russia's economy today. Siberia was also the place of unfulfilled dreams of great riches – the prospect of the riches that would accrue from opening up the Amur river region in the second half of the nineteenth century or the Trans-Siberian railway in the nineteenth century through to the BAM (Baikal-Amur Mainline) railway in the twentieth century. Such hopes were shared by adventurers and hunters in the seventeenth century and by the young, often idealistic, men and women who sought adventure and a new and better life in the remotest parts of the Soviet Union in the 1950s and 1960s. Resources and the overexploitation of resources, hopes fulfilled and hopes dashed, are also part of the Siberian story.

Finally, Siberia is a region of extremes, and in that respect popular perceptions of Siberia are quite correct. This is not, however, merely a question of the vast extent of the lands, extreme temperatures, wild animals and exceptional resources. It is also about the human actions that have shaped Siberian development. The opening up of Siberia in the seventeenth century and the expeditions of the eighteenth and nineteenth centuries were extraordinary feats of courage and endurance, but at the same time they were violent and traumatic, both for the participants and for the indigenous people with whom they came into contact. There are times in its history when Siberia has been at the forefront of economic development and has offered settlers new lives in a new world: in the seventeenth and eighteenth centuries, Siberia offered serfs a less restricted way of life; in the late nineteenth and early twentieth centuries, it was the land of economic opportunity for peasants and industrialists; the exploitation of new resources in the Soviet period put Siberia at the forefront of the creation of a new and exciting industrial and scientific powerhouse east of the Urals; and there are prospects today of opening up Siberia as a gateway to the markets of the Pacific and the Far East.

Siberia has also been a place of extremes in terms of human suffering. This was true for indigenous peoples and settlers who were the victims of the arbitrary actions of soldiers and state officials in the tsarist period and of Soviet attacks on their way of life in the 1930s. It was even more the case for millions of exiles and convicts from the seventeenth to the twentieth century who were dispatched to Siberia. The region was the scene of some of the worst atrocities of the Civil War between Reds and Whites after the Bolshevik Revolution.

The end of the Soviet regime has brought more economic and social disruption to Siberia than to almost any other region in the former USSR.

The cruelty that features so much in Siberian history fascinates and repels at the same time – and makes it all the more important that its story should be told.

* * *

There is a rich literature on Siberia, from early travel accounts through to very detailed archival studies of local history in the Soviet and post-Soviet periods. My account of Siberia has benefited in particular from the publication in recent years of a considerable number of memoirs and collections of correspondence of those who lived through traumatic times in Siberia in the twentieth century. It has been further enriched by having archival sources made available to me and by the people I have met in Siberia.

I have worked in archives in Moscow, Irkutsk, Tomsk, Krasnoiarsk, Omsk and Khabarovsk, and I should like to thank the archivists for their friendly and helpful advice. In Moscow, I used the records of the Siberian Office (*Sibirskii prikaz*) in the Archive of Ancient Acts, and the records of the garrison at Gizhiga held at that archive and in the Military-Historical Archive. I consulted records relating to exiles in the regional archive in Irkutsk, read the records of the Priamur branch of the Imperial Geographical Society in Khabarovsk, and used very revealing clerical records from Krasoniarsk and Tobolsk in the regional archive in Krasnoiarsk. Two very successful visits to the Tomsk regional archive gave me access to a wide range of material on 'the way people lived' in Siberia covering the eighteenth, nineteenth and early twentieth centuries. In the Omsk regional archive, I consulted documents relating to the Omsk Asiatic School,[4] but also found useful material on religious sects and various aspects of administration in the nineteenth century.

I have been helped in my archive work and made very welcome by my academic friends in Russia. In particular, I should like to thank Kirill Anisimov in Krasnoiarsk, Nikolai Serebrennikov in Tomsk, Elena Dobrynina in Irkutsk, Elena Vasileva and Tatiana Saburova in Omsk, and Olga Strelova and Marina Romanova in Khabarovsk for helping to make my visits to their cities both productive and enjoyable. Sergei Iakovlev, at the Higher School of Economics in Moscow, generously shared his childhood reminiscences of Siberia with me, and showed great interest in my work. I should also like to thank Professor Erika Monahan Downs for making her thesis on seventeenth-century trade available to me. My many friends and colleagues at the London School of Economics and Political Science have put up with me chattering about Siberia for the last six years or so, and I should like in particular to thank Howard Davies, the Director of the LSE, for his support and encouragement for my academic work during my Pro-Directorship. Professor Isabel de Madariaga read the draft text with her usual thoroughness and made many valuable and thoughtful suggestions for improvement. My husband, Will Ryan, read the final version and bravely ventured some more criticisms. Finally, I should like to thank all the 'Sibiriaks' whom I have met, in Siberia and outside Siberia, and who have talked to me about their life there, their analysis of Siberia's problems and potential, and their hopes for its future.

CHAPTER ONE

Cossacks and Conquest

On the 23rd of October all the Russian troops went out from the strong-
hold to battle, all proclaiming: 'God is with us.' And again they added:
'O God, help us Your servants.' They began to make an advance towards the
barricade, and there was a great battle. These unconquerable heroes spread
slaughter around them and displayed fierce-hearted daring, and were as
though having the points of spears in their entrails, for they armed themselves strongly with their valour and were all breathing with rage and fury,
clad in iron, holding copper shields, bearing spears and firing iron shot.
Battle was joined from both sides. The pagans shot innumerable arrows,
and against them the Cossacks fired from fire-breathing harquebuses, and
there was dire slaughter. In hand to hand fighting they cut each other down.
By the help of God the pagans gradually began to diminish and to weaken.
The Cossacks drove them onwards, slaying them in their tracks. The fields
were stained with blood then, and covered with the corpses of the dead,
and swamps were formed by the blood which flowed then, as in ancient
times from the city of Troy by the river Scamander, captured by Achilles.
Thus they conquered the infidel, for the wrath of God came upon them for
their lawlessness and idolatry, since they knew not God their creator.[1]

This is one of several chronicle accounts of the triumphal march of Russian
Cossacks into Siberia at the end of the sixteenth century, of the victory of
modern guns against primitive bows and arrows, and of the triumph of
Christianity over paganism. At least this is how it was depicted in a chronicle
written some 50 years after the event by a scribe in the service of the archbishop

of Tobolsk, In fact, some Muslim Tatars fought alongside the Cossacks; indigenous tribesmen continued to resist the Russian advance well into the seventeenth century and beyond; Cossacks were lured east of the Ural mountains by a lust for booty and adventure rather than by a desire to proselytise; and the leader of the Cossacks was killed within a few years and his original band had to retreat. Nevertheless, the chronicles did tell an extraordinary tale – how, in a few years at the end of the sixteenth century, the exploits of a small group of men led to them claiming 'Siberia' for the tsar and starting the remarkable process of exploration and colonisation of vast lands stretching to the Pacific Ocean. Myths have grown up about the Cossack leader and his men, from their personal heroism to the divine protection against the arrows which poured down on them, but the reality of what happened was extraordinary enough.

What caused this invasion and who were the main protagonists? 'Sibir' was an independent khanate centred on the river Irtysh east of the Ural mountains, and was a very small part of what is now considered Siberia. Its 'capital' was called Isker, or sometimes Sibir, and was situated at the juncture of the Irtysh and Tobol rivers, near where the town of Tobolsk was later founded. It was one of the few remnants of what had once been the powerful and enormous Mongol empire of Genghis Khan. By the late sixteenth century, the remaining khanates of this former empire had been severely weakened. Tsar Ivan IV had defeated the khanate of Kazan in 1552 and the khanate of Astrakhan in 1556, and had taken over their territories in southern Russia. The rulers of Sibir had agreed to pay a tribute of furs to Ivan in 1555, in itself a recognition of their weakness and subordinate status. The following year, the Muscovite ambassador returned from Sibir with 700 sables for the tsar,[2] an immensely valuable gift.

In 1563, Sibir was ruled by a new khan – Kuchum – who had ruthlessly deposed and killed his predecessor. At first Kuchum continued to pay tribute to Ivan IV and in 1571 he sent 1,000 sables to the Russian tsar. He was determined, however, to assert his independence from Russia. First, he stopped sending tribute and then, two years later, the ambassador sent to Sibir by the tsar was killed on Kuchum's orders. The scene was set for conflict; yet, when it came a few years later, it was not a Russian army under Ivan IV which crossed the Urals to depose Kuchum, but a group of Cossacks in the service of the wealthy and influential Stroganov family.

The Stroganovs had been a prominent noble family in Russia since the fourteenth century. They remained so up to the Revolutions, and the Stroganov palaces which survive in St Petersburg testify to their immense power and wealth. Their wealth came from their mines – mainly iron and copper – which they established in the Ural mountains and in the Russian north from the sixteenth century. Anika Stroganov (1497–1570) was the main force in developing business interests in the Urals. As well as iron and copper mines, he established saltworks and traded in furs. He was an enterprising and energetic merchant, but also a deeply devout man who took monastic vows before his death, built churches on his lands and began the family collection of religious manuscripts and icons. Under Stroganov patronage a whole school of icon painters developed, known for their delicate and meticulous brushwork. Anika Stroganov's trading links extended to the Arctic and even to Central Asia. After his death, his sons, Grigorii and Iakov, took over the business.

These activities were simply too important, and too valuable, for the Russian government not to be interested, or involved. All land in Russia belonged to the tsar, and the Stroganovs, like any other family, had to seek formal approval from him to extend their property and commercial interests. The tsar was also the greatest trader of all and traded on his own account in furs, precious metals and other valuable goods. Ivan IV was mercurial, if not unbalanced, and the leading nobles knew that their position was always precarious: good relations with the tsar had to be carefully cultivated.

In 1558, Ivan IV granted a charter for the Stroganovs to occupy the 'empty lands, the lakes, rivers and forests' on both sides of the river Kama, that is, east of the town of Perm in the Urals. The Ural mountains are not high but they still constitute a natural barrier rising up from the great north European plain, and they have become the accepted boundary between Europe and Asia. The family was allowed to cultivate and settle empty land with peasants, and to establish saltworks and mine for ores. The charter also recognised that such expansion would not take place peacefully and that the Stroganovs would have to control these territories by force, and authorised the construction of forts on the new lands. The family also sought state approval in 1572 to crush revolts in the Ural mountains by the Cheremis people (people of Finno-Ugric ethnic origin, who live along the Volga and Kama rivers and are now called Mari). Kuchum may have had a part in instigating those revolts. The following year his intentions were made clear when his nephew raided Stroganov lands. The Stroganov family had already demonstrated that they could and would use force to maintain and extend their position, and it was equally clear that further penetration into the lands of the Sibir khanate would be met with resistance.

In order to protect their lands and their trade, the Stroganovs had constantly to expand their area of control and so continued to petition for charters from the tsar to acquire territories further to the east. To this extent, the expansion of the Russian presence east of the Urals was an ongoing process rather than the result of a single, sudden decision. It was the need to get access to furs further north and east, as well as to extend their holdings of iron and silver mines, which drove the Stroganovs to continue with their conquests.[3] In 1574, a further charter allowed the Stroganovs to build strongholds east of the Urals on the Tobol, Irtysh and Ob rivers.

The concept of frontiers was very fluid at the time, but an understanding of landownership was not, and these lands were part of the Sibir khanate. The lands allocated by the tsar to the Stroganovs comprised approximately the northern half of the Sibir khanate. The charter urged Iakov and Grigorii Stroganov to 'persuade' local tribesmen to pay tribute to the Russian tsar instead of to Kuchum, and even invited them to 'gather volunteers' from these tribes and to send them, together with Cossacks, 'against the Siberian Khan'.[4] The interests of the tsar were thus tied to the Stroganovs' – tribute and obeisance from tribesmen for the former, trade and wealth for the latter, which would also benefit the tsar. It was equally clear that, even if they made no formal declaration of war, their activities would inevitably lead to conflict with indigenous tribesmen and with Kuchum.

The Stroganovs did not rush to claim these lands and risk a fight with Kuchum. The latter had proved himself ruthless in power by crushing local revolts, and it was clear that he would resist any attempt to take his lands or diminish his power, and that force would be needed to remove him. When the fight came, in the 1580s, it was conducted on the Russian side by a band of Cossacks under the leadership of Vasilii Timofeevich, who is better known by his nickname of Ermak.

Who was this man who led the Russian penetration of Siberia? Ermak's origins are obscure. There are no contemporary portraits or descriptions of him, although one of the later chronicles described him as 'flat-faced, black of beard and with curly hair, of medium stature and thickset and broad shouldered'.[5] This has not prevented several later portraits or statues being made. He was referred to as an ataman, or leader, of Cossacks in documents, but this probably just signified that he was a leader of a band of Cossacks on the river Volga. We know he had once worked on the Stroganov fleet on the Kama and Volga rivers, and became a pirate. He may well have had a price on his head – pirates on the Volga who were captured were impaled and floated down the Volga on rafts to die in excruciating agony as a gruesome warning to others. Ermak was unlikely to have come from the south of Russia, although he was later claimed as a Don Cossack and there is a statue of him in Novocherkassk, in southern Russia, the capital of the Don Cossacks.

Nothing is certain about who initiated the campaign or its purpose. Was it a determined attempt by the Stroganovs to overthrow Kuchum, or was it a useful way of ridding themselves of troublesome Cossacks who had arrived in their lands? The intentions of the Cossacks were also unclear. Did they see themselves as an invading force and, if so, on whose behalf? Or were they motivated by the desire for booty (furs and other goods), or simply a lust for adventure? What evidence we have comes from a number of chronicles, all of which were written after the event (probably at the earliest in the 1620s, although that too is a matter of dispute among historians). The chronicles give different degrees of prominence to the Stroganov family; the dates of key events are also a matter of dispute – the campaign started in 1581 or 1582; it is thought that Ermak died in 1585, but it could have been 1584.

What is known with a reasonable degree of certainty is that Ermak was in Stroganov service, and that the Stroganovs had already demonstrated their energy and ruthlessness in taking territory by force. Ermak was just the sort of swashbuckling daredevil ne'er-do-well who might well be used by the Stroganovs for a dangerous expedition. It is also clear that Tsar Ivan IV was not directly involved in the military campaign at this early stage. The role of the Russian state in the first formal penetration of Siberia was restricted to permitting the Stroganov family to expand its territories. Granting that permission was, however, to have enormous implications.

It is not certain how many men accompanied Ermak or who they were, and the chronicles differ on this. The normally accepted figures are that the group comprised some 530 men in the first instance, followed by 300 reinforcements. But some estimates drawn from the chronicles are lower (650 in total) and some considerably higher (several thousand). Later stories about Ermak portray him as leading an entirely Cossack force, but it seems that it also included some of Stroganov's men as well as non-Russians such as Tatars and foreign prisoners of war. In addition, it is said that the band was accompanied by three priests and a runaway monk, who was also a cook.

The image of Cossacks in the West tends to be a mixture of romance and repulsion – superb horsemen, wild men, free spirits, ungovernable, fearless, cruel – just the sort of men, in fact, who could conquer and squander lands that were both inhospitable and of great potential wealth. There is some truth in this image of undisciplined but brave warriors, and Ermak certainly fits that description. Cossacks retained a separate legal identity within the Russian state but were not a separate ethnic group (although in the Soviet period they would be classed as such). They were originally mostly fugitive peasants from Russia and Ukraine (which is why it is awkward to speak simply of 'Russians' colonising Siberia) who had formed semi-autonomous military communities on the southern frontiers of the country in the sixteenth century. In the process of settling on the southern frontiers, they had experience of moving into and settling new lands, primarily following the river routes. The main role of Cossacks was to defend the southern and western borders of Russia from marauding Tatars and Poles. In every way, then, they were well suited to the adventure in Siberia.

Although the dates of the campaign are uncertain, we know roughly what happened. Ermak and his men crossed the Urals and spent the first winter camped on the eastern side. When the weather became warmer, and the ice on the rivers melted, they progressed down the rivers on rafts. After a number of victories in skirmishes with tribesmen, they established a base at the town of Tiumen and then advanced down the Tura and Tobol rivers, fighting all the way. The Cossacks seemed to intimidate and dishearten the tribesmen with the power of their weapons and their seeming immunity to arrows. On one occasion they deceived Kuchum's men by floating dummies of soldiers – Cossack clothes stuffed with twigs – down the river, and then attacked and defeated their opponents from behind. The party then fought a Tatar force loyal to Kuchum, a battle which lasted five days before the Tatars retreated. The encounter was ferocious: 'They fought mercilessly hand to hand, slashing one another, so that horses were up to their bellies in blood and corpses of the unbelievers.'[6] The Cossacks then rested and, according to the chronicles, fasted to ensure that their piety would continue to give them divine protection.

Kuchum had meanwhile gathered forces of several thousand Tatars and native tribesmen to resist Ermak. He was, however, weakened by divisions and rivalries within the different tribal groups, some of which were as willing to pay tribute to the Russian tsar as they were to the Siberian khan. These groups included Ostiaks and Voguls (people of Finno-Ugric origin, and now known by the names of Khanty and Mansi) and Chuvash people (people of Turkic origin), who lived in the Volga region and what is now western Siberia.

Kuchum's forces were positioned in his capital in Isker, where the key battle took place in October, probably in 1582. A Cossack assault failed, but a few days later Ermak's men returned and launched an all-out attack. The battle was bloody, and some of the tribesmen took flight. After three days Kuchum had to accept defeat and flee as one of the chronicles graphically recalls:

> the fighting was terrible on the 23rd day of October, hand to hand, cutting down foe. . . . The unbelievers, driven by Kuchum, suffered great losses at the hands of the Cossacks, they lamented, fought unwillingly and died. Kuchum's men had no guns, only bows and arrows, spears and swords. The Chuvash had two cannon which the Cossacks silenced, so they hurled these down the hill into the Irtysh. Kuchum as he stood on the Chuvash hill saw the carnage wrought among his men and lamented with all the unbelievers and ordered his chanters and mullahs to shout their prayers to their idols because their gods were asleep. Helpless and dishonoured, hard pressed by God's might he meditated flight. They fought on ceaselessly for three days without respite. On the 24th day of October the Ostiak prince-lings of the lower reaches were the first to disobey Kuchum's orders and fled on horseback to their homeland without return, to lie there like animals in wild forests. . . . Kuchum, after seeing in the night [a] vision [of] the final loss of his kingdom and wholesale devastation, fled from his city . . . and said to all his people: 'Let us flee immediately so as not to die a cruel death at the hands of the Cossacks.' And without looking back all fled from the city to the steppe.[7]

The next day the Cossacks entered the town of Isker. They had lost over one hundred lives in their bloodiest encounter, but in a single battle they had ended the khanate of Sibir. At the same time, the small group of Cossacks were not able to hold out in Isker without reinforcements and supplies. At this point, Ermak had the good sense to offer his services to Ivan IV, and to claim Sibir in the name of the tsar rather than the Stroganov family, and he did so with the handsome gift of a collection of furs as tribute – all of 2,400 sables, 800 black fox and 2,000 beaver pelts.[8] The offer was timely, as Ivan was in the process of rebuking the Stroganovs for their rash actions in attacking Kuchum instead of limiting themselves to defending their own lands. The arrival of the news of Kuchum's defeat and the collapse of the khanate, along with the immense value of the gift of furs, changed his mind. Ivan promptly added the title of 'tsar of Siberia' to his other titles and sent reinforcements.

Ermak has often been portrayed in Russian and Soviet literature as Russia's Cortés, a symbol of the triumph of Western European technology over backward people, and of Christianity over Islam (Tatars were Muslim) and paganism. The chronicles depicted the campaign as a Christian victory, and described a number of miracles which had protected the Cossacks from the arrows of the tribesmen. According to these accounts, for instance, there took place a 'wonderful miracle!' – 'the arms of those strong in archery who shot at him [a Christ-like figure leading the Cossacks] from afar went dead by divine fate and their bows were shattered'.[9] The chroniclers were not unaware of the mismatch between the two sides in terms of military technology, which also helped to account for Cossack victories. These words were put into the mouths of Kuchum's men:

> The Russian troops are so powerful: when they shoot from their bows, then there is a flash of fire and a great smoke issues and there is a loud report like thunder in the sky. One does not see the arrows coming out of them. They inflict wounds and injure fatally, and it is impossible to shield oneself from them by any trappings of war. Our scale-armour, armour of plates and rings, cuirasses and chain mail do not hold them; they pierce right through them.[10]

Myths about Ermak originated in the Russian chronicles, but then became part of a larger myth about the spirit of the Cossacks and the triumphal progress of Christian Russians against pagans and Muslims in Siberia. The Remezov chronicle, written about 1700, gave Ermak, and his clothing, miraculous powers: 'Miracles were worked by Ermak's body and clothing, the sick were healed, mothers and babes were preserved from disease, success came in war and in fishing and hunting'. The chronicle goes on to claim that native tribesmen were in awe of Ermak's power, and that even his grave had special powers: 'to this day the infidels see on the Saturdays of the commemoration of the dead a pillar of fire rising to the sky, and on ordinary Saturdays a great candle burning at his head'.[11]

Cossack folk legends and songs portray Ermak as a brave brigand, and there is some folkloric merging of Ermak with Stenka Razin, the rebellious late seventeenth-century Don Cossack. Some later Cossack songs see him as someone who opened up the possibility of ordinary Cossacks making their fortune in Siberia:

> Shall we go, shall we not go to the river Irtysh,
> From the river Irtysh we'll take the town of Tobol.[12]

The legends continued into the nineteenth and twentieth centuries. A play by Nikolai Polevoi written in 1845 (that is, at a time when public opinion was in favour of further Russian expansion into the Amur region and far east) about Ermak's conquest of Siberia stresses the triumph of Christianity:

> As the pagan idol fell, so will fall
> The infidel before the Orthodox faith.
> And divine grace and light will shine
> Over the Siberian realm, which hitherto
> Has stagnated in the darkness of idolatry.[13]

The town of Ermak bears his name, and at least eight other towns have names derived from it. In the late nineteenth century, one rail planner stated: 'The Siberian railway will be the culmination of Ermak's work'.[14] Postage stamps have commemorated him, in both the Soviet and post-Soviet periods (his face adorns a 10-rouble stamp issued in 2009). Icebreakers have been named after him, presumably because they also smash their way through the frozen seas to enable goods and people to move around and open up new lands.

* * *

By the time they had defeated Kuchum, only 150 Cossacks were left, so they had to retreat from Isker. Kuchum may have been defeated but he, and other tribesmen, could still inflict losses on the Cossacks. Added to this, the winter of 1583–4 brought famine and the Cossacks were desperate for more supplies. In, probably, August 1585, Ermak and his men were attacked as they slept by a party of Kuchum's men. It is said that Ermak tried to escape by jumping into the river, but was dragged down by the weight of his heavy mail coat, a gift from the tsar. The adventurous foray into the Siberian khanate was over, ending in inglorious defeat and the death of Ermak and many of his men. But once Ivan IV had accepted the title of tsar of Siberia, along with

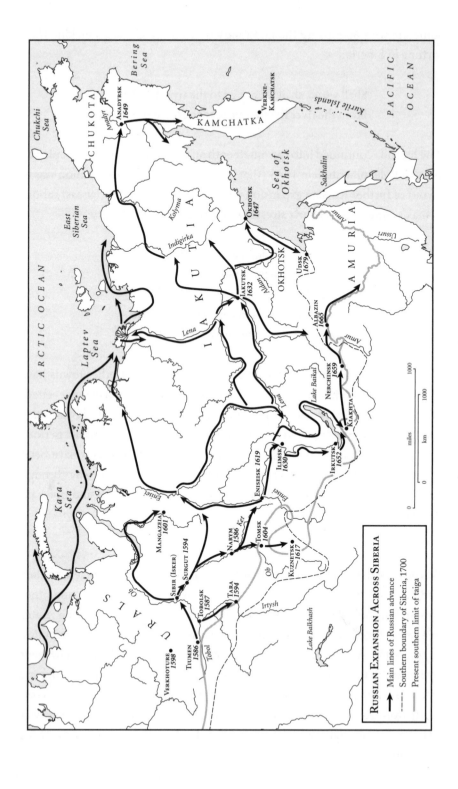

RUSSIAN EXPANSION ACROSS SIBERIA

→ Main lines of Russian advance
- - - Southern boundary of Siberia, 1700
— Present southern limit of taiga

the gift of furs, the colonisation of Siberia had become state policy. The first stage of the opening up of Siberia after 1585 was achieved at astonishing speed and then progressed steadily. By the end of the seventeenth century, Russians had criss-crossed the Siberian rivers and reached the Arctic and Pacific oceans.

The Russians marked their presence by the erection of temporary fortified stockades, which spread out like a fan from the first settlements around the former khanate of Sibir. Forts (a fort was called an *ostrog*) were initially simple stockades made of timber, with watchtowers on each corner. As the settlements grew, and the population required more protection, so the lines of each stockade were expanded, and key administrative buildings erected within. More towers and watchtowers were constructed on the outer walls and moats were dug. The location of the fort was determined by communications – primarily by rivers – but forts became the centres for military presence and to control and intimidate local tribesmen. By the 1620s, over 50 villages in western Siberia were fortified.[15]

In western Siberia, parties of troops were sent out to establish towns at strategic points along the rivers. Tiumen (1586) and Tobolsk (1587) were early foundations. The fort of Tara was constructed on the upper Irtysh (1594) to protect Tobolsk from raids by Kuchum and his supporters. Its strategic importance was demonstrated by the fact that some 1,500 men, including prisoners of war, were sent to build it. They were instructed not only to fortify the town thoroughly but also to build a prison to hold native hostages. This was at a point when Kuchum was still at large and a potential threat. A party of 400 men was sent from Tara against Kuchum in September 1598 and fought him on the River Ob. Many of Kuchum's men were slaughtered, including two of his sons and a number of his leading warriors. Kuchum fled, only to perish at the hands of other native tribesmen.

By this time Kuchum was more of an irritant than a serious opponent, but the Russians needed more forts to control key trade routes along the rivers and to control the tribute-paying indigenous peoples. The town of Pelym was founded in 1593, on a settlement of the Voguls (Mansi). The Voguls were led by a princely family which had encouraged raids on Russians and so needed to be subjugated and forced to pay tribute to the Russians. The instructions for the construction of Pelym made the aims clear: 'Build the *ostrog* first, then try to lure Ablegirim [Abdul Kerim], the Prince of Pelym, his oldest son Tagai, his nephews and grandsons and execute them all'.[16]

The town of Berezov was established in the same year on the river Sosva, conveniently positioned to access both the Ob and the Pechora rivers. The purpose was to strengthen the position of the Russians on the Ob and to better control local tribesmen. The towns of Verkhoture and Turinsk were founded in 1598 to consolidate the Russian hold on the areas between the Kama and Irtysh rivers. Mangazeia was a northern settlement, founded in 1600 by Cossacks from Tobolsk to control the local population, and became an important base for the fur trade and coastal trade with Archangel on the White Sea. Tomsk was founded in 1604 on the upper Ob, also as a base for the collection of tribute.

The less accessible lands further north and east were opened up by expeditions led by hunters/trappers, often accompanied by soldiers. Only after they had established a presence were more permanent settlements set up and 'claimed' by the state. As Russians penetrated further they demanded tribute (tax paid in furs) from indigenous peoples, making conflict inevitable. Expeditions set out north from Mangazeia in the early seventeenth century to explore the river Enisei, collecting tribute on the way. Krasnoiarsk was founded in 1628 on the Enisei to subdue the Buriats (people of Mongolian origin) and other local peoples, although this took time – the garrison was massacred in 1634 by Buriats, who attacked the town again four years later. The area round Lake Baikal and Irkutsk was explored in the 1640s, and a series of forts constructed in the region.

Rumours concerning the richness of the supply of furs in the northern Lena region meant that the river Lena – 2,700 miles (4,400 kilometres) long with some thousand tributaries – became something like a gold rush for a period in 1620s. The town of Iakutsk was founded on the middle Lena after a group of 20 men under the Cossack Petr Beketov were sent in 1631 to build a fort there.[17] For over two years, Beketov explored the remote and dangerous country along the Lena, fighting with tribesmen in his way. He described his experiences in terse language: '[We have] shed our blood, suffered every privation, starved, eaten every unclean thing, and defiled our souls during this two and half years.'[18]

Expeditions from Iakutsk established new bases in the north and the east. In 1639, an expedition had reached the Pacific, led by Ivan Moskvitin with a mere 20 men, resulting in the founding of Okhotsk as a port on the Bering Sea. One of the most daring expeditions from Iakutsk was carried out by Semen Dezhnev in 1647 in order to open up the Anadyr region in the far north-east of Siberia for hunters and to take valuable furs as tribute from the local people. Dezhnev was from a peasant background but had entered military service in Siberia. We do not know much about his companions, except that they numbered only 25 men and comprised hunters and military servicemen. He and his men travelled along the river Kolyma for seven years, collecting tribute in furs and walrus tusks from the tribes they encountered. Dezhnev was almost certainly the first European to sail through the Bering Strait.

We know something about what conditions were like for these men as manuscript records have been preserved for Dezhnev's expedition. His papers show the constant danger and violence of the fighting, not only with local people as they resisted having to pay tribute but also with fellow Russians and Cossacks who were competitors for these valuable offerings. On the river Kolyma, Dezhnev reported: 'we came across the natives' reindeer tracks in the mountains and followed them on the march. . . . We seized a . . . hostage . . . we took the sovereign's tribute of nine sables for this hostage.' However, at this point one of the party, Mikhailo Stadukhin, a merchant with more influence than Dezhnev and clearly a hothead, fired his guns to intimidate the tribesmen. Stadukhin and his men then raided and killed many of these men. Dezhnev recorded: 'I, Semeyka, and my men went to Mikhailo and his men at the Anaul stockade and set about telling him he was acting wrongfully and was killing natives indiscriminately.' The upshot was a fight with Mikhailo, whose men seized food, arms, clothing, dogs and sleds from Dezhnev and his group. Despite the fact that his men were 'starving to death and ate cedar bark', Dezhnev had to continue. As he said: 'We dared not send the sovereign's treasury with a few men across the mountains through the many non-tribute paying natives of various tribes since servicemen and hunters have been killed in the sovereign's service, and other hunters have gone off with Mikhailo Stadukhin.'[19]

Conflict with indigenous peoples was hardly surprising given that tribute was demanded and exacted brutally. This is the way Dezhnev described an encounter on the river Kolyma with settled tribesmen:

We, your sovereign's orphans, began to call this chief to your sovereign's bounty with all his family and tribesmen. . . . That chief Alay and his brothers and tribesmen went into a stockade and resisted and did not obey. 'We will not give tribute to your sovereign', he said, 'because this land is ours and the people are mine.' We, your sovereign's slaves and orphans, begging God's mercy, began to take action against them and to move toward the stockade. [We] laid siege to chief Olay, his brothers, and tribesmen in the stockade. . . . chief Olay, came to us . . . and began speaking: 'Do not kill my son, and I will hunt the sovereign's tribute and pay every year.' We, your sovereign's slaves, erected a small fort in Olay's living area. Olay's son sat as a hostage. On the 28th day of January of the present year 152 [1644] Olay and his brothers and tribesmen came and gave tribute to the great sovereign from himself and his tribesmen.[20]

The one area where Russians were unable to establish a permanent presence in the seventeenth century was the Amur river basin, on the border with China. Vasilii Poiarkov was the first explorer to travel in the region in the 1640s. He travelled down the river Aldan with 133 men and then made his way along the Zeia, a tributary of the Amur, and finally reached the Amur river and then the Sea of Okhotsk (an extension of the North Pacific coast). This expedition showed how difficult it would be to secure this area. Supplies ran short and there were violent clashes between Poiarkov and his men and the local inhabitants. It was a remarkable journey but a very difficult and dangerous one among hostile tribes, during which over half of the group lost their lives. Poiarkov reported that to hold this area and collect the tribute required more forces and the construction of at least three forts.

The Poiarkov expedition was followed by another led by Erofei Khabarov (after whom the town of Khabarovsk on the confluence of the Amur and Ussuri rivers was later named). Khabarov was of peasant stock from north European Russia but moved to Siberia at some time in the 1630s, became a trader and organised a private expedition along the Amur in 1649, fighting and taking tribute as he went. He founded the fort of Albazin (now Albazino) on the river Amur. It became clear to Khabarov that there would be a conflict with China over the right to collect tribute from the indigenous people and, on his return to Iakutsk, he advised that at least 6,000 men needed to be sent to the Amur to conquer the territory. His second expedition, of 1650–3, immediately ran into difficulties as he tried to force local inhabitants to hand over tribute. Khabarov's conclusion was that the Amur region would be of great value to the Russian state, but that an army was required to fight the Chinese if the land were to be secured.

In 1656, a further expedition was undertaken in the region by Afanasii Pashkov. This founded the town of Nerchinsk, on the border with China, but was dogged by disaster, and the men suffered attacks from hostile tribesmen and famine. The foray was significant mostly for the account written of it by Archpriest Avvakum, whose story of exile is told in a later chapter. His memoir talks of the suffering of the party, including one of his young sons:

> we dragged on for another year, living on the Nercha river, and keeping ourselves alive with the roots and herbs that grew on the banks. One after another the folk died of hunger. . . . And in winter we would live on fir-cones, and sometimes God would send mare's flesh, and sometimes we found the bones of stinking carcasses of wild beasts left by wolves, and what had not been eaten up by the wolves that did we eat; and some would eat frozen wolves and foxes – in truth, any filth that they could lay their hands on. A mare foaled, and, in secret, the starving folk devoured the foal together with the caul.[21]

An added problem in the Amur region was that there, unlike in any other area of Siberia, the Russians faced a formidable rival in Manchu China, which claimed both the lands and the tribute. Chinese forces were sent against the Russians and, in 1658, killed or captured 270 men in a party of Cossacks. Russian colonisation slowed after this date, particularly as the news filtered back that much of the land was hard to cultivate. Some areas required forcible settlement to establish that the territory was Russian. In Nerchinsk, for example, the governor had to take measures forcibly to settle exiles and soldiers in the town in the 1680s as it had failed to attract voluntary settlers.[22]

In reality, the Russians could not hold this territory with so few soldiers and settlers. Embassies from Russia to China in the 1650s and 1670s could not establish territorial divisions to the satisfaction of both sides. Chinese military activity against the Russians increased in the 1680s, once a rebellion in southern China had been crushed, and the Chinese demanded the demolition of Russian forts on the river Zeia. In 1685, they attacked the fort of Albazin and, with supplies of gunpowder running low, the Russian abandoned the fort to the Chinese.

Although the Chinese army later abandoned Albazin and the Russians rebuilt it, it was clear that negotiations would have to take place as the Russian position on the Amur was precarious. This led eventually to a meeting at the Russian border town of Nerchinsk in 1689, in the presence of a considerable Chinese military force of 15,000 men (as opposed to only 600 in the

Nerchinsk garrison). The Russians had to accept the loss of the whole of the Amur valley, and that the river Argun should now serve as the frontier. The first attempt of the Russians to take the Amur region had failed.

The Russian penetration of Siberia was an enormous feat of human endeavour. But what were the lands like which had been claimed, who lived there, and how could such an enormous terrain be traversed and maintained? These are the subjects of the next chapter.

CHAPTER TWO

Land, Indigenous Peoples and Communications

ONE OF the chronicles describes the relief of Ermak and his Cossack band after they had survived their first winter in Siberia:

After this the winter time passed, the frost and cold were relieved by the warmth of the sun, a frozen crust formed on the snow, and it was time for hunting wild beasts, elks and deer. . . . When spring arrived and the snow was melted by the warmth of the air, every creature grew fat, the trees and herbs were sprouting and the waters were spread out. Then every living creature rejoiced, birds flew to those lands because of their fruits, and in the rivers fish were swimming because of their fruitfulness, and there was much hunting of fish and birds. By this hunting they were fed, and there was no famine among the people. The tribes who lived around that place, Tatars and Ostiaks and Voguls, who were under the sovereign's hand, both far and near, brought them provisions in great quantity of wild beasts, birds, fish and cattle, and costly goods, and all kinds of furs. Then the men of Moscow and the Cossacks by the grace of God were abundantly supplied with all foods and acquired much wealth for themselves from trading in furs. And being in such great joy and gladness, they gave thanks to almighty God, since God had granted to the sovereign such a land blessed with abundance.[1]

This, it has to be said, is not a typical description of the abundance of the Siberian lands. The chronicle was not only recording the survival of the Cossacks but also providing a justification for conquest – the richness of the land and in particular its fur trade, which benefited both individual Cossacks and hunters but also, of course, the tsar. It foretells some of the assertions which would be made in the mid-nineteenth century about the wealth that would come to Russia if the Amur river basin and the far east were conquered, and the arguments in the late nineteenth and twentieth centuries about the benefits which would accrue if railways were constructed across the whole territory. There was, and is, of course, vast mineral wealth, as well as oil and gas, in Siberia, which was at that time unknown to the Cossacks.

I have defined Siberia in the broadest sense in this book – as the vast land-mass that stretches from the Ural mountains to the Pacific ocean and the Bering Strait in the east, and reaches from north of the Kazakh Steppe to the Arctic Ocean. It covers some 2,900,000 square miles (some 7,500,000 square kilometres), and crosses eight time zones. It comprises 77 per cent of Russian territory and covers some 10 per cent of the Earth's surface. Its vastness can only really be appreciated by flying over it, either to Vladivostok or to Japan, or by travelling by train from Moscow to Vladivostok, a journey of over 6,000 miles (over 9,600 kilometres).

The formal boundaries of Siberia have changed over time. The Kamchatka peninsula was reached at the end of the seventeenth century and the Kurile Islands in the early eighteenth century. Russia won part of, and then lost, the Amur region to China in the seventeenth century; it was only regained in the mid-nineteenth century. The Soviet army captured Sakhalin Island and occupied the Kurile Islands in 1945. In the eighteenth and first half of the nineteenth century, the Russians established a presence on part of the coastline of Alaska and California. The Californian settlement of Fort Ross failed, and Alaska was sold to the United States in 1867, so ending the Russian presence in North America.

There were significant geographical, topographical and climatic differences between regions within Siberia (Siberia as I have defined it is today divided into three administrative divisions: Western and Eastern Siberia and the Far East). Western Siberia is a lowland plain, a great basin to the east of the Ural mountains, drained by the Ob and Irtysh rivers, which create swamp-lands and numerous lakes. The region has rich pasture and grasslands in the south; the woodlands are deciduous in the south and there are vast coniferous forests to the north. In the north, as across all of northern Siberia, the land is permanently frozen and the Arctic Ocean is icebound for most of the year (although now navigable with icebreakers). In the eighteenth and nine-teenth centuries, the bulk of the population of Siberia lived in the west, farming on the steppe and in the rich black-earth regions. The main cities in western Siberia before the twentieth century were Tomsk, Omsk, Tobolsk and Barnaul. Novosibirsk (called Novo-Nikolaevsk until 1926) became a prominent industrial and cultural centre in the last century. Vast coal deposits were found and developed in the Kuznetsk basin in western Siberia in the twentieth century.

Eastern Siberia was less populous, less fertile and more mountainous. The eastern Siberian uplands are drained by the river Lena. The tundra spreads further south and the forest is denser than in western Siberia. The main urban and cultural centre of eastern Siberia has always been Irkutsk since its founda-tion in 1661, but the towns of Iakutsk and Chita have also been significant centres. Lake Baikal, east of Irkutsk, is over 400 miles (640 kilometres) long and is the deepest lake in the world. Over 300 rivers flow into the lake; only one – the river Angara – flows from it. East of Lake Baikal, great mountain ranges, with peaks of over 10,000 feet (3,048 metres), stretch to the Sea of Okhotsk. The great Siberian rivers – the Ob, the Enisei, the Lena – all flow out northwards into the Arctic Ocean. In the twentieth century, vast reserves of oil and natural gas were discovered in eastern Siberia and in the very far north and far north-east.

The Kamchatka peninsula, on the north Pacific coast of Siberia, has mountains of over 15,000 feet (over 4,500 metres) and many active volca-noes. The far east is still the least populous part of the region, and its trade and contacts are becoming ever more orientated towards Russia's eastern neighbours. The climate of the Amur basin is warmer and wetter than further north and coniferous forests give way to deciduous woods. The main city in the Amur basin is Khabarovsk, at the confluence of the Amur and Ussuri rivers, and the main city in the far east is the port of Vladivostok, founded in 1860, the home of the tsarist, Soviet and Russian Pacific fleets.

As we saw in the last chapter, Siberia was not uninhabited when Ermak and his men crossed the Urals. By the end of the seventeenth century, some 100,000 Russians and other 'foreigners' had settled in Siberia but just over twice that number of indigenous peoples already lived in these lands. It has been calculated there are over 500 different tribal groups in Siberia, who between them speak some 120 languages.[2]

Indigenous Peoples in Siberia in the Late Seventeenth Century

Tatars:	14,265
Teleuts and other Altai-Sayan Turks:	11,300
Ostiaks (Khanty) and Voguls (Mansi):	16,260
Samoeds, including Nenets, Tavgi and Selkups:	15,285
Ostiak-Samoeds (Kets):	5,630
Tungus, Evenki and Evens:	36,235
Iakuts (Sakha):	28,470
Kalmyks (Mongols), including Buriats:	37,175
Iukagirs:	4,775
Eskimos:	4,000
Chukchis:	8,500
Koriaks:	11,000
Kamchadals (Itelmen):	23,000
Ainu:	3,540
Nanais and Ulchas:	3,500
Gilikas (Nivkhs):	4,300
Total:	227,235[3]

Western Siberia was inhabited by Samoeds and Ostiaks/Voguls (now called Khanty-Mansi). *Samoed* is a Lapp word; the Russians took it to mean 'self-eater': they thought the Samoeds wild semi-humans who ate their own children, and were semi-aquatic and lived partly in the sea. Sometimes it was said that they shed their skin, or that they were hairy from the waist down, or that they lacked mouths and chewed their food with their shoulders.[4] These fantastical ideas notwithstanding, the Samoeds were a group of Uralic peoples who lived west and east of the Ural mountains. South of the Samoed clans were the Voguls and Ostiaks, Finno-Ugric clans who lived in the Volga and Kama river valleys of western Siberia. Ostiaks were described by the German botanist and traveller Johann Georgi in the eighteenth century as 'Timorous, superstitious, and lazy, dirty and disgusting, but tractable, mild, and a good-hearted people'.[5] Ostiaks and Voguls were mainly semi-nomadic hunters and fishers but some were occupied in agriculture in the southern plains. All these peoples were shamanistic and believed in spirits in the forest or lakes, which could take the form of birds and animals.

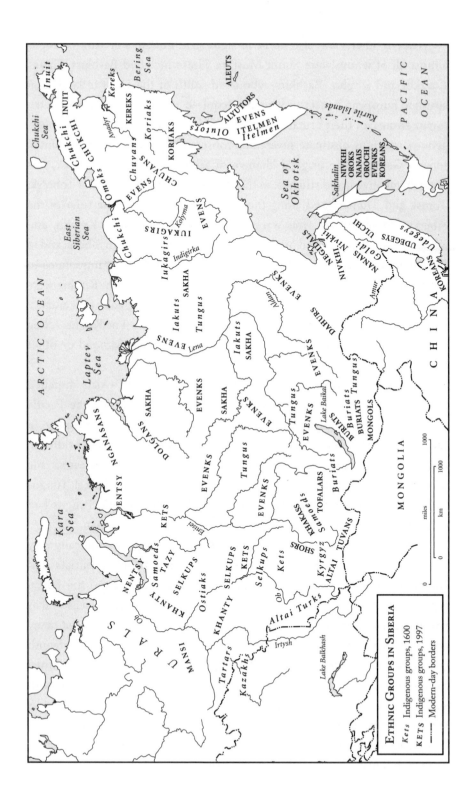

ETHNIC GROUPS IN SIBERIA

Kets Indigenous groups, 1600
KETS Indigenous groups, 1997
——— Modern-day borders

Western Siberia was also home to significant numbers of Turkic people, almost all of whom were Sunni Muslim. These included Bashkirs, Tatars, Kazakhs and Kirghiz. Bashkirs, who lived south of the Urals in lands that spanned European Russia and Siberia, acquired a fearsome reputation in the tsarist armies for their brutality as well as for their courage. 'They are courageous, suspicious, obstinate, severe, and consequently dangerous,' commented Johann Georgi.[6] The original khanate of Sibir, conquered by Ermak, was Tatar. Tatars lived, and still live, in the regions around the towns of Tobolsk, Tomsk and Tiumen, and along the river Irtysh. Kuchum, the ruler of the Siberian Tatar khanate who was defeated by Ermak, was a Kazakh, and Kazakhs had mainly settled on the southern steppes of western Siberia and in the Altai region. Kirghiz settlements extended from the Ural mountains to the Lake Baikal area and to the Chinese border in the south. Kirghiz were occupied in hunting, agriculture and the mining of copper, gold, iron and tin, and also traded in goods across Central Asia and to China. The Kirghiz ruling elite were Turkic, but many of their subjects were from Samoed or other tribes.

Tungus (now called Evenki and Eveni) lived in lands which stretched from south-eastern Siberia across to Lake Baikal and reached the Pacific coast. They were mainly forest-dwellers and lived by hunting and fishing. In the north they had reindeer herds, and had developed saddles and bridles so that they could ride them. Tungus were formed into over 20 tribes, each made up of several clans, scattered over vast distances. South of Lake Baikal, Tungus had become cattle-rearers. Like other north Siberian people, Tungus had animistic beliefs and believed in the magical powers of the shaman.

The mountainous Altai region, south of Lake Baikal, was ethnically very mixed, and included Buriats, Kalmyks and other peoples. Buriats and Kalmyks are of Mongolian origin. Buriats lived mainly around the Baikal region and were involved in trade with Mongolia and Central Asia as well as within Siberia. Buriats were shamanistic when the Russians arrived but many converted from shamanism to Buddhism in the seventeenth and eighteenth centuries. Kalmyks lived in the Volga region, in a territory which spanned European Russia and western Siberia, and had contact, and conflict, with Bashkirs and Cossacks east of the Urals. In the 1770s, some 200,000 Kalmyks left their lands in Russia and attempted to make their way to their ancestral homeland in China. Kalmyks converted to Buddhism in the late sixteenth century, but many retained shamanistic beliefs alongside Buddhism.

In the north-east lived Iakuts (now called Sakha), who are of Turkic origin. Iakuts were occupied mainly in hunting and fishing but had also settled along the river Lena. Iakuts remained shamanistic unlike other people of Turkic origin in Siberia. In the far north lived the Dolgan people, whose ancestors were Tungus but whose language had become a dialect of Iakut. Iukagirs lived to the north and east of the Iakuts. More settled Iukagirs lived by the rivers and fished or hunted; nomadic Iukagirs herded reindeer and hunted in the tundra.

Further east lived Chukchis, Koriaks and Eskimos, who also held shamanistic beliefs. The Chukchis have given their name to the far north-eastern peninsula of Chukotka. The islands in the Bering Strait were home to Aleuts, who speak a language similar to Eskimo. Koriaks, Kamchadals (sometimes called Itelmen) and Ainu occupied the Kamchatka peninsula. Kamchadals were distinctive in not having shamans, although they held similar animistic beliefs. According to a French traveller in the late eighteenth century, they were:

> in general below the common height; their shape is round and squat, their eyes small and sunk, their cheeks prominent, their nose flat, their hair black, they have scarcely any beard, and their complexion is a little tawny. The complexion and features of the women are very nearly the same; from this representation, it will be supposed they are not very seducing objects.[7]

Ainus lived on Kamchatka and the Kurile Islands – they are rare among Asiatic peoples in having thick, wavy, dark hair. Those who had settled on the coast lived by fishing and the hunting of walrus, whales and seals in the Bering Sea. Others lived a nomadic existence herding reindeer or hunting. In total, in the seventeenth century, the Iukagirs, Chukchis, Koriaks, Itelmen/Kamchadals, Eskimos and Ainus comprised only some 40,000 people out of an indigenous population of Siberia of some 220,000 but inhabited a vast, and mainly hostile, terrain. Sakhalin Island, which was not completely occupied by the Russians until the late nineteenth century, was home to the Ulchi people.

Siberia may be more fertile, and more populous, in reality than it is in popular imagination, but the sheer size and nature of the terrain hindered communications, and this has had a profound effect on its development. The first settlements in Siberia were wooden forts, which were positioned at key points on the rivers. Forts were constructed in the seventeenth and eighteenth centuries along a 'Siberian line' running across the south (on roughly the later route of the Trans-Siberian railway), with spurs along the rivers in order to found settlements to the north.

The main highway across Siberia was a 'post road'. Post houses, with horses, were established along its route so that travellers could change horses and coachmen. The short distances between post houses, however, indicate that travellers progressed only slowly. There were 20 post houses between the towns of Tara and Tobolsk in 1745,[8] a distance of only 240 miles (384 kilometres). The traveller John Ledyard took two and a half months to get from St Petersburg to Irkutsk in 1787, using post stations every 26 miles (42 kilometres). The journey in 1858 undertaken by a party of peasants who were settling in Tomsk province required 17 post stations to cover a journey of only 300 miles (480 kilometres).[9] The distance from St Petersburg to Iakutsk, in north-eastern Siberia, is some 5,700 miles (over 9,000 kilometres), but even in the 1860s that journey required as many as 368 post stations.[10]

In Russia, there was a special legal category of people called 'post-drivers' or 'coachmen', who lived in separate settlements and were obliged to provide post horses for officials and other travellers on these major state roads. It was a duty often poorly and grudgingly performed, but it was nevertheless a vital means of ensuring communication by road and an important state service. It is significant then that some of the earliest settlements in the seventeenth century in western Siberia were villages comprising 50 families of post-drivers, each responsible for a stretch of road in return for a small payment and a plot of land.[11] By 1662, there were some 3,000 post-drivers in Siberia.[12] They were relatively few in number but crucial in maintaining lines of communication – not so different from railway workers in the late nineteenth and early twentieth centuries.

The difficulties of travel are well illustrated by the first Bering expedition, which took one and a half years to move men and supplies across Siberia to the port of Okhotsk on the Pacific coast.[13] Vitus Jonassen Bering set off with 33 men in January 1725 on the route through Vologda and reached Tobolsk on 16 March. He then had to wait until May, when the ice finally melted on the river Irtysh, to navigate through dangerous rapids to the settlement of Ust-Kut on the river Lena. The party had to winter there as, in his words, 'we could not get through to Iakutsk owing to the snow and cold'. They constructed heavier barges, which took them to Iakutsk in the spring of 1726. The unwillingness and inability of local inhabitants to help them (they did not have dogs to pull the sledges) slowed the party. Local people were also poor carpenters as 'not many were capable of this work because they were blind or limping or suffering from diseases'. There were many desertions en route and outbreaks of sickness. Bering had five soldiers whipped 'to serve as an example', but then recorded: 'On December 19 I examined all the workmen and military men. . . . I found 11 of the workmen and 15 of the military men from Iakutsk to be ill, had the shivers or had other diseases. 59 of the workmen and military men were in good health.'

Individuals, however, were easier to transport than goods. Bering travelled further with a small party of men with packhorses to Okhotsk, but it was 'impossible to make use of wagons owing to the mud and the hills' so the equipment and foodstuffs required for the expedition had to be transported separately. Bering had to leave Lieutenant Chirikov and some of the equipment behind at Iakutsk. Chirikov finally arrived in Okhotsk in January 1727 but had had to leave material behind in four places as the party: 'had been on the road ever since 4 November and during that time had suffered greatly from hunger, having been compelled to eat the dead horses that had dropped by the wayside, the harness, their leather clothing, and boots.' The return journey to Moscow, at the end of the expedition and without the supplies, took nine months.[14]

Travel continued to be slow and treacherous well into the nineteenth century. In the 1830s, Major-General Termin reported that the roads between Iakutsk and Okhotsk in the east were 'everywhere in a bad condition and the journey could only take place on saddle horses'.[15] Ferdinand von Wrangel, manager of the Russo-American Company, a trading company which established trading posts on the North American coast, and in effect governor of these settlements, commented on the difficulty of acquiring supplies for Russian settlers in North America, which had to be transported across Siberia and then shipped from the port of Okhotsk; he noted that 'in Siberia the Okhotsk road means the most fatiguing and the most dangerous journey'.[16] As if the physical conditions were not bad enough, travellers also had to contend with corrupt officials, who cheated them, and escaped convicts, who attacked them. The trail to Okhotsk was strewn with the carcasses of dead horses and skeletons. It was said that up to half of the horses died on each trip, particularly during rainy summers. Even in the 1830s it took up to two years to complete the journey and, by the time the goods reached the colonists in Alaska and California, much of the flour and meat was spoiled. It was easier to transport goods by sea round the Cape of Good

Hope in South Africa to Russian North America than to take the overland
route across Siberia.

Convicts travelling to exile in Siberia before the completion of the Trans-
Siberian railway were supposed to walk 15 miles (24 kilometres) a day. Their
sentence only technically started on the day they arrived at their destination,
and in 1863 it was commented, tragicomically:

> The majority of prisoners come from distant Russian provinces, and to get
> to assigned locations takes them two years, but in case of illness and conva-
> lescence in hospital, all of three years. There are examples of some pris-
> oners taking four or five years, and I know of one example where a prisoner
> came to Irkutsk only after eight years, and when he entered the factory this
> marked the first minute of his sentence of eight years.[17]

And Irkutsk was still over 660 miles (1,056 kilometres) from Nerchinsk,
where convicts were sent to work in the mines.

In 1890 an intrepid British nurse, armed with a revolver, visited leper colonies in remote parts of Iakutsk province. Even she found the journey across
Siberia almost too much:

> Bump, jolt, bump, jolt – over huge frozen lumps of snow and into holes, and
> up and down those dreadful waves and furrows made by the traffic – such is
> the stimulating motion you will have to submit to for a few thousand miles.
> . . . You ache from head to foot; you are bruised all over; your poor brain
> throbs until you give way to a kind of hysterical outcry. . . . You are then, in
> a semi-comatose state, dragged from the sledge; and, on gaining a footing,
> you feel more like a battered old bag of mahogany than a gently-nurtured
> Englishwoman.[18]

Even after the construction of the Trans-Siberian railway at the end of the
nineteenth century, and the BAM (Baikal-Amur Mainline) railway in the
twentieth century, the journey across Siberia to any settlement located any
distance from the railway line remained difficult. Prisoners in the 1930s and
1940s could take several weeks to reach the Kolyma camps in the far north-
east of Siberia by rail and sea. Inmates in the Kolyma camp referred to other
cities, in southern Siberia as well as in European Russia, as the 'mainland'.
Railways in Siberia are still painfully slow: it takes seven days to complete the

journey by the Trans-Siberian railway from Moscow to Vladivostok. The aeroplane transformed travel to and within Siberia in the twentieth century, but even today the remoteness of the deposits of oil and natural gas makes extraction very difficult, and the distance and expense of air travel to Moscow mean many Siberians feel divorced from events and life in the capital.

Despite the physical difficulties of communications within Siberia, many Russians/Ukrainians chose, or were obliged, to leave their homes in the seventeenth century and start a new life east of the Urals. The reasons for this are presented in the next two chapters.

CHAPTER THREE

Traders and Tribute-Takers

I T WAS the immense value of furs and pelts which made Siberia attractive to trappers and traders (and the tsar). It was the value of furs which gave the Stroganovs their great wealth and made formal possession of the territory east of the Ural mountains so important, and lucrative, and precipitated the Cossack incursions into Siberia. It was the gift to Tsar Ivan IV of thousands of valuable pelts by Ermak, with the additional promise of tribute from tribes, which persuaded the tsar to support further conquest of Siberia and to establish a state presence to consolidate Russian control. Without the sables and the furs, or, put another way, without the prospect of rich resources and revenue, there would have been no Russian Siberia.

The advance of hunters to the east and the north was relentless in the decades after Ermak, and was closely followed by the construction of a chain of forts and stockades which established a tenuous claim to the area. The trade patterns established in the seventeenth century lasted at least until the advent of new forms of transportation – railways, refrigerated shipping and then air transport.

Hunters and traders moved through the waterways of Siberia, transporting themselves, their animals and their equipment on flat-bottomed boats in the summer and on sledges in the winter months when the rivers were frozen. Trade routes followed the rivers. In the north, goods reached the port of Archangel on the White Sea in European Russia from sea routes along the Arctic coast and from routes along and linking with the northern rivers.[1] Moscow was not only a main centre for the sale and exchange of goods but also the centre of administration where central government offices collected and registered the tax, and where the tsar personally inspected furs and other goods.

There were two main routes to Moscow from Siberia – a northern one through the town of Vologda and a southern route which gave access to the Volga river system. Overland routes in Siberia fed into the main river routes – the Pechora (in European Russia), Ob, Enisei, Kama and Tobol rivers. In the south, overland routes traversed the steppes from Mongolia to the town of Tiumen in western Siberia and from there crossed the Ural mountains. Iakutsk, on the river Lena, was the centre of the northern trade routes. From Iakutsk, trade routes reached the Arctic by land or via the river Kolyma. Another route followed the Tobol, Irtysh and Ob river network to the Enisei river in the north or down the river Ob to Berezov in the west to the Urals via the river Pechora, and then joined the Volga river network.

The quality and availability of furs attracted the first settlers to Siberia. Furs were immensely valuable, and a man could become rich as a result of a few successful expeditions. Hunters and trappers were not, however, the only beneficiaries of this trade, and governors and customs officials took their 'cut'. Indeed, the early state apparatus in Siberia was almost entirely designed to control and benefit from the fur trade. The key towns in the early seventeenth century for the fur trade were Mangazeia, which was the main entry point for hunters to the lower Enisei river region and for the trade to Archangel in the north, and Tobolsk, which was strategically placed on the southern route.

The period of acquiring great wealth from hunting was, however, short-lived. The search for quick profits led inevitably to overhunting, and sables and foxes became rarer and rarer. In 1627, there were already reports of sables and beavers being 'hunted out' in the regions of Mangazeia and the lower Enisei region.[2] Hunters moved further east, but the same pattern was repeated and, by the 1670s, shortages were being reported here as well. By 1690, even the area around Iakutsk in the north began to suffer from the shortage of pelts.

Siberia developed a trade in other goods as well as furs during the seventeenth century. Most of Siberia was inaccessible by river or road, or uninhabited, or only inhabited by nomads or native hunters and trappers. Nevertheless, significant trade routes were established and brought valuable products to European markets. As well as furs, Siberians traded in livestock and foodstuffs, including fish, meat, butter and honey. A specialised, and very lucrative, trade in mammoth tusks (for ivory) and mammoth bones (for magical purposes) had existed as far back as the twelfth century.

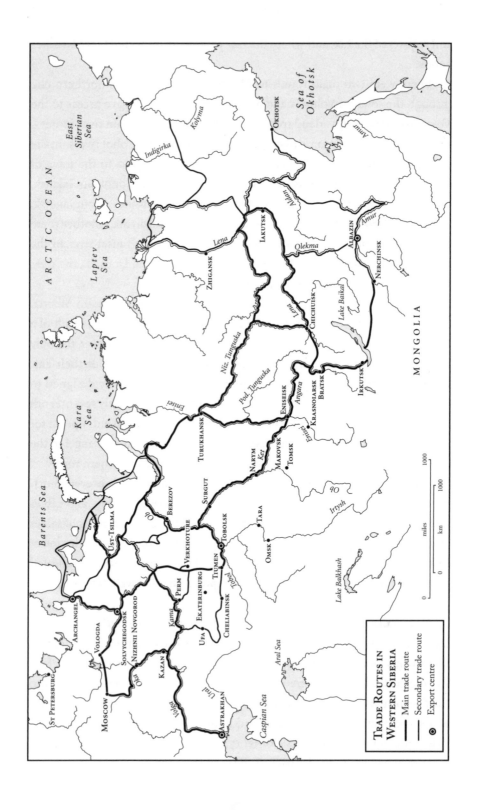

TRADE ROUTES IN
WESTERN SIBERIA

Main trade route
Secondary trade route
Export centre

ARCTIC OCEAN

East
Siberian
Sea

Sea of
Okhotsk

Laptev
Sea

Indigirka

Kolyma

OKHOTSK

Amur

Kara
Sea

Lena

IAKUTSK

Olekma

ALBAZIN

Amur

ZHIGANSK

NERCHINSK

MONGOLIA

Barents
Sea

Niz. Tunguska

CHICHUISK

Lake Baikal

Enisei

Pod. Tunguska

Lena

Angara

IRKUTSK

USTʹ-TSILMA

BEREZOV

TURUKHANSK

ENISEISK

KRASNOIARSK

BRATSK

Ob

SURGUT

NARYM

Ket

MAKOVSK

TOMSK

Enisei

ARCHANGEL

VOLOGDA

Ob

VERKHOTURE

TOBOLSK

TIARA

OMSK

Irtysh

Lake Balkhash

St PETERSBURG

SOLYVYCHEGODSK

NIZHNII NOVGOROD

PERM

TIUMEN

Tobol

CHELIABINSK

EKATERINBURG

UFA

Kama

Irtysh

MOSCOW

Oka

KAZAN

Volga

Ural

ASTRAKHAN

Aral Sea

Caspian
Sea

miles   1000

km   1000

0

0

It was the grain trade, however, that became most important in the seventeenth century, as grain was exported from Siberia to European Russia and beyond. Towns grew as centres for the collection and dispatch of grain. In the 1620s, the largest centres for grain trade were the towns in western Siberia. In 1657, over 7,000 tons of grain[3] passed through Tobolsk;[4] by the end of the seventeenth century, the town had emerged as the centre for the grain trade.

Trade routes crossed Siberia to bring goods from the east to European Russia and, at least in the first third of the seventeenth century, to Europe from the port of Archangel on the White Sea (Russia acquired ports on the Baltic Sea only in the early eighteenth century). Chinese goods came in caravans from Beijing through Mongolia to the town of Selenginsk, and from there to Tobolsk, or through Manchuria via the border town of Nerchinsk. Between 1639 and 1674, caravans of traders arrived annually in Tobolsk from the east. A caravan of 90 camels laden with goods arrived in Irkutsk in 1685.[5] In 1689, the Treaty of Nerchinsk established a state monopoly of trade caravans. Between 1689 and 1697, seven Russian state caravans carried goods from Beijing through Siberia to European Russia. The goods included silks, cotton, tea, medicinal rhubarb, cinnamon and anise. As late as 1820, a traveller from Orenburg, in the southern Urals, commented that he had seen 'camels coming over the hill bringing tea from China'.[6]

One of the most significant items exported from China through Siberia to Europe was rhubarb or, more precisely, rhubarb root, which was highly valued for its medicinal qualities and was widely believed to aid digestive ailments, asthma, fevers and problems of the nervous system. Medicinal rhubarb was seen as particularly beneficial in that it was believed to purge the body without causing any harmful side effects. It could be used by itself or mixed with other herbs and was therefore prized by doctors in Europe, and of enormous monetary value. Rhubarb was imported from Turkey and India, but it was 'Russian rhubarb' that was considered the best quality and commanded the best price. 'Russian rhubarb' did not refer to rhubarb actually grown in Russia but to rhubarb transported by merchants across Russia from China (although some was also grown in Siberia).

Siberia became the main overland route for the export of rhubarb from China to the West. Rhubarb was transported through Siberia to the northern port of Archangel and thence to western Europe, where Amsterdam was the emporium for the rhubarb trade. In 1652, the Russian government declared rhubarb a state monopoly. Only goods that were deemed to be of particular monetary value or of state importance became monopolies. In practice, however, it was not possible to stop private trade in rhubarb and it was smuggled through Siberia to the West. The Treaty of Nerchinsk in 1689 attempted to regularise this trade and confirmed that rhubarb was a state monopoly. From this date, regular state-sponsored caravans took rhubarb along with other goods from Beijing to Moscow.[7]

Who were the men who traded in Siberia? The early pioneers were hunters and trappers. They were known in Russian by the term *promyshlenniki*. Strictly speaking, the term meant men who worked for themselves and who exploited the natural resources of the land. This meant that they were hunters and trappers, but they were also more than this. They could also be explorers, adventurers, exploiters of indigenous people, and conquerors of new lands and peoples. They could act alongside military men to obtain furs and tribute from indigenous people by force. They moved into new lands in a constant and restless pursuit of furs and wealth, and then claimed these lands for the state. They were the true pioneers who opened up Siberia and made its colonisation possible.

Most fur trappers and hunters acted alone or in small groups (artels). The fur trade, and other trades that followed it, required others to transport and market the goods. In seventeenth-century Russia, all members of society were categorised by means of a formal legal status which designated their role or occupation and also brought privileges and obligations. In effect, everyone was a servant of the Russian tsar, but served in different ways, with different responsibilities and different rewards. Merchants were a distinct social group but were categorised within this group according to their wealth, status and occupation. Merchants were given both rights and restrictions in trading (according to the capital which they possessed, and declared, and not just in the seventeenth century; this lasted into the eighteenth century and to some extent up to the late nineteenth century). In practice, it meant that the activities of less elite merchant groups and non-merchants were carefully controlled and regulated.

To many later commentators, both Russian and Western, the rigidity of the categorisation of social groups, and the curbs this imposed on their activities, acted as a brake on the modernisation of Russian society and its economy. It has been claimed that this is what held Russia back, made it 'backward', and in general hindered the development of modern economic and political systems. It is certainly true that Russian society was rigidly divided: the award of privileges to one group inevitably meant the denial of privileges to another group. Everyone needed permission to move from one part of the country to another, from one town to another and from one village to another (only the elite, and wealthiest, merchants could travel abroad freely). Indeed, restrictions on movement lasted well into the nineteenth century, and, to some extent, into the twentieth and twenty-first centuries as well. This did not, however, stop trade from developing in Siberia or stop some men from getting very wealthy through this trade. It must not be forgotten that the craft guilds (and, later, trade unions) in Western Europe could also be very restrictive. In practice, there was always some social mobility in Russia and able, and lucky, men were able to join the ranks of elite merchants and, occasionally, to acquire land.

In the seventeenth century the top merchants were termed *gosti*, (the word means 'guest' or 'visitor' in modern Russian). This elite merchant group was very small and select, numbering some 25 members in the 1650s, and 56 in the 1680s. Most lived in Moscow, but they, or their agents, also conducted operations in Siberia, trading in furs and importing goods from the east. Merchants were servants of the state, or rather the tsar, and personal relations with the latter could be used to their advantage in their commercial operations. In the seventeenth century, the tsars were, in any event, traders themselves. It was the tsars who established state monopolies for particularly valuable goods from which they took a personal cut.

The way the relationship between the tsar and his wealthy merchants worked can be seen from one Siberian example. The Sveteshnikov family came originally from the town of Iaroslavl, north-east of Moscow. In the 1630s, they had trading interests in southern Russia and in the northern port of Archangel as well as in Siberia. The Sveteshnikovs had trading stalls in Tobolsk and exchanged furs for European goods. By 1644, the head of the family, Nadei Sveteshnikov, had assets of over 35,000 roubles – that is, he was an immensely wealthy man. He was also exceptional in that he owned landed estates with serfs (personal peasants) in European Russia, which was very unusual for any merchant family, at this date or later. He nevertheless had to seek government help when he ran into difficulties with his agents, who were out of his reach. At one point he even petitioned the tsar to ask the Siberian governor to search for some of his agents when they went missing, with his goods, on the river Lena.[8]

Few merchants from outside Russia and the country's immediate neighbours penetrated Siberia in this period. A handful of merchants from the

Baltic provinces (then under Swedish rule) and from the Black Sea coast traded in Siberia. English merchants were active in the Ob river region in western Siberia from the late sixteenth century, and exported goods back to England via the northern port of Archangel.[9] They established a trading base at Putozersk, on the river Pechora, and expressed an interest in the following 'Siberian' goods: feathers (from geese and ducks); fish (mainly salmon); furs; ivory from mammoth tusks. In 1611, one of the English merchants, William Pursglove, travelled inland with a caravan of 210 sledges to ascertain where he could best obtain furs and ivory. The English merchants found, however, that local merchants were hostile to their attempts to enter their trading zone and caused 'no little hindrance to the sale of our goods'. They were protected in the short term because John Merrick, the head of the English Muscovy Company, a London trading company which had established a monopoly over English trade in Russia in the mid-sixteenth century, offered English mediation to the new tsar, Michael, in a conflict with Sweden. Within a few years, however, this advantage had been lost and the Russian government became suspicious of English activities which might lessen the profits from the fur trade which accrued to Russian merchants and, most importantly, reduce the tax revenues which would accrue to the tsar. In 1616, the tsar ordered that all Siberian goods had to be traded by the southern route and not exported from the north by the sea route. Russians were now only allowed to trade with foreigners in Archangel and not in inland Siberian towns – under threat of execution if this were violated.[10]

Between the hunters/trappers and the merchants who lived in Siberian towns came the middlemen who handled most of the goods, transported them along the routes and, in particular, formed caravans that carried goods overland from China through Siberia. This trade was often in the hands of Tatars, and most notably in the hands of so-called 'Bukharans'.[11] This term sometimes simply meant traders from Central Asia, or even just Tatars, but strictly speaking it referred to traders from the Bukharan khanate, an area encompassing territory a bit larger than contemporary Uzbekistan, including the cities of Bukhara and Samarkand. The Bukharans had been trading in Siberia since the fourteenth century; they therefore preceded the arrival of Cossacks in the late sixteenth century, before the establishment of any Russian state apparatus and the founding of Russian towns in Siberia. Tsar Ivan IV had recognised their value and, in 1574, had instructed the Stroganovs, and then Russian officials, to treat the Bukharans well and to allow them to trade freely. The Bukharans also supplied the new settled population with goods. Bukharans were most active in western Siberia. They brought between one and four caravans of goods to the towns of Tobolsk and Tara every year throughout the seventeenth century. They came with goods from China and traded goods from Europe in return. They dominated the Siberian fairs, in particular the fair held every August at the town of Iamysh, on the river Irtysh. They handled the slave trade, luxury goods and daily foodstuffs of almost every type, with the exception of grain.

Some Bukharans became very wealthy. In 1666, an anonymous European officer described Tobolsk Bukharans as follows: 'These wealthy people, they live in wonderfully constructed wooden homes, with large windows and doors in the German [that is, foreign] style. Their rooms are decorated with beautifully carved stucco work and expensive Chinese carpets; they live cleanly and tidily, dressing in beautiful clothes.'[12]

Bukharans settled in the towns of Tobolsk, Tiumen, Tara and Tomsk, where they had trading stalls and warehouses. In the 1630s, 59 Bukharans were permanent residents in Tobolsk. By the end of the century, there were some 3,000 in Tiumen and Tobolsk. The nature of their activities meant that they had to interact with Russians, but they also maintained a separate identity, not least because they were Muslims. They tended to live in separate areas, either in villages or, more commonly, in specifically designated parts of Siberian towns. The latter were arranged in sections, with each section originally being surrounded by a separate stockade for defence, so it was relatively easy for different sections of the towns to be occupied by different social groups, or for individuals to pursue distinct occupations and to have distinct styles of dwellings (including yurts instead of wooden houses).

In the mid-seventeenth century, a church official complained that Muslim homes were too close to Orthodox homes in Tobolsk. 'Such impure living . . . is found nowhere else in Russian towns as it is in Tobolsk,' he asserted. In particular, he feared that Orthodox Christians would be disturbed during their fasts by their Muslim neighbours: 'While Christians are fasting, those unfaithful ones are having their weddings and big celebrations, and . . . Russians are badly influenced in a variety of ways.'[13] Despite these complaints, no attempt was made to move the non-Russians in Tobolsk. In 1703, the Siberian Office in Moscow ordered that mosques were to be built at a suitable distance from churches so that Christian services would not be disturbed. In reality, Russians and Bukharans worked together or for each other.

Some of the newly founded Siberian towns grew rapidly in size and significance during the seventeenth century. By the 1690s, Tobolsk had an annual
customs turnover of 50,000–60,000 roubles, which put it on a par with long-
established towns such as Pskov and Smolensk on the western borderlands of
Russia and the Polish-Lithuanian Commonwealth (a dualistic state in the
seventeenth and eighteenth centuries, and one of the largest countries in
Euope). On the other hand, some settlements in Siberia disappeared altogether as their trade dried up (as, indeed, they have done in Soviet and post-
Soviet Russia). Mangazeia, a prominent town in the early seventeenth
century, had collapsed by the end of the century through a combination of
political and economic factors: the tsar, as we have seen, closed the trade
route to Archangel because he feared further foreign penetration of Siberian
trade; in addition, the supply of furs diminished. After a fire in 1678 the town
was abandoned and the remaining population moved to the village of
Turkhansk, on the river Enisei, which was known as New Mangazeia until the
1780s. Pustozersk, where the English merchants had based themselves,
declined rapidly after they departed. The last inhabitants left that settlement
in the 1960s.

Trade, and the revenues that came from it, were of great value to the state,
and to the tsars personally. At least in the early years of the seventeenth
century, the fur trade delivered enormously lucrative revenues: one in every
ten pelts was taken by the state. Ensuring that this revenue was collected, and
then passed on to the tsar in Moscow, required in turn a state administrative
structure. Custom houses were set up in the new towns or forts in the early
years of the seventeenth century.[14]

The Russian government was all too aware that customs officials might
avail themselves of goods for their own benefit or take bribes. It tried, not
entirely successfully, to address these problems by restricting the categories
of people who could take these posts and the length of time they could
continue in them. Officials in the custom houses were supposed to be
appointed for a set period of time only from merchants and good citizens and
to serve in towns other than their home town, but achieving such a separation
was not always possible, particularly in the more remote forts. Governors
who administered vast areas of land were supposed not to be involved in the
fur trade, but in practice the opportunities for self-enrichment were too
tempting for many. This could lead all too easily to open corruption. The
whole customs process could also be evaded by smuggling goods either

through or round the customs points. In 1699, for example, a Bukharan merchant from Tobolsk, a certain Tatzimko Iatipov, attempted to smuggle 228 sable tails through the Verkhoture customs by hiding them inside pillows. On this occasion, the goods were discovered, confiscated and sent to Moscow.[15]

The government also attempted to regulate trade, which was to be conducted only in towns or forts. This restriction enabled the state to claim its share of the value of furs from indigenous hunters Left to their own devices, the indigenous hunters and trappers would naturally trade their best furs for goods with merchants and leave substandard sables for the state.

The state also tried to restrict the sale of certain goods to indigenous people. No arms could be sold to them. The sale of tobacco in Russia had been banned in 1613 by Tsar Michael because it was regarded as a harmful drug (a ban which was supported by the Church and reiterated in the Law Code of 1649 in the reign of Aleksei Mikhailovich under threat of execution). Peter I re-established the tobacco trade but sales to indigenous peoples continued to be banned because they were thought to be particularly susceptible to trances induced by smoking. A traveller described the effects:

> they swallow the Smoak, after which they fall down and lye insensible, like dead men with distorted Eyes, both Hands and Feet trembling for about half an Hour. They foam at the Mouth, so that they fall into a sort of Epilepsie: and we could not observe where the Smoak vented itself, and in this manner several of them are lost.[16]

To this extent at least, the state acted to protect native peoples, albeit treating them like children who could not be trusted to look after themselves. The prohibition was reiterated in 1697, after a certain Martyn Bogdanov was found to have traded tobacco with tribesmen in return for sables.[17]

From the very beginning, the Russian government was aware that indigenous peoples had to be incorporated into the state, and sought to win over the chiefs of tribal groups and their families, allowing them to continue to exercise control over other tribesmen. Governors entertained native chiefs lavishly, and some leading men were given ranks in the armed forces or became in effect Russian officials. Converts could join the Cossacks and serve in the armed forces. In fact, in this early period the lack of Russian government troops and Cossacks in Siberia meant that indigenous troops could outnumber Russians in active service and in garrisons. In 1659, an expedition in the north against Chukchi tribesmen numbered 150 Iukagirs and only 19 Russians.[18] As the century progressed it became easier to conscript Cossacks and other categories of military service men who had already settled in Siberia to the Russian army, so reducing the dependence on tribesmen.

The relationship between state officials and indigenous peoples was, however, marked from the start by conflict arising from the value of furs and the 'tribute' (*iasak*) which the state exacted from them. Taking 'tribute' was an indication of the inferior status of native peoples. Tribute was the form of levy which had been imposed by Mongol Tatars on subject peoples. To this extent, the tsars simply followed the practice that already existed in Sibir and other lands which had been under Mongol rule before Cossacks and hunters started to colonise Siberia. The taxation system in Russia at the time was complex and difficult to apply to primarily nomadic peoples. In 1600, there were approximately 280 different taxes in Russia including ones on buildings (bathhouses among them), goods, livestock and the postal service. The main tax, however, was based on a unit of ploughed land, replaced in 1679 by a tax on households. It is significant that there was no consideration of whether this taxation should be applied to native peoples as it was to new peasant settlers in Siberia from European Russia. The reason for this was simply that the tribute in furs was more valuable.

Tribute was extremely lucrative in the early years since it was initially paid in furs and in the early decades sables and arctic foxes were so plentiful. In the early seventeenth century, tribute could be as high as 16 to 22 sables per man.[19] But in time, as the supply of furs became exhausted, the tribute began to be paid in cash.

The collection of tribute was easiest in western Siberia, where the practice was already customary and where indigenous peoples were for the most part sedentary and easier to track and exploit. In western regions, local people sometimes came voluntarily to administrative centres to hand over furs as tribute. In more remote areas, where most people were nomadic, tribute was harder to collect and carrot-and-stick tactics had to be employed. Taking hostages and holding them at local forts to ensure payment was one such tactic; gifts of copper goods, cloth, and food and drink was another. Elaborate 'tribute books' recorded all the dues and payments, and also served to register members of households.

Tribute collection was regularly marked by violent conflict as furs were often taken by force from indigenous people who had few means to resist and little protection from excesses. The government far away in Moscow was aware of the violence; regular decrees were issued instructing governors and officials to treat indigenous people well. As early as 1601, Tsar Boris decreed: 'The inhabitants of Siberia are to live in our Tsarist favour, and not be oppressed, and are to be allowed to live in peace and tranquillity without fear.'[20] This instruction was repeated throughout the century, which indicates that such practices must have continued. In 1695, the Siberian Office in Moscow instructed officials not to 'execute or torture natives' and noted that many had been killed, whipped to death or tortured, that bribes had been demanded from them and livestock stolen, leading to the 'ruin of many tribute-paying people'.[21]

Cossacks and other soldiers were unruly and ill-governed, and could use their weapons on indigenous peoples. In 1635, Cossacks in the Krasnoiarsk region were alleged to have 'slaughtered many tribute Tatars'. In 1638, the governor of Krasnoiarsk, Petr Potasev, sent the Cossack ataman Miloslav Koltsov and Emelian Tiumentsev with 300 men to collect tribute; it was claimed that 86 native men were killed or captured in the process.[22]

Most violence would have gone unrecorded, and the victims had few means to protest against their treatment. It is perhaps remarkable that records are preserved of complaints by indigenous peoples about the violent behaviour of Cossacks made in the hope that action would be taken against them, and perhaps even more remarkable that on some occasions perpetrators were punished. In 1679, 280 sables were confiscated from a Cossack called Mukhoplev which 'he had taken for himself instead of state tribute'.[23] In 1688, two other Cossacks were investigated and punished for violence and theft in a village of Iakuts during the collection of tribute, where, according to a witness, 'they beat my father and my brothers and my relatives, and maimed them. They tortured them. They tied their hands behind their backs and tied them to the woodpile and out of insatiable greed stamped on their chests and beat them and stole everything possible by force.' One of the Cossacks involved was a prominent explorer but, surprisingly, that did not save him or his companion from a painful and humiliating flogging.[24] In 1690, a minor official called Poluekhtov was flogged because he stole sables and fox pelts.[25]

The violence over the collecting of tribute has to be seen in the context of the lawlessness of seventeenth-century Siberia and the fact that violence was endemic in this undergoverned land. The brutality of I. P. Golovin, the governor of Iakutsk, towards indigenous people in the seventeenth century was notorious. He 'flogged many Iakuts to death, used torture and starved others to death in a dungeon'. In 1606, officials in Tomsk were alleged to have 'tortured the natives and extorted exorbitant gifts'. In the town of Pelym, the local governor flogged many Ostiaks to death. A certain official called Pushkin, in order 'to satisfy his greed, flogged the natives with rods and kept them in irons'. A minor official in Okhotsk was said to have hanged and flogged Tungus, and mutilated them by cutting off their ears and noses.[26] In 1646, in the Lena region, the Cossack leader Vasilii Kolesnikov and his men attacked Buriats, took their wives and children captive, and stole horses and cattle.[27] The following year, a Cossack called Vaska Firsov attacked two Kalmyk tribesmen with an axe and robbed them.[28]

The violence was not one-sided: indigenous people also attacked soldiers, officials and peasants, and some of these conflicts were long-lasting and bloody. In 1604, a major uprising took place around the Ob river area involving Tatars, Kirghiz and Ostiaks. A native army was raised in 1612, in part because the leaders were vaguely aware there was a crisis of rule at that time in Moscow – that, in their words, there was 'no tsar'. Kirghiz and Buriat tribesmen conducted attacks on settlers in the Enisei region throughout the 1620s and the 1630s. In 1683, 13 tribute collectors were killed by tribesmen.[29] In 1645, a battle raged for two days on the river Oka. The battle led to the fortification of the town of Krasnoiarsk to defend the inhabitants. In 1658, Buriats revolted around the fort of Balagan. There were uprisings in the vicinity of Krasnoiarsk in the 1670s. In September 1700, Kirghiz attacked Russians and Kalmyks, killing six people and wounding far more and stealing horses and cattle. The following month the slaughter continued, including 12 Cossack children, 16 women and 7 Kalmyks.[30] In 1706, Kirghiz tribesmen attacked the fort of Aninsk, near Lake Baikal, and killed Cossacks and other inhabitants, including women and children.[31]

Traders were both subject to and involved in violence with other ethnic groups. In 1625, a whole party in a caravan from Tobolsk to Central Asia was murdered by the Kalmyks who were travelling with it.[32] In 1672, Ermamet Tachkalov, a prominent Bukharan trader, complained, along with some Tatars, that Russians had assaulted them as they watered their animals, and that as a result 'their women and children could no longer use the spring'. In 1682, a petition from Tiumen Tatars complained that other Tatars and

Bukharans had let their livestock trample on their fields. A Cossack complained that a Bukharan called Shadru Utiakov from Tiumen had attacked him without justification.[33]

While Siberia was a source of wealth, or at least was perceived as a source of wealth, for hunters, traders and tribute collectors in the seventeenth century, the victims of the penetration of Siberia were primarily its indigenous peoples. Siberia also had to be colonised by administrators, lawkeepers and, most importantly, farmers. Some of these settlers came to Siberia to find employment, prosperity and freedom; others were sent there against their will. All of them had to come to terms not only with the climate and the terrain but also with the presence of the original inhabitants. It is to these settlers that we now turn.

CHAPTER FOUR

Early Settlers: The Free and the Unfree

IT WAS Cossacks and hunters who first came to Siberia from European Russia. They were soon followed by other soldiers and officials as the Russian government tried to establish at least a tenuous presence in this vast region. A Russian state presence could, however, only be more firmly established if colonists settled the land. Peasants soon outnumbered other groups of settlers during the seventeenth century. Officials and military men in the town of Krasnoiarsk rose from 377 in 1669 to almost 700 by the end of the century, but in the same period the number of state peasants in the districts around Krasnoiarsk rose from some 200 families to over 900 families.[1]

Who were the early settlers and was it their choice to relocate to Siberia? And how did they interact with each other and with the indigenous population?

Military men inevitably dominated in the early colonisation of Siberia. Governors, or *voevody*, were important noble officials with military backgrounds, who were sent by the tsar to rule territories in Siberia, which in the seventeenth century might be relatively small areas around towns or vast, almost uninhabited regions in the north and east. In Russia, there were several categories of military men who had traditionally been rewarded with land, peasants or other privileges in return for service in active campaigns or garrison duty on the frontiers. In European Russia, these groups gradually became absorbed into the regular army or the state peasantry in the late seventeenth and early eighteenth centuries. They played a crucial part, however, in the early settlement of Siberia in the seventeenth century and continued to exist there as separate groups well into the eighteenth century.

These groups included so-called 'boiars' sons', or 'boiars' children', who were originally impoverished or younger sons of military men who had not achieved the rank of a *boiar* (or *boyar*), that is, a member of the higher nobility. At this time Russia had a complex and elaborate system of ranking of nobles in military and civil service, known as 'placing by preference', which lasted until 1682, whereby nobles could refuse to serve under anyone considered to be of a lower rank or standing. Within this system, 'boiars' sons' were the lowest-ranking nobles. In addition, military service-men on so-called 'provincial lists' were ranked lower than military service-men in Moscow. The 'nobles' in Siberia were therefore the lowest-ranking nobles in the country. These 'nobles' were also few in number, which had an effect, as we shall see, on both rural and urban life in Siberia.

'Boiars' sons' were nevertheless higher in rank than ordinary Cossacks, and Cossacks were sometimes promoted by the governors to the rank of 'boiars' son' and some 'boiars' sons' even became governors. In 1627, there were 37 'boiars' sons' in the town of Tobolsk, along with 10 Poles and 3 'Germans' (often in Russian before the nineteenth century the word 'German' was used to describe any European who could not speak Russian). Their numbers in Tobolsk rose to 40 by 1638, 129 by 1660 and reached 229 by 1681.[2] The title of 'boiars' sons' lost its original meaning during the eighteenth century and some of the families were renamed 'Siberian nobility', but that title also indicated that they were regarded as lower in status than nobles in European Russia. In 1822, the legal categories of both 'boiars' sons' and 'Siberian nobility' were abolished and the members of these groups were reclassified as Cossacks.

Cossacks had been the main driving force in opening up Siberia in the late sixteenth century and in bringing it under the tsar. However, they could also be transported at the will of the state to defend other borders as the need arose. As a result, Cossacks from the Don and Volga regions of European Russia ended up in far less comfortable frontier posts in Siberia. This also explains why their numbers continued to grow during the seventeenth century. There were some 2,000 Cossacks in Siberian service by 1631.[3] They could also be moved around Siberia. In 1640, for example, an infantry Cossack called Kirilov was sent to Atbash (an occasionally garrisoned fort in the Tiumen region) for a year.[4]

Cossacks were committed to a specific period of military service, normally 20 years although only about half of that would be in active service. When they were not serving in garrisons or engaged in other military duties, Cossacks and their families in European Russia lived in communities as peasants. Siberia was too far away for Cossacks to return to their original communities in European Russia after they had completed their military service, so they had to petition for their families to be allowed to join them in Siberia. Even when not on military service, Cossacks were expected to guard the settlements – villages and forts – as well as to become colonists. This meant that Cossack communities developed differently in Siberia from Cossack settlements in European Russia. Siberian Cossacks often lived with the peasants rather than in separate communities, and many became residents of new towns, although they could still be occupied in agriculture as well as in crafts and petty trade. In time, and through the next generations, they came to acquire a separate identity among Cossacks as 'Siberian Cossacks' and lost the links to their original birthplaces.

Another group of military men in seventeenth-century Siberia was the so-called *strelt'sy*, a term usually translated as 'musketeers', who were primarily infantrymen who had been used in auxiliary regiments for the cavalry in the sixteenth century. The number of musketeers in Tobolsk rose over the seventeenth century, from 53 in 1647 to 455 by 1693.[5] Along with Cossacks and 'boiars' sons', these musketeers became a major component of the armed forces in Siberia in the seventeenth century. They could, like Cossacks, simply be transported from areas of European Russia to Siberia for service. Many seem to have come from the northern region of European Russia bordering the Arctic Ocean, but they might originate from any town or region. Like Cossacks, the musketeers who were sent to Siberia were male and, again like Cossacks, they had to appeal to the government for their families to be allowed to join them. In the early eighteenth century, in the reign of Peter I, the musketeers were replaced by a more modern army of regular officers (drawn from the nobility) and conscripted men. Musketeers, however, continued to exist, with obligations and privileges, in the more remote parts of the Russian empire – such as Siberia.

Military men in Siberia also included a number of men categorised as 'foreigners' or sometimes as 'Lithuanians', comprising prisoners of war who, voluntarily or otherwise, had entered the military service of the tsar. In the seventeenth century, these men were usually Poles, Lithuanians or Swedes (although they could include other nationalities – there were Turkish prisoners of war in the Narym garrison, on the river Ob, in the 1630s).[6] Some 'foreign' prisoners of war served for 20 or 30 years in Siberia and became part of the armed forces. Other 'foreigners' arrived in Siberia as voluntary settlers or as exiles and remained as permanent settlers.

The Polish-Lithuanian Commonwealth (founded in 1567 and dissolved in 1795) was one of the largest states in Europe in the seventeenth century, and was involved in a number of wars with Russia during the latter period. Many Polish and Lithuanian prisoners entered Russian military service after they were captured in these conflicts. In 1633, the Tobolsk garrison included 140 'foreigners' among its 1,175 men. In Tomsk in 1657–8, 95 of the 847 military residents were listed as 'foreigners'. It is not clear how many of these men stayed in Siberia voluntarily when the wars ended, although for many it would have been no worse than service in other armies of the time, and possibly offered them better conditions and opportunities. In 1654, a Pole called Fedor Kozyrevsky was captured and entered Russian service. He was sent to Iakutsk to serve as an ordinary Cossack. By 1668, he was in Tobolsk, ready to be returned to Poland, but the Tobolsk governor apparently persuaded him and two other Poles to remain in Siberia 'for permanent service' and awarded him the rank of 'boiar's son'.[7] Poles continued to be 'involuntary' settlers in Siberia – we will see that Polish rebels in the late eighteenth century and in the 1830s and 1860s were exiled to Siberia as forced labourers and settlers.

The existence of these military men resulted in towns in Siberia having a quite different social composition from towns in European Russia. Siberian towns in the seventeenth century were primarily military bases and administrative centres. For example, in 1663, the town of Tiumen in western Siberia comprised 29 'boiars' children', 68 'Lithuanians', 187 Cossacks, 297 musketeers, 10 gunners (another category of military service-man) and 107 serving Tatars.

Siberia, as we have seen, was not an empty land when Cossacks, soldiers, officials and traders from Russia first began to arrive. Russians and non-Russians had to live side by side. The town of Iakutsk in northern Siberia was founded in 1632 on the river Lena. By 1641, there were 46 yurts (that is, dwellings of Iakut design) and 24 wooden huts (that is, dwellings of Russian design). At this time the population of the town numbered 280 males, of whom 68 were military service-men (including Cossacks), 86 were hunters/trappers, 3 were traders and 123 were Iakuts. Men from different social groups lived together in huts or yurts. In one hut, a trader, Semen Strekalovsky, lived with another trader, Vasilii Vologzhanin, two hunter/trappers called Motor

Afanasev and Foma Semenov, a Cossack called Timofei Blokhin and a cook called Karpunko Semenov. In another hut lived seven hunters/trappers and two native women.[8]

The state presence in Siberia – officials, Cossacks and other soldiers – determined the distinct social composition of seventeenth-century Siberian towns. Many of these men were involuntary settlers with little chance of returning to their homes in Russia, Ukraine or Poland-Lithuania. The Siberian countryside also had to be farmed, and that required peasants to undertake the hard and often dangerous journey eastwards across the Ural mountains to settle and cultivate the new lands.

Some peasants migrated voluntarily from European Russia and Ukraine. They came to escape impoverishment; a few perhaps fled to escape retribution for disobedience and crime. Peasants came from all parts of European Russia but particularly from the south and the lower Volga region. Flight could be determined by local conditions, as peasants escaped not only grain shortages but also local disturbances and conflicts.

Until the mid-seventeenth century, all peasants in European Russia had some freedom to move, although those rights became more and more restricted until finally they were only able to move off the land on a limited number of fixed days of the year, normally after sowing or harvest time. In the primitive Russian economic and political system, peasants *were* wealth. Military men who were rewarded with land for their service measured their reward by the number of peasants living on the land they had been given rather than by the size of the plot. These military men, especially the large number of poorer ones, constantly urged the tsar to give them permanent ownership of their peasants and to forbid them from leaving their land. In 1649, Tsar Aleksei Mikhailovich, under pressure from these poorer military service-men at a time when his throne was vulnerable, issued a Law Code of enormous significance which institutionalised serfdom by abolishing the right of these peasants, and of all peasants of private landowners, irrespective of their wealth or status, to leave of their own free will and in effect made them the chattels of their landowners. Such peasants became known as serfs – and were distinct from peasants who lived on state land.

From this date, serfs who fled to Siberia could be returned to their owners. Some were indeed so returned but, in practice, Siberian officials were very reluctant to seek out and return peasants when their labour was so valuable. It is impossible to enter the mind-set of a seventeenth-century Russia peasant, but there is some evidence from the petitions from peasants against their return to owners that their perception was that once they had crossed the Ural mountains into Siberia they were no longer serfs but state peasants – that is, they now lived on land owned by the state.[9]

No serfs – is that what made Siberia special, and free? That is certainly part of Siberian self-perception, and it is certainly true that the social structure in Siberia was different from that in the heartland of European Russia. It is not quite true, however, that there were no serfs in Siberia. There was a very small number, living on land owned by 'boiars' sons', or other military service-men, or by the few nobles who had landed estates, including, of course, the wealthy Stroganovs. Some peasants also hired land from other peasants or from military men, along with horses and agricultural implements, in return for half their produce: an arrangement which was not very different in practice from serfdom. Some serfs from European Russia were also forced by their often wealthy noble owners to resettle next to large factories and were, in effect, enserfed in the factories (this is discussed more fully in the next chapter). The majority of peasants in Siberia, however, were so-called state peasants, who lived on land owned by the state and not by individual landowners, and who owed obligations, such as taxation and labour dues, to the state rather than to individual landowners.

Central to later Russian, and Western, perceptions of Russian backwardness in the eighteenth and nineteenth centuries was the assumption that the institution of serfdom in the mid-seventeenth century retarded Russia's development. Serfs were bound to their landowners, whether they were wealthy, established, noble families or impoverished military service-men. Serfs had to work for a number of days per week on the land of their owners; they had to pay dues directly to their owners; they were not allowed to leave the land of their own free will; they could be moved, with or without their families, to other estates; minor offences were dealt with by noblemen rather than the state courts; they could be obliged to work in the household of wealthy noblemen rather than in the fields. In sum, they were 'owned' by their landowners. This is certainly true, and militated against agricultural modernisation and social mobility, but in purely economic terms state peasants in European Russia were often worse off than serfs because the land owned by wealthy nobles was, unsurprisingly, usually of better quality and more productive than state land. More state peasants than serfs abandoned their homes in European Russia to make their way to Siberia.

State peasants in European Russia lived where there were few noble landed estates: where the quality of the soil was poor or in the borderlands, mainly on the southern frontiers and in the far north. In the far north, the climate and the terrain made for a primitive and subsistence agriculture of slash and burn, where forests or vegetation were burnt to create fields but the quality of the soil was so poor that the process had to be continually repeated.

Furthermore, the 'freedom' of state peasants, whether in European Russia or Siberia, did not mean that they were simply free to go where they wished and claim any land as their own, or that they were free from taxation and other obligations to the state. Some state peasants were in fact moved en masse to empty lands in Siberia from state lands in European Russia. Indeed, restrictions on movement applied not only to peasants but also, as we have seen, to Cossacks and military men, and applied not just in the seventeenth century but throughout the whole period of the tsarist empire, and to individuals and some groups of people in the Soviet period as well.

Once settled, peasants had to petition for the right to move to another location in Siberia. When they arrived in any region of Siberia they were allocated plots of land which came with obligations to pay the state certain dues – in kind or, later, in cash – in return for the use of the land. In other words, dues were owed to the state on 'state' land, instead of to nobles on noble-owned land. That peasants were in effect tenants of state land can be seen both in the privileges they initially received as well as the obligations they owed. New settlers were often given seed and agricultural implements by the state as well as exemption from taxation for a number of years. In fact, in the early years of the seventeenth century, it was relatively easy for peasants to farm extra unused land in addition to land allocated by the state and then claim it as their own, but this became less common as the regions became better administered.

It may seem odd that restrictions should be placed on peasant landownership, given the vastness of Siberia and the wish for the land to be cultivated. These restrictions, however, have to be understood in both legal and fiscal terms. Land was allocated per male peasant on a rough understanding of how much it could yield, which it was assumed would both sustain the peasant household and provide dues for the state. Peasants could and did petition the Siberian Office (the main administrative office for Siberian affairs) in Moscow with requests for more land per person or for less onerous dues for temporary or permanent reasons. They could not, however, escape the allocation process or the obligations and restrictions on movement which came with their land. The same happened in the eighteenth and nineteenth centuries, and even during the mass migration to Siberia at the end of the nineteenth century.

Siberia was also settled by so-called 'Church peasants', who were owned by the Church and, like serfs, had to work the land for and/or pay dues in cash or kind to their owners. Orthodox churches and monasteries were established in Siberia as soon as the land was secured, however tenuously. A monastery was set up in Tobolsk with a charter and land granted by Tsar Fedor as early as 1596. In all, 36 monasteries and convents were established from Tiumen in the west to Irkutsk in eastern Siberia in the seventeenth century.[10] Lands held by monasteries could be extensive; by 1686, the Epiphany monastery (founded in 1622) had almost 900 acres of land cultivated by almost 100 peasant households.[11] Some of these Church peasants would have been moved eastwards from monasteries in European Russia. Other peasants 'fell' into this category when they settled on land owned by monasteries.

For all that peasants were not 'free' in a modern sense, the majority of them had chosen to settle in Siberia and, in doing so, many had been released from personal bondage to noble landowners. From the early years, however, Siberia was used as a place for penal exile, and has continued to be used as such ever since. These 'unfree' men, sometimes accompanied or joined by their families, were sent to Siberia as a punishment or, strictly speaking, as a supplementary punishment, either for a short period or permanently as settlers.

In 1582, a supplement to an earlier Law Code permitted the state to use exile as a punishment.[12] The number of exiles in Siberia in the seventeenth century was small compared with other groups, but still not inconsiderable. Some 28,000 men and women were exiled in the period 1662–1709. Exiles came from all sections of society. At one end, high-profile rivals to the throne were exiled; at the other, vagrants and criminals. In 1635, a woman in the entourage of the wife of Tsar Michael confessed under torture that she was in possession of a magical root which she had been given by the wife of a musketeer. The wretched woman claimed that she intended to use it to restore her husband's affection for her, and not to harm the tsar's family. All the same, she and her husband were exiled to Siberia, an early and little-known case of political exile for anti-tsarist activity.[13] An early exile on grounds of his religious beliefs was Prince Semen Shakhovskoi, who was tried and found guilty of heresy in the 1640s but whose death sentence was commuted to exile to Siberia.[14]

The most notorious exile in the seventeenth century was Archpriest Avvakum, who wrote one of the first accounts of exile to Siberia and of his brutal treatment at the hands of his jailer. Avvakum was the most high-profile opponent of the changes to the liturgy, text and ritual of the Orthodox Church in the mid-seventeenth century, in the reign of Tsar Aleksei Mikhailovich. The changes involved what may seem relatively trivial matters of liturgy and outward forms (for example, the number of fingers used when making the sign of the cross) but they were seen by Avvakum and his supporters as a heretical attack on the purity of Russian Orthodoxy. The changes were implemented in the 1660s with the support of the tsar, but the Church split irrevocably over them, and those who did not accept the new practices became known as Old Believers. Siberia became closely linked with Old Belief: Old Believers, and other religious nonconformists, were forcibly exiled to Siberia but they also chose to flee to the forests of Siberia as a safe haven in which they could practise their beliefs. Their communities still exist today.

Avvakum's experience of exile in Siberia was harrowing. He set off with his family (his wife and four young children) in September 1653 on a 13-week journey to exile in Tobolsk. At first, this proved a relatively civilised existence, and Avvakum was appointed archpriest at one of the churches in Tomsk. He apparently lost support of local officials because of his rigid position on religious observance. In any event, in 1655, he was exiled further east and made chaplain to an expedition which was exploring the lands east of Lake Baikal under Afanasii Pashkov. Both his commander and jailer, Pashkov tormented Avvakum, and on one occasion had him brutally flogged (with 72 blows of the knout, a fearsome whip of rawhide with metal tips) and then imprisoned under appalling conditions, as his victim recounted:

> there I lay till Advent, in a freezing tower. . . . Like a poor dog I lay on the straw; and sometimes they fed me, and sometimes they did not; there were many mice and I would strike at them with my biretta. . . . I lay all the time on my belly, my back was covered with sores, and of fleas and lice there was abundance.[15]

Avvakum, incidentally, having returned from his Siberian exile to Moscow in 1662, was unrepentant in his opposition to the reforms. He was exiled again,

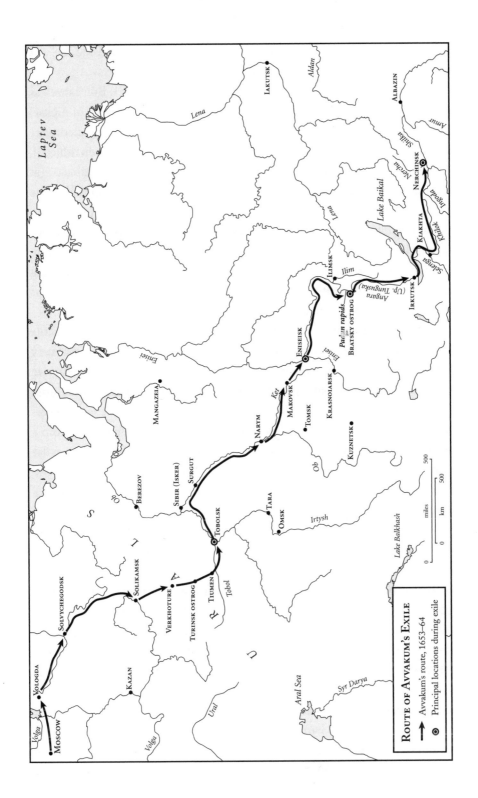

ROUTE OF AVVAKUM'S EXILE

→ Avvakum's route, 1653–64
⊙ Principal locations during exile

this time to a prison in the far north of European Russia; in 1682, he was condemned to death and burnt at the stake.

Before 1649, few ordinary criminals were exiled to Siberia. But, as well as institutionalising serfdom the Law Code issued in 1649 in the reign of Aleksei Mikhailovich detailed the crimes for which perpetrators could be exiled, after brutal corporal punishment and in many cases mutilation had been inflicted. These included murder, banditry and theft but also possession of tobacco (at the time a banned substance). Corporal punishment was supposed to be excruciatingly painful and act as a warning to others, as well as providing a gruesome public spectacle. Those who survived it (a man could be killed with seven blows of the knout, but sentences of several hundred blows were common) were expected to provide economic benefit for the state by settling distant lands (not unlike convicts sent to Australia from Britain). It was assumed that these convicts could and would become useful subjects.

Convicts were supposed to be provided with land, seed and implements for farming in Siberia, like free peasant settlers. In reality, however, it was very hard to turn these poor wretches into useful subjects. Many did not survive the initial journey out, made more difficult by the fact that exiles were used to colonise remote regions in the north and east rather than the more accessible and more heavily populated western Siberia. Only 9 members from a group of 19 exiles survived the journey to Iakutsk in 1685.[16] In practice, exiles often failed to receive either sustenance en route or the promised land and implements if and when they finally arrived at their destination. A group of 28 penal settlers on the river Lena in 1648 was described as 'poor, without grain and without clothing'; 'none of them had anything'.[17] It was not so different, as we shall see, from the experiences of the kulaks exiled to Siberia in the 1930s.

Exiled penal settlers were dependent on the state supplying necessary goods for agriculture; in 1676, forced settlers in the Amur region petitioned Moscow for the provision of basic tools, including 129 axes, 100 ploughshares, 200 scythes and 200 sickles.[18] Life in the remoter areas of forced settlement was harsher than in the western, more fertile and more settled, part of Siberia, and many exiles were victims of crop failure and attacks from local tribesmen. Some exiles simply fled from their place of settlement and became vagabonds and bandits.

It is hard to assess the contribution made by exiles to the colonisation of Siberia in the seventeenth century. It is possible that forced exile to the more remote, and less productive, northern and far eastern regions of Siberia helped maintain a Russian presence there. Individuals and families of exiles were settled in the Lena river region, although they were never in the majority. Penal settlers and free settlers could live together. One list of peasants on the river Lena in 1656 noted that 3 of the 48 were 'exiles' who had been convicted of theft.[19] As 'free' settlers could also include fugitive serfs who had fled from their noble landowners as well as impoverished peasants, such distinctions may have meant little in practice. Between 1640 and 1653, 296 people were moved into the Iakutsk region, including 47 Cossacks, 14 retired Cossacks, 111 exiles, 7 military service-men and 76 'vagrants'.[20]

Another group of 'unfree' people in Siberia was indigenous slaves. The Russian government tried in the early decades of the seventeenth century to restrict the practice of enslaving indigenous people who were prisoners of war, or who had simply been taken by force from their villages and families. However, a combination of ingrained habit and immediate need in Siberia and the formal institutionalisation of serfdom in European Russia in 1649 meant that slavery continued in Siberia. Slavery already existed in any event within tribal groups. Ownership of slaves was common, for example, among Iakuts. In 1675, an Iakut called Kurdiage Totoev sold his daughter for a horse and two cows with calves.[21]

Impoverished families sold their children into slavery to Russian settlers. A tribute book in 1698 recorded that 'many Iakuts are poor and have neither necessities nor livestock and tribute'.[22] Some peasants employed native boys to look after livestock, which may have been very little different from slavery in practice. Enslavement also enabled some able boys to find a respectable position in society. Russian merchants in the seventeenth century bought native boys as assistants. The wealthy Kalmykov merchant family purchased a Tatar boy called Kabulaik who grew up to be a trusted agent.[23] As late as 1732, an Iakut called Dydarov (a Russian name so he was almost certainly a convert to Christianity) sold his five-year-old grandson for seven roubles to a Russian, Vasilii Stupin.[24] Slavery largely died out in European Russia in the early eighteenth century, but continued in Siberia into the early nineteenth century.

A striking aspect of the composition of early settlers in Siberia – free or unfree – was that it was overwhelmingly male. In 1648, peasants in Tomsk stated that 'they were in need and poor and have no wives or children'.[25] Military men and other settlers had to petition to allow their wives and families to join them. A certain Fedoseev, who had been a 'vagrant' (probably a fugitive peasant) before getting a job as a clerk, asked permission in 1650 to travel to the town of Velikii Ustiug, on the other side of the Urals, to fetch his wife and children.[26] Exiles were also predominantly male: in 1709, two-thirds of exiles were men.[27] In its own way, the state tried to address the issue in the seventeenth century. The Siberian Office in Moscow recorded in 1631 that 39 women voluntarily arrived in Enisei for 'marriage to Enisei servitors [military service-men] and ploughing peasants'.[28] Six years later, another 150 girls were dispatched to Siberia as wives for Cossacks.[29]

Gender imbalance continued to be a problem in Siberia, both after as well as before the end of the imperial regime. It was even claimed in the seventeenth century by Patriarch Filaret that men had incestuous relationships with their sisters, mothers and daughters as there was such a shortage of women.[30] Mixed marriages, or relationships, between settlers and indigenous peoples took place, particularly in the more remote, less settled, regions. In the eighteenth and nineteenth centuries, and even in the Soviet period, as we shall see, there were further attempts to attract, or force, women to settle in Siberia.[31] But what sort of life awaited these settlers – male and female – after the first century of settlement? This is the subject of the next four chapters.

CHAPTER FIVE

Life in a Siberian Village

A VILLAGE in Siberia in the eighteenth and the first half of the nineteenth century differed little from a village in north European Russia. The houses would be made of wood; the window frames would be in blue or white and sometimes carved; each house would have a small plot for vegetables; there would be tumbledown barns and outhouses; there would be some chickens running around and a horse tethered to a fence; the paths would be rutted and unpaved; the village would be on a river bank; there would be a wooden Russian Orthodox church and a communal bathhouse. The settlers in Siberia were ethnically Russian, or possibly Ukrainian or Belarusian; they brought seed and agricultural implements with them and continued with much the same farming, occupations and way of life as they had done at home. The state demanded much the same dues and obligations from peasants in Siberia as it had done in European Russia; peasant society and peasant households were organised in much the same way as in European Russia; the vast majority of peasants were Russian Orthodox.

Siberia was nevertheless different from European Russia. The environment, the climate, the natural resources, the terrain, the distances and the difficulties of communication all affected the way peasants worked, dressed and lived. The particular social composition of Siberia discussed in the last chapter – the small number of serfs compared with state peasants, the presence of so many Cossacks and military men, the indigenous peoples – all had an impact on village life, on personal relationships and on the way peasants governed themselves.

In the Russian empire as a whole the proportion of serfs and state peasants changed over the eighteenth and first half of the nineteenth century: in 1719, there were two-and-a-half times as many serfs as state peasants, but that proportion then changed in favour of state peasants, who became the majority by 1850. Part of this change was owing to the recategorisation of almost all Church peasants as state peasants after the secularisation of Church lands in 1762–4. As we have seen, the vast majority of peasants in Siberia were state peasants, who lived on state land and paid dues to the state rather than to noble landowners. The fourth census (which recorded only male inhabitants) in 1782 recorded that there were 297,698 male state peasants in Siberia, who comprised some 77 per cent of the population (in the Russian empire as a whole serfs outnumbered state peasants at this date: over 5 million male serfs compared with just under 4 million state peasants).[1] In addition, the census recorded 17,266 male monastic peasants and 3,097 male serfs in Siberia.

Serfs lived on the small number of noble estates in Siberia, mostly on lands near the Ural mountains. In the mid-nineteenth century, the state tried to establish just how many noble landowners there were in the area. In 1850, 65 nobles were recorded in western Siberia, who owned over 250,000 acres of land, but there were only two noble landowners in eastern Siberia. At that time it was estimated that there were 2,367 male serfs on 33 noble estates in Siberia.[2] By 1861, there were some 3,700 male serfs in Siberia. Some of those would have been domestic serfs, that is, they would have worked within the noble households.

All members of society in Russia were put into legal categories which not only determined their privileges and status but also their obligations to the state (including their taxation status). In time, occupations became divorced from legal status – peasants could live and trade in towns or work in factories, Cossacks could work in the fields as peasants. This had an impact on the composition of the Siberian village, which was often mainly peasant and Russian, but rarely exclusively so. It did not mean that Cossacks, artisans or soldiers were not occupied in village agriculture, or that they lived any differently from their peasant neighbours, or that they were ethnically different. Their obligations to the state and taxation status were, however, different. It has been estimated that at the beginning of the eighteenth century approximately one-third of cultivated land in Siberia was worked by non-peasants. In 1703, it was found, for example, that 51 of the 53 'boiars' sons' registered in the Tomsk garrison were in fact involved in agricultural pursuits.[3]

Villages in the Krasnoiarsk region in the late eighteenth century included retired Cossacks and soldiers alongside peasants. As retired military service-men, these Cossacks and soldiers could be elderly, and probably no longer able to farm the land. The records also suggest they had married, or remarried, in retirement and that their children were young enough to work as peasants, although they could not change their legal status. For example, in the village of Ust Botoiskoe, in the Krasnoiarsk region, lived a 75-year-old retired Cossack who had five children aged between 5 and 18.[4] Some Cossacks in Siberia did live in separate settlements (called a *stanitsa*) but many were in effect peasants and lived with peasants and worked on the land with them. Soldiers and their descendants lived in Siberian villages alongside peasants. In the village of Barabanov, again in the Krasnoiarsk region, 2 of the 20 houses were occupied by retired soldiers. A retired soldier and his wife lived in one of the huts, but the other housed a family of nine with a retired soldier aged 75 as the head of the household.[5]

We will see in the next chapter that crafts and trade developed in Russian towns. 'Artisans' were a legal category of townspeople, but they also lived in villages in the countryside. The difference between 'village' and 'town' was very difficult to define in Siberia – large villages and small towns were much the same. Peasants needed basic goods which they could not make or grow themselves – some items of clothing, leather goods and agricultural imple-ments, salt, tea, etc. – and many artisans also had garden plots and livestock. The village of Gorshek in the Krasnoiarsk region included 11 artisan fami-lies.[6] Cossacks and artisans might be competitors for land as well as fellow villagers. In 1788, peasants in the Krasnoiarsk region complained that 'many artisans from Kuznetsk district and retired Cossacks' were occupied in haymaking, which was causing hardship for peasants.[7]

The Kolyvan area in the Altai mountains had a large number of industrial enterprises, mostly mines, some of which were enormous. Most of these enterprises were owned by noble families, such as the Stroganovs, although some were owned by the state. It was very difficult to recruit workers for them. In the rigid social structure of imperial Russia it was almost impossible for any serf, state peasant or townsman to freely leave their village, or town, to work in a factory and, in effect, to change their social estate from peasant or artisan to factory worker. In any event, the work was very hard and conditions were very poor, so only the desperate would volunteer to become factory workers.

The result was that factories were partly manned by convicts who had been sentenced to hard labour, partly by army deserters and fugitive serfs, and partly by serfs who had been forcibly removed from European Russia by their owners to work in their factories. Some of these serfs worked for a limited period in the factories and then returned home. Others were forcibly resettled in new villages specially created near the factories, where agricultural work was undertaken alongside factory work. These former serfs were identified as a separate category of 'possessional' or 'assigned' peasants, but I will refer to them as 'factory peasants'. The number of these peasants rose in the Altai region over the eighteenth and first half of the nineteenth century from 121 males in 1746 to 54,750 in 1781, 63,355 in 1807 and 145,584 in 1857.[8] Factory villages could be particularly large and of very mixed social composition. The village of Krivoshchekova, for example, in the Altai, comprised 1,307 factory peasants, 62 artisans, 9 retired soldiers and 13 families of clergy.[9]

Factory peasants were close in status to serfs because they could be moved from place to place by their owners and forced to work in factories. Poor conditions meant there were frequent disturbances at factories, as at other places of forced labour, and also that some workers simply fled. Some of these fugitives ended up in villages, where they were often used as hired labour for menial tasks. A few examples demonstrate how the existence of factories contributed to the complexity of the composition of peasant communities in Siberia as well as the fate of unfortunate individuals who tried to escape factory bondage. Three men fled from one of the Kolyvan factories in 1738, and were hidden for a couple of days in a peasant village before being caught and returned to the factory.[10] One Arkhip Tetenev registered as a peasant and lived in a village but was then discovered to be a fugitive from a Stroganov iron factory and returned to the factory in 1741.[11] A certain Stepan Durygin fled from a Kolyvan factory and registered as a peasant, but was caught in 1824, beaten and returned to his place of work.[12]

Peasant settlers also encountered non-Russian, and non-Christian, original inhabitants. Taking and farming land which had previously been used by indigenous peoples inevitably led to clashes. We have seen in the previous chapters that there were violent clashes between settlers and indigenous people in the seventeenth century. Conflict continued, at least in part because there were rival claims to land.[13] Impoverished indigenous people also hired themselves out to peasant settlers: for example, it was reported that

impoverished Tungus 'from need' lived in Russian villages and hired themselves out for work for Russian peasants or in the Nerchinsk factories.[14]

For the most part, Russian settlers and non-Russians lived apart. The tiny
village of Shiverskie in the Krasnoiarsk region in the late eighteenth century
listed only two households, both of 'tribute people'.[15] In the mid-nineteenth
century, there were separate 'Muslim villages' in the Kainsk district, in western
Siberia, which varied in size from a small settlement of 15 households to a
large village of 208 Muslim households.[16] The lists of households in the
Siberian archives suggest that Russians might live with converted indigenous
people in the same village. The village of Gutova in the Kolyvan region
comprised 771 factory peasants, 160 artisans, 16 members of the clergy and
their families, 15 retired soldiers and 116 'tribute-paying' people. The latter
had Russian, or semi-Russian, names, which means that they had almost
certainly converted to Christianity.[17]

How well did peasants live in the eighteenth and the first half of the nineteenth century? Some exiles in Siberia were favourably impressed by the
conditions they discovered there. A Polish exile commented in 1770 that 'we
found everywhere abundance, prosperity, and villages populated with a
people more humane than in Russia'. In 1791, the exiled writer Aleksandr
Radishchev commented: 'In many places the peasant lives in abundance; the
old inhabitants are often wealthy from raising grain and cattle.' But could it be
that reformist political exiles wanted to believe that peasants were better off
in Siberia because there was no (or very little) serfdom? State peasants in
Siberia were not in bondage to noble landowners: they were free from their
jurisdiction for petty offences and, indeed, from physical and sexual abuse at
their hands, which certainly occurred in estates in European Russia and
which writers such as Radishchev found so offensive. 'The common people
seemed to be much more free, more clever, even more educated than our
Russian peasants', commented another political exile in the 1820s.[18]

Peasant settlers certainly moved to Siberia looking for prosperity, or at
least relief from poverty, but had little intention of farming in any other way
than that they had farmed at home. If they were able to, they brought seed
with them to grow the main staple crops of European Russia, as well as their
own livestock and agricultural implements. Impoverished peasants and
forced settlers were supposed to be provided with these basic supplies by the
government. In western and southern Siberia, much of the land was fertile,
and the water supply was plentiful, although the growing season was shorter

than in central or southern European Russia and weather conditions could be more extreme in the winter. In these regions, peasant settlers were able to adapt relatively easily to the new conditions and their agricultural practices changed little. The main grains of European Russia were grown: rye, oats, barley, wheat. The same vegetables were also cultivated – in particular, cabbages, onions, peas, carrots. Barley was grown more than wheat in northern Siberia. The climate and terrain in the extreme north and in parts of eastern Siberia meant that traditional agriculture had to be replaced by more primitive subsistence slash-and-burn agriculture and by hunting, trapping and fishing. This could be a precarious existence, but it was little different from the way peasants lived in the north of European Russia, and the shorter growing season in Siberia was compensated by the abundance of fish and game.

There were vast expanses of land in Siberia, but abundance of land did not in itself change peasant agriculture. The amount of land that a peasant could farm was limited to what it was physically possible for a man, his family and his horses to cultivate. Peasant land was divided into strips, each strip being no wider than could be ploughed by one man and a horse. An individual's strips were scattered across the available village lands so that peasants had a share of both good and poor land. It made no sense for peasants to acquire more arable land than they could plough. That was important not only for the peasant but also for the state, as taxes and other obligations were allocated according to a rough understanding of the ability of the peasant household to pay.

The land was used by peasants in Siberia in much the same way and employing the same implements as in European Russia. The usual plough used in Siberia was a *sokha*, a wooden plough with metal shares, which was drawn by one horse and which dug a shallow furrow. Heavier ploughs (which were used in Ukraine) were more effective and cut a deeper furrow but required more horses, or oxen, to pull them. The wealth of peasants was typically measured in terms of the number of horses per household – that remained the custom until the early twentieth century, when ideology determined that different measures had to be used to define wealthy peasants as kulaks.

Yields were low throughout Russia compared with central or western Europe, although it is difficult to make precise comparisons because statistics are unreliable. This was primarily a subsistence economy, limited as much by poor transport and communications as by agricultural methods. The three-field system was used in western and southern Siberia, which meant one field always lay fallow. This caused problems in the 1920s but the abundance of land made it effective in the eighteenth and nineteenth centuries. Peasants were naturally cautious because they could not afford to take risks; this was particularly true in Siberia, where extreme weather might ruin crops and epidemics could devastate livestock. Distribution of strips of good and poor land between peasants was itself a way of sharing risk. Attempts by Peter I in the early eighteenth century to persuade peasants to use the scythe rather than the sickle for harvesting met with only limited success. A later attempt by the government to encourage cultivation of new crops, in particular potatoes, encountered resistance and led to so-called 'potato revolts' in the 1760s. Potatoes were condemned by Old Believer sectarians as the apple of Eve or the Devil, but they were also unpopular as yields were initially very poor. Potatoes were, however, being grown in Tobolsk province by the end of the eighteenth century.

The location of villages was determined in Siberia, as elsewhere, by topographical features. Water was the crucial resource, and most villages were situated on river banks or by lakes. Roads, as we have seen, were few and far between but villages grew up on post roads and trade routes. They could vary enormously in size but some Siberian villages were very large and their remoteness meant that they had to become self-sufficient centres for foodstuffs and local crafts. Industrial villages, situated near mines and factories, were often particularly large.

Village houses in Siberia were built in much the same style as in northern European Russia, despite the fact that settlers came from all parts of European Russia and Ukraine. They were constructed of wood, with pitched roofs so that snow could be cleared easily, and could comprise up to three rooms plus various outhouses and barns. In Kolyvan, in the Altai region, where there were brick factories, the foundations of houses might be made of brick. A small log cabin (called a *klet*) was often built in the yard and used as a storage hut in winter and as a spare bedroom for a young married couple in summer.

Large peasant houses were built in Siberia during the eighteenth century. Some certainly looked well cared for, and were very skilfully decorated on the roofs, shutters and window frames. John Parkinson, who travelled from Moscow to Tobolsk in the 1790s, was impressed:

The Farm houses were larger than we had been accustomed to see; and though built on the usual model, do not stand as in Russia in a regular line but [are] dispersed. Their cattle also instead of being under cover are in open Crutch Yards; and each farm Yard is surrounded by a high Palisade. The People themselves have much finer countenances than the Russians have on the other side of the Oural mountains. The cottage where we breakfasted this morning in point of neatness would have been no disgrace to Norway; but my indisposition rendered the heat of it insupportable. Several pretty girls who belonged to it could not lessen my impatience to leave it as soon as possible.[19]

There was little attempt in Siberia to build dwellings in the style of the indigenous people. For the most part, settlers simply transported their style of buildings in the same way that they farmed the same crops with the same implements. In the far north tundra region, however, where wood was in short supply, earth was packed on to the roof, and the houses were sunk into the earth for warmth, in imitation of local houses, and translucent fish bladder was used to cover window spaces. Nomadic settlers also used yurts, as did poorer settlers in villages and towns. The museum in Khabarovsk has a replica of a nineteenth-century peasant hut with carvings for good omens on the eves of the roof, which copied carvings used in indigenous dwellings.

The main room inside the Siberian peasant hut was dominated, as in other peasant huts in European Russia, by a clay stove (only the richest peasants had brick stoves) for cooking and heating and sleeping on in the winter, which could occupy up to a quarter of the room. Sleeping lofts might be built above the stove and wooden benches were placed against the sides of the room for sitting and sleeping on. Livestock could be kept in the hut during the long winters in the area below the sleeping loft. Poorer huts had only a hole in the roof for the smoke to escape, so walls became blackened. The room was normally divided into female (where the stove was located) and male areas.

Most furniture was handmade and hangings on the walls helped to keep out the cold. All huts included an icon corner, where one or more holy images were kept. This was always in the corner of the male area of the hut, diagonally opposite the stove. Peasants bowed and crossed themselves in front of it when they rose in the morning and when they retired to sleep and, as a traveller reported in the 1780s: 'Every peasant also, upon entering the room, always paid his obeisance to this object of worship before he addressed himself to the family.'[20] Most peasant huts were very simply furnished but, in 1827, the exile V. M. Shakhovskoi found 'furniture of beautiful wood, in the corner an English table-clock', inside a rich peasant hut in the Baikal area.[21] In the far east, mica was used for windowpanes but, by the nineteenth century, glass was to be found in richer peasant houses.

Peasant diet is an indication of prosperity or otherwise. Foreign commentators in Russia often considered that peasants ate well, at least compared with peasants in western Europe. Part of this related to quantity: 'A Russian consumes as much bread in a month as a Frenchman in a year,' commented one English traveller to Siberia in the 1790s.[22] Russian peasants never lost their reliance on bread in Siberia, even when local conditions did not lend themselves to grain cultivation. The Russian peasant diet was also regarded as nourishing by foreign visitors as it included so many vegetables. The number of fasts observed by the Orthodox Church, which could occur in over thirty weeks of the year, meant there was less reliance on meat. Indeed, the generous use of onions and garlic by peasants in cooking meant that one visitor to Russia commented: 'you may know the Approach of any of them by the Scent before you see them, especially in Lent'.[23] Cucumbers and other vegetables were pickled and preserved, and were an important part of the Siberian peasant diet in the long winter.

In general, the Siberian peasant diet did not differ dramatically from the European Russian peasant diet as the same crops were grown. The great rivers and lakes of Siberia, and the east coast, also provided a great variety of fish, and the forests supplied not only game but also a wealth of mushrooms, nuts and berries. Contemporary commentators suggested that the Siberian peasant diet included more meat, possibly a sign of wealth but more probably a result of the availability of wild game. In 1858, Petr Semenov, a member of the Imperial Geographical Society, was 'startled' by the wealth of Siberian peasants in the more settled western parts and compared their diet favourably to that of peasants in European Russia: 'Meat dishes, including beef and veal, domestic fowl and wild game, as well as fish, were part of the peasants' daily diet.'[24] Travellers in Siberia commented on the abundance of fish, particularly in Kamchatka, where it was said that nets broke owing to the weight of fish caught in them. Fish could be kept for up to two years if frozen or salted.

The traditional Russian peasant preparation of pancakes, soups (particularly *borshch*, made from beetroots, and *shchi*, made from cabbage) and *kasha* (a porridge made from grains) was replicated in Siberia. Siberian peasant food was known for its pies (*pirogi*), filled with meat, fish, vegetables, fruit or mushrooms, and also for its *pelmeni*, a kind of large filled ravioli. The latter came from the Ural region but soon became known as a Siberian dish, and was most commonly eaten in the winter, when, I can testify personally, it is a very substantial and warming dish. Peasants ate butter and drank milk and soured cream, but cheese was rare. They drank beer and *kvass* (a lightly fermented beer made from malted grains, bread or fruit), as they did in European Russia, but these were flavoured with Siberian berries and honey. Tea was transported across Siberia from China and became part of the Siberian peasant diet.

Peasant dress in Siberia was much the same as in northern Russia and changed little over the eighteenth and nineteenth centuries. For both men and women it was practical – loose and easily-made clothing which allowed them to go about their business and protected them from the elements. Peasants wore local variations for special occasions, which they brought with them from their original villages in European Russia and Ukraine. Across the eighteenth and nineteenth centuries, some specific Siberian variations developed. One estimate is that there were 130 different elements of peasant dress in Siberia in the first half of the nineteenth century – including blouses, belts, skirts, buckles, aprons, headdresses – although these were all based on traditional European Russian peasant dress.[25] Unmarried girls wore their hair in a plait, sometimes tied with a ribbon; married women wore their hair in two braids and a headdress under which the plaits were attached. Peasant men in Siberia, as elsewhere in Russia, cropped their hair short but grew their beards long.

Siberia has precious metals, and wealthier peasants used precious and semi-precious stones in jewellery and buttons and for decoration on waistcoats for special occasions. Some even acquired silks from China. John Parkinson came across Russian peasants in their best outfits and compared the 'goodness and neatness of their cloaths with the rags and tatters of the populace of Italy'.[26] Settlers had to adapt to the colder climate in Siberia and in some respects copied the dress of indigenous peoples. Siberians used more fur, especially in the north, including fur leggings, fur boots and native 'parka'-style fur coats with big hoods. Good leather and fur boots were particularly important in the Siberian climate, although bast shoes (woven from the fibres of birch trees) were worn in the summer. In the far east, Russian settlers adopted the protective hoods for fishing used by local people.

Peasant households in the Russian empire varied enormously in size from nuclear families to large, complex groups including the families of sons and brothers. Some of this depended on fate – fertility, family tragedy, the loss of sons in the recruit levy – but purely practical reasons often determined attitudes to ideal household size. A larger household could provide able-bodied men to work the fields and increase landholdings. Small households might be unsustainable economically and be unable to pay dues to the state. On the other hand, smaller units were sometimes spared obligations such as the recruit levy as they would collapse economically without their adult males.

It is hard to generalise about the size of the peasant household in Siberia. New colonists in Siberia tended to arrive as smaller family units than in European Russia. As western Siberia became more settled in the first half of the eighteenth century, so households grew in size, but households remained smaller in less settled eastern Siberia. In Russia as a whole there was a decline in household size in the early nineteenth century, and this was also true of western Siberia. Household records in Siberia show, however, that much depended on personal circumstances, and that a village could contain both small and large households.

Records of the Krasnoiarsk region in 1795 show that some households comprised nuclear families but there were also some very large peasant households. In the village of Tavesikh, one household comprised 16 people, aged between 1 and 66; in the village of Ozerskoe a household of 10 varied in age from babies to an 80-year-old. While it is difficult to generalise from a single set of records, the artisan families seem to be smaller than peasant families, possibly because they were allocated less land (although an artisan household of 25 people lived in the village of Vysotinov). The families of priests (Orthodox priests had to marry) seem to have been particularly large – in the Kolyvan region, the priest Afonasii Boroshin, aged 49, had 9 children aged between 1 and 29.[27] Although priests farmed plots of land, they were not solely dependent on their produce for their livelihoods, and at least some of their sons could hope to find positions in churches in other villages.

Households of factory peasants in the Kolyvan region of the Altai might be very large, possibly because these households had to cover obligations both in the factory and in the fields. One factory peasant household in the village of Chauskii comprised 19 people: the head of the household had four sons, three of whom also had families. In another factory village there were several households of over 20 persons and one of 30.[28] On the whole, house-hold sizes were larger in the Kolyvan area than in the equivalent industrial villages in the Urals, although there is some evidence that average household size decreased at the beginning of the nineteenth century. This may have been because by this time many of these peasants had become permanent employees of factories and had dropped agricultural pursuits completely.

The peasant family hierarchy in the village was no different in Siberia than in European Russia. The head of the household (the *bolshak*) was normally the eldest male member of the family, although the widows of former heads sometimes managed to claim this position. Heads of household had the power to determine how responsibilities were shared within the family and, crucially, which boys were dispatched to the army as recruits (so allowing them to save their own sons from that fate). The eldest son was most likely to succeed his father as head of household.

It was in the interests of the household that children married early so that the family could be extended – the statistics suggest that the age of marriage was a little higher in Siberia than in European Russia, but it was still common for children in their early teens to be at least betrothed and it was not uncommon for young boys marry older, or widowed, women in order to acquire property. Brides customarily moved into the houses of their husband and the position of a young daughter-in-law was often difficult as she had to please her mother-in-law and was sometimes subjected to sexual advances from the head of the household (there is a special word in Russian to describe a sexual relationship between a father-in-law and daughter-in-law). Sometimes, family disputes could be complex. In 1797, Agrafena Epifanova, from the Omsk region, alleged that her mother-in-law had beaten her so forcefully that she had miscarried. The case ended up in the highest court in Tobolsk, which was in itself unusual, but on this occasion the claims of the daughter-in-law were found to be false and the wretched Agrafena was sentenced to a birching.[29] The weakest members of the household were orphans and the abandoned wives of men who had been conscripted as soldiers.

Relations between parents and children, and husbands and wives, were again no different in Siberia from what they were in other peasant families in European Russia. Children were expected to contribute to the household economy from an early age: boys tended livestock from the age of five or six, were working in the fields from the age of seven or eight, and took on a full workload from the age of 15. Girls helped in the home and the fields from an early age. The reality was that infant and child mortality was high; there was some evidence of infanticide of girls as boys were more valuable workers; life was hard and often dangerous for children; sons taken as conscripts were often regarded as dead; but children were also guarantors of the survival of the family unit. Attitudes of parents to children in Siberia are impossible to reconstruct because of the lack of written evidence.

Corporal punishment was common, and not simply for children. Wife-beating was common throughout Russia in all classes, to the extent that it became a popular myth that it was a sign of affection. An anonymous English commentator stated that, in Russia, 'when Marry'd, the Wife Loves her Husband the better if sometimes he Corrects her; and concludes, he Loves her not, if he altogether declines it'.[30] In reality, such beatings were often brutal and had nothing to do with affection or love. One Siberian peasant woman, Matrena Andreeva, allegedly used 'impertinent words' to her husband, for which he 'beat her with a switch and when the switch broke in his fury he took an axe from the axe store and beat her three times with the blunt end on her head and shoulders'. Another peasant, Arafiia Ivanova, left her husband because he 'constantly beat and maimed [her] for no reason'.[31] On the other hand, European Russians considered that women were held in esteem among Siberian peasants and that relations were rather formal. The governor of the Enisei region in the 1830s commented: 'The women hold the first place among them at banquets, and if the room is crowded all the men stand.'[32]

Peasants had some leisure time and many celebrations and festivals took place throughout the year, coinciding with significant days and events in the Christian and agricultural calendar. Popular pastimes included singing and dancing, and villages, in Siberia and elsewhere, developed their own songs and forms of dance (circle dances were said to be particularly popular in Siberia). Young people played a number of games, including ball games of various sorts and a form of Aunt Sally where stones were thrown at a spike in the ground. Wrestling contests were also popular, and it was not uncommon for organised fights to take place within and between villages.

All kinds of peasants in Russia – serfs, state peasants, Church peasants, factory peasants – were organised into self-governing communities known as the commune (or *mir*, a word which also means 'world' in Russian). The commune was the essential organ of administration for peasants, for the state and, in European Russia, for noble landowners. It was the commune which determined the obligations of peasant households, which included state taxes, the levy of young men to serve in the army and other obligations such as bridge-building, carting and road repairs. Peasants had a collective responsibility for taxation and other obligations, but these were distributed roughly according to household size. Within the village, the commune could divide and redistribute land to align tax obligations with household size (and, in particular, with the number of 'labour teams' comprising a male and female unit which worked the land), in an attempt to ensure that all peasants were able to meet their obligations. Peasants had to sow and harvest collectively, and the communes fixed the timetable of this work in the fields and determined the use of common land for pasture (although factory-peasant communes could not determine work obligations in factories). Communes determined who could leave the village to earn an income elsewhere (this was important as the village retained collective responsibility for the taxes of peasants who departed) and elected representatives who acted as peasant officials in the village. The commune also acted as a court for petty offences and resolved disputes over property and inheritance according to peasant customary law. Communes could censor unacceptable behaviour, including relations between parents and children and husbands and wives. The case concerning Marfa Zogzina, however, who complained that her husband beat her 'every day', came to a commune in the Tiumen region, not because of his behaviour but because she had run away from him and had thereby become a fugitive peasant.[33]

Siberian peasant communes performed the same functions as peasant communes in European Russia but had some distinct characteristics. The extent of land redistribution by communes varied within European Russia according to local conditions but the practice became more common in the eighteenth century when the state, and noble landowners, increased taxation and other obligations. There was less pressure on land in Siberia than in the most populous regions of European Russia, which militated against redistribution. In practice, land distribution only began to take place in Siberian villages in the nineteenth century, and was more common in the more populous western regions.

The most obvious distinction between communes in Siberian and European Russia is that there was no involvement by a noble landowner in the allocation of duties or obligations in the former. In practice, nobles in European Russia rarely interfered with the commune's responsibilities over the allocation of labour dues or state taxation, agricultural activities or their settlement of petty disputes, although some attempted to raise the level of labour and/or monetary obligations and more radical nobles sometimes attempted to modernise these practices. It was not uncommon, however, for nobles to interfere in the selection of young males for conscription to the army as the interests of the commune and the noble sometimes diverged: both wanted to lose the least productive members of the peasant community but differences arose over such matters as to whether married men should be conscripted.[34] Siberian peasants were truly self-governing in this respect, and this may account in part for the perception both inside and outside the region that Siberian settlers were and more independent than their counterparts in European Russia.

We have seen that Siberian villages included members of different social groups, who might also be represented in communes, and even elected as their officials. Communes in the mines in the Kolyvan region included representatives from the merchant and artisan classes. Representatives from Siberian village communes were sent to district communes, where attendance might be several hundred strong, but we know little about how these larger communes functioned.

Communes were dominated by the wealthiest peasants and the heads of household, who would either attend in person or select poorer peasants to do their bidding. It is possible that women played a more prominent and vocal part in Siberian communes than in communes in European Russia. In 1763, a Church peasant woman, Vassa Semenova, spoke at a district commune meeting in western Siberia and declared that the recent decree on the obligations of Church peasants to the state was a 'false decree'. In 1812, the commune of the village of Agafonikha, in the Kolyvan region, assembled to investigate an accusation of theft by a peasant and noted the presence of two 'wives', Avdotiia Berezovskaia and Matrena Kislova.[35]

Peasant life did not change significantly in Siberia over the course of the eighteenth and the first three-quarters of the nineteenth century. In the late nineteenth century, the arrival of the Trans-Siberian railway led to a dramatic increase in peasant settlers and opened up new economic opportunities for export of their produce. But it was a change of political regime and ideology in the early twentieth century that would change the Siberian village for ever.

CHAPTER SIX

Life in a Siberian Town

'S IBERIA IS simply Siberia, that is, a wonderful place for exiles, convenient for several types of trade, curious and rich in metals; but not a place for life and higher civic education.'[1] This disparaging comment was made by Mikhail Speransky, Governor-General of Siberia, to his daughter in 1819. A Decembrist exile wrote about Irkutsk that it 'was an absolute wilderness, almost no education at all'.[2] Certainly, Siberian towns were not comfortable and Siberian urban society was not sophisticated. To a high official from St Petersburg or a noble, however, any provincial Russian town would have appeared barbaric and the idea of living there would have been unbearable (as, indeed, it would be today to fashionable and sophisticated Muscovites). The engineer Samuel Bentham, brother of the English philosopher and reformer Jeremy Bentham, may have been reacting against this sense of metropolitan superiority when he commented in 1790, while employed in Russian service: 'Here in Tobolsk at last I can associate with people of philosophy, talent and amiability which I could find but with difficulty in the Capital.'[3]

Towns nevertheless played a crucial role in Siberia's development. The earliest fortified settlements, as we have seen, performed essential military and administrative functions. In the course of the eighteenth and the first half of the nineteenth century, these towns also began to develop an economic and cultural life of their own. In such a vast and inhospitable territory, however, they remained tiny outposts of 'Russianness' – in architecture, population, occupations and cultural and educational institutions – in an otherwise very alien land.

The population of the Russian empire was overwhelmingly rural. The urban community – that is, merchants, artisans, and unskilled town-dwellers (mainly labourers and workers, but not peasants) – represented only 4 per cent of the male population of the whole Russian empire in 1719 and had only risen to 6.6 per cent by 1833.[4] Some 90 per cent of the Russian population was classified as peasants in the census of 1782. At this date, there were only some 27,000 (male) members of the urban community in Siberia, compared with almost 300,000 state peasants. The urban population in Siberia grew in the first half of the nineteenth century, and increased overall from 112,500 to over 200,000 males between 1825 and 1858.[5] Siberia nonetheless remained a predominantly rural society until the great wave of industrialisation in the Soviet period.

By far the largest towns in the Russian empire were Moscow and St Petersburg, which were both key administrative as well as commercial centres. Several Siberian towns, however, grew quickly: by the mid-eighteenth century, Tobolsk and Eniseisk had urban communities of a similar size to those in major second-ranking European Russian towns such as Simbirsk, Kazan and Tver.

Siberian towns retained their military and defensive functions. All were built with defensive walls, watchtowers and gates. Towns were originally built of wood and the only stone kremlin, or citadel, in Siberia was constructed in the eighteenth century in Tobolsk, and still survives today. Each town had a military garrison: Omsk had a garrison of 4,000 men in the 1820s.[6] The town was later described by Dostoevsky (who passed through it during his Siberian exile) as 'a nasty little town. ... dirty, military and depraved to the highest degree'.[7] Such towns were also centres of administration, housing not only a governor or major officials but also a treasury, custom house and law courts.

Siberian towns also developed as commercial centres during the eighteenth century. By 1775, 813 members of the urban community in Tiumen, in western Siberia, were listed as being engaged in over 40 different occupations. They worked and traded mainly in leather and wooden products, that is, in goods which could be made and traded locally and which were used by the local population in the town and in the countryside. Tobolsk, a little further to the east, developed as a trading centre for goods coming from China and European Russia during the eighteenth century. Merchants from Tobolsk traded all over Siberia, and the town attracted merchants from the main towns of European Russia as well as Bukharans and other traders from

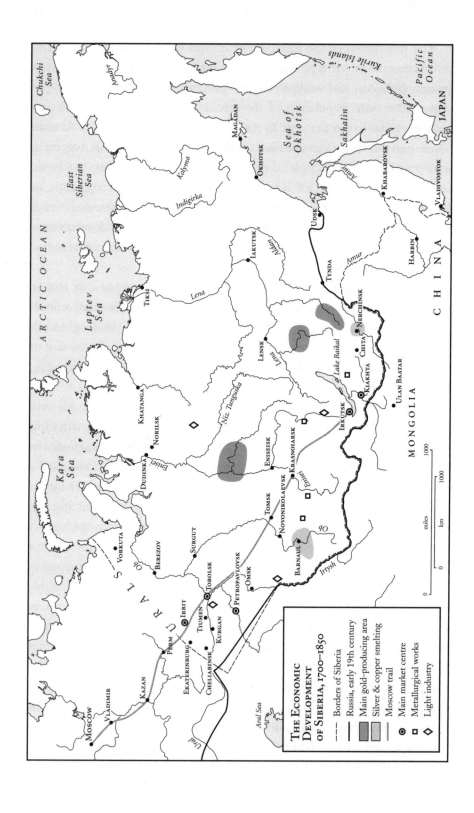

THE ECONOMIC
DEVELOPMENT
OF SIBERIA, 1700–1850

- - - Borders of Siberia
──── Russia, early 19th century
▰▰▰ Main gold-producing area
▰▰▰ Silver & copper smelting
──── Moscow trail
◉ Main market centre
▢ Metallurgical works
◇ Light industry

the east. Merchants traded in basic goods, such as grain, salt and wood, and also in luxury goods from China. Tomsk developed as the other major commercial centre in western Siberia.

The towns of Eniseisk and Krasnoiarsk developed as centres for trade on the river Enisei and attracted merchants from other towns in Siberia and from China and Mongolia. Further east, Irkutsk became an important trading centre: 1,388 merchants were registered there in 1767. By this time, the town was holding two fairs a year – in March–May and November–December – where a great variety of items were traded, including leather goods, cloth, silks, soap, clothing, salt and spirits.[8]

Kiakhta was established as a border town and customs post between China and Russia. By the second half of the eighteenth century, it had also developed as a commercial centre in its own right, trading in furs, porcelain, cloth, silk, cotton, medicinal rhubarb and tea. By 1772, the town had 60 shops. It was described by a German scientist and explorer as follows:

It consists of a fortress, and a small suburb. . . . There are three gates, at which guards are constantly stationed: one of the gates faces the north, a second the south towards the Chinese frontiers, a third the east close to the brook Kiachta. The principal public buildings in the fortress are a wooden church, the governor's house, the customs house, the magazine [store] for provisions, and the guard house. It also contains a range of shops and ware-houses, barracks for the garrison, and several houses belonging to the crown; the latter are generally inhabited by the principal merchants. . . . [The Chinese town] is situated about a hundred and forty yards south of the fortress of Kiachta, and nearly parallel to it. Midway between this place and the Russian fortress, two posts about ten feet high are planted, in order to mark the frontier of the two empires: one is inscribed with Russian, the other with Manshur [Chinese] characters.[9]

Rural and urban fairs were important throughout the Russian empire, but they were particularly important in Siberia because the great distances between settlements made regular exchange of goods difficult. Fairs were also where goods from Asia were traded and bartered. During the eighteenth century, Irbit, in western Siberia, established itself as home to one of the major fairs in the whole empire, second in importance only to that held at the town of Nizhnii Novgorod in central Russia. This three-week winter fair became an important centre for the exchange of goods from Europe and Asia. In 1734, it attracted merchants from 26 towns in European Russia and the Urals, as well as Bukharan traders from Central Asia. By the 1770s, there were over 200 permanent shops or stores in the town.[10] In the late nineteenth century, the journalist, author and traveller Thomas Wallace Knox noted the 'many sledges laden with goods en route' to Irbit and estimated that 40 to 50 million roubles' worth of goods were exchanged there annually. The town comprised enormous wharf areas for storage and dormitory-style buildings to accommodate traders, and continued to thrive until a combination of the Trans-Siberian railway, the Revolutions and the Civil War diminished its importance; the fair ceased trading in 1929.[11]

Not all towns in Siberia developed as commercial centres. Some forts simply remained as military outposts. And some so-called towns were more occupied with farming than with commerce. A visitor to the small town of Ialutorovka in western Siberia in the mid-nineteenth century commented: 'here artisans are occupied for a large part in grain growing, haymaking, carting and some cattle breeding, the women – in market gardening and needlework. In the town there are 542 garden plots, 943 horses, 1,165 cattle, 760 sheep and 10 pigs.'[12] The rural appearance of some Siberian towns was not, however, exclusive to Siberia. Peasants lived in all Russian towns, and traded in food-stuffs and locally produced goods. Townspeople had their own plots for vege-tables and some livestock but were often also occupied in agriculture. It was estimated that there were 20,000 head of cattle in St Petersburg in the 1760s.

Indeed, as we saw in the last chapter, there was often very little distinction between towns and villages in this period. The small town of Narym in western Siberia decided that it was too small to have elective urban institu-tions. By 1829, the trading activities of the town had declined so much that the population of 32 registered artisans declared they could no longer pay state dues and support an urban court, and requested to be classified as state peasants.[13] The town thus in effect became a village.

The main weakness of towns in imperial Russia was the fact that the legally-defined members of the urban community were outnumbered by other social groups living in the town. This reduced the income from urban taxes, because only people formally categorised as 'townspeople' paid them. It also meant that it was impossible for merchants and artisans to protect their trade from unfair competition – from nobles, who owned factories and mines and who exported grain and other agricultural products, and from peasants who sold their agricultural products and homemade crafts in towns without contributing to urban dues or other obligations. Merchants and artisans also lived in villages, so the boundaries became blurred between town and village and between the social groups which lived there. Attempts by tsars in the eighteenth century to establish a western European-style guild structure foundered as they could not force certain crafts to be the exclusive preserve of the urban community.

In this respect Siberian towns suffered from the same general weaknesses as towns in European Russia. Their social composition was, however, different. Despite the growth of economic activity, merchants and artisans could be minorities in Siberian towns until well into the nineteenth century. Towns were dominated by military men (soldiers, Cossacks and their descendants), by officials and, if they were on major road routes, by post-drivers. There were few nobles in Siberia to compete with merchants, which may explain why some merchant families became so prominent and wealthy in areas of trade, such as distilling, which were sometimes in the hands of nobles in European Russia, but many peasants also lived in the towns and traded there. There were also considerable numbers of non-Russian traders and settlers in Siberian towns.

The distinct social composition of settlers in Siberia was reflected in the population of Siberian towns. Krasnoiarsk in 1730 comprised 755 artisans but also 30 'boiars' sons', 610 Cossacks, 345 children of Cossacks, 30 Tatar military service-men, 1,174 tribute-paying Tatars, 586 state peasants and 127 Church peasants.[14] In Tobolsk in the same period, some 40 per cent of the town's inhabitants were soldiers, Cossacks or officials. By 1782, over half were merchants and artisans (348 merchants and 2,761 artisans) but there were still significant numbers of other social groups, including exiles (725), post-drivers (487), indigenous peoples who had converted to Christianity (151) and retired military service-men (300).[15] In smaller towns, the urban groups might still be a minority at this date. In the 1780s, merchants and artisans made up less than half of the population of Tiumen, which was dominated by peasants and post-drivers. By the early nineteenth century, Tomsk had a majority of urban-dwellers, but also a significant number of Cossacks, tribute-paying Tatars, Bukharans and post-drivers.[16]

Some important Siberian merchant dynasties emerged in the eighteenth and nineteenth centuries. Contemporaries considered Siberian merchant families to be less specialised in their activities than their counterparts in

European Russia. That may have been because some areas of Siberian trade naturally went together – grain and distilling, for example – but was primarily owing to the fact that there was only a small number of commercial centres which handled a great variety of goods. In Tiumen in the 1730s and 1740s, one of the wealthy families was the Perevalovs. They had interests in leather, salt and distilling, and traded in a wide range of goods, including tobacco. By the mid-eighteenth century, the Stukalovs, who owned fish, soap and distilling factories, also dominated in Tiumen.[17]

The nature of Siberian society allowed for some social mobility. The children of Cossacks and other military men could move more easily into other activities than they would have been able to do in their more segregated communities in European Russia; the sheer distances involved meant it was more difficult for government officials, urban authorities and peasant communes to monitor the movement of people in Siberia. A list of merchants and artisans in the town of Krasnoiarsk in the 1780s shows that a significant number had begun life as peasants. Some of these had become successful merchants and served as urban officials in the town. Fedor Pianov, for example, had become a merchant, had accumulated capital of over 1,000 roubles and traded in the towns of Eniseisk, Irkutsk, Tomsk and Krasnoiarsk. Semen Zhizhin, who became a merchant in 1769, served as town head (the head of the urban administration) from 1775 to 1781. Grigorii Krasikov became a judge in the oral court (a low-level court for minor offences). A former Cossack, Ivan Cheepanov, also became a merchant in Krasnoiarsk.[18]

Merchant households tended to be small and nuclear, unlike the larger, more extended, peasant households. Fathers, in towns as in the villages, dominated the household and dictated the careers of their sons, the behaviour of their children and the choice of their spouses. It was common in European Russia for marriages to take place within the merchant community and this pattern was repeated in Siberia, although the lack of resident nobility meant that when marriages took place outside the merchant community they could be with Cossacks, children of clergy or even wealthy peasants.

Widows of merchants could play an important role in business affairs; this may in part have been because there was a tendency in Russia for merchant husbands to be older than their wives. There is a suggestion that wives, and particularly widows, played a more significant part in commercial life in Siberia than in European Russia, although this is hard to prove. There were certainly powerful merchant widows in Tomsk in the eighteenth century. One such powerful woman was Elena Grigorevna, aged 62 and illiterate, who ran her deceased husband's firm of Morozov for 14 years in the late nineteenth century.[19]

There had been very few Jews in the Russian empire until the late eighteenth century, when Russia acquired lands which had formerly been part of the Polish-Lithuanian Commonwealth. There was also a substantial Jewish population in Bessarabia (modern-day Moldova), which Russia acquired in 1811, and in the Congress Kingdom of Poland (the rump of what had been the Kingdom of Poland in 1807), which was formally attached to the Russian empire in 1815. The Russian government sought to confine the Jews to a 'Pale of Settlement' in the eastern part of the former Polish-Lithuanian lands and the south of Russia (Jews comprised some 10 per cent of the population of the port of Odessa by the end of the eighteenth century).

As far as the Russian government was concerned, Jews posed particular problems: they might be effective traders; on the other hand, there were concerns that Jewish settlement might be disruptive. Many Jews were originally rural but were forced into urban categories in the early nineteenth century by the Russian government, which was convinced that Jewish innkeepers and traders in spirits were harming the Russian peasantry.

Government policy towards Jewish settlement in Siberia was inconsistent. Jews were forbidden to leave 'the Pale' in the late eighteenth and early nineteenth centuries. In 1827, Nicholas I then allowed Jews to settle in distant parts of the empire, including Siberia, and, in 1836, 1,377 Jewish families moved to Siberia from Russia.[20] Alexander II also allowed certain categories of Jews to reside outside the Pale of Settlement. Local rules could, however, restrict settlements. In 1831–2, the town authorities in Tomsk and Tobolsk decided not to let Jews or Roma register as merchants in the town. Most Jews in Siberia settled in towns rather than the countryside, and a survey of Tobolsk province in 1838 found that 48 out of 57 Jewish households in the province were in the town of Tobolsk.

The number of Jewish merchants in Siberia rose in the first half of the nineteenth century. By 1827, there were 327 in Kainsk, 128 in Tobolsk, 69 in Tomsk and 17 in Tiumen. By 1835, the number had risen to 681 in Tobolsk province and to over 1,000 in Tomsk province. A synagogue was opened in Tomsk in 1859. Some of the Jewish families became very wealthy – the Mariupolskys, for example, became one of the richest merchant families in

Omsk and became town councillors. In Tomsk, the leading Jewish family was the Fuksmans, who were involved in distilling and the grain trade.

The small town of Kainsk,[21] near Tomsk, particularly attracted Jewish settlers. Governor-General Speransky commented: 'Kainsk – a small town … many Jews and gypsies.' Ivan Zavalishin, an exile, called it the 'Siberian Jewish Jerusalem'.[22] By the end of the nineteenth century, almost half of the Kainsk merchants were Jewish. The traveller John Dundas Cochrane noted in the 1820s that some of the Jews in Kainsk were 'very rich'.[23] The majority of Jewish urban dwellers, however, were very poor.

It is hard to know if toleration of Jewish settlers was greater in Siberia than it was in European Russia. Certainly, Jews took advantage of the opportunity to move to Siberia when they were allowed to do so. There were already dissident religious sects in Siberia, some of which had been persecuted in European Russia, which may have made urban residents more tolerant of other faiths. Russians in Siberia were also used to living and trading with Muslims and other non-Christians. Jewish merchants, however, did not dominate trade and commerce in major Siberian towns and this was probably the main reason why they lived relatively peacefully among other towns-people in this period – Kainsk was a very small town.

Towns were governed by town officials, councils (dumas), administrative offices and law courts which were largely staffed by urban representatives. These offices were established by the Russian tsars in an attempt to raise the status of towns, and to stimulate trade and growth. Some of these posts were highly regarded, as their occupants could influence town policy and were remunerated; others were simply seen as burdens. Either way, the posts were supposed to be filled by the various legal categories of the urban community – that is, the top posts were to be taken by merchants (who, in the eighteenth century, were divided into three 'guilds' according to their declared capital, with the wealthiest merchants becoming members of the first guild), and representatives in dumas and lower level law courts were also drawn from artisans or simple town-dwellers (labourers and other workers).

In reality, it was difficult to fill all of the available posts in many towns in the Russian empire (and only the largest Russian towns had any merchants wealthy enough to be members of the first and even second guilds), but Siberia posed particular challenges because the distinctive social composition of its towns distorted the membership of these institutions in a way that was not intended by legislators in St Petersburg. In Tobolsk in 1788, one

town duma included elected representatives drawn from retired soldiers, officials and post-drivers as well as from artisans. Tomsk urban institutions
included representatives from soldiers, Cossacks, past-drivers and 'state peasants'. In 1803, the Tomsk town duma even had a representative from tribute-
payers, that is, pagans.[24] Omsk's urban institutions included representatives
from Cossacks and the clergy. The town of Tara elected representatives from
the clergy and the military.[25] This representation was repeated at parish level:
parish assemblies in Tobolsk in the second half of the eighteenth century
were dominated by officials and military men, who outnumbered merchants.[26]
This mixed representation reflected the slow economic development of
Siberian towns but it did allow different social groups to participate in
decision-making in the towns. To an extent this made the urban administration more 'open' in Siberia than in European Russia.

Did Siberian towns develop a distinct lifestyle or culture – or, indeed, any
cultural life at all in this period? Life certainly continued to have a rough-and-
ready quality in Siberian towns in the eighteenth and early nineteenth centuries. Violence and drunkenness were common, and townspeople might fall
victim to the vagrants, brigands and deserters who plagued the countryside.
These gangs were sometimes referred to as 'General Cuckoo's army', as the
first call of the cuckoo in spring was often a signal for brigands to begin to
descend on the towns. Tiumen in particular was notorious for the camps of
vagrants and brigands which formed outside the town in the summer months.

A visitor, the French astronomer the Abbé Chappe d'Auteroche, wrote a
very negative account of Russia in the 1760s. Of Tobolsk he observed:

> It is scarce possible to walk along the streets in this city, on account of the
> quantity of dirt there is even in the upper town. . . . At Tobolsky [sic] men
> are very jealous of their wives, as they are throughout the greater part of
> Russia beyond the city of Mosco . . . however, they are seldom in company
> with them, spending most of their time in drinking, and generally coming
> home drunk. The women seldom go out; they live wholly sequestered from
> society, given up to laziness and indolence, which are the causes of the
> depravity of their manners.[27]

Some changes took place in at least the larger Siberian towns in the eighteenth and early nineteenth centuries. It is difficult, however, to find distinc-
tively Siberian features in this development. In reality, pockets of European

Russian culture existed alongside more traditional ways of life. Furthermore, most of what we might regard as more 'civilised' European cultural features and institutions came into being as a result of the need to implement government policy rather than owing to any local initiatives in Siberia.

One clear example of this is the architecture of Siberian towns. The houses were originally all wooden, and the wooden defences lasted well into the nineteenth century, even after they came to be surrounded by new buildings. The first houses were built in wood in the north Russian style, and tended to be simple, with steep roofs and small windows. Churches were constructed in the same way as in European Russia. Arcades of trading stalls were constructed from the early eighteenth century onwards, modelled on those of European Russian towns. In sum, there was very little that was distinctive about early eighteenth-century Siberian towns compared with provincial towns in European Russia, except that there were fewer stone buildings, and styles of churches and stone buildings were probably slower to change than in European Russia. Baroque-style churches, for example, came late to Siberia.

In the late eighteenth century, Catherine II ordered all Russian towns to develop plans for reconstruction to make them more 'European'. Streets were broadened and straightened, formal squares were created, and new state buildings, schools, trade arcades and private houses were built in a classical style. These European Russian innovations were simply transported to Siberia, without any consideration of whether the construction materials or the style were suited to the climatic conditions there. In this way, the 'Russian town' (and, for that matter, the Soviet town in the twentieth century) was simply duplicated in Siberia, in the same way that under the British empire colonial buildings in Africa and the Indian subcontinent were erected in the style of the 'home' country.

Fires plagued Russia's wooden towns; new roads and buildings were often planned after fires had destroyed old town centres. A fire in Tomsk in 1770 led to the construction of new government buildings. The same happened in Irkutsk after a fire in 1775. In 1788, a fire in Tobolsk burnt down nine churches, a monastery and the governor's house, and resulted in the rebuilding of the centre with two-storey stone buildings in a classical style.[28] Despite these changes, the number of stone buildings remained small. In 1825, there were only 17 stone buildings in Tomsk, 32 in Tobolsk and 56 in Irkutsk.[29] Most merchant homes continued to be wooden two-storey buildings until the late nineteenth century. In the mid-nineteenth century, further remodelling of Siberian towns took place – more town bridges were built, pavements were laid and statues erected. Towns could still, however, be damaged by fire – Tobolsk suffered further fires in 1839 and 1845.

The lifestyle in Siberian towns did not differ greatly from that in provincial towns in European Russia, but there were some specific features determined by local circumstances. Statistics seem to indicate that life expectancy was slightly higher for Siberian merchants than for their counterparts in European Russia, but by the end of the nineteenth century the average was still low – somewhere in the 30s.[30] A high death rate at birth and in infancy, insanitary living conditions, extreme cold in the winter, poor medical provision and the inability to control epidemics all helped to account for low life expectancy in Siberia and elsewhere in Russia – and, indeed, to account for the relatively slow growth of towns until the late nineteenth century.

Food in the towns was much the same as Siberian peasant food, except that more meat was consumed by wealthier merchants, partly as a sign of their wealth and partly because urban dwellers tended to observe religious fasts less conscientiously than peasants. Diet was governed by the availability of foodstuffs in the market and by the produce of cottage gardens. Most food was produced and consumed locally, but many Siberian towns were on key trade routes. Imported foreign luxury foodstuffs, however, were expensive and could be of poor quality. At the end of the eighteenth century, the traveller John Ledyard found 'French & Spanish wines here: but so mutilated that I was told of it before I knew it to be wine'.[31]

Tea was imported from China and Siberians acquired a reputation as great tea drinkers: 'Siberians love to drink tea with passion, which they do several times a day usually without sugar.' It was said that Siberians drank tea with milk, which was unusual in European Russia. A popular saying was that a Siberian could go without food for a day but could not go without tea.[32] 'The samovar was on the table with night-time being the only exception,' claimed a visitor to Irkutsk in the late 1850s.[33] An account written in the early twentieth century claimed that Chinese tea was 'used in some parts of Siberia instead of money as a medium of exchange, and the value of a horse or cow or plot of land is estimated as so many bricks of tea [blocks of finely ground tea]'.[34] What is sometimes known as 'Siberian tea', and still sold, is in fact a herbal drink and not made from tea leaves.

The tsars genuinely believed that they could legislate to change the cultural habits of their people. Peter I forced nobles to adopt Western-style clothes and shave their beards as part of his attempt to modernise the country in the early eighteenth century. Russian merchants were, however, slow to adopt these fashions, and many wore traditional kaftans until at least the end of the century, even in Moscow. In Siberia, these coats were popular for practical reasons as they were warmer than short coats. New fashions and trends came from noble society but there were very few nobles in Siberian towns apart from governors and chief officials. As a result Siberian urban dress changed only slowly.

Russian merchants, and in particular their wives, had a reputation for liking exotic cloth and decoration, something which contemporaries saw as an indication that they were more 'oriental' than the nobility, who by the mid-eighteenth century looked and dressed like gentlemen elsewhere in Europe. Merchant wives in the early nineteenth century presented themselves in their finery at Easter, as an Anglo-Irish visitor commented from European Russia: 'Headdresses of pearls & veils of muslin embroider'd with gold & silver, or silk embroider'd with ditto, their pelisse of gold silk lined with the most expensive furs, their faces painted red & white altogether give them very shewy & handsome appearance.'[35] In Siberia, the trade from China gave merchants the opportunity to buy silks and other luxury goods, and wealthier merchants took advantage of this. Those in Irkutsk were said to look oriental rather than Russia, and were noted for wearing Chinese-style hats in the 1830s.[36]

Material and decorative goods – furniture and furnishings, clocks, mirrors, crockery, paintings, pianos – could be found in Siberian towns, although it took time for the latest fashions to reach the more remote centres. The intrepid wife of Vitus Bering, who, along with their two children, accompanied him on the second Kamchatka expedition, lived in Iakutsk in 1734–7, and then in the port of Okhotsk in 1737–9. These must have been very primitive settlements at the time and it is hardly surprising that she apparently found life there 'dull'. She did, however, manage to acquire, as well as bring with her, some material comforts. When she left Okhotsk for Tobolsk her luggage comprised 11 chests on seven carts – including furs, Chinese fabrics, and silver from Siberia but also her personal clavichord, which she had brought with her and which had crossed and recrossed Siberia with her.[37] Urban life became rather more comfortable over the course of the next century. In 1842, it was said that rich Siberian merchants lacked nothing of 'European comfort': 'they thirst for luxury objects, which they import from each point of the earth, and pay excessive prices for them.'[38] A 'provincial society' was slow to develop in Russia. The largest European Russian towns in the eighteenth century – above all, St Petersburg and Moscow – staged theatrical and musical events and had a social calendar of balls and fine dining. Much of this was stimulated by the tsars themselves. Peter I believed he could create modern social habits simply by forcing young nobles of both sexes to meet at 'assemblies'. His successors staged theatrical and musical events at court, and held elaborate balls, masquerades and other social gatherings for the elite. Catherine II wanted to stimulate the development of a provincial society through the participation of the local landed nobility in such events. In 1775, she increased the number of posts for provincial nobles in local administration and courts. Social events were timed to coincide with elections for nobles to these posts, when the nobles came to town from their country estates for a few weeks and used the occasion to socialise and enjoy themselves. In time, rich merchants also became involved, in the first instance by holding parallel events for themselves at their own elections. Siberian towns, however, as we have seen, had few resident nobles. As a result, it was more difficult to encourage cultural gatherings of this nature, and much depended on governors and local officials to create some sort of social life, often by holding events in their residences.

Some cultural institutions were nevertheless established, at least in the major towns. Tobolsk became the major cultural centre of western Siberia. In the 1780s, Governor-General Iakobi brought a 40-piece orchestra to the town.[39] In 1793, the traveller John Parkinson visited the theatre there and commented: 'There was an opera in the evening at the theatre which did not go off ill. Their prettiest and best actress was a common girl taken from the Streets.'[40] Another traveller, John Dundas Cochrane, contrasted the 'good society' in Tobolsk to the 'bad' society in Tomsk, which was a 'most miserable place'.[41] Speransky attended a ball in 1820 in Tobolsk, where he noted the 'female society'.[42]

Catherine II tried to broaden knowledge in the provinces by encouraging the setting-up of local printing presses. Tobolsk had a printing press by the end of the eighteenth century. In the 1790s, it published an early literary journal, Irtysh, which lasted for a couple of years and included literary contributions from teachers and pupils from the Tobolsk national school.

Irkutsk became the centre of cultural life in eastern Siberia. The first public library opened there in 1782, in a brick building designed in the latest

European Russian style. A senior administrator visited the theatre in Irkutsk in the 1780s and found that 'the actors are local people. . . . Their perform- ances are excellent.'[43] Speransky also saw some evidence here of merchant social activities and attended a merchant dinner and ball, at which, he wrote to his daughter, 24 couples danced.[44] The Decembrists also established a social and cultural life for themselves in exile in Irkutsk, which is discussed more fully in Chapter 9.

Schools were established in Siberian towns (but not in the villages) during the eighteenth and early nineteenth centuries. This was rarely due to local initiatives, although a private donation led to the opening of a school in the small town of Kainsk in 1817; it had 64 pupils by 1833.[45] As with so many other cultural matters, it was the tsars who largely determined national educa- tional policy, including who and what was taught. The particular conditions in Siberia, however, did have an impact on schools, both on the syllabus and on the recruitment of pupils and teachers.

The first school in Siberia was set up to educate the sons of the lower clergy in 1702–3 in the home of the bishop of Tobolsk. Thirty-three boys studied there between 1703 and 1726;[46] the number of pupils had risen to 285 by 1791.[47] The sons of clergy had to acquire a basic education to take even minor posts in the Church. Boys were educated on the cheap and semi- naries had a reputation for brutality, which seems to be borne out in an account of the Tobolsk seminary in the late eighteenth century. Two brothers were found out of class in the home of a soldier's wife, a certain Avdotiia Semenova. They were flogged, with 25 blows inflicted on the elder and 15 on the younger boy. Another boy was flogged with 40 blows for drinking and ended up being dispatched as a soldier (the worst fate that could befall anyone) 'because of bad behaviour'. Other pupils, not surprisingly, fled.[48]

National secular schools were first established in the reign of Peter I (the children of nobles were usually tutored at home) in the early eighteenth century. Peter took a very pragmatic approach to education, which in his view should teach basic technical and military skills. Schools were set up in his reign in garrisons, including major Siberian towns.[49] There were 150 pupils, the sons of Cossacks and soldiers, in the Omsk garrison school in 1767.[50] Peter was particularly keen that naval skills should be taught so that Russia could develop a powerful navy. Navigation schools were established in the far eastern port of Okhotsk and in Iakutsk, on the river Lena, in the 1730s, and in Irkutsk, on the river Angara and near Lake Baikal, in 1754. These schools taught foreign languages as well as mathematics and practical navigational skills. Specialist schools for surveying were also established and mining schools were opened near or in the large factories and mines in Kolyvan in the Altai region and in Nerchinsk in eastern Siberia.

In 1786, Catherine II established more national schools in towns. The main town in each province was to have a major school (or higher school) comprising four classes, and each major district town was to have a minor school (or lower, or primary, school) with two classes. Major schools were set up in Siberia in Tobolsk, Irkutsk and Barnaul, and ten minor schools were opened in smaller Siberian towns. Almost all the pupils in these new schools were male (although Catherine did not in principle exclude girls from national schools) and were the children of officials, nobles, merchants and even some peasants.

Catherine II determined the syllabus of national schools, and specified that Asiatic languages should be taught in Siberia. The Tobolsk national school ran a Tatar 'class' in 1793. The Irkutsk major school claimed to teach German, French, Mongolian, Chinese and Japanese, at least for a few years. In 1789, an 'Asiatic' school was opened in Omsk, which taught Tatar and some Mongolian to some 20–30 boys, primarily the sons of Cossacks but also a few sons of Tatar officials. The aim of the school was pragmatic – to produce interpreters and translators to deal with military and administrative contacts with Tatars and Kalmyks.[51]

Towns in Siberia, as elsewhere in the Russian empire, were not always enthusiastic about supporting the national schools financially. Nor were townspeople convinced that it was necessary for their sons, let alone their daughters, to have more than a basic education. 'In our trading life we don't need much knowledge . . . the main thing is reading and writing,' commented an Irkutsk merchant in the second half of the nineteenth century.[52] The minor schools in Krasnoiarsk and Kuznetsk had closed by the end of the eighteenth century. In 1788, there were 88 pupils in the major school in Tobolsk. Numbers rose to 149 in 1792 but then dropped back to 76 by 1796.[53] By then, however, there were some 500 pupils in Tobolsk (in the seminaries and national, garrison and surveying schools) and about 300 pupils in Irkutsk (in the seminaries and major and minor, garrison, navigation and surveying schools).

Alexander I founded new universities and extended the national school system. Schools in Siberia were reorganised and came within the orbit of the newly established Kazan Imperial University, in the east of European Russia. Grammar schools, or gymnasiums, were set up in Tobolsk, Irkutsk and Tomsk. By the time of Alexander's death in 1825, Tobolsk gymnasium had 22 teachers, including a German and Frenchman. There were 35 pupils in the Irkutsk gymnasium in 1806, rising to 149 in 1850.[54] Some schools were also set up for non-Russians – in 1804, a Buriat minor school was opened in Balagan, although it only lasted for a short time. The Tobolsk Marianskaia girls' school was founded in 1845 and girls were accepted into the Kainsk school from the 1850s. There were, however, few other educational opportunities for girls until the 1860s.[55]

It was hard to find suitable teachers for the national schools throughout Russia, not least because teachers were poorly, and sometimes only infrequently, paid, and it was particularly difficult to attract anyone to posts in remote Siberia. Records from Tomsk in the 1830s show the practical problems on the ground. Inspectors found that there were serious shortages of teachers at this date in the Tomsk district minor schools. There were only 16 pupils in the Kainsk minor school, but there were 40 in the Kuznetsk school and 55 in the Tomsk school. Minor schools should have had a complement of six teachers, but the Tomsk school had only three, and Kainsk only two. Both schools used a priest to teach religious education, but lacked teachers for other basic subjects. In Kainsk, there were vacancies for teachers of Russian language, geography, history, writing and arithmetic. The Kuznetsk school also had three vacancies for teachers of Russian language, arithmetic and writing. The Tomsk provincial board advertised its own vacancies in European Russia, and offered posts to candidates from all over European Russia, including three from Kharkov (in eastern Ukraine), two from Vilnius (in present-day Lithuania) and others from St Petersburg, Smolensk and Moscow. Almost all the candidates were sons of priests.[56]

In 1812, during the dark days of the Napoleonic invasion of Russia, all members of the 'privileged' social groups – nobles, merchants, clergy – were urged to donate money and goods to the patriotic cause, both then and in subsequent years to help the devastated populations of the towns and villages of the western provinces of European Russia. Over 170,000 roubles were collected from Irkutsk province, and almost 150,000 roubles were collected from Tobolsk and Tiumen provinces.[57] In addition, cloth, pistols and articles made of gold and silver were donated. The donors were primarily officials and merchants, although they also included artisans, retired soldiers, peasants and even indigenous people. In Tobolsk, for example, donations were received from 24 officials, 32 artisans and 59 peasants. In the smaller town of Tara, donations were received from 4 officials, 10 artisans, 2 post-drivers, but also from 77 peasants and 2 house serfs.

The year 1812 was exceptional, of course, and it is hard to draw more general conclusions from it about the extent to which a sense of civic responsibility was developing among the urban community or within society more generally in Siberia. It showed, however, that inhabitants of Siberian towns participated fully in the patriotic sentiments of the country as a whole and contributed money as well as conscripts to the cause. This was despite the fact that the campaigns and battles took place so far from Siberia. In 1814, when the news that Russian troops had entered Paris reached Irkutsk, it was reported by a contemporary:

Despite the remoteness, the hearts of the Irkutsk [inhabitants] did not beat with any less joy than those in the centre of Russia. Siberia looks to Russia, as to its mother, and a Siberian has never separated, never separates and will never separate himself from the common fate of his fatherland.[58]

This is almost certainly a bit of patriotic hyperbole, but it is also an indication that by this time Siberian towns, and Siberian town-dwellers, had much in common with their counterparts in European Russia while also developing some distinct social and cultural characteristics of their own.

CHAPTER SEVEN

Life in a Remote Siberian Garrison

I was deep in reflection, for the most part of a gloomy nature. Garrison life held little attraction for me. . . .

'Is it far to the fortress?' I asked my driver.

'Not far,' he replied. 'You can see it over there.'

I looked around me in every direction, expecting to see menacing bastions, towers and a rampart: but all I could see was a little village surrounded by a thick wooden fence. On one side of it stood three or four haystacks, half-concealed beneath the snow; on the other, a dilapidated windmill with idly-hanging bark sails.

'But where is the fortress?' I asked in surprise.

'There it is,' replied the driver, indicating the little village, and as he spoke, we drove into it.

At the gates I saw an old cast-iron cannon; the streets were narrow and twisting; the cottages small and for the most part thatched. I ordered the driver to take me to the commandant, and a minute later, the sledge stopped before a small wooden house. Built on a rise in the ground near the church which was also made of wood. Nobody came out to meet me. I went up to the entrance and opened a door into the front hall. An old soldier, seated at a table, was sewing a blue patch on the elbow of a green uniform. I told him to announce me.

'Go in my good chap,' the old soldier replied. 'Our people are at home.'[1]

This is the way Pushkin describes his young hero Petr Andreevich arriving at the remote fort near Orenburg in the Urals in the mid-1770s in his historical novel *The Captain's Daughter,* published in 1836. The young officer's mood and first impressions were no doubt typical. Who would want to serve in a remote and inhospitable garrison fort, far from the excitement of real warfare or the glamour of the social life available for officers stationed in Moscow or St Petersburg? Petr Andreevich lacks the social connections to get a more prestigious posting with the Guards and laments: 'Instead of a gay life in Petersburg, boredom awaited me in some dreary and distant part of the country.' He finds that one of his fellow officers has been transferred from the Guards to garrison duty in disgrace after killing someone in a duel.

Pushkin's story goes on to show, however, that life in such a backwater could be dangerous as well as tedious. The last major Cossack revolt in Russia took place in the years 1773–5 under Emelian Pugachev, who, leading a motley force of some 10,000–15,000 Cossacks, peasants and deserters, wreaked havoc throughout the province of Orenburg, sacking garrisons, murdering local officials, and bringing terror to the local landowners and clergy. The fort of Tatishchev, on the river Iaik, manned by 1,000 men, was sacked by the rebels and subjected to a three-day drunken debauch. The towns of Orenburg and Kazan fell to rebels in the same year. The largely Tatar town of Kazan was subjected to an orgy of looting, rape and violence lasting from six in the morning until midnight, and then was set ablaze with the loss of almost all the wooden buildings. In Pushkin's story, the garrison is overrun almost without a shot being fired: the soldiers immediately swear allegiance to Pugachev; the elderly commandant is hanged on the spot; his wife dragged naked and screaming from the house and struck down by a Cossack; and the hero and his love surviving simply by a chance set of circumstances.

The reality of garrison life in the eighteenth and early nineteenth centuries is captured in Pushkin's story: boredom week in, week out in a desolate outpost and always with the threat of danger. But there were far more remote postings than Orenburg. Who served in remote Siberian forts and how did they spend their lives?

The garrison 'lines' in Siberia were set up to assert Russian military presence over a vast territory, from Orenburg in the Urals to the Kamchatka peninsula in the far east. From Orenburg, a chain of forts followed the Volga and then the Kama river through territory occupied by the Bashkirs across the steppes north of the Caspian and Aral Seas to the town of Omsk. From Omsk, forts were strung across the steppe, swamp and forest to Irkutsk on

Lake Baikal and then eastwards across the mountains along the Chinese border to the Kamchatka peninsula. Smaller forts were established on the river networks, asserting Russian control over the main trading routes as well as borders. The presence of non-Russians on the borders could always pose a security threat. In 1791, concern was expressed to the government about the presence of 300 Kirghiz in nine villages very near the border with China.[2]

Supporting this vast network of forts required considerable manpower. Some 50,000–90,000 men served in garrison regiments in the second half of the eighteenth and early nineteenth century, but this included garrisons in the Caucasus and western frontiers of European Russia as well as Siberia. The Siberian forts were very lightly manned throughout this period. In reality, there was no serious attempt to dominate this vast territory; the plan was simply to establish a strategic presence on the main waterways, trade routes, natural frontiers and international borders. The Orenburg 'line', which ran from Orenburg across the north of the Caspian Sea, was manned by an Orenburg corps of five infantry and two dragoon regiments, supported by some 10,000 Cossacks. Individual forts on this line could be manned by as few as 30 men, and some had no permanent garrison at all. Even then, in 1793 Bashkir elders asked if their people could be relieved of service on the Orenburg line as the men would be leaving 'small children behind to their arbitrary fate' and 'their parents without any help'.[3] It is no surprise that Pugachev was able to overrun such outposts with little resistance.

The Orenburg line, however, was almost 'civilised' in comparison with the more remote posts to which men – Cossacks and regular soldiers – could be sent. Forts in Siberia could be substantial, and had to be maintained at vast cost. The fort in Tobolsk was reconstructed in 1783 at a cost of 11,000 roubles;[4] some 50 million roubles were spent on fortresses in the first quarter of the nineteenth century. Many forts were, however, little more than a wooden stockade surrounding simple huts for barracks, with a church and some sort of hospital building inside but with most of the soldiers billeted in local peasant huts (as at the fort in Pushkin's story). The garrison on the Kamchatka peninsula represented the imperial presence in the very far east. It was manned by just 56 men in 1812,[5] all of whom were quartered in the huts of local inhabitants. It may seem surprising that some postings could be regarded as even more remote and less desirable than Kamchatka (which could at least be reached by sea from Okhotsk, the port on the west coast of the Sea of Okhotsk). One of those was a small fort called Gizhiga.[6]

Gizhiga is a settlement on the left bank of the river Gizhiga, which flows into the Sea of Okhotsk from the north. The fort was founded in the 1750s in order to establish a military presence on the land and sea route between the ports of Okhotsk and Kamchatka; it is at roughly the midpoint by land between the two ports. That was the rationale behind the settlement and the reason the Russian government continued to send men there and spend a not inconsiderable amount of money on its fortifications and supplies (by the early nineteenth century, it was costing some 80,000 roubles a year to maintain the fort and the men inside it).[7] That does not explain, however, what it was like to live, or rather exist, in this dismal spot.

Gizhiga is about as remote as can be, even within Siberia – over 3,000 miles (4,800 kilometres) from the town of Irkutsk and over 8,000 miles (12,000 kilometres) from St Petersburg. The journey from Irkutsk could take over six months; the sea route from the port of Okhotsk could take many weeks. The entrance to Gizhiga harbour was in any event ice-free for only half the year. The climate was appalling – damp, cold, snow, sea fogs – and the permafrost meant that the water never drained away from the fields or the streets. There were more huskies in the little settlement than there were people. As we will see, the local garrison troops faced serious problems staying alive – not so much from hostile tribesmen, although that was a factor, but more from starvation when foodstuffs ran out. A British traveller summed it up in the early nineteenth century: 'a dismal, half-starved place, where drunkenness seemed the only amusement, or rather consolation, the inhabitants enjoyed'.[8]

The number of men in the garrison rose slowly. In 1762, there were only 43 soldiers and Cossacks in the fort, that is, fewer than in Kamchatka. By 1773, there were 83 regular troops (officers and ordinary soldiers) but also 245 Cossacks manning this desolate spot. In 1809, there were 298 soldiers and Cossacks and their wives and children living in or around the fort.[9]

Who were these men who ended up in Gizhiga and other Siberian forts? To state the obvious, garrison service was not an attractive posting. For young officers such as Pushkin's fictional hero, the glamorous part of army life was the life of action and, not least, the smart uniforms of the prestigious Guards regiments, which might impress the ladies and peers alike. 'My heart throbbed when I saw him with all his little cords and laces, with a sword, and four-cornered shako worn a little on one side and fastened with a chin-strap,' recalled the writer Alexander Herzen enviously in his early nineteenth-century memoirs when a cousin with a commission with the Guards regiments visited his house.[10] For officers, a distant posting normally came about as a result of poverty or a lack of influence, or was given as a punishment for some indiscretion, or simply was a placement for someone who was no longer young or fit enough for active service. Most Russian noblemen were not wealthy and simply needed a posting somewhere, anywhere, for economic survival. The immensely wealthy nobles with lavish lifestyles and armies of house-serfs like the Stroganovs, and who sometimes feature in anecdotes about Russia and in nineteenth-century literature, were in reality few and far between.

Garrison service could provide the basis of a career for the few members of the impoverished Siberian nobility who lacked social connections in European Russia, although it almost certainly meant remaining in Siberia. In a country without a developed civil service, and with almost no tradition of formal legal training, nobles could move from a military to a civilian career without taking examinations, undergoing training or providing any real indication of aptitude as far as we can tell. Service in a Siberian garrison, however, was not a passport to a glittering career.

Garrisons were manned mainly by Cossacks. Most Cossacks could expect to serve for most of their adult life – for up to 20 years although almost half of this was normally in initial training or, at the end of their career, in the reserve – and could be sent wherever the state wished, either individually or as part of a Cossack group. Siberian Cossacks had become a significant and separate group since their penetration into Siberia at the end of the sixteenth century, but Cossacks from elsewhere continued to be posted to Siberia in the eighteenth and nineteenth (and even early twentieth) centuries. Many local Siberian Cossacks sought a posting simply to survive, and were happy to accept one in even the most unattractive location. Petitions for service could be pitiful. In 1778, a 16-year-old Cossack called Ivan Kolmogorov begged the fort commander in Gizhiga for a position as his father had died and he needed 'food to maintain my mother, brothers and sister'.[11] In 1795, a Cossack called Nikolai Smisar in western Siberia asked for his son to have a posting or 'he would die from hunger'. Some impoverished rural Cossacks were so desperate they were 'eating grass from which their children had swollen up'.[12] In these circumstances, a posting anywhere was a blessing. Cossacks were paid very little for service in the garrisons but they were given a grain allocation on which they, and their families, could survive.

Ordinary soldiers, in the regular army of course, had no choice about where they were posted. We do not know much about them; this was an essentially illiterate society and soldiers did not write letters home, or their memoirs. Some may have been local men, but equally they could have ended up in a distant garrison purely by chance. There is, however, one striking feature about a number of these soldiers and Cossacks which tells us something significant: their age. Many of them were much older than would normally be expected in the armed forces. A considerable number of men in Siberian garrisons (and in other garrisons in Russia, for that matter) were in their 50s and some were even in their 60s. In 1809, a number of soldiers or Cossacks in Gizhiga were in their 60s and one, a certain Stepan Nizhegorodov, was 82.[13] It is hard to imagine some of these men defending the wild frontiers against hordes of armed native tribesmen.

Service for conscripts to the regular army was for life throughout most of the eighteenth century. In 1793, in theory this was reduced to 25 years, although for most that effectively meant life as they would have had nowhere else to go after spending a quarter of a century as a soldier. At the point of conscription they normally lost contact with their family and village. Indeed, even if these men had wanted to return to their village after they left service they would have been unwelcome as they could no longer contribute to its economic life and, by extension, to the tax levied on it. This was not only because of their age but also because at the point of conscription they were no longer 'peasants' but had become 'soldiers', that is, they had changed their social categorisation(marked symbolically by shaving off their beards), and could not revert to becoming peasants again. Such men could all too easily end up on the streets of Moscow as pitiful beggars. In an age, and a country, where there was little provision for elderly and infirm soldiers, the garrisons acted as an outdoor relief for men who had nowhere else to go. It is no coincidence that the garrison hospital in Gizhiga always held a number of sick men, some of whom never left. In 1762, only 32 of the 43 soldiers/Cossacks listed in the garrison were classified as healthy.[14] Garrison life was certainly not a comfortable occupation for retirement, but it provided a home of sorts with companionship and basic medical services for when men fell sick so very far from their place of birth.

Indigenous peoples also served in Siberian garrisons. Bashkirs, Kalmyks and Tungus were formed into special regiments which served on the frontiers in the same way as the Cossacks. Much of this was enforced service, of course, but there were a few advantages to be gained from it. Bashkirs were paid a small fee for two years' service in the garrisons – 20–30 roubles for service on the Orenburg line and 30–50 roubles for service on the Siberian line.[15] Tribesmen could become Cossacks or enrol in the regular army, in Siberia as elsewhere. For pagans, this almost inevitably meant conversion to Christianity. Muslims could retain their own faith within the army, although some were nonetheless baptised. The army, and the garrisons in particular, could act as a means of assimilating non-Russians into Russian service, willingly or otherwise.

Forts were intended to assert Russian control – military, political and fiscal – over a hostile land and an often hostile people. A very small number of men – some elderly and frail, as we have seen – with no means of communication with other forts therefore had the impossible task of defending the empire, or at least holding the line, and collecting tribute from the local population, not only to assert Russian overlordship but also to offset some of the costs of being there in the first place. It is not surprising in these circumstances that interaction with the local population often involved conflict.

Violence was endemic in relations between soldiers and civilians anywhere within the Russian empire and, for that matter, in other European states as well. The lack of other forms of restraint – legal redress or a police force – in the more remote areas of the empire, and the real physical threat posed by local tribesmen, meant that such violence could be extensive and extreme. Local tribes were commonly referred to as 'the enemy' in official garrison records. Conflict led to the taking of 'prisoners' from hostile tribesmen. Between 1759 and 1774, the Gizhiga garrison killed no fewer than 141 male and 105 female Chukchis and Koriaks, the local indigenous peoples, and took over 90 prisoners. Most of the deaths took place in the earlier part of the period – 52 were killed in 1759, 46 in 1760, 64 in 1762 – but sporadic killings took place throughout the 1770s.[16] Conflicts took place between tribal groups as well as between indigenous peoples and soldiers. The garrison could serve as a haven during intertribal conflicts. In Gizhiga, it was the Chukchis, and not Russian soldiers, who were said to have 'devastated' the lands of the Koriak people. As a result, some Koriaks took refuge within the walls of the fort – nine were there in 1773.[17]

Violence between soldiers and civilians was a daily occurrence. As we saw in Chapter 5, Russian peasants were responsible for the collection and allocation of tax in their own village communities, but in Gizhiga it was the troops who collected the 'tribute'. The sums were relatively small – in Gizhiga, they ranged from 25 copecks to 1 rouble, that is, less than the various taxes paid by state peasants in European Russia. (The poll tax, the main tax on state peasants, was 2 roubles in 1810, while townspeople paid more: 2 roubles in 1796, rising to 5 roubles in 1810 and 8 roubles in 1812.) Because the indigenous population practised little more than a subsistence economy, any demand for cash proved onerous (and, as we have seen, by this date the supply of pelts had dried up). Indeed, even being required to pay only these relatively small sums, the local Koriaks still ran up large arrears. The fort always cost the government far more to maintain than was ever recouped in tribute.

With the former taking money from the latter, and often by force, contacts between soldiers and local people were inevitably hostile. In 1774, there was a fight in the Gizhiga garrison between troops and a number of Chukchis who seem to have come to swear an oath of loyalty to the tsar. At least one Chukchi was killed, and women and children were injured. This particular case was investigated formally by the army: as a result, one Russian officer was condemned to the savage sentence of running the gauntlet six times through a rank of 100 men, and a Cossack was ordered to be flogged 'mercilessly' (brutal sentences which later commuted to demotion to the ranks for the officer and resettlement for the Cossack).[18]

On the Orenburg line, there were constant clashes between serving Cossacks and local tribesmen – Kirghiz and Bashkirs. Cossacks were attacked, their children were kidnapped and ransomed, their daughters were raped, and their horses, cattle and goods were stolen. Cossacks in turn were accused of various crimes including theft, unruliness and rape. Kidnapping of troops and their families was common, and ransom was always demanded in silver roubles rather than in paper roubles, the value of which depreciated rapidly in the eighteenth and early nineteenth centuries. One Cossack paid as much as 1,000 roubles to have his son released from captivity.[19]

Drink was one obvious source of comfort, and drunkenness and violence went together. Savage punishments within the Russian army – of which the most notorious was running the gauntlet several times between rows of soldiers who rained blows upon the backs of the unfortunate culprits – did little to prevent this. Government decrees which tried to restrict troops' access to alcohol proved ineffective. Drunkenness was almost endemic in the army and navy – among officers as well as men. Life in a remote garrison was particularly bleak, of course, and drink was one of the few reliefs or pleasures available. Drunkenness inevitably gave rise to crime and conflict with fellow soldiers and local inhabitants. In 1776, a soldier called Gavril Kuznetsov in Gizhiga stole vodka from a local Russian merchant, Mikhail Skorniakov; he was found guilty by a military court and sentenced to be flogged.[20]

Not all relations, however, involved conflict. The garrisons gave local people opportunities for trade. Soldiers needed basic foodstuffs and supplies, including candles and wood, and they paid in money or kind. The latter might be vodka; it might also be tobacco, which, as we saw in Chapter 3, was popularly thought to induce trances among the indigenous people. A contemporary traveller to Gizhiga noted: 'Tobacco is their great commodity, which they eat, chew, smoke, and snuff at the same time.'[21] Soldiers also needed somewhere to live, unless they stayed within the confines of their wooden fort. Small houses and barns were rented out to garrison troops in Gizhiga for sums ranging from 10 to 70 roubles.

Local people worked for the troops, again for small but probably very welcome payments. A Cossack in Gizhiga called Iakov Alekseev employed a converted Aleut to work for him for seven years for 79 roubles. That was quite a substantial sum, considered in light of the small sums noted above demanded in tribute. Another Cossack paid 10 roubles to a newly baptised Efrimov and a 'pagan' Akherin for 'domestic work'.[22] Garrisons could also be an escape from extreme poverty for local people as well as for the Cossacks living there. The Scottish Missionary Society set up branches in Siberia in the early nineteenth century, and one travelling missionary, William Selbie, noted the extreme poverty of the Kirghiz, who had moved near the forts for survival:

> several of the poorer of them who have no flocks & who consequently are not able to support themselves in the steppe, come & live near the Forts; along the borders of Russia, but beyond its boundaries, & by trade, or labour, or begging miserably support themselves – Such poor families are found scattered along the lines.[23]

Soldiers needed companionship, of course. Very few wives and children accompanied ordinary soldiers and Cossacks, or even officers, to such remote garrisons. Cossacks might be conscripted for a limited time and so leave their wives and children at home, but ordinary soldiers were in effect cut off from their families for good at the point of conscription. Having a son (or father or husband) go off as a recruit was regarded as tantamount to losing them for ever: conscripted boys left their home village to the accompaniment of songs which were akin to funeral laments. The wives of conscripts were often left in a desperate position, not infrequently with small children, and they often married again, even while their husbands were still alive, with the connivance of their parish priests.[24] In principle, bachelor soldiers had to ask permission to get married (as was the practice in most other European armies), and for the most part marriage was discouraged as it was thought to lead to indiscipline. In practice, however, these requirements had to be relaxed in remote garrisons where men could be stationed for many years.

The records of Gizhiga unfortunately tell us very little about the personal relationships formed between troops and local women. They do show, however, that a large number of soldiers were married and had families. In 1809, 176 males and 122 females were listed in the fort – a very high proportion of women. Gizhiga also had a garrison school which was attended by sons of Cossacks and soldiers. There were 82 boys at the school in 1809, aged between seven and 17.[25] Given the almost complete lack of settled Russian traders and peasants in this remote area, it can be assumed that the wives were indigenous Koriaks or Chukchis, who would have had to convert to Christianity. A hint is given by the formal records of the Gizhiga fort, which suggest that at least some of these were late, or even second, marriages. A soldier called Petr Belousov, who was aged 51, had a wife aged 23 and children aged 2 and 5; Ilia Kuiarev was aged 57 and had a young wife aged 24. Russian records are not always reliable but if they can be believed then one Stepan Nizhegorodov, aged 82, had a daughter aged 16.[26]

Cultural assimilation between garrison troops and the local population in Siberia was almost nonexistent. The garrison schools, known for their brutality, were not open to outsiders. Garrisons had an Orthodox church but there was no evidence of any attempt in Gizhiga to proselytise among tribesmen. There was no interest in the culture of the indigenous people, who were regarded as primitive and backward when they were not regarded as 'the enemy'. Western travellers found the Chukchis 'wild and rude' and 'a bold, suspicious and irascible people'. One British visitor described the Koriaks as 'the most rapacious barbarians I ever saw, although I have seen the savages of many parts of the world'.[27] They must have seemed a fearsome foe when they were attacking small parties of soldiers who were collecting tribute or foraging for berries, or when they were launching a full-scale assault on a tiny fort manned by a motley crew of Cossacks and soldiers.

Companionship, marriage and children must have been a great comfort in dismal spots such as Gizhiga. But they also meant that, when disaster struck, it affected whole families and not just individual soldiers. Troops had to adapt to the climate and ecology in their diet, but this was easier in western Russia and the northern Caucasus than in the hostile environment of eastern Siberia. The climate of Gizhiga meant that it was almost impossible to grow any type of grain, so the garrison depended largely on fishing. Cossacks were accustomed to fishing – that was their main activity on the river Iaik in the Urals. In good years this could be very lucrative: in 1776, Gizhiga Cossacks were said to have caught almost 5,000 sturgeon as well as other fish.[28]

When the fishing failed, however, the whole garrison found itself in desperate straits – lacking any other source of food and months away from receiving additional supplies by sea or road/sledge. In 1773, the river burst its banks and the fishing was ruined. Troops and locals alike were threatened with starvation – in 'extreme need', 'hungry' and 'ravaged', as the garrison records tersely report.[29] An officer, Pavel Mordovsky, petitioned for help as the failure of the fish catch meant he could no longer support his family of seven. In 1778, disaster struck again and the garrison was without food for 16 days. Some supplies were purchased from Koriaks but they too were heavily dependent on fishing. Desperate messages went from Gizhiga to Okhotsk begging for grain and warning that as many as half of the 800 men, women and children in the garrison could starve to death if they did not receive help.[30] A further famine occurred in the years 1815–19. Some 5,000 Koriak reindeer were slaughtered to try to offset the lack of other foodstuffs, and the government moved to establish a network of state stores and to encourage different types of cultivation.[31] However, the harsh climate and the constant dampness of the earth caused by the permafrost meant that little could grow (including potatoes). The government allocated a further 5,000 roubles to purchase supplies from Irkutsk to provide essentials for the fort but it could take many weeks, or even months, for supplies to reach Gizhiga.

The economic situation was unsustainable. By the early nineteenth century, the fort had fallen into an irreversible economic decline and the number of troops in the garrison and traders in the town fell. When Mikhail Speransky was sent by Alexander I to review Siberian administration, it was reported to him that villages had been ruined, that the natives had fallen into 'apathy and drunkenness', and that Gizhiga had 'in consequence of sickness, famine, etc., been much reduced in population'.[32] The settlement never thrived. A 'Russian-American Trading Company of New York and Gizhiga' existed briefly in the 1890s but then ceased trading. It was never connected by rail to any other town, either in the 1890s or during the Gulag period; in 1921, a White Don Cossack established a base there to 'conquer' Chukotha, but was caught and executed. Collectivisation in the 1930s destroyed the local economy. The settlement is now shabby and desolate as the young and educated have left; the population in 2000 was said to be 700, mainly Chukchis.[33] This was indeed Russia's Wild East.

CHAPTER EIGHT

Governing and the Governed

'A S FOR justice 'tis a joke. No such thing exists and its shadow covers vice enough to make me shudder,'[1] stated an Anglo-Irish visitor to Russia at the beginning of the nineteenth century. Russian provincial administration was poor: officials were often incompetent, ignorant or corrupt; the powers of higher officials all too often went unchecked; there was no effective police force to maintain law and order; bribery was rife; overlapping jurisdictions led to confusion and delays; court cases languished unresolved for years; taxes went uncollected; government decrees were not implemented. The country was, in fact, severely undergoverned. In 1763, the whole Russian empire had some 16,500 officials in central and local government offices, while Prussia, with less than 1 per cent of Russia's land area and a far smaller population, employed some 14,000 civil servants. The difficulties experienced in European Russia were often exacerbated in Siberia.

Siberia was an excellent example both of the issues which had to be tackled and of the difficulties of resolving them. The inadequacies of provincial administration were fully exposed in Siberia, but this was also the territory within the empire where the most significant efforts were made to improve administration in the early nineteenth century. New posts and structures were established in the early 1820s, many of which lasted until the February 1917 Revolution. This process also, however, exposed the limitations of institutional reform in preparing Siberia for the challenges of the late nineteenth and early twentieth centuries.

Siberia posed particular problems. The sheer distances involved meant that it could take not just months but years for government decrees to be received, let alone implemented. In distant Gizhiga, a case of so-called 'word and deed of the sovereign' (a denunciation of treason against the tsar) was investigated in 1765 – three years after this archaic procedure, which included torture for both the accuser and the accused, had been abolished.[2] The difficulties of communication were exacerbated by the nature of the population of Siberia. This had risen to circa 760,000 people by 1762 and continued to grow steadily: 1,070,000 by 1795, 1,330,000 by 1811 and over 2 million by 1833.[3] The population was very thinly spread over vast distances. Furthermore, it was almost impossible for administrators in towns to know what was happening in the countryside when tax, tribute or recruits were being levied, and sometimes impossible to implement government policy. In 1780, for example, the army reported to Moscow that it had proved impossible to levy men at all from 'distant villages in the Irkutsk region and on the Sea of Okhotsk'.[4] State granaries had been set up but in practice it was very difficult to supply the population with grain and other goods if the harvest failed in one area. Governors often had little idea of what was happening when local officials, or soldiers, tried to conscript in the villages, or exact other state obligations. Central government had little idea of what was happening in offices in towns or how officials were behaving, unless petitions reached it or the behaviour was so extreme that it was brought to its attention

Violence and disorder were endemic throughout Russia but there was even less control by government officials in remote areas such as Siberia. Some of the worst excesses took place during the collection of tribute from indigenous peoples, as we have already seen, and this continued during the eighteenth century and beyond. In the 1730s, reports reached the government of disorders concerning the collection of tribute 'so that the inhabitants here have been completely ruined in a few years and are in such a condition that they will not be able to pay tribute any more'.[5] In 1733, 'devastation and injuries' were inflicted on the tribute-paying people in Iakutsk and Kamchatka.[6] Three years later, two Cossacks were accused of taking bribes during the collection of tribute – one had taken 592 roubles and the other 400 roubles, and between them they had acquired gold and silver and over 8,000 pelts – an absolute fortune.[7] In 1745, Kamchadals in Kamchatka suffered 'harm and ruin' (this was the normal phrase used in official documents to signify that irregularities had taken place) during the collection of tribute.[8]

One of the reasons for the violence was the exceptional levels of poverty and desperation of some of the indigenous peoples of Siberia, who frequently alleged that they were too poor to pay the tribute of furs. In 1702, Kalmyks in Kuznetsk district in south-western Siberia petitioned to be exempted as 'illness' meant they were unable to pay.[9] In 1741, a group of Iakuts stated that they had no pelts and had to buy them in the town of Iakutsk to fulfil their obligations.[10] Massive arrears of tribute built up as a result: in Tobolsk province alone, the arrears were 342,835 roubles by 1822.[11]

Contact between Russian peasant settlers and state officials was rare – and was often unwelcome and violent when it did occur. 'According to the notions of the Siberian people, the human race is mainly divided into two classes – people and government officials,' stated one Russian observer in the late nineteenth century.[12] The main contact between peasants and the state came during the recruit levy, when peasants could 'pay off' local officials to save their sons from conscription. In 1719, the official Aleksei Dioltovsky was accused of taking bribes during the levy – he took minor sums of 3 to 4 roubles from each peasant and amounts of grain.[13] In the 1730s, an official called Matvei Beiton was accused of taking much larger sums – 1,500 roubles.[14] In 1780, bribes of 20 copecks per peasant were paid to the treasurer Aleksei Trubnikov in Dolmatovskii district in western Siberia. Many such bribes no doubt went unreported and undetected, but on this occasion Trubnikov was investigated and beaten 'with sticks without mercy'.[15]

The Russian government was not unaware of the problems of governing Siberia. During the seventeenth and eighteenth centuries, the territory was divided and redivided into different administrative units under different officials in an attempt to govern the region better. In the seventeenth century, Siberia was divided into four large administrative units: Tobolsk, Tomsk, Eniseisk and Irkutsk. In 1637, a Siberian Office was set up in Moscow (and finally closed in 1763), but it had little control in practice over the affairs of the separate Siberian units. In the first half of the eighteenth century, a number of restructurings of the administrative boundaries of Siberia took place. In Peter I's reign, new provinces were established and governors appointed to administer them. In the reign of Catherine II, Siberia was divided into two provinces – Tobolsk in the west and Irkutsk in the east – and then a third province was created in the Altai region, each under the authority of a governor-general. Paul I, Catherine II's son and successor, reverted to the administrative structure of the two provinces of Tobolsk and Irkutsk. In the early nineteenth century, in the reign of Alexander I, a further restructuring took place, and new regions and sub-regions were established under one overarching chief official, the general-governor of Siberia.

This constant changing of administrative boundaries reflected the difficulties of trying to administer such large and diverse lands, but it rarely solved any problems or made life any easier for the people who were being governed. One major difficulty was finding the right calibre of men to represent the authority of the state in territory so far away from St Petersburg. It was difficult enough to find able people to fill administrative posts in European Russia. How much more difficult must it have been, then, in Siberia where it was hard to attract outsiders to posts in remote and unsophisticated towns and where there were very few resident nobles?

Who governed in Siberia? The governors (the governor was called *voevoda* until 1775) of large administrative units in the seventeenth and eighteenth centuries were powerful men throughout Russia, but in Siberia there was little check on their authority and they could rule over vast territories almost like satraps. One Siberian governor was described in the following way: 'ignorant, hot-tempered, greedy, he flogged hunters and trading people who did not give him gifts, persecuted clerical staff and he loved to entertain constantly and drink different spirits until drunk'.[16] Governors everywhere had wide-ranging military powers, but in Siberia these were again more pronounced as they were responsible for commanding troops, and for the construction and defence of forts and towns. They also had overall responsibility for civil government, for implementing the tsar's edicts, maintaining law and order, administering justice and ensuring that trade was conducted legally. It was only in the later eighteenth century that there was an attempt to separate the military from the civil functions of the governors, but even then it was impossible to make a clear division. In practice, the only way their power could be checked was to make sure the posts were temporary and to make an example of the most notoriously corrupt governors. Prince M. P. Gagarin, governor of the Nerchinsk region in the 1720s, described in official documents as a 'rogue and an evil man', was investigated by the government and eventually executed for his abuses.[17]

We know little about the clerks and other minor officials who staffed the administrative offices in Siberia. Posts everywhere lacked glamour, but even more so in remote, uncomfortable, and sometimes dangerous towns in Siberia. Life for petty clerks there was grim – poorly paid, of low status and with few comforts. An Austrian diplomat in the early eighteenth century noted how clerks were 'trained' in the reign of Peter I: 'The clerks, after the manner of outrageous criminals, were chained with iron to their places, and fettered, to teach them how to write night and day.' They were punished, he said, with 'a kind of cudgelling'.[18]

Some office clerks were fugitives, either peasants from European Russia or factory workers. Others were 'foreigners', that is, prisoners of war who had ended up in Siberia, or sons of clergy who had been unable to find a position within the Church. Many were very young and it was not unusual to find boys of 15 working in offices.[19] It is hardly surprising that these clerks took petty bribes when they could, were often corrupt and incompetent, and turned to drink. In 1799, a Siberian clerk called Igumen, aged 39, was investigated for 'drunkenness, laziness and disobedience' and sentenced to be kept on bread and water for a month.[20]

Under Peter I, all nobles were required to serve the state in some capacity. Most, however, wanted to serve in the army rather than in a civilian post. Army life, whatever its dangers, was more appealing than a dull life in a provincial backwater taken up with writing endless reports. Even that dull occupation required some skills, such as basic literacy, which some nobles lacked. In 1762, in the brief reign of Peter III (the husband of Catherine II), nobles were freed from compulsory service to the state. Most of them, however, still needed employment, either in the armed forces or in administration, to supplement the income they received from their estates. 'Service' became the distinctive characteristic of the nobility, and a way to divide them from 'non-privileged' members of society who had no choice other than to pay taxes or be conscripted into the armed forces. Every post in the armed forces and the civil administration had been assigned a 'rank' in the reign of Peter I, and these were listed in a special Table of Ranks on a scale of 1 to 14. The 'rank' acquired through service defined not only the occupation but also the status and prestige of the nobleman (characters in nineteenth-century Russian novels are always given their title and rank), but military service and its ranks were always more prestigious than those in the civil service.

Those who ended up in local administration were usually not fit for active military service, were sometimes elderly, were often from less wealthy backgrounds, and were sometimes there against their wishes. This was particularly true in Siberia, especially in the remoter and less settled east, which was an unattractive posting. Colonel Adrian Voznitsky, aged 57, for example, had a small estate in European Russia comprising only seven peasant households and wanted to retire, but was declared fit for civilian service and sent in 1722 to Eniseisk as a judge. His successor was Grigorii Opukhtin, who owned only ten peasant households. Opukhtin became the governor of Eniseisk in 1727.[21]

In 1775, Catherine II implemented a significant reform of local administration throughout the empire and created new institutions at both provincial and district levels, including new advisory boards for the governors, new financial institutions and three tiers of local courts for all sectors of the population. This was an attempt not only to improve local administration but also to find 'useful' posts for nobles who, since the abolition of compulsory service, no longer had to serve in the armed forces but needed an occupation in the provinces and, in many cases, an income.

Military service, however, seemed much more glamorous to young nobles, who continued to enter the civil service only if they were too poor, lacked social connections or were not physically fit to undertake military service. N. Tolubeev, the son of a poor provincial noblemen, joined the civil service as his health was poor but had

little enthusiasm when serving in the criminal chamber. Whatever I did was like present-day peasants on labour obligations, especially when I saw two sons of our neighbour who had been appointed to a regiment in uniform – with lace on their red collars. I lamented for a long time that I could not follow them and could not be transferred to a regiment.[22]

In reality, posts in local administration were often only sought by army officers after retirement. They have therefore been referred to as a 'pension system'.

The social composition of Siberia, however, also accounted for the failure to fill some vacancies in Catherine's new structure of administrative offices and courts. At the end of the eighteenth century, the empress sent trusted senior noblemen to the provinces, including to Siberia, to see if her new institutions had been properly established and were fully staffed. They found that in Tobolsk it had proved impossible to fill elected posts in local courts reserved for members of the nobility.[23] In Kolyvan, in the Altai region, a 'great shortage' of suitable candidates meant that not all institutions could be opened, and retired Siberian nobles and administrators from the mines had to be recruited to the new posts.[24]

It is hard to put together a picture of the type of men who ended up 'governing' Siberia in the late eighteenth century after Catherine's reforms. Senior administrators there came from a variety of backgrounds, reflecting the distinct social and ethnic composition of Siberia and the dearth of resident landed nobility. Some were members of the less prestigious 'Siberian nobility' and/or had previously served in Siberian regiments or garrisons, which were again the least prestigious in Russia. A significant number of senior administrators had served in the navy (which was less popular than the army; service in the galley fleet was a punishment for criminals). I. O. Selifinov, who became the general-governor of Kolyvan and Irkutsk provinces in the late eighteenth century, was educated in the Naval Cadet Corps, served briefly in the British fleet, became a brigadier in the Russian navy, and then served as president of Perm criminal chamber in the Urals (the highest criminal court in the provinces). After his service in Siberia he was rewarded with a post as Governor-General in European Russia.[25]

The difficulty of filling posts in Siberia did lead to some social mobility, possibly more than in European Russia. A list of 165 lower-level officials in Irkutsk in 1789 shows that the majority were of noble origin from inside and outside Siberia, including Ukrainians and Belarusians, but officials were also recruited from clerical, church and merchant backgrounds and included one son of a peasant and one converted Jew.[26] The son of a priest, Ivan Zakharzhevsky served as a soldier and rose to the level of major; he then retired and became a councillor in one of the new local government institutions in Irkutsk.[27] A. I. Losev, the son of a soldier, had been educated at the Irkutsk navigational school and became a surveyor and then the architect of Irkutsk.[28] Ia. Ia. Pavlutsky, the son of an army officer in Tobolsk, joined the army at the age of 13 and rose to the rank of major, became the Tobolsk postmaster, retired, but then came out of retirement to become a judge. In a rare example of extreme social mobility, P. A. Taskaev, born a serf of Count Stroganov (who, as we have seen, had vast wealth and lands and factories in Siberia) in 1735, had been conscripted as an ordinary soldier at the age of 15, rose to the rank of sub-lieutenant through service in Prussia, Silesia and Pomerania, became treasurer in Okhotsk, and then *noble* assessor in Okhotsk conscience court in 1794 with the title of titular councillor (the same rank as an army captain).[29] Siberia was certainly the land of opportunity for some able, or lucky, individuals.

Poor communications, an ethnically diverse population, poverty, recruitment difficulties – all these factors exacerbated the problems of local administration in Siberia. The Siberian experience, however, exposed more fundamental problems within the Russian state as a whole. The lack of able administrators arose from the fact that the civil service did not develop within Russia, as it did in other European states such as Prussia, France, Austria and Britain. The first Russian university had been founded in 1755, in Moscow, but higher education was only expanded in the early nineteenth century, in the reign of Alexander I, and there were no universities in Siberia until the late nineteenth century.

A more fundamental problem was the slow development in Russia in establishing modern legal procedures and unified codes of law and the absence of trained lawyers. Laws were not properly codified until 1832 in the reign of Nicholas I. Before that time, courts used the Law Code of 1649, supplemented by later laws and edicts covering particular areas (such as Peter I's military code of 1716, which was applied in the courts for, among other things, allegations of witchcraft). Legal training developed very slowly in Russia. The first Russian professor of jurisprudence, S. A. Desnitsky, was trained at Glasgow University in the 1770s.

In the eighteenth century, it was considered appropriate for retired army officers without any legal training to act as judges in provincial courts. An American traveller to Siberia in the 1780s noted 'two old discharged officers (colonels) who at their own request have quitted the Service, and constituted Judges and Justices of the Law'.[30] These judges were assisted by clerks who prepared the evidence in a series of legal proofs or testimonies, which were normally presented as a series of questions and answers. This evidence was often in the form of confessions, which were sometimes achieved by torture (at least up to the reign of Catherine II, when torture was forbidden, but even after that time the way prisoners in remote towns were treated could go unchecked), and the judge then handed down punishment according to whatever law seemed most appropriate.

Both Peter I and Catherine II had attempted to improve local administration and the quality of local officials. Neither, however, addressed the specific problems of governing Siberia. It was Alexander I who finally addressed these in the early nineteenth century, and he chose Mikhail Speransky to undertake the work on his behalf. Speransky had been the chief minister in the first decade of Alexander's reign and in 1809 had devised a 'constitution' for Russia, which, had it been implemented, would have divided executive, judicial and legislative functions in the state, that is, it would have followed the most 'modern' constitutions of the day which had emerged from the French Revolution. The tsar would have retained the highest executive power, assisted by his ministries, and the Senate would have become the highest court of appeal. It would also have established a 'legislature' for Russia, a State Duma. At a local level, there would have been local dumas, with members elected from property owners, whose representatives would have elected members from their number to serve in a Provincial Duma. The tsar would then have chosen from lists of representatives at provincial level to make up the State Duma.

This type of 'constitution' was not untypical of the Napoleonic-style constitutions of the early nineteenth century. The introduction of such a constitution would have been a radical move in Russia, where there were no pre-existing modern-style representative institutions and where the ruler had few effective curbs on his or her power. One major issue which Speransky did not address in 1809 was serfdom and its compatibility (or otherwise) with a modern, representative, political system, although it is clear from his private writings that he abhorred serfdom. He believed that a proper framework for administration and law had to be in place before more radical proposals to modernise society could be implemented. It was not lost on Speransky, or other Russian reformers, that the United States had a constitution and also had slavery.

In the event, Speransky's plans were not implemented by Alexander I. They were kept secret quite possibly because the tsar considered them a threat to his power. Speransky fell from power in 1812, on a rather feeble charge of treason, in part because the reforms which he had enacted had made him unpopular with the noble elite and smacked rather too much of Napoleonic France at a time when it looked likely that war would break out between France and Russia. He was sent into internal exile.

In 1819, however, he was recalled and sent to Siberia as governor-general with the instructions:

> you will correct everything that can be corrected, you will uncover the persons who are given to abuses, you will put on trial whomever necessary. But your most important occupation should be to determine on the spot the most useful principles for the organisation and administration of this remote region.[31]

Speransky did not welcome what he probably regarded as a second exile (his first exile was in European Russia), rather than being restored to the heart of the decision-making process in St Petersburg. But he understood that Siberia was different, as he had stated back in 1801, because of its size and 'the conditions of the people that inhabit it and the great variety which prevails in their mores, customs, industries, and ways of life'.[32] Had he had any doubts that Siberia needed attention, then they were shed when he heard of the high-handed and arbitrary behaviour of the incumbent Governor-General, Ivan Pestel (father of Pavel Pestel, who led the army revolt in southern Russia in 1825), and his assistant, N. I. Treskin, which had led to many complaints of bribery and corruption.

Speransky took his duties seriously and travelled extensively within Siberia before putting substantial proposals to Alexander I, all of which were accepted and implemented in 1822. He also became convinced that despite its problems – not least the small number of resident nobility and what he saw as the backwardness of its merchant class – Siberia represented enormous untapped potential wealth.

The aims of Speransky's reforms were to eliminate corruption and arbitrariness in administration, establish the rule of law, set up effective and clear organs of administration, and improve the quality of officials in local administration. He divided Siberia into two general-governorships, Eastern Siberia and Western Siberia, both of which were to be supported by an advisory council of appointed senior officials. These two regions were further subdivided into new provinces, each with its own administrative structures, and administrative regions were established in the most remote and sparsely populated areas At the local level, administrative units were determined by the density and composition of the population, but the number of police and their responsibilities were increased. Speransky made sure the most notorious corrupt officials were arrested: in all, 681 officials were charged with various misdeeds.[33]

Speransky took a particular interest in the scientific resources of Siberia and encouraged expeditions and the collection of proper information and statistics. He helped to establish more schools, supported the study of oriental languages and established branches of the (Protestant) Bible Society, which printed and disseminated copies of the Bible in Russia. His home in Irkutsk became the centre for social and cultural events. He established a special office in Tobolsk and new regulations for settling exiles on the land in Siberia,

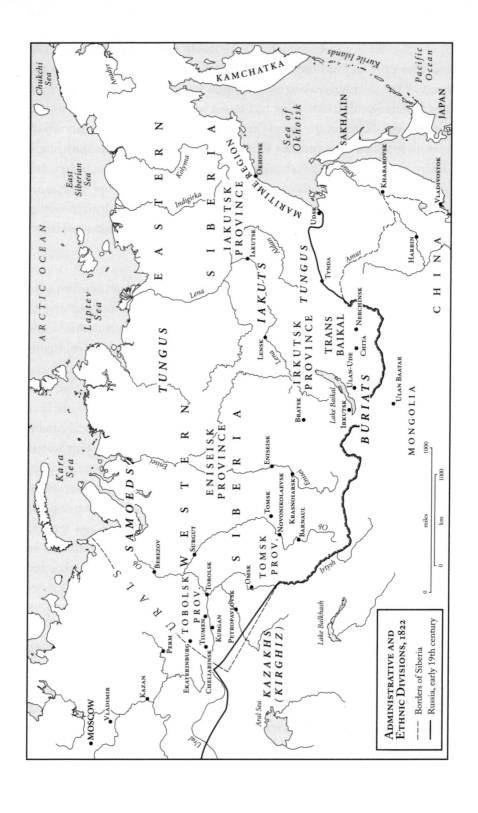

ADMINISTRATIVE AND
ETHNIC DIVISIONS, 1822

--- Borders of Siberia

—— Russia, early 19th century

and modernised tax collection from indigenous peoples and state peasants, replacing dues in kind (pelts, foodstuffs) and service obligations (such as carting and road building) with cash payments. He reorganised the operation of state grain (and fish) stores in Siberia, which were essential to supply inhabitants with provisions when harvests failed but which in the past had all too often been controlled by corrupt officials. He took measures to liberalise Siberian trade with China and proposed reductions in customs duties, and clarified the duties of the Siberian Cossacks, in effect equalising their rights and obligations with those of state peasants. Cossacks were for the most part freed from military duties and encouraged to become more settled and engage fully in agriculture. Henceforth they would be subject to the normal state courts (rather than military jurisdiction).

All this was both necessary and helpful for Siberia's administration and economic development. However, what it represented essentially was an exercise in tidying up the administration, refining the classification of social groups and defining their activities more closely. How traditional Speransky's approach was can be seen most revealingly in his policies towards indigenous peoples in Siberia. Speransky studied their customs and way of life, established good relations with tribal leaders and considered that in time they would evolve to the same cultural level of Russians. At the same time, he thought they should be treated differently from other inhabitants but within an administrative framework imposed from above. In the first instance, this required him to categorise the indigenous peoples, drawing distinctions between them according to their level of 'civilisation'. They were thus divided into three groups – 'settled people' (Bashkirs, Tatars, Kazakhs), 'nomads' (Buriats, Tungus, Iakuts) and 'vagrants' (Samoeds, Koriaks, Chukchis, Kamchadals) – all with their own rights and obligations.

Settled peoples – that is, the more 'advanced' peoples – were treated more or less like state peasants. Kazakhs in particular were encouraged to settle on land specifically allocated to them. The other groups – which were of greater concern to Speransky – were to handle most matters themselves according to their own customs, including minor offences and disputes, with the state's role limited to a supervisory policing function and the investigation of serious criminal offences (such as murder, rebellion or theft of goods above a certain value). Each group of 15 families was to form a clan administration comprising an elder and senior members of the clan. The clan representatives were brought together in a Steppe Duma, with limited, primarily fiscal functions: it was supposed to be responsible for conducting the census and accounting for monies, property held in common and supplies of foodstuffs. The main contact between these institutions and the state was the Lower Land Court, which was an administrative and police office rather than a judicial court as we would understand it. The Lower Land Court transmitted serious cases to the Russian courts and major concerns to the Provincial and Governor's Offices and passed back national or local instructions to the clan administrations. Speransky also started the process of codifying local customary laws, which resulted in a Code of the Laws of the Steppes in 1841, which, although never formally sanctioned, in practice remained the basis for legal relations with indigenous peoples until 1917.

Speransky also attempted to end the practice of enslaving indigenous people by Russian settlers. Speransky was practical: he tried to buy out slaves from Russians for 150 roubles each and suggested setting up foster homes so that nomads would not sell children into slavery. Records which I found in the Omsk archive show that in the 1820s this resulted in a spate of requests from slaves of Kalmyk, Kirghiz and even one of Persian origin (the son of a former prisoner of war), all of whom had converted to Christianity, to be granted freedom from 'slavery' in the households of Russians. These requests were handled by the local courts which had to disentangle the 'ownership' rights. Some petitions were rejected as the supplicants had become categorised as peasants and were therefore legitimately 'owned'; one Nikolai Alekseev, a converted Kirghiz, was judged to be a house serf and therefore birched for making a false slavery accusation against his master. Two Kalmyk women were, however, freed from their owners on the grounds that they were older than 35, and their masters were each given 150 roubles in compensation.[34]

Speransky's reforms were comprehensive, and put in place a more efficient and less corrupt system of administration in Siberia. They nonetheless represented an *ancien régime* approach by a man who had once favoured far more radical political and social solutions for Russia. It was, in fact, very much the approach taken by the tsars Peter I and Catherine II in the eighteenth century – that is, based on a belief that institutional reform could lead to the social and economic development of the county and that classifying and defining social groups and functions helped to bring about modernisation.

The judicial system continued to operate on the understanding that not only indigenous peoples but also other non-Russians and non-Christians, and particular social as well as ethnic groups, were governed by their own laws. Not only indigenous peoples but also peasants (serfs and state peasants) dealt with minor offences and land and property disputes by customary law until the late nineteenth century. In reality, many abuses continued unchecked in local administration, not only in Siberia but throughout the empire. In 1824, an official called Loginov took 50 roubles from a peasant called Kutenov in a village in the Kolyvan region. The money had apparently been handed over to the official 'out of fear'.[35]

Russian literature provides some of the most acute (and humorous) descriptions of the failings of the administration. The play *Chicanery*, written by Vaslii Kapnist in 1798, features a court prosecutor by the name of Khvataiko, which means 'Grabber', a great bribe-taker, who sings the following song:

> Take, you'll learn the art with ease!
> Take, whatever you can seize!
> God for this your hands did make,
> That you may take.[36]

The best depiction of corruption, venality, greed, general incompetence and ignorance is provided by Gogol's *The Government Inspector*, written in 1836 and set in an unnamed, but distant, province. In one scene, the various local government officials offer bribes to the young man wrongly assumed to be the inspector from St Petersburg. It is the reaction of the two main officials to the idea that the 'inspector' might have already been in town for two weeks and might want to see what they are actually doing which is most revealing:

Mayor: Two weeks! Holy saints and martyrs! In the last two weeks the sergeant's wife has been flogged! The convicts haven't had their rations! The streets are filthy, covered in rubbish!
Judge: Who on earth would want to inspect the courthouse? If he does read any of the papers in there he'll bitterly regret it. I've sat 15 years on the bench and every time I look at one of those legal documents I throw up my hands in despair. I can't make head or tail of it.[37]

The reality was that reforms such as those undertaken by Speransky could only improve the *mechanics* of administration. More fundamental change was stymied by the Russian social structure, in particular the lack of development of towns and commercial classes, by the slow development of jurisprudence and an independent judiciary, and by the structure of government whereby the ruler's powers remained unchecked by representative institutions. This was true throughout the empire but was exacerbated in Siberia by the region's vast size and social composition. This meant that it was ill prepared to face the new economic, social and political challenges which arose several decades after Speransky's reforms.

CHAPTER NINE

Exiles and Convicts

IN 1591, Dmitrii Ivanovich, the ten-year-old youngest son of Tsar Ivan IV, was murdered in Uglich, a town on the river Volga north of Moscow. There were suspicions about who had done this, but punishment for the crime was meted out in the first instance on the bell of Uglich. The latter had tolled and raised the alarm at the death of the boy, and was held to be responsible for triggering the riots which followed. It therefore had its clapper (that is, its tongue) and its 'ears' cut off and was exiled to Siberia. It was only pardoned and returned to Uglich in the late nineteenth century. Another bell in Moscow was punished in the same way by Catherine II after being held responsible for the plague riots of 1771.[1]

We are concerned with the people, and not the bells, who were exiled to Siberia, but the incident in Uglich demonstrates that from the very beginning of the opening up of Siberia people understood that it was a place of punishment and banishment. We have seen that unfree as well as free settlers populated Siberia in the seventeenth century. The idea of Siberia as a prison has remained a powerful image, and reality, ever since. The 'exile system' arose essentially because Russia lacked a 'prison system'. Unlike in some other European states, most local prisons in Russia simply held people waiting for trial or for their punishment to be inflicted (or in prison hospitals after punishment). A small number of high-profile prisoners – claimants to the throne, rebels, insane nobles – were normally held in fortresses or monastery prisons. One aspect of the exile system was certainly punishment – the harshness of the journey across Siberia on foot and shackled, the terrible conditions of forced labour in mines, the floggings inflicted on convicts, so vividly described by Dostoevsky in his *Memoirs from the House of the Dead*, published in 1862. The other side of the exile system, however, was a belief that convicts and exiles might prove valuable settlers in the remoter parts of Siberia and that they could be 'reformed' in the process and turned into useful citizens. These two conflicting aims had a profound impact on the development of Siberia and helped to mould not only the nature of settlements there but also affected its social and ethnic composition, its cultural development, and the image of 'Siberia' that was projected to the rest of the Russian empire, and to the world beyond.

It is impossible to calculate the number of exiles accurately, although they never constituted more than a small proportion of the overall Siberian population. It has been estimated that there were some 7,400 exiles in Siberia in 1662. That number grew slowly in the eighteenth century; in the period 1760–80, some 30,000 men were exiled, that is, somewhere between 1,500 and 2,000 a year. Some 8,000 a year were exiled in the period 1823–60. One estimate is that between 1863 and 1888, over 300,000 exiles and their families were sent to Siberia, which would be in the region of some 12,000 per year, although the number was higher than this in some years.[2] It has been estimated that, by 1898, there were just over 300,000 exiles in Siberia out of a total population of some 5,760,000, that is, about 5.2 per cent.[3]

In reality, Siberia may have been more the land of the 'free' rather than the 'unfree' but that was not the perception of travellers who saw parties of wretched convicts walking in chains across its main routes or lodged in transit prisons in major towns. An American traveller reported from Irkutsk in the 1780s: 'Not a day passes scarcely but an exile of some sort arrives here.'[4] Nor, as we shall see, was the resident population of Siberia insulated from contact with exiles in the imperial Russian period, something which contrasts with the limited contact with prisoners in the Gulag camps in the twentieth century.

The Russian government always distinguished between different types of exiles, even if some of the niceties were lost on those charged with guarding parties of convicts. There are sad stories of some naive exiles being conned on the journey across Siberia by hardened criminals in their party into 'swapping' their sentences for some small payment or some pathetically small luxury and ending up performing horrendous forced labour in their place. Speransky, as part of his reforms in the 1820s, had grouped exiles into six categories according to the nature of their crime. The main distinction, however, was between people who had been convicted by the courts of a

crime for which exile was a punishment, and those who through alleged idleness, unruly behaviour or minor non-criminal offences had been dispatched
to resettle in Siberia. Nobles were given the right to exile their serfs to Siberia,
provided they were under 45 years of age. The power of nobles to wreck the
lives of their serfs in this way has sometimes been seen as symbolic of the
arbitrariness and cruelty of the serf system, and it is certainly the case that
nobles exercised this right – and that their main concern was that these serfs
were counted as part of the recruit levy.[5] The same power, however, was also
given to, and exercised by, state-peasant and urban communities. Indeed, it is
not untypical of the way in which the Russian, and then the Soviet, government simply moved individuals and whole communities to remote parts of
the country. These so-called 'administrative exiles' were supposed to increase
settlement, particularly in the remoter areas of eastern and northern Siberia.
In practice, the distinctions between exiles were blurred by the fact that
sentences could involve both types of penalties: for example, a specified
period of forced labour in a mine followed by a period of forced settlement in
a specified location in Siberia.

The reality was that exiles comprised a wide range of people, from hardened criminals, murderers and brigands, to petty thieves, fugitives from the
army, work-shy peasants, members of religious sects, aristocratic political
prisoners, veterans from the army caught begging on the streets, prostitutes,
and young children accompanying their parents. The list of a party of 29
exiles in 1736, for example, included murderers, thieves, peasant deserters
from the army, a clerk who had failed to turn up at the conscription post, and
Cossacks and artisans who had moved location without permission from the
authorities.[6]

By the mid-nineteenth century, the largest group of exiles – some 40 per
cent – was described loosely as consisting of 'vagabonds' or 'vagrants'. Lest
we forget that exiles did indeed include those who had committed horrific
crimes as well as those we might regard as innocent victims of the 'system', the
second largest group of exiles in the mid-nineteenth century were those
convicted of serious crimes, such as murder (8 per cent) and robbery.[7] The
latter group would almost certainly be sentenced to forced labour (often
followed by forced settlement in Siberia); the former group might be the
people who became forced settlers. It has been estimated that about half the
exiles were resettled on the land in some form, but exact figures are lacking
precisely because of the blurring of categories noted above.

The number of women and children among 'ordinary' convicts and forced settlers is unknown. Female prostitutes and beggars were rounded up in European Russia and sent to Siberia. A list of 28 women, widows and girls sent to settle Siberia in 1765–6 for 'idleness' and 'dishonourable deeds' included artisans but mainly comprised soldiers' wives, that is, those who had been separated forcibly from their husbands or who were widowed, and who, without any other support, were the most vulnerable in society.[8] In the period 1854–60, over 2,400 children entered the exile system.[9] Women, however, constituted a minority of exiles; for that matter, they also represented a minority of free settlers, as we have already seen.

It is the political prisoners in Siberia who have inevitably caught our imagination, because so many of them were, or became, prominent and some wrote about their experiences. In 1790, Aleksandr Radishchev, a well-educated, wealthy noblemen, was sentenced to death by the St Petersburg criminal court for publishing his *A Journey from St Petersburg to Moscow*, but his punishment was commuted to ten years' exile in eastern Siberia by Catherine II herself. His book was presented as a travelogue and written in a sentimental style (which is why it initially passed the censors) but was really an indictment of the whole social and political structure of the state. Radishchev's traveller witnessed the cruelty and corruption of conscription in particular and serfdom in general, which he proposed should be abolished. In a powerful dream sequence, the rottenness of the judicial structure, and by extension the whole state, is revealed to him. To Catherine, already shaken by the French Revolution in 1789, this book was 'infected with French poison'. Radishchev's subsequent interrogation was based in part on the notes Catherine had made in the margins of her copy of the book.

In the nineteenth century, Siberia became an undesired home for many more political prisoners. The most famous were the Decembrists, but they had many distinguished successors, from the Petrashevsky circle in 1849 – a clandestine radical discussion group whose members included Dostoevsky, then aged 27, who was led out with others to be executed at dawn on Senate Square in St Petersburg and at the moment that the firing squad raised their rifles was informed that his sentence had been commuted to exile and hard labour in Siberia – through to the anarchist Mikhail Bakunin in 1857 and the socialist and Marxist thinkers at the end of the nineteenth century.

The Decembrists were adopted as the heroes of later socialist thinkers and became favourites of the authorities in the Soviet Union, although their admiration was tempered by a consciousness of the rebels' mainly aristocratic backgrounds. They had certainly challenged the political and social order. In December 1825 (hence the name 'Decembrists'), officers appeared in Senate Square in St Petersburg with some 3,000 troops and refused to take the oath of loyalty to the new tsar, Nicholas I. Popular myth has it that when they demanded a 'constitution', some less sophisticated soldiers and onlookers thought they were calling for the wife of Constantine, Nicholas's elder brother who had refused to take the throne, to be adopted as head of state instead. In any event, the 'revolt' was put down with a single salvo from the artillery. Poorly organised and badly led, the rebels were dispersed with ease, and the leaders rounded up. A parallel revolt in the south was also easily put down.

This was, then, an attempted revolt against the tsar and not simply a provocative discussion group. The hope of these officers that Nicholas I might listen to them and agree voluntarily to their demands proved naive and futile – and the lesson was learnt by later revolutionaries – but this was none-theless a direct, armed challenge to the state. The Decembrists were influ-enced by the ideas of the French Revolution, developed in secret societies formed in the wake of the Napoleonic Wars by mainly army officers, many of whom had been stationed in France or the German lands during and after the campaigns. The Decembrists demanded a 'constitution', which was either monarchical (as proposed by the Northern Society in St Petersburg) or republican (as favoured by the leaders of the more radical Southern Society); whatever form it took, any constitution would inevitably have limited the powers of the tsar. More extreme members of the Southern Society supported the abolition of the monarchy altogether ('There is no compact with kings', declared one of them after the suppression of revolts in Spain in 1820). Both societies wanted serfdom to be abolished, although moderates thought it could be achieved without taking land from nobles (that is, creating a landless peasantry) while the leaders of the Southern Society proposed a redistribu-tion scheme that would have in effect nationalised land.

In the event, 579 demonstrators were interrogated, most of them in the Peter and Paul Fortress in St Petersburg, five of the leaders were sentenced to death and hanged, and over 90 nobles were exiled to Siberia, either as forced labour or as settlers. Ordinary soldiers who took part in the revolt were also banished to Siberia.

Poles were another distinctive group of exiles in Siberia. A traveller there in the 1790s noted: 'the Poles and Exiles form a very numerous body. The

Poles were sent thither after the first partition [in 1772]. . . . [People] spoke highly of their honesty in that country. The Poles are the most industrious and best farmers.'[10] Prisoners of war were regularly sent to Siberia but returned to their own country at the end of hostilities (Lithuanians in the seventeenth century, Swedes during the Great Northern War of 1700–21 and Turks in the eighteenth century). Catherine II, however, regarded the Poles as 'rebels' who had rejected the control of the kingdom of Poland-Lithuania by Russia and had involved Russia in a war with the Ottoman empire from 1768 to 1774. In the 1770s, there were 32 Poles in Tara and 21 in Tiumen in western Siberia.[11] One group of Poles was sent to distant Kamchatka, given provisions for three days and told to fend for themselves.[12] Catherine had even less sympathy with the Poles after 1791, when they introduced their own revolutionary-style constitution which she regarded as a threat to the political and social order. Russian troops were sent to crush the 'rebels' and some 13,000 were slaughtered when the Russians took Warsaw in 1794, including many civilians. Polish prisoners arrested in this uprising were dispatched to Siberia or to garrisons on the frontiers. Some Poles remained in Siberia, either in work battalions or as forced settlers in towns and villages.

One hundred thousand Polish troops accompanied the multinational Napoleonic armies that invaded Russia in 1812. Captives of many nationalities were taken by the Russians and held in towns throughout the empire, including some in Siberia (there were particular concentrations of prisoners in Orenburg and Perm in the Urals), but Poles and Frenchmen predominated. A party of some 2,000 prisoners passing through the western provinces of Russia included 1,053 Frenchmen and 622 Poles.[13] Polish memoirists claimed they were treated worse than other prisoners – something which is hard to prove, though it is certainly the case that the government and the noble elite saw the Poles as treacherous neighbours in 1812, unlike the French, with deference sometimes shown to French officers and men. Poles, unlike other nationalities, were conscripted to serve in the Caucasus and in garrisons on the Siberian lines, and repatriated only in 1814, whereas French prisoners of war were repatriated in 1813. Some 50,000 prisoners of war died while being held in the provinces in Russia, and many others are likely to have died en route.

Some prisoners of war settled in Russia, even in Siberia. Omsk was a main centre of Polish prisoners in 1812–13, and 689 (from a total of 2,459) asked if they could take Russian citizenship. In part this was a practical step because

Russian citizenship made it easier for them to take up posts in the regular army of government offices, but some of these Poles nevertheless asked to be repatriated to Poland in 1814. Some Poles stayed and married 'the daughters of Cossacks'.[14] In 1817, it was reported that 'three French prisoners of war have already settled in Biisk district in the Altai, become Orthodox and are occupied in farming'.[15] A report in 1824 on 'French' prisoners of war in Tomsk province listed three French names but also included a Josef Frankiewicz, a Pole.[16]

Polish revolts in 1830–1 and 1863 led to a further influx of Poles to Siberia. A so-called 'Congress Kingdom' of Poland, comprising a rump of what had been the former Kingdom of Poland-Lithuania, had been established at the Congress of Vienna in 1815. The Congress Kingdom was nominally independent but in practice was firmly tied to Russia through the person of the tsar, who was also king of Poland. In 1830, when Poles revolted to restore the independence of their country, the Russian government regarded them as rebels and treated any captives as such rather than as prisoners of war (in the same way that the British government regarded Americans in the War of Independence as rebels). One consequence of this was that Poles were not repatriated at the end of the campaigns as prisoners of war would have been, but were made to remain in Siberia. It seems that some 20,000 Poles were sent to Siberia after the 1830–1 revolt,[17] although some estimate that as many as 50,000 Poles were exiled there at this time. After 1863, a 'deluge' of a further 16,000–20,000 Poles were sent to Siberia, of whom about half were forcibly and permanently resettled on the land irrespective of their aptitude for farming (and had to be fed and housed by the local peasants), while others were dispatched to forced-labour battalions, prisons and military service in Russian regiments.[18]

Some Poles were lucky – a certain Anton Gankel was amnestied and allowed to return to Poland from Eniseisk province in 1864.[19] Others were less fortunate and remained or were exiled to more remote parts of Siberia. In 1866, 65 Poles were resettled from Tobolsk and Omsk to the fort of Semipalatinsk (now in Kazakhstan) to relieve overcrowding.[20] Some never left. Frederick Baedeker, who undertook missionary work in Russia, commented in the 1890s of Tiumen: 'This place is full of descendants of Polish exiles, and many who have themselves been exiled from Poland.'[21] Poles became engaged in commercial and industrial enterprises in Siberia; one owned a chocolate factory in Tomsk.[22] Lenin met Polish settlers from the

1863 revolt when he was exiled at the end of the nineteenth century. It has been estimated that there were some 150,000 Poles in Siberia on the eve of the First World War, but that figure included free settlers as well as exiles.

The Decembrists and Polish prisoners were male, although exiled revolutionaries in the late nineteenth century also included women. Wives and children did accompany men, particularly members of the more privileged classes, into exile. Radishchev was joined by his children and his sister-in-law (his wife was deceased), by whom he had a further three children in Siberia. Some of the wives of the Decembrists volunteered to join their husbands in Siberia, often with their children, both at the Nerchinsk mines and in the villages and towns where they were later settled. A party of 4,728 Polish prisoners in 1863 included 441 female (wives and daughters) camp followers.[23]

Political prisoners and Polish exiles were 'special'. More privileged exiles enjoyed some comforts, although these were often made available only by chance. Catherine II was shocked to hear that Radishchev was shackled and personally ordered that his shackles should be removed. But the experience of most exiles was brutal. Anyone who had been convicted of a serious crime – murder, theft, desertion – would have been flogged before being dispatched to Siberia. The death penalty was abolished in 1753, in the reign of Empress Elizabeth, for all but the most serious crimes (murder, rebellion and brigandage), but corporal punishment was not, and this in effect could be a death penalty. The most fearsome implement of punishment was the knout, a three-tailed rawhide scourge with metal tips. An experienced flogger could kill a man with a few blows; sentences of hundreds of blows of the knout were nonetheless common. Nobles and merchants were exempted from corporal punishment in 1785, but it could still be inflicted on criminals who were stripped of their social status on conviction. To put this in a wider perspective, flogging continued in the British navy until 1879 and all European armies used the gauntlet in the eighteenth century (indeed, Peter I copied this punishment from the 'modern' armies of the time). Nevertheless, Russian punishments were particularly brutal, even by the harsh standards of the day. Flogging was followed by branding on the cheeks or forehead and, at least in the eighteenth century, could be accompanied by mutilation such as slitting of the nostrils. The knout was banned in 1845, but its use continued in Siberia and in any event its replacement, another three-tailed whip without metal tips, could still kill or maim victims.

Conditions for exiles on the journey through Siberia were horrendous and, as mentioned above, distinctions were rarely made between different types of exiles. The journey could take up to two years on foot (barges were only used from the 1860s, and rail from the 1890s), and sometimes longer to reach remote destinations – and the official sentence commenced only on the day the exile arrived. The party went on foot in winter and summer, whatever the weather. Food and medical assistance were inadequate. Convicts (though not 'administrative exiles', that is, those who were exiled for poor behaviour but not convicted of crimes) were shackled, and the shackles cut into the ankles and often resulted in gangrenous wounds unless the convicts could afford to purchase leather leggings for protection. The Dostoevsky Museum in Omsk has a replica of the shackles used – they are extraordinarily heavy. Corporal punishment on the march was common (Dostoevsky was flogged twice), and anyone who tried to escape was brutally punished (fellow convicts, who risked the loss of small concessions if members of their party escaped, could be even more brutal than the guards).

Speransky ordered that special lodges should be built to house parties of exiles overnight. This created particular problems because the huts were poorly built and maintained, and usually far too small for their specified purpose. Parties slept on wooden benches, and those who were unable to secure a berth slept on the floor, enjoying little ventilation and lying close to an open pit used for human waste. The dangers for women and children travelling in these parties were particularly serious – rape and molestation were common. Separate parties of women and children were instituted only in 1883. There were few hospitals en route for the sick and many failed to survive the journey.

Exiles were deliberately scattered over the vast territory, in part out of fear that they might plot together if they were allowed to communicate. No more than three Decembrists were kept together in any one place. The administrative problems this caused were immense. To give just one example: a party of 13 Decembrists arrived in Irkutsk in 1826 – whereupon its members were sent to 13 different locations, including distant Gizhiga (discussed in Chapter 7).[24] Polish prisoners also had to be scattered so that they would not conspire together. In 1830–1, Polish exiles were divided between settlements in Eniseisk, eastern Siberia and Omsk. One party of 538 Polish prisoners in the 1860s had to be distributed between towns and villages: 106 to Tobolsk, 86 to Omsk, 57 to Tara, 6 to Kugan, 61 to Ialutorovka, etc.[25] The same policy was applied to revolutionaries exiled in the late nineteenth century.

Forced labour was concentrated mainly in the silver and lead mines of Nerchinsk, where conditions were particularly harsh. Food and accommodation were poor, corporal punishment was common and men could be permanently chained to wheelbarrows. The mines were spread out over a large area and included many separate prisons and settlements. When Mariia Volkonskaia arrived in Nerchinsk she tried to find the mine where her husband, a convicted Decembrist, was working:

> The town seemed to consist of only one street, running along the foot of the mountains. ... I noticed something that looked like the entry to a large cave; a soldier, armed with a halberd with a steel pike mounted on the end of a long shaft, was guarding the door. 'This is the door through which the Gentlemen Princes go' whispered a peasant woman who passed me.[26]

It is hard to know the number of convicts in Nerchinsk, especially as so many died and escaped. It could have been as few as 1,000 in 1774.[27] By the late nineteenth century, forced labour of this nature had become less useful, and even unwanted by the mines, so special prisons had to be set up to house the convicts instead.

Exiles could be sent anywhere. Forced resettlement was more common in eastern Siberia than in western Siberia, simply because fewer free settlers chose to move there. Some exiles were settled in separate villages – there were whole villages of Poles or vagrants or 'self-castrators' and Old Believer sectarians (described in the next chapter) – while others were intermingled with free settlers. Individual exiles could be sent to any village, seemingly on the whim of the administrators in centres such as Tobolsk or Irkutsk, while new settlements could be established anywhere with apparently little thought given to the practicalities of agriculture.

The administration of the exile system put a strain on local officials. Speransky had established that certain towns – Kazan, and then Tobolsk and Irkutsk – should act as centres for the reception and dispatch of parties of exiles. In practice, some exiles waited weeks or months before being dispatched further. Each exile incurred a financial and administrative cost for their home town or village. A report in 1819 from Tomsk noted that the town duma had to pay to dispatch one convict called Mikhail Mylnikov.[28] Rules were also set about the number of soldiers used for convoys. Instructions to the Selenginsk regiment in 1826 specified that one convoy of 55 exiles required 24 soldiers and another convoy of 123 men required 58 soldiers.[29]

Once the exiles had reached their final destination, the local authorities were obliged to check and report on their activities. There was a particular concern that Decembrists would spread pernicious ideas. In scenes reminiscent of Solzhenitsyn's later descriptions of the secret dispatching of prisoners to the Gulags, the first parties of convicted Decembrists left St Petersburg by night and were supposed to reach their destinations by a secret route. Care continued to be taken once they were in exile. Decembrists were not allowed to correspond at all; even letters to them from their wives were read.[30] Monthly reports had to be written on their activities. Some of these reports from poorly educated officials were almost comical. The head of police in Kurgan, a man called Tarasevich, reported that D. A. Shchepin-Rostovsky was 'constantly reading the newspapers and talking about political events, the change of ministers, the reasons for this and his conclusions of the matter', and that he had tried 'to show that ranks and power which did not come from the people cannot be respected'. The consequences of such reporting could be serious for the exiles. After reports alleged that the Decembrist S. M. Semonov was 'very dangerous' and 'harmful for the whole region', he was moved to a more remote settlement.[31]

The cost of the exile system, and even the sufferings of individuals, might have seemed justified had exiles become productive settlers and contributed to the industrial and agricultural development of Siberia. In reality, however, they were more of a burden than an asset. The forced labour in mines was not economically productive and the forced settlement of exiles did not fulfil economic expectations and often proved burdensome for the local peasantry.

By the 1780s, there were some 30,000 forced settlers in Siberia, some in separate villages and others lodged with peasants or post-drivers.[32] In the mid-nineteenth century, during the reign of Nicholas I, more use was made of 'resettlement' for 'undesirables', who included petty thieves, beggars, Roma, peasants who had evaded conscription and anyone whose lifestyle was generally considered to be disruptive, immoral or corrupting. In the period 1827–46, almost 50,000 such people were exiled for resettlement.[33] By 1835, there were 30,243 such settlers in villages in western Siberia and 14,769 in eastern Siberia.[34] The practice of nobles, serf and state-peasant communes, and urban institutions dispatching people whose behaviour they regarded as harmful or unruly continued after the emancipation of the serfs in 1861. Of the 4,417 'administrative exiles' who passed through Tiumen between 1882 and 1898, 1,584 had been banished by their peasant commune for 'misconduct' and 2,541 had been 'exiled after non-acceptance by the commune'.[35]

Beggars and vagabonds did not easily transform themselves into good farmers. A report in 1830 stated that 'there are not many good householders among the exile-settlers: their principal vice is drunkenness'.[36] Many 'administrative exiles' were physically incapacitated, elderly, or physically or mentally disabled, which was precisely why some had become beggars or outcasts. The horrendous journey to Siberia, or resettlement after a period of forced labour in the mines, only exacerbated their problems. Some ended up as agricultural labourers or wandered from village to village seeking work. Peasants resented giving land to these new arrivals who contributed little to the economy of the village. Dues and obligations were levied on peasant communities collectively, so the commune could not afford to carry non-productive members. Indeed, this is often why these people had been banished by their communes in European Russia in the first place.

Many of the forced settlers were wretchedly poor as a result. Death and suicide rates in Siberia were generally higher than in European Russia, and were probably highest among exiles, although precise figures are lacking. In 1855–6 in Tobolsk province, 59 exiles killed themselves. Far from bringing benefits, the forced settlers were all too often a burden. By 1836, the tax arrears of exiles in western Siberia (where the land was more settled) totalled 1,830,000 roubles.[37] Forced settlement proved to be an expensive failure.

How did the free settlers in Siberia regard exiles? Dostoevsky wrote from his own experiences of the kindness of ordinary people when convoys of prisoners passed through their village or town:

> There is in Siberia, and the supply is practically never exhausted, a number of people who seem to have assigned to themselves as their mission in life a brotherly care of the unfortunate and a disinterested and holy sympathy and compassion for them, as if they were their own children.[38]

He also described the generosity of local people at Christmas when people of all circumstances gave the prisoners gifts:

> They were brought in extraordinary quantities. . . . I think there did not remain one housewife in the upper and lower middle-class houses in the

town who had not sent food as a Christmas greeting to the 'unfortunates' shut up in prison. There were rich gifts – bread made of the finest flour, with butter and eggs, and sent in large quantities. There were also poor gifts – a cheap white loaf and two black buns of indifferent quality barely smeared with sour cream: a gift to a beggar from a beggar out of his last small store.[39]

Charity is a Christian duty, and it was hard for the settlers not to be moved by the sight of wretched parties of convicts or prisoners in mines. It was rather different, however, when these convicts threatened the livelihoods and security of local people. Fights took place between Poles and local youths in towns where prisoners were held during the Napoleonic Wars. Large numbers of convicts also fled from the mines or their place of settlement and became outlaws and brigands. It was extremely difficult in practice to keep track of all the exiles and it has been claimed that up to 40 per cent of them simply 'vanished'. Once they had fled from their place of exile it was almost impossible for exiles to settle anywhere legally in Siberia (although some ended up in the gold mines). As such, they were forced into a life of crime. Some of the convicts were, of course, hardened criminals, and easily reverted to their former way of life. Others were driven by desperation or had become brutalised by their own experiences in Siberia.

The result was that Siberia was popularly perceived in European Russia as violent and lawless, a situation exacerbated by the remoteness of many settlements and the lack of an effective police force. Gangs of robbers were able to torment not only villages but also towns. Journeys by road or water were hazardous as travellers could be attacked by escaped convicts. Siberia had a high incidence of violent crime – murder, theft and rape – and convicts were often the perpetrators. In the period 1838–47, convicts and exiles were alleged to have committed 1,190 violent crimes in Siberia, including 327 murders, 19 acts of brigandage and 86 robberies.[40] In 1873, for example, the widow of an Irkutsk merchant, her daughter, a workman and a janitor were murdered; a young cook was assaulted in the same incident but survived and was able to identify the assailants – three forced settlers and three exiled vagabonds.[41] Convicts were described as 'the terror of the Trans-Baikal province' by a traveller in the early twentieth century.[42]

Economically unproductive, disruptive, dangerous – how could convicts and exiles be regarded as anything other than a disaster for Siberia and as a moral stain on the region and on the Russian empire in general? Nevertheless, exiles also brought cultural benefits to Siberia. Some of these were only short-lived, but there were longer-lasting consequences too, both for the develop-ment of Siberia and for the perception of Siberia, both in European Russia and within Siberia itself.

At least some of the more sophisticated exiles tried to improve the lives of Siberians. Swedish prisoners in the Great Northern War (1700–21) set up a school in Tobolsk; 63 boys were studying there in 1717, including three sons of nobles and one Kalmyk.[43] The philanthropic activities of the Decembrists have often been idealised, and individual members did indeed attempt to bring enlightenment and modern thinking to remote corners of Siberia. Ivan Iakushkin opened a 'modern' school in 1842 in Chita. This used the British Lancasterian method of teaching, by which, essentially, older pupils trans-mitted knowledge to younger pupils, mainly by rote. The model school forbade corporal punishment (as it already was forbidden, at least in prin-ciple, in Russian national schools), adopted an ambitious syllabus including Greek, zoology and botany, and opened the school to the children of peasants and to Buriats.[44] Iakushkin supplied books, globes and other equipment at his own expense. He also set up a school for girls with a similarly ambitious syllabus. In the period 1842–56, his schools educated 594 boys and 531 girls.[45] Chita became popularly known as an 'academy' as Decembrists set up a substantial library as well as schools there. Schools were also set up around the Nerchinsk factories. The governor-general of Eastern Siberia noted in 1836 that children near the factory were being taught to read and write.[46]

Of course, these schools were a drop in the ocean, and many were short-lived. The Decembrists who settled in towns such as Irkutsk also brought some sophistication to urban culture and provided a focus for cultural events. The handsome houses of Princesses Volkonskaia and Trubetskaia became centres for social and musical gatherings in the 1840s and early 1850s. Princess Volkonskaia encouraged donations from local merchants, which led to the construction of the town's first theatre and concert hall. Their houses have been preserved as museums in Irkutsk.

This educational and cultural tradition was continued by later exiles. Poles exiled in the 1830s were employed as tutors and as teachers in local schools,[47] and Nerchinsk had a library of 3,000 Polish-language books in the 1830s.[48] The Petrashevsky exiles also became teachers and a school was founded at the Aleksandrovsk factory in 1853 which taught arithmetic, geography and history.[49] In the late nineteenth century, political exiles involved themselves in academic work. In the 1880s, Aleksandr Kropotkin, the brother of the anarchist Petr Kropotkin, lived with his wife in a small town on the river Enisei where he was 'devoting himself chiefly to reading and scientific study'. He had amassed a large geological collection, and later acquired a library of 200–300 volumes.[50] Nadezhda Krupskaia joined Lenin in Siberia in order to marry him and they spent their first few months together there happily: 'In the mornings, Vladimir Ilych and I set to work and translated the Webbs' [*History of Trade Unionism*]. After dinner we spent an hour or two jointly rewriting *The Development of Capitalism in Russia*.'[51]

Possibly the greatest benefit for Siberia derived from the presence of the Decembrists and later political exiles was perhaps psychological rather than practical. Many Decembrists found Siberia liberating or, at least, they claimed they did, and portrayed the region in a way that began to change perceptions of it in sophisticated circles in Moscow and St Petersburg. 'In Siberia I spent the best years of my life,' claimed Matvei Muravev-Apostol.[52] 'I so love eastern Siberia,' wrote Baron Shteingel in 1848.[53] The message was clear: Siberia was not just an icy prison and a dumping ground for undesirables.

In a sense, the Decembrists 'discovered' Siberia. The near-absence of serfdom there convinced at least some of them that this accounted for what they perceived as freer and happier Siberian peasants, and comparisons were made with the United States of America, another new world to which people had been banished for their beliefs. Aleksandr Muravev considered that Siberia was free because there was no serfdom: 'in the whole vastness of this region there were no more than 1,000 people in the unhappiness of belonging to their lord.'[54] Nikolai Basargin commented: 'The common people seemed to me to be much freer, cleverer, and even more highly educated than our Russian peasants, especially the serfs. The Siberians better understood the dignity of man, and valued their rights more highly.'[55]

Exiles also contributed to scientific and ethnographic data about Siberia, and made others aware of Siberia's unique fauna and flora and mineral resources. The Decembrists gathered scientific, statistical and ethnographic material, some of which was published after they were amnestied. Dmitrii Zavalishin, for example, not only helped to set up schools, but also made a collection of geological and natural-history materials from the Baikal and Amur area.

Above all, Decembrists and later political exiles became convinced that Siberia had great untapped wealth. The Decembrist Zavalishin, in fact, had visited the Russian colony at Fort Ross on the coast of California in 1823–4, shortly before the revolt, but his experience strengthened his conviction of the economic potential of expanding even further east. General Muravev, who was convinced of the potential wealth of the Amur basin, was acquainted with Volkonskys who were living as exiles in Irkutsk and had discussions with their circle. The Petrashevsky exiles came to the same view of the potential richness of the Amur. Such activities and opinions influenced perceptions of the potential benefits of expanding further eastwards and into the Amur region.

Finally, Siberia awakened in exiles the belief that liberty could be achieved, and would be achieved through their sufferings. The Decembrist poet Aleksandr Odoevsky wrote:

> Beating our shackles into swords,
> Liberty's torch we will relight,
> And she will overwhelm the Tsars,
> While nations waken in the night.[56]

Dostoevsky's Siberian exile was fundamental to the development of the spiritual philosophy which underpins his writings. Later radical exiles, including Lenin, formulated and refined their views in exile in Siberia. The presence of radical exiles there also had an effect, albeit one that is impossible to quantify, on the psyche of Siberians. Exiles brought with them new ideas about culture, politics and society as well as crime and economic burdens. Intellectual Siberians took pride in their presence among them, perhaps more in retrospect than at the time, but their legacy was important to Siberians' own self-identity. In the early 1990s, while the Soviet Union was undergoing economic collapse, I asked an archivist in Irkutsk about her sense of identity as a 'Siberian'. Initially she struggled to define what a Siberian was – and whether she personally was European, Asian or something in-between – and then she burst out: 'We are the children of the Decembrists. That is who we are.'

CHAPTER TEN

Religion and Popular Beliefs

THE MAJORITY of settlers in Siberia identified themselves as Orthodox Christians. The Orthodox Church, however, never had a monopoly of religious or spiritual life in Siberia. From the earliest days, Siberia was a place of exile or a place of refuge for Orthodox Christians who did not accept the changes within the official Church – the Old Believers – and for members of dissident sects. Siberia was also home to Muslims, Buddhists and people with animistic beliefs. The clergy of the Orthodox Church had to try to convert non-Christians but also had to live alongside other faiths. The relationship between the official state religion and pagan and magical practices was complex in Russia, as it was, and still is, in other parts of the world. It was made more so in Siberia by the scarcity of clergy, the remoteness of many settlements and the existence of strong traditional beliefs among the indigenous population.

Orthodox clergy in Russia were divided into 'black' monastic clergy, from whom bishops were appointed, and married 'white' parish clergy. Monks could come from any social group, including the nobility. Some were well educated and became members of the upper hierarchy of the Church, but others lost their vocation or simply behaved badly. For example, in 1752, a monk called Ilarion in a monastery in Tiumen province was fined for smoking tobacco and getting drunk.[1]

In Russia, the parish clergy was almost a closed social estate. Clergy had to marry before they were ordained and were desperate to find posts in the Church for their sons so that they would not be conscripted by the army. A large parish might have, beside the priest, a deacon and one or two more sacristans, all of whom had clerical status. Nearly all marriages took place between children of these clergy, and as such the parish priesthood became almost a hereditary caste. In Siberia, however, the size of the population meant that, in the eighteenth century, Orthodox priests had to be recruited from other social groups, including peasants and artisans. In 1739, the Church permitted the recruitment of members of clergy in Irkutsk, Okhotsk and Kamchatka from non-clerical backgrounds as there was an 'extreme need'.[2]

Poor behaviour by priests existed throughout the Russian empire, but could take a more extreme form in Siberia. The remoteness of many settlements meant that such behaviour of priests could not be easily rectified by the bishop. Two priests in Ialutorovka who were found guilty of theft had apparently stolen the money in order 'to buy spirits'.[3] Peasants in a Siberian village complained in 1774 that their priest Ivan Zagibalov was 'found daily physically incapable, drunk and in such vileness, that he cannot walk, but crawls on the ground with his hair undone like some extraordinary beast'.[4]

The unattractiveness of posts in Siberia meant that it was often difficult to find anyone to take them. In 1815, the priest Andrei Tarkov asked if he could leave his post in a small Siberian settlement of artisans and Cossacks 'because his small salary and provisions were insufficient even to feed his family'.[5] The state had to offer additional salaries and provisions in an attempt to attract priests to the remotest parts of Siberia, including Kamchatka, Okhotsk and Gizhiga. Sons of clergy who had some ability could escape by taking administrative posts or becoming teachers in the state schools. It was rarely possible for members of other social groups to become priests but getting out was always possible for able priests or their sons – Mikhail Speransky, whose role in Siberia was discussed in Chapter 8, was the son of a priest. Badly educated, poorly and irregularly paid, based in often large and very dispersed parishes, and living much like a peasant, the village priest was often treated with little respect by his congregation.

Western travellers to Russia, and to Siberia, commented on the depth of Christian belief there, especially among the common people. This was marked by their regular attendance at church, and by the way they maintained an icon corner in their peasant huts, celebrated saints' days and other festivals, and observed many fasts (up to 30 a year), and, above all, by the way they crossed themselves publicly. 'After rising from the table the Russians first cross themselves and bow to their images and then to each other,' commented John Ledyard from Siberia in the 1780s.[6] This did not mean that it was easy for Orthodox priests, or the Church, to assert their authority over their congregations. Priests in Siberia faced more rivals to the official Church than did their counterparts in European Russia – from Old Believers, extreme Christian sects and non-Christians alike.

The Russian Orthodox Church had split over the changes in Church texts and liturgical practices introduced in the mid-seventeenth century (see Chapter 4). Those who did not accept those changes became known as Old Believers. They believed that the purity of Russian Orthodoxy could only be maintained through the preservation of existing rituals, forms of words and other traditions. To Old Believers this was not only, or even, a scholarly debate. To them, the reforms represented a heretical challenge to sacred symbols and a 'Western', 'Latin' and even devilish attack on the true, uncor- rupted, Eastern Church. The proposed change of using three instead of two fingers to cross oneself aroused particular opposition as it was the most frequently repeated gesture during religious services. The conflict took on an apocalyptic flavour, not least as the reform proposals were being considered in 1666, and the Book of Revelation had stated that the number 666 was the key to the identity of the 'Great Beast', commonly assumed to be the Antichrist.

In the second half of the seventeenth century, whole communities of Old Believers burnt themselves to death rather than accept the changes, in part influenced by the belief that the world was about to end and that salvation would be attained through suicide. In the Paleostrov monastery in north European Russia, over 2,000 Old Believers killed themselves as Russian troops approached. The practice died down in the eighteenth century in European Russia, but continued in Siberia. Three hundred Old Believers died by self-immolation in the Altai region in 1739 to 'save their souls'.[7] In the same year, 24 Old Believers burnt themselves to death in Tiumen;[8] a mass self-immolation took place again in the same town in 1750. In 1756, 200 Old Believers burnt themselves to death in Tomsk region: 'In the Church is heresy; they serve [communion] with five wafers, they stamp the wafers with a Latin cross, they shave, they smoke tobacco, and the priests do not hold that to be a sin. What are you doing standing and listening to the servants of Antichrist?'[9]

Old Believers created a permanent problem for the state and the official Church, serving as a rallying point for opposition generally, as they did in the mid-1770s in the Ural region during the last great Cossack/peasant uprising by the Don Cossack Emelian Pugachev. The Church thus had to contend

with a large number of Orthodox Christians who did not accept their liturgical practices, and were, to all intents and purposes, beyond their influence
and control. Isolated parish priests in Siberian villages could not prevent Old
Believers from building their own chapels. They were dependent on their
parishioners for financial support and in practice often had to cooperate with
local Old Believers and perform baptisms and marriages for them. One priest,
a certain Zemlianitsyn, was accused of taking bribes from Old Believers in
order not to hear their confession.[10] Indeed, some parish priests may have
sympathised with some of the beliefs of Old Believers.

No one knows how many Old Believers there were in the Russian empire
as a whole, as records are unreliable, but it could have been as high as 10 per
cent of the Orthodox population in the nineteenth century. We do know that,
from the mid-seventeenth century onwards, Old Believers fled to form
communities in Siberia and others were exiled there. Speransky commented
in 1819 that it was difficult to open a Bible Society in Tomsk as the 'merchants
and almost all of the inhabitants in reality are ingrained schismatics'.[11] It was
estimated in the 1820s that half the merchants in Tiumen were Old Believers.

Old Believer communities moved to remoter regions to escape persecution from what they regarded as an oppressive and ungodly state. A number
of large Old Believer communities formed around factories in the Altai
region. Some factories had a workforce made up entirely of Old Believers:
some had been sentenced to carry out forced labour; others had settled
voluntarily. In 1856, 45 Old Believers were reported as living in one village
and 70 in another village in the Altai region, a number which included
peasant converts.[12] Some 18,000 Old Believers lived in the Baikal region
in 1851, most of whom were concentrated in a few villages. By the mid-
nineteenth century, there were established Old Believer communities in the
Iakutsk region in the north, comprising exiles and settlers. In 1853, there
were over 100 Old Believer families – 323 men and 266 females – listed in
one village.[13]

More Old Believers moved to Siberia in the late nineteenth and early
twentieth centuries as part of the great peasant migration described in Chapter
12. It has been claimed that there were some 1 million Old Believers in Siberia
by 1900. 'All of Siberia is in the hands of [Old Believers] and the Baptists,'
stated one traveller.[14] In Khabarovsk, I was shown a restored Old Believer
church in which there were sixteenth-century icons – taken from European
Russia in the seventeenth century to Bessarabia, and from there to Siberia in
the early twentieth century and kept hidden during the Soviet period.

Old Believers were accused of converting Orthodox Christians to Old Belief and their movements were closely monitored.[15] In 1795, for example, a retired soldier and his wife and four children in Selenginsk in the Baikal region reportedly 'became Old Believers'.[16] In Tomsk in the mid-nineteenth century, Old Believers were accused of a number of 'crimes', including converting local people to Old Belief, failing to attend church and engaging in 'insulting behaviour' during religious services.[17] On the other hand, Old Believers had a reputation for clean living, particularly as they rejected tobacco and alcohol, and for hard work, be it in the countryside or in factories. Catherine II pragmatically saw them as useful settlers in remote parts of Siberia. In 1830, the exiled Decembrist Baron Andrei Rozen came across some Old Believer women in the Baikal region and commented on 'their beauty' and that they 'appeared content, orderly, hard-working'.[18] In 1841, a visiting Englishman commented on Old Believers in Irkutsk: 'Their villages are remarkably well built, and their houses ... neat and clean. Their dress, food, and especially their personal appearance, is greatly superior to that of any other of the neighbouring people.'[19]

Siberia also became the home for members of other dissident and more extreme Christian sects – either as exiles or as voluntary settlers. These included 'milk-drinkers', or *molokany*, so-called because they continued to drink milk during Lent, 'spirit-wrestlers', or *dukhobory*, who rejected the Bible and icons and tried to re-create a simpler faith based on the catechism, and the 'self-castrators', or *skoptsy*, so-called as they castrated men (cutting off the testicles and, in more extreme cases, the penis) and amputated women's breasts in an attempt to return to a state of purity before Adam and Eve. The numbers of members of sects were carefully recorded and their movements and activities monitored, just as those were of convicts and political exiles (discussed in the last chapter).

Members of these other dissident sects considered that they were following a simpler, more spiritual life, but they also posed a potential challenge to the Church and the state. Like Old Believers, they could lure parishioners away from the official Church. In 1858, Nataliia Petrova, a 'milk-drinker' and widow, was taken to court in Tomsk for 'her crimes', and it was noted that peasants were being converted by milk-drinkers.[20] They were also regarded as a potential threat to state security and to society in general. In 1836, Nicholas I decreed that both spirit-wrestlers and self-castrators had to be carefully supervised so that their 'heresy' did not spread among Orthodox peasants or soldiers, and instructed that both groups had to be resettled in the remotest part of Siberia to protect others.

Spirit-wrestlers were regarded as seditious because they refused to under-take military service (at least up to 1895). In 1802, a priest reported that in the village of Ustiug in Tobolsk province, children had not been christened, did not know basic tenets of faith, did not recognise the icons of saints and did not cross themselves, all of which he blamed on the influence of local spirit-wrestlers.[21] Material relating to the latter in western Siberia in the years 1817–20 shows the harshness with which members of the sect were treated but also the sheer pointlessness of state policy. Spirit-wrestlers, often simple peasants and soldiers, were knouted or whipped for their heretical beliefs and exiled to settlements or forced labour in mines or distilleries. Egor Popov, a soldier, was found guilty of 'heresy' in 1812 at the age of 27; he was knouted, his nostrils were slit, he was branded and sent to the Nerchinsk mines for forced labour. In 1819, he was pardoned and allowed to return home – but by this time he had died in the mines.

In Siberia, spirit-wrestlers were then closely supervised and punished or exiled to even more remote spots if they converted others, but they could not be eliminated as a group or as proselytisers. Peasants among whom spirit-wrestlers were settled were influenced by their beliefs; so too were convicts in the mines. One Martyn Kokodaev had been knouted for murdering his owner in 1801 and had been sentenced to forced labour in a Nerchinsk mine; in 1809, he was accused of becoming a spirit-wrestler and given a further 60 blows of the knout.[22] The spirit-wrestlers were eventually encouraged to leave Russia en masse at the end of the nineteenth century and settled in Canada (with financial help from Tolstoy, among others).

Self-castrators were seen as harmful to society. Perhaps unsurprisingly, the state regarded their activities as not only harmful but also disgusting; their religious 'services' where these castrations took place included wild dances which were said to induce a sense of ecstasy. One of the founders of the self-castrator sect, a serf called Selivanov, had been exiled to Siberia in the reign of Catherine II. There he posed as both the son of God and as Tsar Peter III (Catherine's deposed husband). He was rearrested and confined as a madman in a monastery where he died in his hundredth year. Other original members of the sect, who included nobles and army officers as well as peasants, were knouted, had their nostrils slit and were sent to work in the mines in Nerchinsk. Self-castrators posed a particular problem for the state as it was difficult to inflict further physical punishment on people who had already mutilated themselves, but they were deprived of civil rights and obliged to stay in Siberia after their sentences had ended. Self-castrators were not allowed to participate in petty trade – which might have allowed them to spread their ideas to other settlers – until the 1870s. They were only allowed to leave Siberia in 1905.

Self-castrators in Siberia worked on the land like other peasants, and lived in villages which were like other villages. In 1857, there were 643 self-castrators living in eastern Siberia, most of them in Eniseisk province.[23] In the nineteenth century they were exiled to Iakutsk; their number had risen to over 1,000 by the 1880s. Initially most self-castrators were poor, not least because they had been settled in remote areas on often infertile land, although some individuals flourished. In 1854, a local described the living conditions of self-castrator Aleksei Sorokin: 'his household is full of livestock. . . . Sorokin lives in a crowded home; he gave us beef, game and cream.'[24]

By the end of the nineteenth century, many self-castrators had become prosperous. A report in 1902 to the Imperial Geographical Society noted:

> The wealth of the Markha Skoptsy [village] is particularly striking in comparison with the half-starved Iakuts and their dispersed yurts smeared with clay, which seem to emerge from the earth. . . . [They have] attractive new houses, with big windows, wood and iron decorations on the roofs, carved figurines, glass verandas, and garden plots under the windows.[25]

Contemporaries also, however, noted the sometimes odd physical appearance of boys, who were hairless and often described as having bloated faces, as well as the sterile and lifeless character of self-castrator settlements, where it was claimed there were 'no songs, no children's chatter'. Many self-castrators left the villages in 1905 when the opportunity arose.

Missionary activity towards non-Christians – Muslims, Buddhists, pagans – had been pursued by the Orthodox Church from the very beginning of the Russian presence in Siberia. The Russian government had assumed that it would be easy to convert Muslims, but in reality it was far easier to persuade (or force) pagans to convert to Christianity than Muslims, as the latter had a much more developed theology and organisation.[26]

Tsar Peter I's approach was, like so many of his other domestic policies, a heady mixture of incentives, persuasion, threats and punishments. Male converts were given 10 roubles each, 5 roubles for their wives and 25 copecks for each child, and were allowed to retain their lands. They were also given exemption from the poll tax and military service for a number of years. Many pagans did convert at this time to Orthodox Christianity but there was also some resistance. Pagans fought over conversions: in 1722, 200 Samoeds fought and killed converted Ostiaks (Khanty). Four years later, it was reported from Obdorsk in Tobolsk province that Ostiaks and Samoeds 'with extraordinary stubbornness held firm as heathens and not one of them became Christian'.[27] Peter I's reaction to the reluctance of pagans to convert was typical of the brutal way he dealt with other groups in Russian society which refused to adopt the 'Western' or 'modern' ways which he believed were necessary and beneficial. He instructed the new metropolitan members of Siberia to:

> find their seductive false god-idols and burn them with fire and axe them, and destroy their heathen temples, and build chapels instead of those temples, and put up holy icons, and baptise those Ostiaks . . . and if some Ostiaks show themselves contrary to our great sovereign's decree, they will be punished with death.[28]

This combination of threats and gifts led to the conversion of some 40,000 indigenous people in the next two decades.

Missionary activity continued over the next two centuries. The Russian tsars were keen to incorporate the elite non-Christian princes as loyal servants of the state. When, in 1742, a pagan prince converted, the christening ceremony – at which his mother, his brother and both his wives were present – was attended by the governor of Tobolsk himself.[29] Missionary activity became more active from the 1820s onwards, after Alexander I underwent a spiritual experience during the final campaigns of the Napoleonic Wars. In 1828, the synod of the Orthodox Church set up a special Tobolsk and Kazan mission. Two years later, it was claimed that almost 5,000 conversions had taken place in the Baikal region.[30] Alexander also encouraged missionary activity by the Protestant, British and Foreign Bible Society. In the 1830s, British missionary schools were set up in the Altai region, where there were Muslims, pagans and Buddhists. Buddhists had originally been tolerated, and had even been encouraged to convert pagans,[31] but from the 1840s there were more attempts to convert Buddhist Buriats to Christianity.

There is no doubt there were individual priests who were committed to making conversions in Siberia and were prepared to suffer considerable hardships to reach out to the unconverted. One priest in the 1850s described the conditions of 'travelling in the winter without roads through the tundra and marshes ... in danger of dying from the northern winds ... and ill from plague'.[32] A decade later, another intrepid missionary reported:

> It can be said that for our sins we suffered on the Okhotsk Road ten tortures similar to those of Egypt: rapids, quagmires where land turned to water; nocturnal darkness amidst thick woods; branches threatening us with blindness; hunger, cold; mosquitoes; gadflies – truly *biting* flies; dangerous river crossings and sores on horses.[33]

How genuine were these conversions? Missionaries in Siberia admitted it was difficult to convert and teach indigenous peoples. One commented that it was difficult to teach the local people Christian tenets as they 'saw neither churches, nor clergy, nor images of the Christian worship' and he had 'not the means to educate ... boys and had not the time to talk with the society and to learn their language or their customs'.[34]

Missionaries were constantly instructed not to force non-Christians to convert. There were, however, material incentives for converts, a fact that raises doubts about the genuineness of their conversions. Converts were exempted from paying tribute for three years and then transferred from paying tribute to the poll tax (that is, the tax paid by Russian state peasants whose status they now adopted). They were also given cash and goods – clothing, food and religious items such as crosses. Converts to Orthodoxy could enter Russian military service on an equal footing with Russians and could own land on the same basis as them. In the 1680s, converted Iakuts with Russian names claimed land and one, Mazaryka Lenkoev, claimed not only land, but also his 'hut, out-building, barn, and yurt and horse'.[35]

Conversions were indeed often only nominal. Many indigenous people either ignored Christianity in practice or continued to worship their gods as well. Priests complained that pagan converts 'did not have even the slightest understanding of the faith'.[36] Sometimes this was brutally punished. In 1745, two newly converted Ostiaks (Khanty) were whipped and sent to do forced labour in a monastery for idolatry.[37] In 1747, Father Pykhov reported:

I beat the new Christian, Ostiak Fedor Senkin, with a whip, because he married his daughter off at the said time and celebrated the wedding feast during the first week of Lent. I also beat ... his son-in-law with a whip, because he buried his deceased son himself, outside the church and without the knowledge of the priest. . . . Semen Kornilov Kortyshin was beaten with a whip because he never went to the holy church. . . . I also beat the widow Marfa and her son Kozma with a whip ... because ... they kept in their tent a small stone idol, to whom they brought sacrifices ... and I broke the said idol with an axe in front of an Ostiak gathering and threw the pieces in all directions.[38]

The shortage of women in Siberia was an incentive to convert native women so that they could marry Orthodox settlers, but in practice converted men also married settlers. A traveller commented on his journey through Siberia in the 1780s: 'I have passed some of the Calmucs [Kalmyks], who are married with the Russian.'[39] Converted non-Christians also married other non-Christians. In 1787, a strange case reached the Krasnoiarsk clerical consistory. This involved one Vera Mikhailovna, from the village of Minzenov. She was of indigenous background but had been baptised (hence the Russian name), but was married to a pagan native man. She petitioned the clerical board in Tobolsk, claiming that she had been forced to marry him and requested that the marriage be annulled so that she could return home to her father. It is interesting that the grounds for the request were twofold: first, that she was a baptised Christian and her husband had not been baptised; second, that he beat her and she 'feared for her life'.[40] It is not clear when her conversion had taken place and whether it had been undertaken to escape an abusive marriage.[41]

The prevalence of 'conversion' of small children and babies demonstrates that this was a decision taken by the head of a household on behalf of his dependants. In one village in the Krasnoiarsk region, 43 people were converted in 1800. The age range of the 'converts' shows that these were whole families – 22 were under the age of five and one was just a week old. Whole family units converted together in this village. For example, the family of Ivan Pakarakov (his Russian name) converted, including 4 children, aged 19 (Akilina), 13 (Kirill), 7 (Timofei), 3 (Fedor) and his 1-week-old grandson, Ioann. The 'converts' in the family of Nikolai Chavydaev included children aged seven, three and one. The 'converts' in the Sykin extended family

1. Vasilii Surikov's painting of Ermak's conquest demonstrates the superiority of the Cossacks as their firepower overcomes the Khan, Kuchum, and the tribesmen fighting alongside him. The battle took place near Isker in 1582.

2. A Siberian fur trader at a fair in Leipzig, c.1800. Furs were an immensely valuable commodity but much of western Siberia had been 'hunted out' by this date.

3. Demidov factory in Barnaul region, 1747. The Demidovs were a prominent industrial family who owned mines in southern Siberia (the Altai region) and the Ural mountains. It is significant that the mine is fortified; the mine owners had to control their own workers and defend the factory complex from attacks from indigenous tribesmen.

4. Engraving of a shaman from Witsen's *Noord en Oost Tartarye*, 1785. There were some 200,000 indigenous people in Siberia at the end of the seventeenth century, when the Cossacks crossed into Siberia. Many had shamanistic beliefs. This is the first depiction of a shaman by a foreigner in the late seventeenth century, but shamans, with their distinctive dress and their wild dances, continued to be a source of fascination for foreign travellers.

5. Cossacks collected tribute from indigenous people from the moment they entered Siberia. The collection was initially in furs, as shown here in Eniseisk, and was immensely valuable. In time this was replaced by a cash tribute. The collection of tribute was often marked by violence; both sides in this picture have weapons.

6. Tobolsk, founded in 1587, became one the most prominent towns in western Siberia in the eighteenth century (along with Tomsk). All towns were founded on key points of the rivers, and were fortified. The Tobolsk Kremlin is the only stone kremlin in Siberia and has a commanding position over the confluence of the rivers Tobol and Irtysh.

7. Irkutsk developed from the second half of the seventeenth century as the most prominent town in eastern Siberia. It became the administrative centre of the newly-created province of Eastern Siberia after Speransky's reforms in the 1820s and the residence of the Governor-General of Eastern Siberia. The house of the Governor General was also culturally important to the town, because there were so few nobles in Siberia, and balls and other social events took place there.

8. This painting depicts the fate of some 20,000 Poles who were exiled to Siberia after the 1863 rebellion. The artist, Aleksander Sochaczewski, was himself exiled to Siberia and remained there until 1883: he has painted himself to the right of the obelisk marking the divide between Europe and Asia. Poles formed a distinctive group of exiles in Siberia, and were exiled there as prisoners of war, rebels or political dissidents throughout the Tsarist period.

9. Tomsk was the first university in Siberia; it was founded in 1878 and opened its first faculty in 1888. It had been a source of complaint by intellectuals and members of the regionalist movement that Siberia had no higher education institutions. Today Tomsk State University has over 20,000 students. Tomsk was the cultural and administrative centre of western Siberia in the nineteenth century but its economic importance was diminished when it was bypassed by the Trans-Siberian Railway.

10. Jews came to Siberia in the nineteenth century and most of them settled in towns. This Jewish store is in the town of Nerchinsk, in eastern Siberia, not far from the Chinese border. Nerchinsk developed as trading post between Russia and China in the eighteenth century; it then became a place for exiles sentenced to forced labour in its gold mines.

11. This photograph, from a selection of photographs of indigenous peoples, shows a prosperous Buriat family in eastern Siberia. Buriats are of Mongolian origin and the majority converted to Buddhism in the seventeenth and eighteenth centuries.

12. This is from an album of watercolours of Siberia, now held in the Russian State Library in Moscow. The painting shows Khanty people (now called Khanty-Mansi people, but before the twentieth century known as Ostiaks) who mainly lived in the Volga and Kama river valleys in western Siberia, with a Russian official; the portrait of the Tsar is on the wall and an animal skin is on the table, presumably being offered as tribute.

13. A station buffet on the Trans-Siberian railway, from *The Graphic* of 1905. The construction of the railway started in 1893 and was a colossal undertaking – the longest railway in the world.

14. Vladivostok was founded in 1860, after Russia acquired the territory north and east of the river Amur from China at the Treaty of Beijing. It was the main port for the Russian and then Soviet Pacific fleet, and was also the end of the line for the Trans-Siberian railway. The railway station was re-built in 1912 in the style of the station from which the train departed in Moscow, almost 6,000 miles away, with an extravagant mural on the ceiling.

15. By the early twentieth century, with the arrival of the Trans-Siberian railway, Omsk had become a major economic centre in western Siberia, rivalling Tomsk. The main street shows the development of trade and commerce and the growing prosperity of the city. It was to become the capital of the Whites in the Civil War.

16. A convoy of exiles in Siberia, postcard, c.1905.

17. St Petersburg and Moscow were the centres of the Revolutions in 1905 and 1917 but demonstrations took place in all major Siberian cities. Vladivostok had a particularly high concentration of radicalised soldiers and sailors.

18. The Allies intervened in Russia after the new Soviet state signed a peace treaty with Germany at Brest-Litovsk. By the end of 1918 there were some 70,000 Japanese soldiers in the Far East, a larger contingent than any of the other allied forces.

19. Some 40,000 Czech prisoners from the Austro-Hungarian army played a significant part in the resistance to the Bolsheviks in Siberia during the Civil War. This photograph depicts the Czech Legion about to embark across Siberia in the hope of getting home by sea.

20. Identical five-storey buildings were constructed in the 1950s in a massive post-war housing pro-gramme. Urbanisation in Siberia took place on an enormous scale as mineral resources were exploited and migrants and peasants flooded into existing and new cities.

21. A street sign in Krasnoiarsk in western Russia displays history through its changes. It reads: 'Main Street' (eighteenth century), 'Resurrection Street' (nineteenth century), 'Soviet Street' (from 1924), 'Stalin Avenue', and 'Peace Avenue' (from 1961).

22. The city of Norilsk, in the far north of central Siberia, grew rapidly from a settlement in the 1920s to a town of over 170,000 people by the 1980s. The Norilsk mining complex exploits the largest deposit of nickel in the world. It is the world's northernmost city and also one of the most polluted places on earth.

23. Kolchak was the leader of the Whites in Siberia and his headquarters were in Omsk. There is controversy today about whether a statue should be erected to Kolchak in Omsk – but no difficulty about opening an Irish pub in his name!

24. Iakutsk is the capital city of Iakutia (now called the Sakha Republic), in north-eastern Siberia, about 300 miles south of the Arctic circle. The city was founded in 1632 on the Lena river and now comprises over 200,000 people.

25. Fishermen and former Russian Navy sailors fish in the ice beside abandoned Russian military submarines in Vladivostok.

26. Iakut and Russian schoolchildren.

included two one-year-old girls, Marfa and Nadezhda, and the Dushnin household included four children under the age of five.[42]

Some natives were disappointed with what conversion could offer them and became suspicious of the missionaries. Adopting Christianity with its miracle-working saints often did not miraculously improve their lives. In 1754, converts in the village of Uvatsk 'cast down and crushed the holy images ... since this year at winter and spring time there had appeared few wild animals at hunting time and few fish'.[43] A century later, little had changed. An account by a missionary in the Amur region in the 1850s noted the conversion of one native aged 100. He visited some women in a yurt and tried to convince them of the importance of converting before they died. One woman, the oldest and a widow, said: 'all mine have died: father, mother, husband, children; I love them greatly and after my death I want to see them again and I do not want to be christened'. Others objected to being christened as they thought it meant they had to take their clothes off.[44]

Christianity and paganism could merge, sometimes in strange ways, among the pagan peoples who had supposedly converted. The people of the region of Indigirka, north of Iakutsk, were converted early to Christianity. But research in the 1990s found that their lives were still governed by superstitions and rituals that predated their conversion to Christianity. Shamans and wizards were still relied upon for healing and for telling fortunes, and were present not only at deathbeds but also at christenings. Moreover, pagan and Christian elements had merged in local sayings and superstitions. The word 'heretic' had come to mean the godless living dead who were thought to wander about at night. This had led to a bizarre contemporary expression: 'What are you wandering about at night for, like a heretic?' The Christian God and the Devil had merged with 'the spirit' and malicious sprites. A local man, aged 75, stated in 1973 that people 'every morning needed to wipe the dust off the table, as during the night Satan-Antichrist left his imprint, which could lead the Orthodox astray against Christ or lead them to all sorts of sin'.[45]

Present-day Ostiak (Khanty) cemeteries display a mixture of Christian and pagan symbols – Orthodox crosses side by side with carved birds and animals and artefacts, such as sledges, stacks of firewood and discarded vodka bottles.[46] Shaman drums might be decorated with images of St Nicholas, and shamans might carry crosses, bells and images of saints as well as their pagan symbols. Animal sacrifices took place close to, and even inside, churches.[47]

Russian Orthodox priests had to live with the pagan practices of their congregations. This has sometimes been seen as something exceptional to Russia – the parallel existence of pagan, magical and Christian practices whereby the Church absorbed some ancient elements into its rituals. The Russian word *dvoeverie* means 'double faith' and suggests that paganism survived under a veneer of Christianity and, indeed, that this was the way in which the Church was able to ensure the allegiance of its congregations. This does not mean, however, that there was a conflict between Christianity and paganism, which could exist together at least in harmless and popular activities and rituals. For that matter, many of the religious festivals in the Catholic and Protestant Churches also retain elements of a pre-Christian world and links with major events in the agricultural year and the solstices. But in Russia, and in particular in Siberia, there was less control by the official Church over the development of local practices within the Church and even less control over pagan and magical practices outside it.

Pagan and Christian festivals coincided at key points in the agricultural and Christian calendar, in Siberia as elsewhere in Russia. Holy ('Clean') Thursday was a preparation for Easter that also involved a ritual purification of the farms by circling them with an icon to prevent penetration by evil spirits. Magic coincided with religious beliefs at this time. 'Holy Thursday pitch' was put out on tables in memory of the torches in the garden of Gethsemane, but guns and fishing tackle were also put under the table for luck so that their owners would be successful.[48] In Siberia, Easter heralded the end, or the beginning of the end, of the winter, and was celebrated with special songs and games, in towns as well as in the countryside. Easter involved Church services and processions but also older rituals. The decoration and exchange of painted eggs at Easter are symbolic of spring and (re) birth. Customs and songs came from European Russia but villages in Siberia developed their own variations, which sometimes had only tenuous links with Christianity.[49] Old Believer villages in Siberia in particular developed their own rituals at Easter and at other major religious festivals.[50] In some Siberian villages it was believed that wizards became visible on Easter Sunday; in one report it was suggested that if hunters and card-players shouted out 'I have a bullet!' or 'I have an ace!' when the priest sang 'Christ is risen' during the Easter service they would be lucky the whole year.[51]

The festival of Semik or Rusalnaia (Trinity Week) was celebrated around the time of Pentecost throughout Russia and combined religious services

with pagan festivals; there were special songs in which the pagan goddess
Lada was invoked. Churches, houses and cattle were decorated with branches
and flowers. In Siberia and north Russia, this marked the first time the cattle
went into the fields after the winter. A special branch was decorated with
ribbons and flowers and floated in the river at the end of the festival, on
Trinity Sunday. A particular feature of this festival everywhere was a straw
doll, which was made and then destroyed, and which was supposed to represent a female sprite. Sviatki, a pagan festival to celebrate the winter solstice,
coincided with the 12 days of Christmas, but the songs included invocations
to Koliada, a personification of the season, and contained almost no Christian
motifs. Siberian villages, like villages in European Russia, collected special
local herbs on saints' days. Peasants in the Enisei region collected 'twelve
different herbs' in midsummer on St John's Eve (sometimes known in Siberia
as the day of John the Herbal or John the Magic). These were to be placed on
a pillow so that one's dreams that night would be prophetic.[52] Irkutsk had a
special harvest festival: 'at the end of August and in September [that is, after
the harvest] songs and knocking rang out throughout the town'.[53]

Magical and pagan rituals might also be performed at Church services,
and particularly at weddings to bring luck throughout Russia. It was customary
for the best man to perform various rituals, such as clearing the path from the
bride's house, shooting in the air and cracking a whip to ward off evil spirits.
Windows were shut in churches to keep out evil spirits. The Abbé Chappe
d'Auteroche attended a wedding in Tobolsk in 1761 at which a 'wizard' was
present to counter hostile magic from other magicians; he actually led the
wedding procession.[54] Sometimes these activities could overstep the mark, in
Siberia as elsewhere. In 1794, the best man at a wedding in Tobolsk fashioned
a cross out of wax and read a prayer over it 'so that the simple people consider
him a wizard'. He was reported to the clerical consistory and obliged to
perform a penance.[55]

People of all classes in Russia, including priests, believed in magic. The
major difference was that for wealthier members of society divination and
charms represented harmless superstitions or were used as entertainment;
peasants, and sometimes merchants, took omens and magic much more seriously. Almost all Russian villages had bathhouses that engendered rituals and
superstitions – including rituals for brides before their marriage ceremony.
The bathhouse was where childbirth normally too place. The most magical
hour of the day was midnight, and the most magical places were bathhouses,

although magic also happened at churches, cemeteries, thresholds and crossroads.

Magical invocations and rituals could be an integral part of important activities such as putting animals out to pasture, trying to keep animals free of disease, ensuring good weather in which to sow seed and harvest the crops, or undertaking a journey (which could be hazardous in European Russia but particularly so in Siberia). There were special magical sayings to help bring good weather in Siberia. A period of wet and windy weather could reputedly be banished by throwing a piece of mammoth bone into the fire and reciting the words 'Be clear, be clear.'[56]

Most magic is concerned with the fundamental matters in life – love, marriage, happiness, childbirth, prosperity, death. Most women, then as now, speculated about who their future husband would be, and songs, spells and oracles were used in an attempt to determine the answer. The images of future husbands were sought in mirrors and dreams, and in Siberia rings were also regarded as having power. One variant among Old Believers was that the girl would look through the ring in a cellar until the face of the groom appeared. Old Believers in the Baikal region believed that circles could be used as oracles. They drew a circle on the ground and uttered: 'Circle, circle, tell me the real truth, what is my fate?' Another Siberian custom involved a girl placing a ring on the little toe of her right foot and dipping it into water through a hole in the ice, rotating it in an anticlockwise direction three times and saying a spell: 'Intended one, come and ask me for the key to the lock on the hole in the ice, so that you will be able to water your horse and ask for the ring.' She would then see her future husband in a dream.[57] Some concerns expressed in spells were the same the world over. One can only pity a certain Daria Karganova from the Omsk region who in 1812 admitted adding 'magical remedies' to her husband's food so that 'he would not torment her, but love her.'[58]

Magic was as concerned with evil as with good. In 1833, two peasant women in the Kolyvan region were accused of trying to harm another peasant woman by throwing a bundle into her hut 'containing women's hair, a small piece of brocade, and head of snake.'[59] Special rituals were employed in Siberia to protect new-born babies from the Evil Eye. Ethnographic studies in the late nineteenth century found that Siberian peasants believed that the Devil feared circles as well as crosses and blessings. Some people confessed to communing with the Devil – often, it has to be added, after interrogation and torture. A certain Maksim Malygin was kept in solitary confinement in the early eighteenth century in a remote monastery in Iakutia for 'secret and blasphemous communing with the Unclean Force'. In 1770, Artemii Sakalov was accused of interpreting dreams, murder, arson, robbing churches and pagan graves, dealing with the Devil and making magic spells by invoking the Devil (whom he called father), Christ and three ancient pagan gods of the Slavs.[60]

These pagan and magical customs came with the settlers from European Russia and Ukraine to Siberia. (I was told by a colleague in Tomsk that his family still celebrated weddings and other family occasions according to Belarusian customs because that was where his family originated from.) It might be expected that local pagan customs would also have an impact on the Russian/Ukrainian settler population. Almost all the indigenous people of Siberia had shamans, who were believed to have access to the spirit world, particularly when they danced, which induced a trancelike state which gave them special powers of divination and healing. A foreign traveller in the 1790s described a shaman with a mixture of fascination and disgust:

> Dressed in a habit that was ornamented with bells and plates of iron, which made a deafening noise, he beat besides on a *bourbon*, or tabor, with a degree of force that was terrifying. He then ran about like a maniac with his mouth open, and his head turned in every direction. . . . at one moment real groans, the next tears and sobs, and then loud peals of laughter, the usual preludes of those revelations.[61]

There was a tradition throughout Russia of wandering 'holy fools' whose often wild and dishevelled appearance was not dissimilar to that of shamans. Wandering jesters and minstrels, called *skomorokhi*, told jokes (sometimes against the authorities) but also performed dances and used a drum similar to that of the shaman. They were distrusted by the authorities not only because they could be disrespectful but also as they were often associated with rowdiness and thefts and because their music and dances were said to induce trances during which sorcery and divination took place.

These jesters had their origins as far back as the eleventh century but had only appeared in Siberia in the seventeenth century, along with the first settlers. Their activities were condemned by Tsar Aleksei Mikhailovich in the mid-seventeenth century as 'drunken and devilish amusements'. Anyone caught indulging in such activities was to be flogged and some were burned at the stake. In 1649, the governor of Verkhoture reported that people were listening to jesters, getting drunk, singing devilish songs, fortune-telling, and calling on witches and wizards to cure illnesses.[62] These jesters could still be found in remote parts of Siberia in the early eighteenth century. They then died out, but their reputation did not die. In 2012, one of the defendants in the trial of the rock group Pussy Riot defended their actions in an Orthodox cathedral with the words: 'We are jesters, *skomorokhi*, even holy fools.'

There is some evidence that Russian settlers also adopted some of the spirits of the pagan population and merged them with their own pre-Christian spirits. The belief in people changing shape and becoming birds, animals or forest spirits, was animistic in origin. Like shamans, witches in Siberia were thought to be able to change shape and become birds (usually magpies) or animals.[63] Russian hunters made offerings to pagan spirits before setting out on expeditions; sick Russians were not averse to seeking cures from herbs or chants from shamans. It was only in the post-Second World War period that a combination of persecution and the establishment of provincial hospitals and spread of medical provision diminished the healing role of shamans.

At the same time, however, the habits of pagans in Siberia served to convince Russian settlers of their own separate identity and their superiority over the 'savages'. Almost all Russians/Ukrainians were Christians, and this became their badge of identity. *Inovertsy*, 'people of other faiths', could be used as a collective term for all the native tribes of Siberia and marked their difference from Christian Russians/Slavs. Indigenous people, whether they had converted or not, were seen as the 'other' by the settlers: dirty, eating raw food, polygamous, naked, lustful, slothful, promiscuous, nomadic. In short, the contrast was between the civilised Christian and the non-civilised pagan world, between civilised man and the savage. This in turn links with the mission of the Russians in Siberia, the subject of the next chapter.

CHAPTER ELEVEN

Explorers and Imperialists

My eyes see clearly our future destiny!

Across Siberia, to distant seas

Our fellow Russian is travelling and will there find

A new world. . . .

Our eagle's wing has touched

The diamond mountains of rich India.

The other is resting on the floes of ocean ice.

Waves of gold are flowing from the mines and sands of Siberia.

The Bashkir, the Persian, the Mongol, the Indian, and the Chinaman

Will bring us tribute. O, how clear and bright

Is your future destiny, Mother Russia![1]

These were the dying words attributed to Ermak in an 1854 play by Nikolai Polevoi about his conquest of Siberia. We have seen how rapidly and how successfully hunters and Cossacks penetrated Siberia during the seventeenth century. Further exploration of Siberia and the acquisition of new lands continued in the eighteenth and nineteenth centuries. By 1860, the Russians had regained control of the left (northern) bank of the river Amur, ceded to China in 1689. At its peak, the empire extended as far as the west coast of North America, with settlements on islands and on the coast of Alaska down to Fort Ross on the coast of California. It is no surprise that these conquests were seen at the time as comparable with those of Cortés in the New World in the sixteenth century and with the opening up of the American West, not only in terms of the achievements of explorers and soldiers but also as an indication of the superiority of Russians over the indigenous peoples in these regions. In the nineteenth century, expansion became characterised as a Russian 'mission' to bring enlightenment and civilisation to pagan peoples. This was an 'awakening', projecting Siberia as a land of promise and destiny and not simply as an inhospitable dumping ground for undesirables and criminals.

The explorations of the Arctic seas in the 1720s and 1740s were by any standards extraordinary feats of daring and heroism, undertaken in the most appalling conditions. They demonstrated that Russia, if not always Russians, had as great a capacity, if not a greater capacity, to chart and conquer the unknown as other European countries. The expeditions were intended not only to chart the coastline and the islands between Russia and America but also to discover the 'passage' between the two continents. These intentions were seen clearly in the terse instructions given to Danish seafarer Vitus Bering by Peter I for his first expedition:

1. You are to build one or two boats with decks at Kamchatka or another place there.
2. You are to [sail] on these boats along the land which goes to the north and it is expected (because its termination point is unknown) that the land will appear to be part of America.
3. You are to search for where it adjoins America and then proceed to some city under European control, or if you see some European vessel, find out what the coast is called, and record it; then go yourself and collect original information, record it on the map and return here.[2]

The first Bering expedition (1728–30) sailed from the Kamchatka peninsula up the north coast of Siberia, charting the coastline and the mouths of the rivers. Bering established that there was a sea passage to the east of the northern tip of Siberia (the Chukotka peninsula) but dense fog meant that he was unable to see land on the other side of what is now known as the Bering Strait, and fierce storms prevented him from getting any closer to the Alaskan coast. The charting and mapping of the Aleutian Islands between Siberia and North America also asserted Russian control over this territory.

The second Bering expedition (1733–43) was an ambitious attempt to chart the whole Arctic coastline from the Chukotka peninsula down to

EXPLORERS AND IMPERIALISTS

the northern tip of Japan, and to complete the charting of the Aleutian and Kurile Islands. The expedition was divided into several units, each charged with exploring and charting one area, but all of them faced horrendous conditions – blizzards, gales, freezing temperatures, frostbite, scurvy, snow-blindness and near-starvation. Bering reached Kodiak Island off the coast of Alaska but failed to make shore. He died in intense pain brought on by scurvy and was buried on a small island, which now bears his name, just off the Kamchatka peninsula.

The expedition failed to land on Alaska or to make its way through the passage between Russia and America. All of that had to wait until 1879, when a Swedish expedition sailed through the northern passage in a steam-powered ship (today, the passage can be navigated without icebreakers). Bering's two expeditions had nevertheless achieved a great deal in terms of maritime charting and land mapping, and had established a Russian presence on the Aleutian Islands. The expeditions were also a testimony to the technical ability of the Russian government to mount significant scientific expeditions and to the extraordinary endurance of the seafarers and soldiers involved. The logs of Bering's voyages are terse but the appalling conditions and the extent of the suffering can be gauged from the reports of Lieutenant Sven Waxel in 1741:

It became very difficult to run the ship because, in addition to those who died, 40 were ill and those who were still about were very feeble. ... We and our men were greatly weakened from the severe attack of the scurvy. ... We had only six barrels of water on board. As to provisions we had no sea biscuit or such like and only a little flour, butter and meat. On top of this the shrouds on the mainsail above the cartharpings [lines for tautening shrouds] on the right side were all torn, and therefore we could not carry any sail on the mainmast. ... During the whole winter our food, because we had no other provision, was. ... very poor, difficult to obtain, and not fit to eat. ... If we could not find live animals to kill we had to content ourselves with the dead ones that were washed ashore, such as sea cows and whales. ... On the island where we lived there were violent winds and even blizzards during the winter. It may be said that between December and March there was seldom a fair day. From March and during the spring and summer months there was almost continuous fog and damp-ness and little pleasant weather.[3]

The Russian government wanted to extend both its knowledge of, and its authority over, islands and lands east of Siberia; it also wanted to know more about the lands it had already acquired. A number of significant scientific expeditions were undertaken in the eighteenth century within Siberia. In 1719–21, Daniel Gottlieb Messerschmidt, a German in Russian service, on the orders of Peter I travelled in Mongolia, the Baikal region and along the river Lena. He recorded a lot of natural history and scientific data, including making a description of silver and lead deposits and of a skeleton of a mammoth, which he discovered near Tomsk. His assistant, a Swedish prisoner of war exiled to Tobolsk, Philipp Johann von Strahlenberg, continued his work. It was von Strahlenberg who determined that the Ural mountains should be regarded as the boundary between Europe and Asia.

A further large-scale exploration of Siberia was undertaken in the 1730s by Gerhard Müller and Johann Gmelin, two foreign scholars whose expedition was commissioned by the Russian Academy of Sciences. Gmelin was a brilliant professor of chemistry and a scholar of natural history; Müller was a distinguished historian. They were accompanied by some 600 men, including draughtsmen and instrument-makers. They travelled extensively through the Altai region, along the river Enisei, through the Baikal area and up to Iakutsk. Together they recorded the fauna and flora of Siberia, its physical geography, its demography and its archaeology. Such ambitious expeditions were not organised without difficulties. At one stage Müller and Gmelin needed to force local people to row ships for them on the river Lena. In an act worthy of Peter I, they induced some to serve them – and then erected gallows on the river banks as a warning to others.[4] This was a truly significant expedition: Gmelin collected over 100 species of flowers and plants; Müller's collections of historical documents, abstracts, maps and drawings filled over 40 volumes.[5]

The Kamchatka peninsula was a source of particular fascination to explorers and travellers, with its volcanoes, dramatic mountains, hot springs, and unique fauna and flora. Its inhabitants repelled and intrigued visitors at the same time. Stepan Krasheninnikov, born and educated in Moscow, was originally a member of Bering's second expedition, and the assistant to Müller and Gmelin. He spent three years exploring the Kamchatka peninsula, from 1737 to 1740. He recorded the animal and plant life, fish, metals and minerals. Krasheninnikov was fascinated by the habits of the people there, the Kamchadals (Itelmens). They survived the appalling wet climatic conditions by living in the summer in tent-like shelters raised above the ground on posts and in the winter in dwellings half-sunk into the ground. The primitiveness of the Kamchadals – their almost total nakedness in the summer months, their strange dwellings and their diet of fish, which could be rotten and putrid, and their their personal habits – was noted by Krasheninnikov with horror: 'the Kamchadel do not keep themselves clean at all, do not wash their hands and faces, do not cut their fingernails, eat off the same plates as dogs and never wash them, all smell like fish.'[6] 'They are so filthy and vile ... they are so infested with lice ... that using their fingers like a comb, they lift their braids, sweep the lice together into their fists and then gobble them up.'[7]

In 1740, he was joined by Georg Steller, a German professor of natural history who published an account of the fauna, fish and wildlife of Kamchatka. He agreed with Krasheninnikov's view of the Kamchadals – they had an innocence as a result of their isolation and lack of contact with other peoples, but they also suffered from 'excess and gluttony', had 'no concept of shame', were 'lecherous', and their primitiveness was demonstrated by their careless attitude towards human life: 'they throw away their new-born children if they were born in bad weather or the mothers did not want to be bothered with raising them.'[8]

The expeditions in the mid-eighteenth century followed a pattern. They were very large enterprises, lasting several years and involving many people. They were sponsored from the centre – by the government and by the Academy of Sciences (founded in 1726) in St Petersburg. This was quite different from the smaller-scale explorations of the seventeenth century, carried out by individuals or small groups of hunters and Cossacks. The Academy of Sciences was heavily dependent in its early years on scientists from German lands, which accounts for the large number of German specialists in their expeditions. Russia lacked institutions of higher education – the University of Moscow was founded only in 1755 and a university network only established in the reign of Alexander I, and then only in European Russia.

Some Russians were involved in these expeditions – Krasheninnikov was Russian, although he was originally an assistant to Müller and Gmelin. The Russians Fedor Minin, Vasilii Pronshishchev (and his wife), and Khariton Laptev attempted to chart the Taimyr peninsula in the far north of Siberia in the 1730s. The expedition was not successful and, for his pains, Minin was investigated by the Academy of Sciences and punished by having his officer rank taken away from him. The Sea of Laptev (between the Kara Sea and the East Siberian Sea) in the Arctic is named after Khariton Laptev. Petr Lasinius charted the river Anadyr coastline in the far north-east of Siberia (now Chukotka) in the 1730s – and died there from scurvy. 'Siberians', including indigenous peoples, were only involved in these expeditions at the lowest level, as soldiers or porters.

The later expeditions had different aims from the exploits of hunters and Cossacks in the seventeenth century. Not only did they want to open up new land for settlement and acquire new tribute-payers, they also had serious scientific aims, typical of the eighteenth-century desire to acquire and record information about the natural world. Of course, charting and mapping the terrain also established a political claim to the land and its people.

In the late eighteenth century, Catherine II continued the practice of using German scientists to explore Russia. In the 1770s, she commissioned another German scholar, Peter Simon Pallas, to record flora, fauna, wildlife and geological finds in Siberia, a journey which coincided with the passage of Venus. Pallas's collections of plants and seeds were sent to the St Petersburg botanical gardens and to Kew Gardens in London. Some of his vast collection of specimens has ended up in the Natural History Museum in London. Another German scientist, Johann Adam, found the first complete mammoth skeleton in 1806. Imperial Russian naval officers, however, participated in naval expeditions. Catherine commissioned an expedition to map the coast-line of the Sea of Okhotsk and the Aleutian Islands, this time led jointly by Joseph Billings, an English sailor who had sailed with James Cook, and Gavriil Sarychev, a Russian naval officer. At the beginning of the nineteenth century, Ivan Kruzenshtern (Adam von Krusenstern), a Baltic German, and Iurii Lisiansky, a Ukrainian, both naval officers in the imperial navy, successfully completed the first circumnavigation of the globe via Cape Horn and the Cape of Good Hope.

In the later nineteenth century, the internal exploration of Siberia continued. After the 1863 Polish uprising, able Polish scientists exiled to Siberia made a significant contribution to knowledge. A. L. Czechanowski, for example, during his march in irons from Kiev to Tobolsk, made a collection of ants which he studied with a magnifying glass made from a broken decanter. He later went on to conduct serious geological work in Irkutsk and the river Lena region. The Czechanowski range of mountains is named after him.[9] A voyage in 1877 from the river Enisei to St Petersburg was funded by the millionaire Russian industrialist Mikhail Sidorov to help with the export of his Siberian graphite. The ship, the *Dawn*, was greeted with celebrations when it arrived in St Petersburg (only partly marred by the arrest of one of the crew members who, as an exile, had broken the rules of his confinement in Siberia by entering European Russia) and the voyage's success was enthusiastically greeted by the geographer Fedor Suditskii: 'the *Dawn* will be a dawn for all Siberia and for our merchant fleet. We can boldly declare that navigating out of the Siberian rivers is a new dawn for Siberia.'[10]

In the nineteenth century, it was Russian administrators and entrepreneurs, and not foreign academics, who pushed the frontiers of the Russian empire eastwards, into the Amur basin and as far as the west coast of Alaska and California. The empire reached its furthest extent eastwards in this period and its possessions in North America gave it an overseas 'colony'. Only after the sale of Fort Ross in California in 1841 and then the sale of Alaska in 1867 to the United States did Russia revert to being a continuous land empire.

We have seen that Bering was not able either to establish the existence of the northern passage or to chart land in Alaska. Georg Steller, a German botanist, was probably the first European step on the shore of Alaska in the 1740s. By the time the Russians established proper settlements on the coast of North America in the late eighteenth century, they already faced a rival in Spain, which had claims to California. Grigorii Shelikhov, who was born in European Russia but had moved to Irkutsk as a young man and established a business there, became the first to set up a proper base on Kodiak Island, just off Alaska, in 1784. In 1804, Aleksandr Baranov, the business partner of Shelikhov and later the governor of Russian America, opened a base further down the coast which he captured against fierce local resistance and which he named New Archangel (now called Sitka).

These men, like their predecessors in the seventeenth century, were drawn to the Alaskan coast by the lucrative fur trade. The Aleutian Islands had already proved good hunting ground for sea otters, whose pelts were so valuable that they were referred to as 'soft gold'. Shelikhov appealed to Catherine II to claim the Alaskan coast for Russia. The empress was loath, however, to upset other powers – Spain, Britain and the United States – which had claims on the coast of North America and trading interests there. It was only in 1799, in the brief reign of Catherine's son Paul I, that Shelikhov was granted permission to found the Russian-American Company, a joint-stock company which was officially under the 'protection' of the tsar and in practice under the direct authority of the Ministry of Commerce (its flag included the imperial eagle). The 'colonies' were in effect run by the Company, and by a

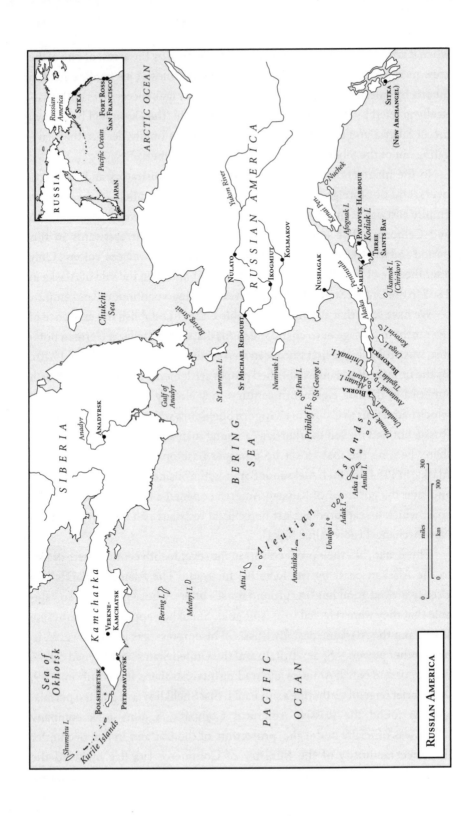

RUSSIAN AMERICA

colonial administration comprising the Company's founders and a small number of naval officers. It had jurisdiction over the Alaskan coastline, islands off the coast and the settlement of Fort Ross, originally a sea otter hunting station, on the Californian coast, just north of San Francisco.

The Russian government was always reluctant to harm relations with the United States, Spain or postcolonial Mexico (which became independent in 1821) and was unresponsive to a proposal from Dmitrii Zavalishin, the future Decembrist, in 1824 to establish a larger and more formal presence in the area by annexing part of California. To this extent, the Russian government was in the same position as it had been in the seventeenth century when it unsuccessfully claimed the Amur territory – colonisation was always restricted when Russia faced competition from another state rather than from scattered indigenous peoples.

Russian America was some 12,000 miles (over 19,000 kilometres) from St Petersburg, so Siberia was an important link with the overseas 'colonies'. The Russian-American Company maintained a recruiting office for colonists in Tiumen, in western Siberia. The colony needed settlers with a range of skills, as can be seen from the somewhat comical request from the governor of Russian America in 1827 for Russian dairy maids since 'Aleut women are not at all capable of such an occupation and have asked me to provide them with Russian women'.[11] The furs and pelts from Russian America were traded in Irkutsk.[12]

Most of all, the colonies needed foodstuffs and other supplies since they were never self-sufficient. It had been hoped that Fort Ross would be able to supply the northern settlements around New Archangel with wheat and meat, but repeated crop failures and the long distances between settlements meant a continuing reliance on Russia – or Spanish America and later Mexico – for supplies. The goods – including butter, flour, beef, caviar, clothing – came from Irkutsk by a precarious route, which was little different, or better, than the route taken by Bering's men (described in Chapter 2). The route from Irkutsk to Iakutsk on the river Lena was manageable but the road from Iakutsk to Okhotsk, the main Russian port on the Pacific coast which supplied the Russian colonies, was treacherous, with dangerous river crossings, made worse by snow in the winter and by attacks from wild animals, hostile indigenous people and bands of escaped exiles and convicts. The journey could take two years, by which time much of the food would have gone putrid. The goods that were usable were very expensive. The journey only improved with the opening up of the river Amur route in the 1860s, although, as we will see, there were still difficulties in navigating the Amur. Indeed, apart from some trade with Spanish California and later Mexico and some grain imports from Chile, Russian America had to be supplied from Russia and the easiest way proved to be the extraordinarily long sea route from St Petersburg via Cape Horn or the Cape of Good Hope.

The Amur river basin was the other main area of Russian expansion in the nineteenth century. This was the one region in the seventeenth century in the east where the Russians had been unable to establish a foothold and had had to cede the area to the Chinese in the Treaty of Nerchinsk in 1689. Expansion into the Amur area in the mid-nineteenth century was driven by the determination of Nikolai Muravev, the governor-general of Eastern Siberia. Muravev saw this as a wonderful opportunity to take advantage of the fact that the Chinese had failed to settle and exploit the area. In his view, Amur would bring great riches to Siberia and Russia, but it would also establish vital political control by Russia over the east and protect Siberia: whoever controlled the Amur basin would also control eastern Siberia. Certainly, descending today by plane into the Amur valley at Khabarovsk after flying for hours over uninhabited mountain ranges and seeing the great sweep of rivers of the Amur and its many tributaries and the confluence with the Ussuri river, one can not only appreciate why Muravev considered the region to be of such strategic importance but also understand something of the challenge of controlling this vast region.

The 'conquest' of the Amur was swift and conclusive, taking advantage of the fact that China was weakened by domestic and foreign conflicts and unable to resist Russian encroachment. In 1850, Muravev established the port of Nikolaevsk at the mouth of the Amur. Four years later, he commissioned expeditions down the Amur, which reached and reclaimed the fort of Albazin, abandoned and destroyed as part of the Treaty of Nerchinsk. By 1858, the Russians had established effective control of the river and the territories to the north and east. Khabarovka (renamed Khabarovsk in 1893) was founded in that year. The weak Chinese government recognised Russian ownership of the left (northern) bank of the Amur and of the Ussuri region in treaties signed in 1858 (Aigun) and 1860 (Peking). New administrative regions were created with the acquisition of territory in the far east: in 1856, a new Amur (Priamur) region was established; after 1860, this was enlarged to form a new Ussuri region.

The town of Vladivostok was founded in 1860. It was located at the end of Golden Horn bay, not far from the borders with Korea and China. Standing on the hill above the town, looking to the wide gulf of the Amur to the west and the many sheltered bays to the east and south, it is easy to see why this was chosen as the ideal spot to provide a safe location for both trade and the fleet. The name 'Vladivostok' means 'rule the east' and was a deliberate asser- tion of the newfound Russian power and aspirations in the far east. It paral- leled the naming of Vladikavkaz ('rule the Caucasus') in the south Caucasus, founded as a fort in 1784, which asserted Russian power in that region.

In the nineteenth century, the Russian 'civilising mission' was used, as it was by other European imperialist powers, to justify the Russian presence in other lands and their rule over the indigenous peoples who lived there. Russian/Ukrainian peasant settlers did not articulate a racial justification for their acquisition of such lands. Indigenous peoples were drawn into the Orthodox Church, as we saw in the last chapter. Practical realities meant that settlers and soldiers had relationships with, and married, local women, both in the Amur region and in the colonies on the American coast. But there is little doubt that settlers regarded themselves as superior to native peoples. They were disgusted by their pagan practices, but perhaps more by their eating habits, lack of cleanliness, nakedness and perceived promiscuity. These views were articulated by the archbishop of Tobolsk in the mid-seventeenth century:

> these people are worse than animals, for even dumb animals do not eat beasts, fowl or grass that God forbade them to eat, while these people, not knowing God who dwells in heaven and refusing to accept His law from those who bring it to them, are raw eaters who eat the meat of beasts and vermin, drink animal filth and blood like water, and eat grass and roots.[13]

Similar views were expressed by Russian and foreign explorers and travellers, as we saw above in relation to Kamchatka. Bering said of the inhabitants of the Kurile Islands: 'A few of them worship idols, and others do not believe in anything and are alien to any decent customs.'[14] These views were not unique to Russians, of course, and the 'civilised' European commonly contrasted himself with the 'savage'. Evert Ysbrant Ides, a Dane in Russian service who was the Russian ambassador to China in the 1690s, had the following to say about the Siberian peoples. Ostiaks (Khanty) fed their idols with milk and

thrust it into their Mouths with a Spoon made for that purpose; but [as] . . .
the Idols cannot swallow this their Milk diet it runs out again at both sides
of their Mouth, down their whole Bodies, in such a filthy manner as is sufficient to disgust one from eating of this Diet.

He also said of the Tungus: 'Both men and women go naked in the Summer,
except only a leather Girdle of three Hands breadth, that they deeply cut in
the shape of Ribbands, which they wear about their wast, and covers their
Privities.'[15]

    The 'civilising' mission was inextricably linked with an attempt to convert
the pagans, as we saw in the last chapter. Priests were sent out to Kamchatka
as early as the 1740s. It was not, of course, an attractive posting and additional
salaries were paid in an attempt to attract applicants. Missionary work was
carried out with great determination, at not inconsiderable personal cost,
in Russian America. One of the first acts of Shelikhov was to found an
Orthodox church and set up a school for native boys on Kodiak Island – the
latter taught religion as well as Russian, arithmetic and navigation. The first
Orthodox mission to the American colonies was dispatched in 1792. The
missionaries not only tried to convert pagans but often also described the
geographical and climatic features, animals and lifestyle of indigenous people.
Later missionary work was carried out by Father (later Bishop) Ioann
Veniaminov, a true 'Siberian' who had been born in a village on the banks of
the river Angara in Irkutsk province and arrived in Russian America in 1823.
He founded a new church and school, and translated the catechism and the
Gospel of St Matthew into the Aleut language. He travelled extensively in the
far east in the 1840s and 1850s, and accompanied Muravev on his expedition
to the Amur.[16] He was a considerable scholar and preacher, which led to his
appointment in 1867 as metropolitan of Moscow under his monastic name of
Innokentii (he was canonised by the Russian Orthodox Church in 1977).

    Russian identity formed itself as Christian and Orthodox against the
'other', during the conflicts with, and then defeats of, the Mongols and
khanates from the thirteenth century onwards. Their identity was founded
on Russians' perception of themselves as the only true heirs of the Byzantine
Christian empire after the fall of Constantinople (now Istanbul) in 1453. In
the wars of the eighteenth and nineteenth centuries, this came to be seen in
terms of the triumph of Christianity over the Muslim Turks in the Ottoman
empire. In Catherine II's reign, the conquest of the Crimea was seen as the

rightful return of Muslim lands to Christianity. Catherine even wrote a play on the triumphant campaign of Prince Oleg in the year 900. It was performed as an opera in 1791, at the end of the Russo-Turkish War, and the programme notes portrayed the empress as fighting as the heir of Oleg to regain Constantinople. She named her grandson Constantine in the hope that he would regain Constantinople for the Christian faith and Russia.[17]

Soldiers' ditties (whether written by or for them) make this mission clear. This particular one below referred to Turks, but could equally be applied to the conquest of indigenous peoples in the east:

> For God and the faith
> We crash against the savage
> In a new blaze of glory.[18]

By the 1840s, the presence of the Russians in Siberia, in particular in the far east, had become something more than an assertion of Russian control over the less sophisticated 'other', and had turned into a full-blown civilising mission. The link with the Christian triumph over the Turks remained. 'The East belongs to us . . . it has been welded to Russia by her Cossacks, and it has been earned from Europe by [the Russian] resistance to the Turks,' stated one Russian triumphantly in the 1840s.[19] Russia's version of the 'white man's burden' was expressed in 1840 by Vasilii Grigorev, a distinguished Russian orientalist, who declared that Russians had a 'noble calling' to enlighten 'the tribes of Asia': 'We are summoned to put these peoples' lives in order, having taught these rude children of the forests and deserts to acknowledge the beneficent power of the laws. ... We are summoned to enlighten these peoples with religion and science.'[20]

This new attitude can be seen in particular in relation to the Amur region, which was never viewed simply in terms of the economic and political opportunities it presented. The area had some potential for agriculture and for imports and exports but was portrayed almost as a Promised Land or Eldorado, offering fabulous wealth and a solution to all of Siberia's problems. It would provide land for Russian settlers (based on the assumption that the land was empty), would feed Siberia (as grain would be grown in the Ussuri valley), would solve all transport problems (the other major Siberian rivers ran the wrong way – north), as the Mississippi river had in North America. It would in short be a new beginning for Siberia, and promised progress, wealth and happiness. As the anarchist Mikhail Bakunin stated in the 1860s: 'Siberia is now connected to the ocean, it has ceased to be a locked-in desert. . . . With the Amur, Siberia has for the first time come to its senses.'[21] One steamship captain on the Amur went even further, stating hyperbolically that 'we are spreading Christianity and civilisation among wild tribes and people.'[22]

This confidence and sense of superiority came in part from contrasting the adventurous Russians – from Ermak down to explorers in the eighteenth century – with the Chinese, who were portrayed as indolent and part of a decaying culture. The acquisition of the Amur basin coincided with the Second Opium War in 1856–60, during which the Chinese government was humiliated by Western powers. Russians also compared themselves with the Americans who opened up the Wild West. The Russian 'mission' was therefore a potent if rather confusing combination: the triumph of Russian culture; the triumph of Christianity and/or Orthodoxy; the triumph of Europe and Europeans over the East.

The reality of expansion in the Amur region and North America severely disappointed the supporters of the idea of a 'Russian' or 'European' mission. Hopes that either or both regions would rapidly provide great economic benefits were soon dashed. Contrary to some Russian assumptions, there were already indigenous peoples living in these territories, and they were hostile to the new settlers.

The new settlements by the Amur river often failed as they were established too hastily. As a result, people had to be resettled. In practice, this meant forcible resettlement in the Amur region from the Baikal area. Even members of persecuted sects were not enthusiastic about moving so far into unknown lands: a small number of Old Believers moved from Samara, on the river Volga river, to the Khabarovsk region, but more substantial settlement only took place in the early twentieth century. It is even said that Muravev rounded up prostitutes from public bars in Irkutsk, sent them in barges down the Amur to provide wives for the men who had settled there and had a priest marry them all in one ceremony on the banks of the river.[23] The same policy had been attempted to address the lack of women in the far east in the mid-seventeenth century, and it was to be attempted again in the 1930s.

The new settlements in the Amur region were too small to produce goods for export to the east or to absorb imports. But the main problem was the river Amur itself. It was too shallow for oceangoing ships and only navigable by flat-bottomed barges and rafts. Furthermore, the river was frozen for half the year, from October to May. Communication along the river banks was further hindered by the dense forest on both sides and by the uneven ice cover, which made it difficult to use sledges in winter on the river. There were also difficulties with access to the sea and the location of a suitable port. Nikolaevsk, at the mouth of the Amur, proved to be unfit, as the harbour was too shallow and the many sandbars made it dangerous for shipping. The port was also icebound in the winter and the climate was dreadful. Moving the port to Vladivostok, further south, in the 1870s was an improvement, but could not solve the fundamental difficulties of navigation on the river Amur, and Nikolaevsk declined rapidly in the late nineteenth century as a result. Most of the population, including the Japanese residents, were massacred by a rogue Bolshevik commander during the Russian Civil War. It is now a small town, with a population of around 23,000.

Russian America was never seen as quite the Eldorado that Amur promised to develop into, but even so it was still a failure. The number of settlers in Russian California, for example, grew slowly, reaching only 563 in 1833.[24] The population rose to some 10,000 by 1862, but the Russians there still only numbered 577; there were far more creoles (1,892) and indigenous people (7,681).[25] As this shows, colonists from Russia were hard to attract. The climate was poor and sickness rife. 'Of all the dirty and wretched places that I have ever seen, Sitka is pre-eminently the most wretched and most dirty,' wrote one commentator in 1841.[26] The popular saying 'It is better to go into the army than to go to America'[27] sums up the general attitude.

The economic potential of Russian America was never realised in part due to the overhunting of sea otters in the Aleutian Islands, Kodiak Island and off the Alaskan coast, in a repetition of events in Siberia in the seventeenth century. Sea otters were clubbed to death and destroyed by uncontrolled over-hunting, the effects of which were made worse by the fact that female otters only give birth every two years. The Russians always depended on Aleuts to catch the otters, and they too were depleted by disease. Sales decreased when the Russian army replaced beaver collars with lambskin collars for winter coats. The Russian-American Company could not compete with the Hudson's Bay Company in the treatment and export of skins. The worst example of waste occurred early in the nineteenth century when the Company killed some 900,000 fur seals, but only had the capacity to export 600,000 skins, with the result that the rest were burnt or simply left to rot on the shore.[28]

The American colonies were never self-sufficient. Settlers were dependent on supplies being brought from Irkutsk to Okhotsk and from there by sea, with all the difficulties which that entailed. Hopes that the colony could be supplied with grain by non-Russians – indigenous peoples and Spanish settlers – were dashed. The political situation in North America was difficult and the Russian government was not prepared to engage with either the newly independent Mexico or the aggressive westward push of American entrepreneurs. The Russian-American Company itself ran up enormous debts.

Fort Ross was sold to a Swiss adventurer in 1841, before the Amur project started, for 30,000 piastres, of which only 3,812 piastres were received (the piastre, a Spanish silver dollar, was the currency of exchange in the Pacific). Today, Fort Ross has been partly reconstructed as an open-air museum. In 1867, the Russian government sold Alaska to the United States of America, in part so that it could concentrate its efforts on the Amur region, for 7,200,000 gold dollars (2 cents per acre, as one estimate has it).[29] The commercial interests of the Russian-American Company were sold to Hutchinson, Kohl & Company of San Francisco, which then renamed itself the Alaska Commercial Company. The overseas colonial adventure was over – just as dramatic new economic opportunities were opening up in Siberia, as we shall see in the next chapter.

CHAPTER TWELVE

Railways and Change

Someday this city [Irkutsk] will be a second New York, the capital of an Asiatic United States, a free Siberia from the Urals to the Pacific. This change will probably not be brought about by revolution. The Russian is too law-loving a man to try to free himself by force from the mother country. He will trust to the accidents of diplomacy. Siberia will someday be free. Every Siberian imbibes the notion of freedom with his mother's milk. Though born in Russia, or the child of Russian parents, he repudiates his nationality, calls himself a Siberiate, and is proud of his country. He looks down upon the Russian as the Yankee scorns the Britisher.[1]

This statement, made in 1875 by Henry Seebohm, an English ornithologist who was observing birds in the Enisei region, illustrates the newfound confidence within Siberia in the late nineteenth century. Siberia changed dramatically around the turn of the century, at a far greater pace than European Russia, both in the countryside and in the towns. Over the two decades on either side of 1900, having been a backwater in so many areas, Siberia became the dynamic centre of change within the empire. Such a transformation brought inevitable social and economic strains and there were, of course, revolutions – although those started far away in St Petersburg.

The root cause of the transformation of Siberia was the construction of the Trans-Siberian railway. The Great Reforms of the 1860s and 1870s in the reign of Alexander II had an impact on villages and towns in the region, as we will see, but it was the opening up of Siberia to mass migration and commerce, and the improved ability to move troops as well as civilians and goods, that changed the region forever. The significance of the railway was not lost on contemporaries or foreign travellers. A local Irkutsk paper in 1898 recorded its arrival as a 'fateful moment,' the end of the old Siberia; the 'new future in front of us' brought both hopes and fears.[2] 'The future of Siberia,' commented a foreign traveller in 1902, 'obviously depends on the success or failure of the Trans-Siberian railway.'[3] Indeed, flying to Vladivostok and seeing the Trans-Siberian railway from the air as it snakes across the Amur valley and then crosses the river into Khabarovsk allows you to appreciate its significance in making this area accessible from other parts of the Russian empire.

Within educated Siberian society there had been a debate about the role of railways from the 1850s, conducted in newly founded regional papers and journals and associated with the sense of 'mission' described in the previous chapter.[4] The discussion highlighted the main concerns of educated society: the desire to expand trade to the east and west, but also to open up Siberia for development and to integrate it more completely within the empire; the need to support the empire's geopolitical ambitions in the east; and, finally, the fulfilment of the mission to spread Russian, and European, civilisation to the east and the need to show that Russia could compete with the grandiose rail projects of the other great European and North American powers. The railway would be the means of 'taking European civilisation into the East', as an official in the Ministry of Interior put it.[5]

The construction of the railway started in 1891. It was a colossal under-taking – the longest railway line in the world.[6] The original route was over 5,000 miles (8,000 kilometres) long (the northern route through Khabarovsk extended this), including some 70 miles (112 kilometres) of tunnels and bridges. As the track was laid further eastwards, the problems intensified. The route had to cut through steep hills and bogs, and cross the great Siberian rivers. It required 50 bridges to cross the tributaries of the river Angara alone. Lake Baikal proved an almost insurmountable problem. At first, train, freight and passengers had to cross the great lake by steamer and rejoin the railway on the other side. In winter the lake froze. The first icebreaker – an English-made ship called the *Baikal* – was damaged on her maiden voyage. The southern stretch round the lake had to be built into the rock and mountain-sides and required 200 bridges and viaducts and 35 tunnels. This part of the track was completed only in early 1904, just as the Russo-Japanese War broke out. In the far east, the railway had to traverse mountain ranges and cope with

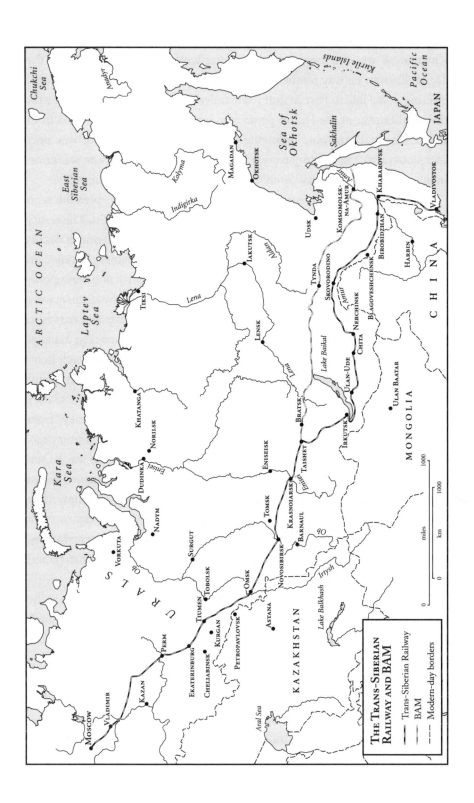

THE TRANS-SIBERIAN
RAILWAY AND BAM

—— Trans-Siberian Railway
—— BAM
- - - Modern-day borders

terrible flooding and landslides. At the time the bridge across the Amur at Khabarovsk was the longest bridge in the world. The first branch of the Trans-Siberian railway reached Vladivostok by cutting through Manchuria, offering a vital link to Port Arthur (now called Lüshun port or Lüshunkou) at the southern tip of the Dalian peninsula, which was leased by Russia from China. The eastern route following the path of the river Amur was only completed after the Russo-Japanese War. The cost of construction was enormous – estimated as 93,630 roubles per *verst* (0.6 miles/1 kilometre).

The luxury compartments on Trans-Siberian trains were splendid, with comfortable beds, soft leather chairs, electric lights and even baths. The reality of travel on the Trans-Siberian, however, was less luxurious than such details suggest. Migrants to Siberia at the end of the century, in contrast, travelled on the line in cattle trucks Furthermore, standards of construction were poor: the line was mainly single track; the rails were too light and the sleepers were made of untreated timber, so they rotted easily; the gradients and curves in the track were too sharp, so the rims of the wheels wore out quickly; many of the smaller bridges were flimsy and needed to be repaired or replaced; there was a shortage of good rolling stock. All this meant that there were frequent derailments and accidents, and that the trains had to go very slowly – as they still do today. The nearly 6,000-mile (9,000-kilometre) journey from Vladivostok to Moscow still takes seven days; it took nine days a century ago. Journeys were subject to many delays, and the capacity of the line was far too limited. In the 1905 Revolution, the first demand of the Chita garrison of soldiers and Cossacks was for more trains to European Russia, followed by demands for better pay, improved conditions and an eight-hour day.[7]

For all its limitations, however, the railway opened up Siberia, transformed the geopolitical position of the east and changed rural, urban, industrial and cultural life dramatically.

The Trans-Siberian railway was built to strengthen Russia's position in the east. It helped to increase trade with China, Japan and Manchuria, although the sea route for eastern trade remained more important, especially after the opening of the Suez Canal in 1869. The original rail route to Vladivostok via Manchuria was also a clear statement of Russia's intention to defend and strengthen its military, as well as its commercial, presence in Manchuria. The Russian presence in Manchuria, and its lease from China of Port Arthur – a warm-water port – was a direct challenge to Japan's influence in Korea and China.

Both Japan and Russia were acutely aware of the crucial military role which the railway played in their rivalry. The Russian government realised that the capacity and reliability of the railway had to be improved in order to make it possible to transport troops to the east more effectively. In particular, the track round the southern banks of Lake Baikal had to be completed. It tried, therefore, to postpone the looming outbreak of hostilities with Japan until the track around Lake Baikal was complete and until the weaker sections of the rest of the line had been renovated, the rails strengthened and more sidings constructed.

The Japanese, on the other hand, understood the advantage of acting before this work was finished but when they declared war in January 1904, just at the point when the ice on Lake Baikal was too thick for an icebreaker to operate, the track around the southern shore had just been completed. In any event, the Russians were able to put down tracks on the ice and transport troops and equipment across the lake. All the same, the Trans-Siberian railway was slow and unreliable, and it proved difficult to relieve the Russian troops in Manchuria. The exclusive use of the railway for the military also disrupted trade and civilian travel. The defeat at sea at Tsushima in May 1905 and flawed military tactics sealed the fate of the Russians, but the weakness of the railway also hindered operations. 'Next to the absence of a Russian fleet, the most important factor to assist the Japanese in their offensive strategy and to impede us was the condition of the Siberian and eastern Chinese railways,' said General Aleksei Kuropatkin, commander of the Russian army in Manchuria.[8] Of course, it was the existence of the railway that had in part provoked the conflict in the first place. The Russo-Japanese War curbed Russian ambitions in Manchuria as Russia had to cede Port Arthur to the Japanese. For Siberia, the immediate consequence was the completion of a second line of the railway between Irkutsk and Vladivostok following the route of the Amur and then the Ussuri rivers.

Japanese settlers had come to the Russian far east at the beginning of the twentieth century. In Vladivostok, the number of Japanese residents grew from 50 in 1875 to almost 3,000 in 1902.[9] In February 1904, soon after the outbreak of war, the Japanese residents in Vladivostok held a 'mass gathering' and then decided to leave.[10] It was a wise decision. On Sunday, 6 March 1904, the Japanese fleet shelled Vladivostok and one person was killed. Eleonora Prey, an American resident in the town, heard the gunfire; her husband grabbed his binoculars and rushed to the top of the hill to witness the ensuing battle.[11] In Irkutsk, it was said that when the war broke out 'all the Japanese – cigarette-sellers, launderers and others – had already rushed away from Irkutsk'. During the war, some 2,000 Japanese prisoners of war were transported across Siberia to European Russia.[12]

One definite consequence of the construction of the Trans-Siberian railway was indeed the opening up of Siberia to settlers and traders from East Asia. Khabarovsk station at the turn of the of the century

> was all bustle and noise. The entrance was packed with Chinamen shouting gutturally and bumping about with loads, while meek, white-robed, and quaint-featured Koreans squatted on their heels in corners. Russians, chiefly officials in their greys and blues, gilt epaulettes, white-peaked caps, and top knots of pliable leather, took possession of the buffet with their bundles.[13]

The Chinese came to Russia to Siberia in the late nineteenth century to work and trade. As early as 1878, the paper *Siberia* warned against the 'greater and greater exploitation of the town [Verkhneudinsk, now Ulan-Ude] by Chinese and Jews'. The number of immigrants rose and spread within Siberia following the railway line. By 1897, there were 73 Chinese residents registered in Irkutsk province, and over 2,000 in the Baikal region overall.[14] Irkutsk was said to have 'hundreds of Chinese about, and rows of Chinese shops'.[15] By 1900, the Chinese were said to make up a third of the population of Khabarovsk; they lived in a special 'Chinese village' on the banks of the Amur.[16] Chinese workers were employed as labourers on the Ussuri branch of the railway.[17] Large Chinese and Korean quarters were established in Vladivostok.

Sensitivity to the presence of foreigners in Siberia increased as tensions within Europe grew before 1914. In 1913, the police reported on a party of five Chinese – four adults and a boy – in the town of Mariinsk (in the river Ob basin) about whom there were suspicions as one of them had a notebook in which he had drawn a map of roads with 'secret marks' and 'Chinese marks'. The police feared they were spies, so arrested and held them for a month. They also listed all foreigners in the region, including three British citizens and Germans, Austrians, Danes and one American. Captain Douglas-Pennant from London was studying fauna; other foreigners were attached to commercial firms in various capacities.[18]

The Trans-Siberian railway was as significant for Russia domestically as it was for its international position. In 1861, Alexander II emancipated the serfs. This act was of fundamental importance in the social and political development of Russia, although of less immediate consequence for Siberia, but the Trans-Siberian railway played a vital role in the years after emancipation as peasants moved east from European Russia to Siberia.

Serfs in European Russia were allotted part of their landowners' estates, but the amount and quality of land they received depended greatly on local circumstances and they had to pay for it over many years. There were, however, as we saw in earlier chapters, very few serfs in Siberia because there were very few serf-owners: one estimate is that there were some 3,700 serfs in all of Siberia in 1861. Inevitably, the few estates which were owned by nobles (perhaps in the region of 30, and almost all in western Siberia) were affected by the Act of Emancipation: for example, the village of Tigin in Eniseisk province, owned by a nobleman called Sukhotin, who had first moved seven serfs there in 1703, divided its lands among the peasants after 1861.[19]

There were, however, many so-called 'factory peasants' in Siberia who were originally serfs and who had been moved to the factories by their noble owners in the seventeenth and eighteenth centuries. By 1861, there were probably some 150,000 peasants in the Altai region and over 58,000 in the Nerchinsk mines.[20] Many had in fact become regular factory workers, but after 1821 some of them had lost rights to what had been communal land, such as woods which were vital for timber and firewood. In the Urals, factory peasants complained of hardships in the wake of the emancipation when 'all our former enserfed peasants became artisans', and some asked to be resettled in Siberia.[21] Factory peasants in one village in the Altai region asked if their commune was still allowed to expel unruly members for a variety of misdemeanours, which included 'playing cards, being workshy, wastefulness, drunkenness, and petty theft'.[22] The emancipation of the serfs also had an impact on Cossack communities in Siberia, which lost many of their distinct rights, obligations and structures, so that their members became, in effect, little different from state peasants.

The main impact for Siberia, however, lay in the fact that the terms of the Emancipation Act enabled more peasants to leave their villages in European Russia. The result was a mass migration to Siberia from European Russia, followed by another wave after 1906, as we shall see below. Numbers of migrants rose during the 1890s, with the peak year being 1896, when over 177,000 peasants and their families crossed the Urals.

Migrants were given financial help by the government to travel, although many came without assistance. Transporting such large quantities of people brought its own challenges. Special low fares – along with the use of cattle trucks – enabled more to move. Local authorities set up field kitchens and medical posts to help the most vulnerable.[23] Visitors to Siberia could not help but be struck by this vast movement of people. One commented in 1897: 'Emigration to Siberia is now going on very vigorously'; the traveller 'passes train load after train load of outward-bound emigration'.[24] Three years later, another commented: 'Emigrants meet you at every turn of the Siberian railway and on river steamers.'[25]

Peasants left their homes for the most practical of reasons – poverty and land shortage. Some may have been influenced by the rosy picture of life painted in letters, whether authentic or not, from peasants already settled in Siberia, which were read out by Russian officials to the peasants in villages in European Russia; 'we drink tea every day and only eat white bread; we never bake rye,' claimed one; 'here the peasants live like [noble] landowners in Russia,' asserted another.[26] This was not so different, as we shall see, from the appeal for young people to start a new and enriching life in the far east in the early Soviet period.

The arrival of new settlers and the allocation of land to them inevitably led to strains and conflicts with longer-established residents, whether Russian or indigenous. 'Old' settlers referred disparagingly to newcomers as 'Russians' and to themselves as 'Sibiriaki'.[27] In Tomsk province, 35 'natives' in the village of Zharkovka complained that 100 new Russian settlers had arrived from European Russia in 1887 and had taken their land, and they had been followed by another 300 settlers the following year from Kursk province (in the south). The original settlers claimed they were 'ruined' by the loss of their land.[28] Buriats and Iakuts clashed with newcomers in Iakutsk province in the 1890s. Ethnic Germans who had lived in the Volga region since the eighteenth century now sought their fortune in Siberia. They clashed violently with both fellow new settlers from Russia and Ukraine and with old settlers; in the 'bitter fights' which followed, several German settlers were killed.[29] Repartitioning of land became more common within Siberian villages in the 1880s as pressure on the land increased, in turn increasing the power of the peasant communes responsible for the reallocation.

In 1905–7, there were serious disturbances all over the Russian country-side (and in the towns, as discussed below) during and in the wake of the defeat in the Russo-Japanese War. Outbreaks of violence occurred in the countryside in Siberia between old and new settlers, between new settlers and Buriats, Tatars and Iakuts, and in Cossack villages. Radical thinkers in the towns penetrated the villages and organised political meetings. Some of the demands which emanated from these meetings were clearly influenced by events in St Petersburg. Other demands related to more traditional concerns such as the levels of taxation and other dues (the poll tax was abolished in Siberia only in 1899, later than in European Russia, and tribute as a levy on indigenous peoples was not abolished until 1917). Many related to purely local matters, such as access to fishing and firewood, issues that were exacerbated in Siberia by the influx of new settlers who were also claiming access to these resources. The disturbances were most frequent in western Siberia, where the majority of the new arrivals had settled and where resentments about the loss and redistribution of land were greatest. Clashes between old and new settlers over land, dues and access to communal lands and woodland continued after the war with Japan and Tsar Nicholas II's granting of constitutional reforms in 1905.[30]

Migration of peasants to Siberia was boosted further after 1906 as a result of the agricultural reforms of the new Prime Minister Petr Stolypin. Stolypin was aware of the limitations of the Emancipation Act for the modernisation of agriculture, and indeed for the modernisation of the Russian economy and society in general. He was also aware, particularly after the disturbances in 1905–7, that dissatisfied peasants posed a threat to the social and political order in Russia. He wanted, in his words, to create the 'diligent farmer' who would become an 'independent, prosperous husbandmen, and a stable citizen of the land' – in other words, peasants with a stake in the political system. Ultimately, he hoped that peasants would become fully integrated into the wider social order and help create a genuine 'civic society' in Russia.[31]

The Stolypin reforms in the period 1906–11 encouraged peasant communes to dissolve their collective responsibilities and abandon the strip system of agriculture, reconstituting their whole village as separate farms. If a village were unwilling to do this, then individual peasants were permitted to split off from the commune and set up their own, separate farmsteads. To help communes and individual peasants, financial support from Russian state banks was increased and resettlement facilitated. The Stolypin reforms applied primarily to European Russia but some peasant communes and individual peasants in Siberia did take advantage of them. Some 10,000 peasants, mainly old settlers, set up as independent households in Siberia.[32]

A far greater impact of the Stolypin reforms on Siberia, however, was the increased migration of peasants after 1906 via rail as a result of restrictions being lifted on their movement away from their villages. The eagerness of peasants to take up these opportunities surprised the government. In European Russia, the Stolypin reforms were taken up particularly in the north-west and in an arc in southern Russia leading to the Volga, with many of the poorer peasants from these regions choosing to migrate to Siberia. In one village in Volhynia, in the west, for example, 22 households applied to resettle in Siberia.[33]

The number of migrants rose after 1906 and reached some 600,000 per year over the next three years, and only dropped back again after 1911. The population of Siberia rose from 5.8 million in 1893 to over 10 million in 1913, that is, at twice the rate of the population rise in European Russia.[34] The figures are not precise but in the period 1885–1914 over 3 million people moved to Siberia (of whom only some 500,000 later returned home).[35] This was the Russian equivalent of the mass emigration from Europe to the United States, and it was the construction of the Trans-Siberian railway that made it possible.

More settlers came to western Siberia than to eastern Siberia or the newly acquired Amur basin and the far east: the population density in Tomsk province doubled.[36] Areas in less densely populated eastern Siberia were, however, cultivated for the first time as a result of migration. In all, the amount of land cultivated in Siberia almost doubled in this period. Siberia – portrayed earlier as an involuntary prison for undesirables and unfortunates – had become the land of opportunity and freedom for many peasants trying to escape poverty, and in some case near-starvation, in European Russia.

It is impossible to know what the long-term effects of these reforms would have been on the peasantry, and on the economy and society in general, had there been greater international stability and war not broken out in 1914, followed by the domestic revolutions of 1917. In 1908, a survey was made of peasant agriculture in the villages in European Russia which had broken away from the commune system. It found that crop yields in the southern provinces were not much higher than in the villages where no such change had taken place. There had, however, been some moves to specialisation and diversification of crops in the north-west of the country. Breaking up the commune could only take place where local conditions favoured it, and that included easy access for 'separators' to woods and a water supply. The reality was that few peasants would take the risk of breaking with traditional agriculture.

Peasants who migrated to Siberia had always done so to acquire more land rather than to change their agricultural methods. The land was allocated to them by the state, which also provided them with some initial assistance with grain and equipment (as it had done with earlier settlers in the seventeenth and eighteenth centuries) but there was no particular encouragement for them to change their agricultural methods. Incentives for change came instead from the opportunities which arose with the Trans-Siberian railway.

The railway allowed the export of grain and other agricultural products to European Russia and abroad. The majority of new arrivals settled within reach of the railway line. The output of arable crops, and wheat in particular, increased markedly in the early twentieth century. Grain exports from Siberia tripled from 1900 to 1914. Exports of all Siberian products to European Russia doubled in the same period, and were further helped by the abolition in 1913 of an internal customs duty on Siberian grain which had been levied as goods crossed the Ural mountains. By 1917, Siberia exported some 30 per cent of its grain. One traveller saw Siberia as one of 'the ultimate food-producing regions of the earth. .... I tell you Siberia is going to be another America.'[37] Siberia, from being the icy wilderness of popular imagination, had become the breadbasket of the Russian empire and a valuable source of foreign currency.

Even more striking was the development of dairy exports. Butter production soared and by 1914 had become the most valuable export from Siberia after grain, flax and wood. The first industrial creamery was set up in the Kurgan district of Tobolsk province in 1894; by 1913, there were over 4,000 creameries in Siberia. Peasant communes reconstituted themselves as butter cooperatives. The Union of Siberian Butter-Making Cooperatives represented over 1,000 creameries, supported by capital from Denmark. By 1914, 90 per cent of Russia's butter exports came from Siberia, almost all of it transported along the railway line in refrigerated compartments. Siberian butter was exported all over the world, in particular to Britain, Germany and France.[38]

Were peasants richer in Siberia? This was a popular belief, and a major reason why peasants were tempted to resettle there. It is true that some of the older settlers had very large land holdings and extensive property. A major indicator of wealth was the number of horses owned by a household; these were required for ploughing. In 1912, over half of the households in Siberia had four or more horses, compared with only 10 per cent in European Russia. In the period 1900–13, the sale of agricultural machinery increased sixteenfold in Siberia compared with a fourfold increase in European Russia.[39] All this points to prosperity and the modernisation of agriculture in at least some parts of Siberia. It is less clear that new settlers benefited to the same extent in the short term. Certainly the *perception*, if not the reality, that some Siberian peasants were prosperous underpinned the devastating policies of 'dekulakisation' and collectivisation in the 1930s.

The Trans-Siberian railway also led to the growth of Siberian towns and created a distinction between urban and village life which had not existed in the eighteenth and early nineteenth centuries. The total urban population more than doubled between 1897 and 1917.[40] The largest growth occurred in towns along the railway line. Omsk (which had replaced Tobolsk as the main administrative centre of western Siberia in 1824) tripled in size and became a centre for commerce as the railway arrived. The railway station was the pride of the town:

> You pass into the usual hall which is waiting-room and restaurant combined; well-set tables with tall palms – imitation palms of course – standing in them, and tall crystal candelabra veiled in red muslin. At one side is the tea-counter, its brass samovar purring softly; at another a display of hot dishes to tempt the hungry, with a chef of smiling face and much-stained linen waving his knife above the baked meats.[41]

Irkutsk's population grew from 51,484 in 1897 to 113,288 in 1911.[42] A traveller in 1901 found the streets still dirty and unpaved but commented that the railway had 'done wonders. . . . Its inhabitants no longer feel themselves isolated from the rest of the world.'[43] Thanks to the railway, some towns grew seemingly overnight from almost nothing into lively centres. Novo-Nikolaevsk (renamed Novosibirsk in 1926), positioned at a railway junction on the river Ob, was transformed from a village into a town. By 1912, it had 32 primary schools, a library, a cinema and ten local papers, and boasted a society which supported primary education.[44] By 1914, it had a population of 80,000 people.

At the same time, towns which were not on the main route declined. Tomsk was only linked by a branch line to the Trans-Siberian railway. As a result, one traveller in 1897 suggested that it was 'stranded', with 'the doom of the city almost sealed'.[45] This was an exaggeration – Tomsk remained an important administrative, commercial and cultural centre – but some of its economic importance did shift to Omsk, a town which would play a key role in the Russian Civil War of 1918–21. The town of Kainsk was not only significant as a commercial centre but was also noted for its Jewish merchant population. By 1897, there were 924 Jewish families in the town,[46] and this rose to around 8,000 over the next decade. Kainsk was not, however, on the railway line and as a result declined in economic significance. By 1913, there were only about 1,000 Jews in Kainsk.[47] The town, which had been known as the 'Siberian Jerusalem', was in terminal decline, not because of any government policy towards Jews or as a result of local pogroms or anti-Semitism, but simply because of the route taken by the Trans-Siberian railway.

Siberia remained predominantly rural and agrarian. Most commercial firms remained small and in family ownership, but some industries expanded as a result of new communications, leading to changes in the location and occupations of Siberians. The railway enabled coal to be exported; output increased dramatically from the end of the century to 1917. There was also a significant expansion in the production and export of textiles, forestry prod-ucts, fish, processed food and alcohol. Foreign investment in the mining industry increased, as did foreign imports of agricultural machinery and other goods. By the end of the nineteenth century, there were 12 central banks operating in Siberia, and local banks had opened in larger towns such as Tomsk and Omsk.

The reforms in the reign of Alexander II affected towns as well as villages. In the 1870s and 1890s, new urban institutions were established. Property qualifications were set for elected urban officials, which in effect restricted post-holders to wealthy merchants and entrepreneurs. At the same time, towns were given greater responsibility for their affairs, including social welfare, hospitals, hygiene, fire prevention and education. This was an attempt – and not the first – by the government in St Petersburg to stimulate urban self-administration and create a sense of 'civic responsibility'.

One reason we know as much as we do about the civic and cultural life of Siberian towns is that many of them now had local newspapers and cultural journals which recorded their activities. The *Siberian Spectator*, for example, noted how much was spent in Tomsk on constructing new bridges and restoring public buildings,[48] and how much was spent in Krasnoiarsk on welfare institutions. Local publications could be critical as well as self-congratulatory, in itself a sign of growing civic maturity. *Siberian Questions*, for example, in 1909 criticised the dirty streets in the town of Kurgan and elsewhere.[49]

The physical appearance and material quality of towns improved. Tramways were laid in the larger towns in the early twentieth century. The first telephone system was opened in Tomsk in 1894 with 115 numbers; by 1916, there were 1,236 lines.[50] The museum in Khabarovsk today houses the interior of a prosperous merchant's house from the turn of the century, complete with clocks, books, furnishings, the local paper and a telephone. This period also saw a significant increase in urban buildings – department stores, private houses and public buildings including libraries, museums, theatres and schools. Buildings were in eclectic styles but some of them incorporated regional, Siberian features in the motifs on their façades.[51] A newfound pride in Siberian heritage merged with the best of modern, European style.

The most significant advances came in the expansion of educational and cultural facilities, mainly if not exclusively in towns. Literacy rates at the end of the nineteenth century were lower in Siberia than in European Russia (some 11 per cent in Siberia compared with about 20 per cent for European Russia), a point not lost on one of the contributors to *Siberian Questions*.[52] In 1897, there were only 1,134 schools in Siberia, that is, about 1 school per some 6,000 people.[53] By 1910, the literacy rate had improved to about 18 per cent. By 1911, the number of schools had increased to 4,385, of which 2,136 were state and 2,249 were run by the Church. This represented a significant improvement, although the author of the piece in *Siberian Questions* pointed out that this was still far too few.[54] A report on Omsk in 1881 noted that there were only 10 primary schools in the town while there were 100 establishments for drinking. By 1910, it was estimated that there were 4,656 pupils of both sexes in the town, including small numbers of Muslim and Jewish children.[55] In 1897, some 25 per cent of children in Khabarovsk and 20 per cent of children in Vladivostok were receiving an education, but this figure dropped to 10 per cent in the Okhotsk region.[56] The expansion of schools was in part due to private philanthropy, in itself a sign of an emerging civic society. Mikhail Butin, a prominent local industrialist and silver-mine owner, donated money for schools in Irkutsk and Nerchinsk, including village schools. His home and its library and other collections were bequeathed to the town of Nerchinsk.[57]

One of the main demands of the Siberian regionalists (discussed below) in the late nineteenth century was for a university. The University of Tomsk was founded in 1878 and started teaching in 1888. By 1905, it had 676 students; women were permitted to attend the following year. Private philanthropy was also behind the foundation of Tomsk University. The newly educated young people acquired radical ideas and played a role in the disturbances in 1905. In Tomsk, political discussion groups radicalised both pupils in the grammar school and students at the university.[58] One meeting at the university in 1905 attracted some 5,000 people.[59]

Cultural life flourished in the main towns and even in smaller settlements. Vladivostok was unique as a port on the Pacific Ocean, hosting sailors and traders from all over the world. In 1873, an orchestra from the Siberian fleet performed a musical accompaniment to a performance of *Hamlet* in Vladivostok.[60] In 1879, visiting ships from the United States, Britain, Germany and Japan staged musical shows in the town. By 1906, there were ten military orchestras in Vladivostok. The town opened a music school in 1900; its activities were interrupted by the Russo-Japanese War, but it had over 1,000 pupils by 1914. The town also had two theatres and an opera house. In the 1900–1 season, the latter staged *Othello, La Traviata, Rigoletto, A Masked Ball, Aida, Faust, Romeo and Juliet,* and *Samson and Delilah,* as well as works by Russian composers.

The Russian Imperial Geographical Society was founded 1845 (the British Royal Geographical Society was founded in 1830) and soon established itself as an important patron of expeditions and collections of geographical, scientific and ethnographical materials. The vigour of local intellectual society can be seen by the founding of Siberian branches of the Society in Khabarovsk and Vladivostok. In Khabarovsk, for example, the Priamur section of the Geographical Society was founded in 1894 under the presidency of the governor-general. It immediately acquired members (93 attended the opening meeting and membership had grown to 248 by 1898)[61] and donors, primarily comprising officials and wealthy merchants but also local 'intelligentsia' including doctors, teachers, architects and surveyors.[62] One prominent member was the Chinese merchant Tifontai, who took Russian citizenship and was a key benefactor of the town library.[63] The Khabarovsk branch organised lectures on a range of topics, including local flora, fauna, topography, birds, the indigenous population and non-Christian religious practices, and also funded the town library and museum through subscriptions and donations of money, artefacts and books. In all, over 10,000 exhibits and over 60,000 books were donated to the museum and the library. The Society ceased to function in 1920, after the establishment of the Bolshevik regime.

The range of social activities in Siberian towns can be seen from a survey conducted in 1907 in Tomsk province of theatres, public gardens and societies. The largest number of these – 18 – were based in the town of Tomsk itself, and included a theatre, an exhibition hall, public gardens, a musical society and restaurants which staged plays and concerts. The smaller town of Biisk listed seven establishments, including a public garden, societies and clubs. In Barnaul, there was a winter and a summer theatre, public gardens and cultural clubs. There were even a few societies and clubs in villages in Tomsk province. The large village of Zmeinogorsk (it was granted town status in 1952) in the Altai region, for example, had a building where the villagers put on plays, a cultural society with 50 members and a musical-drama society. Other villages had cultural groups which charged small subscription fees.[64]

Cultural activities could follow the railway line. A special 'railway company' was set up to encourage cultural events. In 1899, it established a presence in Harbin (Kharbin), at that time an ethnically Russian town in Manchuria. Its activities were interrupted by the Russo-Japanese War, but it was operating again by 1911 and staged theatrical and musical events.[65] Travelling groups from other parts of the Russian empire could now reach Siberian towns by rail. A group from Ukraine visited Port Arthur and Khabarovsk in 1900.

Industrial expansion in the late nineteenth century in Siberia led to an increase in the number of industrial workers, both inside and outside towns. It is hard to be precise about numbers – there were ideological reasons why Soviet historians exaggerated the number of industrial workers and their concentration in certain factories. One estimate is that the number of industrial workers in Siberia almost doubled from 250,000 in 1897 to approximately

500,000 in 1913. The largest concentration of factory workers was in the gold mines: there were over 34,000 by the 1890s in western and eastern Siberia.[66] Most enterprises remained small and employed under 100 workers. Conditions in factories could be very poor, and 13- to 16-hour days were common. In Omsk in 1897, a tobacco factory employed boys and girls, aged between 10 and 12, who worked from six in the morning to eight in the evening.[67] Conditions in the gold mines, originally manned by convicts, were particularly poor, and this was the root cause of the strike in 1912, described below.

At the peak of the construction of the Trans-Siberian railway in 1895–6, there were some 80,000 railway workers on the line;[68] they had come from all over European Russia. The majority were unskilled, single young men, displaced from their homes and families, living together in barracks and working in often very difficult conditions. Reports of penalties for offences committed by workers on the Ussuri branch of the railway in 1899 show the extent to which drunkenness, fights and disorderly behaviour were common: one Grigorii Malakhov, for example, was sacked for 'drunkenness, unruliness, fights and abusive language'.[69] In 1896, over 1,000 convicts worked on the Ussuri section of the line.[70] The number of railway workers dropped sharply as the line was completed and may have been as few as 5,300 by 1904.[71] Railway workers could pose a threat to social order as they were concentrated in a few key places on the line; skilled workers on the railway, such as telegraph workers, played an important role in communications.

In 1905, there were large-scale strikes in Chita and Krasnoiarsk on the railway line. Railway workers combined with other workers and soldiers, many of whom were garrisoned in towns along the railway. The Krasnoiarsk strike in late 1905 involved some 3,000 men; a workers' and soldiers' soviet, or council, was set up.[72] It was also claimed that the 'lower ranks' of soldiers in Krasnoiarsk had 'come into contact with political exiles and had shaken hands with them'.[73]

Serious disorders took place in Vladivostok in 1905, involving a potent social mix of industrial workers, soldiers, sailors and railway workers. In October, there were mass demonstrations, initially started by sailors but joined by soldiers in the Khabarovsk reserve regiment stationed in the Vladivostok garrison. The demonstration soon turned violent. Prisoners were liberated from jail and the main guardhouse was destroyed; this was then followed by looting, especially of liquor shops, leading to a 'terrible picture of drunkenness and destruction' in local restaurants, as one eyewitness commented.[74] Railway workers on the Ussuri section of track formed their own revolutionary committee. The imposition of martial law could not prevent further disorders. Another demonstration on 10 January 1906 was dispersed by the army, with some 80 men killed or wounded in the process. The garrison mutinied and for a couple of weeks the town was in the hands of rebel soldiers and sailors, until loyal troops re-entered the town and brutally put down the uprising.

The level of violence dropped in Siberia after 1907, but the tensions remained. A strike was called in April 1912 in the gold fields on the river Lena in north-eastern Siberia over the appalling working conditions and levels of pay. These complaints were more economic than strictly political – about the length of the working day and the requirement to buy food at inflated prices in the factory stores. The factory administration refused to negotiate and the strike committee was arrested. Troops were sent in and fired on workers who were marching to demand the release of their strike committee; 230 people were killed and over 500 wounded.[75] News of the massacre sparked protests all over Russia and reignited worker militancy.

The late nineteenth century saw the radicalisation of some of the peasantry and workers. It was also the time, however, when the first, tentative sense of a separate Siberian identity made itself felt, a product of the new social and economic developments and a corresponding newfound confidence in the future of Siberia.

In 1865, the authorities discovered a publication in Omsk entitled *To the Patriots of Siberia* which called for 'the separation of Siberia from Russia and its establishment as a republic composed of federated states similar to those of North America'.[76] This was an isolated incident, but by the 1880s a regionalist group had emerged.[77] Its members included the intellectuals Petr Slovtsov, a historian whose works portrayed the exploitation of Siberia by the government in St Petersburg, Nikolai Iadrintsev, whose *Siberia as a Colony*, published in 1882, was a powerful critique of the way Siberia had been used and exploited as a 'colony', and the writer Grigorii Potanin. The group called for the reform of the exile system, which they claimed was harming Siberian development, greater investment in economic development within Siberia so that its natural resources were not simply exploited by the centre, the establishment of more educational institutions, especially at the higher level, and the adoption of new, less harmful policies towards indigenous peoples who, they believed, might become extinct if there was no intervention.

This movement was a product of the discussions around the great reforms in Russia of the 1860s and 1870s, which raised questions about the active role that 'society' should play in government at a national as well as a local level. In the Siberian case, this discussion went beyond the desire to participate or mould local institutions, and beyond a local 'patriotism' to a particular region or town. Siberia was so vast that there was a feeling among this group that some regional autonomy was merited and feasible.

At a local level, the group was influenced by the unique social composition of Siberia: the almost complete lack of a landowning nobility and serfdom, the ethnic composition of the population and the presence of educated exiles. It was also influenced by the experience of North America: its members saw parallels between Siberia and the United States and Canada, both in size and in the perceived 'civilising' role played by Europeans in conquering almost empty lands and opening up new frontiers. In this way, the group shared the sense of destiny which was so evident in the hopes placed in the acquisition of the river Amur, and the conviction that Russians, like other Europeans, had a special role to play in the broader global civilising mission. The federal system of government in the United States appealed in particular to Siberian thinkers as this model could give Siberia some autonomy within the Russian empire.

The Siberian group was not extreme in its aspirations: its members did not seek independence, nor did they produce a political manifesto. They had a desire for the region to be regarded as distinct from European Russia – but there was still a dependence on the centre, whether for colonists, supplies, military support or the spread of cultural and educational institutions. They argued that Siberia was different but still wanted the best that European Russia, and European culture, could offer, such as universities and cultural journals. They wanted Siberia and Siberians to share in Russian literature and did not seek to create a separate Siberian literature. They saw the social composition of Siberia as something which made the region distinct and special – but separate groups within Siberia, such as Cossacks, non-Russian groups of settlers and indigenous peoples, as well as industrial workers and peasants, all had their own interests and this weakened an all-Siberian approach. The regions within Siberia were also very different: the west was far more settled and urbanised than the east and the newly acquired territories along the Amur were frontier towns, outposts of Russianness on the Chinese border.

Above all, it was difficult to sustain ideas of regional autonomy at a time when new notions were beginning to penetrate into Siberia as well as into the more economically developed parts of the Russian empire. Iadrintsev died in 1894, by which time Marxism was becoming more influential, making regionalism seem parochial to some. Potanin developed further ideas on Siberian separatism in the early twentieth century; in 1905, he called for an elected regional duma. The next brief flowering of Siberian separatism was to be under very different circumstances, during the Revolutions and Civil War.

By the last quarter of the nineteenth century, Russia and Siberia were both entering a new era. In the early twentieth century, Siberian society was dynamic and self-confident. One traveller in 1903 went as far as to say: 'the influence of the railway, which is rapidly converting insignificant villages into prosperous towns, has done away with the terror of the exile system'.[78] This confidence was to be shattered, however, by events which took place far from Siberia but which were to have a devastating effect on the region and on the whole of the Russian empire.

CHAPTER THIRTEEN

Wars and Revolutions

T HE CAMPAIGNS of the First World War (1914–18) took place far away
from Siberia. The Revolutions of February and October 1917 broke out
in Petrograd, over 2,000 miles (over 3,000 kilometres) west of Omsk. The
sons, husbands and fathers of Siberians were involved in these cataclysmic
events but the region itself was relatively quiet during this time. Siberia,
however, became a key battleground during the Civil War (1918–21). It was
the location of several organs of government which, at various times and in
various towns, challenged Bolshevik rule. Battles between Whites and Reds
were fought in western Siberia, with peasants being conscripted to both
armies. Eastern Siberia was ravaged by the brutal Cossack warlords and the
far east was occupied by Japanese forces. White and Red terror was inflicted
on peasants and townspeople alike. Armies, deserters, prisoners of war, refugees and, finally, the desperate remnants of the White forces crossed Siberia,
trailing destruction, disease and chaos in their wake. Above all, lives were
wrecked: family members killed, injured, infected with disease or trauma-
tised; individuals, families and whole villages uprooted; property, crops and
livelihoods destroyed. Siberia, which had entered the new century with such
confidence, emerged from the Civil War a shattered land.

The outbreak of war in August 1914 led to the immediate mobilisation of
some 4 million men in the Russian empire. During the period 1914–17, at
least 14 million men (and possibly as many as 17 million) were conscripted
from a population of 180 million. Russia conscripted fewer men per head of
population than other powers: France called up a similar number of men
from a population of 40 million and Germany called up more men from a

population of 65 million.[1] Nevertheless, conscription had a significant economic and human cost. Some 24 per cent of all males in the Russian empire were conscripted during the war, and some 49 per cent of able-bodied men served in the army.[2] By July 1916, 600,000 had been conscripted from Tomsk province alone.[3]

By 1915, boys who were only sons were being conscripted, with the result that some peasant households lost all their able-bodied males. In practice, exemptions in place for 'breadwinners' were ignored: wives lost their husbands; children lost their fathers. In a scene which would be familiar elsewhere in Europe, Eleonora Prey in Vladivostok recounted as early as October 1914 coming across a woman with a tiny baby and a small boy of 11. She was weeping, she said, because she had spent all day trying to find her husband whose regiment was leaving for the front and she feared that they would never see him again.[4]

The Russian losses were horrific. Official figures estimate that some 900,000 men died in battle and 400,000 from combat wounds, a total of around 1.3 million, but the actual numbers might be far higher, with perhaps as many as 2 million men dead. The largest single loss of men occurred in the early stages of the war, when the Russian Second Army was almost destroyed by the Germans at the Battle of Tannenberg with the loss of some 80,000 men. Many more soldiers were wounded and maimed, and almost 4 million Russian soldiers were taken as prisoners of war by the Germans and Austrians. An indication of the human cost can be seen in the lists of dead and wounded men in the *Tomsk Diocesan News* for the week 27 December 1914 to 3 January 1915, which also showed how many married men had already been conscripted. In this week alone, 14 local men died (3 of whom were junior officers). Far more men were wounded during this one week – 41 in total. They included, for example, Stepan Leontovich, a rifleman, who had a wife and four children, and who was wounded in the leg and given six months' leave; Vasilii Grigorev, a lance corporal, who had a wife and six children and who was discharged an account of sickness; Fedor Kondrashev, who had a wife and three children, and who was wounded in his left side, his left ear and finger by a shell was also fully discharged. Only some of these 41 men would return to action or be fit to resume work in the village.[5]

Siberia was far from the war zone and did not suffer from the disruption and destruction caused elsewhere by the passage of troops. Nevertheless, the war had a significant impact on agricultural practice and production. The loss of manpower in the countryside was in part made up for by the presence of prisoners of war who could be used for labour, as they had been in Siberia in the eighteenth and nineteenth centuries. In Tomsk province alone, there were 22,451 prisoners of war in May 1915, including Germans, Hungarians, Romanians and 'Slavs'.[6] Prisoners, however, could not necessarily carry out the work required in the village and, in any event, many of them were wounded and sick or brought diseases with them. The army expropriated over 2 million horses during the war, and horses were essential for agriculture. In Tomsk province again, over 50,000 horses were taken by the army in 1914 and 1915 (over 18,000 from Tomsk district alone).[7] Nevertheless, while the area of land sown and crop production probably dropped in European Russia in 1916–17, it grew in Siberia by some 37 per cent.[8]

In the towns, there had been patriotic demonstrations when war broke out. In the war years, however, townspeople suffered badly from economic dislocation and loss of services. The price of basic foodstuffs and other goods rose as supplies worsened. Disorderly behaviour increased and attempts to limit the sale of vodka were unsuccessful. Prisoners of war passed through Siberian towns; groups of prisoners begged for bread, coffee and tobacco in the streets of Tomsk. Refugees fled from the war zones to Siberian towns: 200 were housed in temporary barracks in Tomsk; large numbers arrived in Irkutsk, some of whom had to resort to begging in the main street.[9] Overcrowded prisons and hospitals caring for wounded soldiers and prisoners of war and the presence of so many refugees inevitably led to outbreaks of typhus, diphtheria, dysentery and other infectious diseases. This offered only a foretaste of the far greater disruption and suffering that would afflict Siberian towns during the Civil War.

In February 1917, demonstrations on the streets of Petrograd and Moscow and mutinies among the troops led to the abdication of Nicholas II. The news of the February Revolution reached Anadyr, in the remote north-east, at the beginning of March 1917, when, reported one: 'A Russian worker, Kashirin, told us about the holiday on 1 May and that on this day we join with simple working people of all the world and struggle for happiness and a good life.'[10]

After the February Revolution, the organs of administration in the Russian provinces mirrored those in Petrograd, where there was an uneasy sharing of power between the Provisional Government (comprising some members of the former State Duma, an elected parliament which had been in existence since 1906) and the Petrograd Soviet, comprising workers, soldiers and sailors who were members of socialist parties. In Siberia, the old governing bodies in the towns now coexisted with newly elected local soviets, or councils, of workers, soldiers and sailors, and factory committees.[11] After February 1917, organs of rural self-government, called *zemstva*, were extended from European Russia, where they had been set up in 1864, to Siberia, but they came too late, and in extremely difficult circumstances, to make much difference to peasant representation.

Siberia had only a small Bolshevik presence before the October Revolution. The Socialist Revolutionaries (SRs) were the most popular socialist party in Siberia, and in Russia generally. They had roots in a late nineteenth-century Russian populist movement which believed that the peasants, and peasant communes, could forge a unique path to socialism. The SRs differed from the other socialist parties – the Bolsheviks and the Mensheviks – in that they considered the peasants as part of the larger 'toiling class' alongside workers and believed that they had revolutionary potential.

Most Siberian soviets operating between February and October 1917 had a mixed membership drawn from socialist parties, and were for the most part prepared to work alongside the traditional organs of local administration. Only in Krasnoiarsk, where there were factories and a considerable number of railway workers, was the soviet more radical, calling for an immediate confiscation of private property and an end to the 'bourgeois' First World War.[12] Siberia generally lacked the concentration of urban workers, soldiers and sailors which was so toxic in Petrograd. It has been estimated that there were 960 strikes in Siberia between February to October,[13] but these were not on the same scale as those in European Russia, or the strike by the Lena gold workers in 1912.

One main difference between Siberia and European Russia was that the land question was less acute in the former. There were very few landowners in Siberia, so there was little call for the seizure of their land. Disorders took place between August and October 1917 in the Siberian countryside; many of the underlying causes, as in European Russia, were to do with such traditional matters as the cutting of wood, the use of communal land, and payments of dues and leases.[14] Many of the peasant committees set up after the February Revolution in Siberia were traditional in composition: an analysis of 110 village committees in the period March–June 1917 shows that they included some members of the rural 'intelligentsia' (such as teachers and clerks) and even members of the clergy. The richer peasants dominated these committees, just as they had formerly dominated the peasant communes.[15] This is not to say that there were no tensions in the Siberian countryside in 1917. There were conflicts between wealthier old settlers and poorer new settlers, as there had been ever since 1905. The return of peasant soldiers to the villages from the front could also be disruptive as they might dominate meetings and spread new ideas. There were, however, fewer desperate, land-hungry peasants in Siberia than in European Russia.

Events far away had an impact on workers, soldiers and young people, and gave them a strong sense that they now had a voice. A certain Sviridov, who was at school in Vladivostok in 1917, described the excitement of those days in his memoirs. He recalled 'meetings, gatherings, demonstrations, legalising parties, establishing trades unions, unions of invalids [old soldiers]'. He was chosen as a representative of his local grammar school. He and other students met in a café, in the daytime, because there were fewer customers at that time. 'We all thirsted to be involved in revolutionary activity,' he recalled. He was involved in meetings where Bolsheviks, SRs and Mensheviks all put their views forward. He distributed Bolshevik material at his school, where he declared he was the only Bolshevik in his class, and was involved in a school strike. In 1918, he was sent to western Russia to fight the Cossacks.[16] Eleonora Prey recalled the demonstrations and meetings in the summer of 1917 in Vladivostok, and the naivety of some of those who were involved. They thought 'the money in the banks was theirs and the goods in the shops'. One person in the crowd had a very nice coat and one of the demonstrators demanded it with the words: 'in accordance with these principles give me your coat as I haven't got one'.[17]

The period between the February and October Revolutions also saw a revival of Siberian regionalism. Nikolai Iadrintsev, one the main leaders of the movement, had died in 1894, but another leading figure, Grigorii Potanin, was still alive, now aged 82. In May 1917, an All-Siberian Regional Duma was set up in Tomsk under his leadership. It declared its own authority as a duma, called for self-government and produced its own Siberian flag: it was a rather attractive design comprising two white and green triangles to signify Siberia's most obvious natural features – snow and forest. Other small regionalist groups were set up in other Siberian towns. Most of the regionalists looked to the SRs because they favoured a federal state and some degree of autonomy for non-Russian peoples: 70 of the 179 delegates in the Tomsk Duma identified themselves as SRs and another 25 were sympathetic to the party.[18]

The tragedy for the regionalist groups was that when they at last had a chance to assert their concerns the government and the population were focused on very different issues. Workers and peasants had other, more pressing concerns and, in any event, the regionalists had limited means to get their message across. A peasant resolution made in Novo-Nikolaevsk (renamed Novosibirsk in 1926) in January 1918 was terse: 'the question about autonomy of Siberia is considered undesirable'.[19] The reality was that such aspirations and ideas were limited mainly to a small circle linked to Tomsk University.

The period between February and October 1917 also encouraged ideas of separatism among the indigenous peoples of Siberia, who numbered over 2 million by 1911.[20] Ethnic groups formed their own organisations and declared their autonomy, just as autonomy for the whole of Siberia was being proposed in Tomsk. Buriats established a National Buriat Duma in April 1917 to take over their own judicial and administrative affairs. Iakuts formed their own Public Safety Committee in Iakutsk, made up of Iakut nationalists, SRs, Mensheviks and Bolsheviks (power in Iakutia changed hands several times during the Civil War). In May 1917, a 'People's Assembly' convened in Tomsk with representatives from several groups of native peoples. In July 1917, a Bashkir Congress took place in Ufa and declared Bashkir autonomy. Small and isolated towns in Kamchatka and the far north-east also established their own committees and assemblies.

The Bolsheviks overthrew the Provisional Government in October 1917. Following this, demonstrations against them were held in Omsk, Irkutsk and Novo-Nikolaevsk. In Tiumen, news about the October Revolution reached the town two days after the event.[21] Most people assumed that this was only a temporary state of affairs and that it would be overturned by the Constituent Assembly, the elections for which took place just after the Bolshevik Revolution. It was popularly believed that this new, national, and democratically-elected assembly would have the authority to establish a democratic government in Russia. Political sympathies in Siberia can be judged by the elections to the Constituent Assembly. Almost 42 million people in the country voted, that is, about 60 per cent of those eligible to do so. About 50 per cent of the votes in Siberia were cast for the SRs and only about 10 per cent for the Bolsheviks. In the country as a whole, the SRs (and their allies) received over 50 per cent of the votes, but the Bolsheviks achieved some 22 to 25 per cent, and were particularly strongly represented in the large towns of European Russia and among soldiers at the front.

The rapid assertion of authority by the Bolsheviks after October 1917 illustrated not so much their strength – as we have just seen, they had only about a quarter of the popular vote – as the impotence of their opponents in resisting them. The army was disintegrating; the liberal Constitutional Democrats (known as 'Kadets' from the capital letters K and D) were humiliated in the elections to the Constituent Assembly in which they received less than 5 per cent of the vote; the Mensheviks were deeply divided and had lost popular support during 1917; the SRs, the most popular party, split internally in December 1917 and a new minority grouping, the Left SRs, supported the Bolshevik policy on ending the war.

None of the alternative political parties had any military power: soldiers strongly supported the Bolsheviks, both at the front and in the key garrisons in Petrograd and Moscow. When, in January 1918, the Bolsheviks dissolved the Constituent Assembly, there was little the other parties could do to resist. Dissolution did not even require force – the delegates simply found the doors locked. This did not lead to popular outrage; in reality, few people believed in the Constituent Assembly or saw it as the true representative of the people's will. It now became clear that the Bolsheviks were not going to give up power unless they were forced to do so.

The Bolsheviks did not comprise the most popular party in Siberia, but Siberia became a centre of resistance to the Bolsheviks almost by chance. The Bolshevik government signed a peace treaty with Germany at Brest-Litovsk in March 1918. As a result, the First World War was now over on the eastern front, and between Germany and Russia, but it was not over in the west and the fate of other countries remained to be determined. One of the consequences of this was the uncertain position in which prisoners of war now found themselves in Russia. These included some 40,000 Czechs from the Austro-Hungarian army who had chosen to fight alongside fellow Slavs to create a homeland for themselves. In 1918, these prisoners of war found themselves in the middle of the conflict in Russia.

Although they were few in number, the Czechs were an effective fighting force and, in the absence of any military or effective state power, their presence took on far greater significance. The Bolshevik government agreed that they should return home, but because of the wartime disruption in central Europe the only route they could take was along the Trans-Siberian railway line to Vladivostok and from there by sea. Their progress along the railway line almost inevitably led to clashes. Conflict was provoked with the Bolsheviks when Trotsky tried to disarm the Czechs in Cheliabinsk, in the Urals, in May 1918, and then, when they resisted, ordered that all armed Czechs on the railway line should be shot. The Czechs were therefore almost forced into armed resistance. They quickly took control of key points on the Trans-Siberian railway line and became a rallying point for anti-Bolsheviks. By this time, they were also being encouraged by the Western allies – Britain, France and the United States – to resist the Bolsheviks.

The initial concern of the Western Allies was that the Central Powers of Germany and Austria-Hungary should not take advantage of a defeated and powerless new Russian state to acquire more resources to continue the fight in the west. The allies could only land safely in ports. A small British contingent landed in Murmansk, on the White Sea, the day after the signing of the Brest-Litovsk Treaty with Germany. Later in the summer, the Allies took over Archangel, also on the White Sea. The other port which the Allies could reach was Vladivostok in the far east, and the Japanese, British and United States established a presence in the town. By the end of 1918, there were 70,000 Japanese soldiers in the far east, a far greater presence than that of any of the other Allied forces.

The initial success of the Czechs, and for that matter the unopposed landings of foreign troops, showed how weak the Bolsheviks were. In this power vacuum, a few troops could easily overthrow the small pockets of Bolshevik support in distant towns. Effective resistance to the Bolsheviks, however, required the establishment of an alternative government. The feeble attempts to do this in Siberia exposed the weakness of the opposition and their inability to address, or even recognise, the crucial issues at stake, in particular the land question, the economy and the position of non-Russian nationalities within the state.

After the October Revolution, an Extraordinary All-Siberian Regional Congress was convened in Tomsk, dominated by SRs, which proposed a separate Siberian government and Constituent Assembly. The latter met in January 1918, but was dissolved by the Tomsk soviet, in which the Bolsheviks had gained a majority, and the building was surrounded by troops (paralleling the fate of the Constituent Assembly in Petrograd). The regional leaders fled to Chita in the far east, where Potanin died in 1920, and its members went underground. The dissolution of the Assembly was met with the same indifference that had greeted its establishment.

In the summer of 1918, a Provisional Siberian Government was established at Omsk and the soviet, which had become dominated by Bolsheviks, was crushed. At the same time a Committee of the Members of the Constituent Assembly (known as the Komuch) was established in Samara on the river Volga in European Russia. It proved impossible to bring these administrations together, either as a fighting force or as a coherent political movement. The Komuch had the greatest claim to legitimacy as the successor to the Constituent Assembly, but this became irrelevant in this power vacuum. Communications were poor; it was almost 1,000 miles (1,600 kilometres) from Samara to Omsk, and 2,693 miles (4,309 kilometres) from Omsk to Vladivostok. The railway line was severely disrupted and it took several weeks to cover the journey from Vladivostok to Omsk.

In some ways the emergence of Omsk as the centre of resistance in Siberia was unexpected. As we have seen, it was Tomsk that had become the intellectual centre of western Siberia from the late eighteenth century; Irkutsk had emerged as the intellectual and commercial centre of eastern Siberia. Tomsk had suffered from not being on the main Trans-Siberian line, and Irkutsk – and Vladivostok even more so – were simply too far away from Moscow to be centres for resistance. Omsk had acquired some commercial importance early in the twentieth century as a town on the railway line, but it had relatively few industrial workers; it was primarily the administrative centre for western Siberia. It had a large population of active civil servants and had attracted retired civil servants as it was cheaper to live there than in European Russia and was relatively civilised. Things had not changed much in the couple of decades since George Kennan had remarked: 'the largest building is a military academy and the most picturesque building is a police station . . . there is neither a newspaper nor a public library . . . one half the population wears the Tsar's uniform and makes a business of governing the other half.'[22] Furthermore, the Omsk government was supported by the powerful Siberian butter-making cooperatives, which were broadly SR in sympathy and opposed to the Bolsheviks.[23]

The Omsk government moved to the right during the summer of 1918 and became dominated by the liberal Kadets, which made cooperation with both the SRs in Omsk and with the Komuch very difficult since Kadets were regarded as the privileged remnants of the old regime. The butter cooperatives also moved to the right and formed a so-called 'Omsk Bloc' in the summer which included socialists and non-socialists (and later endorsed the Kolchak regime).[24] At the same time an army began to be raised in the city. In an atmosphere of mutual distrust and suspicion, the Komuch and the Omsk government met in September 1918 in Ufa, in the Urals, about midway between the two towns. There, the two groups nonetheless formed a Provisional All-Russian Government, led by a Directory of five members comprising two SRs, the regionalist head of the Omsk government and two Kadets. Its base was to be in Omsk, but only because Omsk was further from the military front line than towns in the Urals.

Samara on the Volga fell to the Bolsheviks in October, two weeks after the Ufa conference closed. By this time there were some 3,000 Czech troops in Omsk. In this chaotic situation, the Ufa agreement began to dissolve and it proved impossible to form any orderly government from the conflicting factions. The following month the Omsk government was overthrown by Admiral Aleksandr Kolchak, who remained in power as a military dictator until his forces were defeated in the second half of 1919.

From late 1918 to the end of 1919, western Siberia was to be a major battleground between Reds (Bolsheviks) and Whites (anti-Bolsheviks). At first, the numbers of troops on either side in Siberia were roughly equal. Kolchak's forces were divided into three: a northern, or Siberian, army of some 60,000 men under the Czech Rudolf Gajda; a western army of some 40,000 men; and a smaller, southern army around Orenburg of some 30,000 men. Initially, the northern army was successful, taking the key town of Perm in the Urals in December 1918 and pushing forward to the town of Glazov. But neither the western nor the southern army could make much progress. The White armies suffered from poor coordination, poor supplies and poor leadership. Kolchak proved a poor judge of commanders; in particular, the inexperienced General Dmitrii Lebedev was shown to be an unwise appointment to lead the crucial western army. Many White officers were young and inexperienced, their ordinary conscripts were poorly trained and captured Red soldiers made unreliable troops. Cut off from the main industrial supplies of European Russia, the Whites did not have access to the same quality and quantity of equipment as the Reds. The vast distances involved meant few supplies from the Western Allies reached armies in Siberia.

The main problem, however, was the inability of the Whites to coordinate, within and outside Siberia, which was not only a matter of military misjudgements but also a reflection of the inadequacy of their political thinking. The White armies were never able to coordinate with the Czech legion and there was mutual mistrust. In principle, Kolchak could call on considerable Cossack forces in Siberia, but the Cossacks in the Baikal area and in the far east acted separately. In addition, Cossack excesses only alienated the local population and did not help the White cause. The Bashkirs fought with the Whites at first within their own region, and proved excellent troops with a local knowledge of the terrain. Kolchak, however, had rejected the Soviet government's 'Declaration of the Rights of the Peoples of Russia' in November 1917, which offered equality, and seemed to offer self-determination, to non-Russian peoples. He then merged the Bashkirs with his other armies and refused to offer them any degree of autonomy. The result of Kolchak's attitude and policy was that some 6,500 Bashkir troops in the southern army deserted en masse to the Red Army in February 1919. Finally, not only were the three Siberian armies unable to coordinate with one another, they also failed to combine with the other White forces in the north and the south. The southern army in Siberia, the smallest of the three Siberian armies, never advanced to meet the southern army of 'Volunteers' under General Anton Denikin. This failure sealed their fate.

As a result, when the Red Army increased in size and discipline, the Whites were unable to hold it. Sheer numbers favoured the Bolsheviks, as they conscripted and used the resources of the far more populous Russian heartland. By 1919, the Red Army was 780,000 strong and was able to deploy over 300,000 men to the east, with another 195,000 in the Urals and the Volga region.[25] The Reds, better equipped and better trained, were ready to attack by May 1919. They soon retook the towns of Perm and Ekaterinburg in the Urals and forced the Whites to retreat. As a result, the protection offered by the natural barrier between European Russia and Siberia was lost, as were iron mines, causing the White armies to fall back on all fronts. Discipline collapsed and soldiers deserted in droves, saving themselves and even turning on their officers. Omsk fell in November 1919 without a fight and its garrison of 30,000 men surrendered. Kolchak fled eastwards with the remnants of his forces. He was handed over by the Czechs to the Irkutsk Military Revolutionary Committee in January 1920 (which had overthrown the Irkutsk administration loyal to Kolchak) and

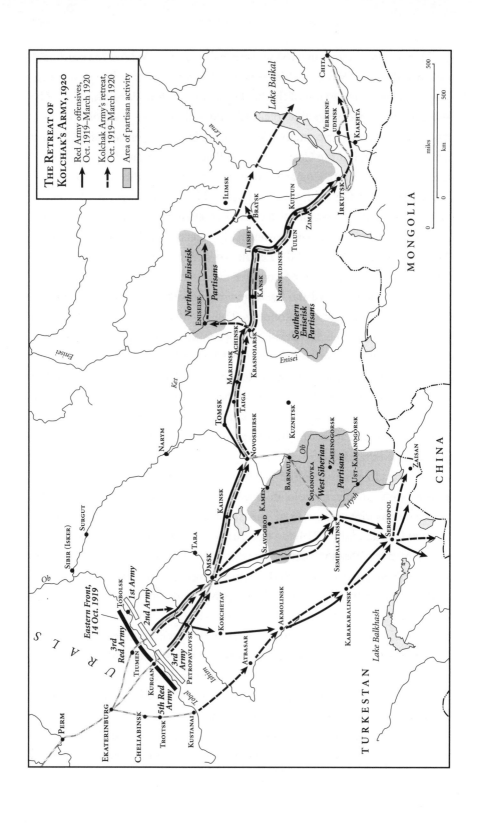

MONGOLIA

CHINA

TURKESTAN

URALS

Lake Baikal

CHITA
VERKHNE-
UDINSK
KIAKHTA
IRKUTSK
ZIMA
KUITUN
TULUN
NIZHNEUDINSK
BRATSK
TAISHET
ILIMSK
KANSK

Lena

Northern Eniseisk
Partisans

Southern
Eniseisk
Partisans

ENISEISK
ACHINSK
MARIINSK
KRASNOIARSK
TAIGA
TOMSK
Enisei
Enisei

Ket

NARYM

SURGUT
SIBIR (ISKER)

Ob

PERM
EKATERINBURG
CHELIABINSK
TROITSK
TIUMEN
TOBOLSK
KURGAN
PETROPAVLOVSK
KUSTANAI

Eastern Front,
14 Oct. 1919

3rd
Red Army
5th Red Army
3rd
Army
2nd Army
1st Army

Tobol
Ishim

TARA
KAINSK
OMSK
NOVOSIBIRSK
KUZNETSK
Ob
BARNAUL
KAMEN
SLAVGOROD
SOLONOVKA
ZMEINOGORSK
UST-KAMENOGORSK

West Siberian
Partisans

Irtysh

KOKCHETAV
ATBASAR
AKMOLINSK
KARAKARALINSK
SEMIPALATINSK
SERGIOPOL
ZAISAN

Lake Balkhash

summarily shot. By this time, the war was already over in western and central Siberia.

The final act was played out in the far east. The Japanese were the only representatives of the Allies there after the small contingent from the United States left Vladivostok in April 1920. A Far Eastern Republic survived under the Japanese army simply because the Bolsheviks were occupied elsewhere and in the short term had to appease the Japanese. In May 1921, with Japanese support, a new administration was set up in the far east called the Provisional Amur (Priamur) Government. In June 1922, the Japanese decided to withdraw, exposing the weakness of the government which they had helped to establish. In July 1922, in the final, few farcical days, a new duma with the old Russian name of *Zemskii Sobor*, or the Assembly of the Land, was convened in a hall lined with imperial flags, and passed a resolution that power lay with the Romanov family. It sent a greeting to Dowager Empress Mariia and Grand Duke Nicholas and received their thanks by wire.[26] General Mikhail Dieterichs, who had commanded White forces under Kolchak, was nominated as the regent until tsarist power was resumed. The Bolsheviks finally entered Vladivostok unopposed in October 1922.

An account of the military campaign does not reveal the horror that many Siberians and soldiers in Siberia had to live through during the Civil War. Soldiers of both armies, peasants and inhabitants of White towns all suffered as law and order and the economy collapsed around them.

Thousands of Red Army prisoners of war were put in cattle trucks and simply moved along the Trans-Siberian railway line without any medical assistance, sanitation or even food and water. One such train sat in the sidings for two days in Chita, with 1,000 prisoners and women and children on board. Local people were forbidden to help the starving and desperate human cargo, and after five days the train moved back west. Indeed, it was not even clear that there was an intended destination for these poor people, or whether they had simply been consigned to a living death. A foreign commentator from the YMCA, Edward Heald, witnessed the arrival at Chita of one such train filled with starving and sick prisoners: 'They looked more like animals than any group of human beings I ever saw. They fought with each other for the pieces of bread which some of them were able to buy . . . . When I asked where they were going, the reply was "Back and forth".'[27]

Towns which were taken and retaken by armies inevitably suffered in the immediate aftermath of each capture. The Bolsheviks executed about

150 people when they took the town of Verkhneudinsk (now Ulan-Ude), and they targeted the 'bourgeois' such as shopkeepers and anyone who could be classified as 'intelligentsia'. It was claimed that over 1,000 people were massacred when the Bolsheviks entered Blagoveshchensk in the far east. When the Japanese entered Novo-Nikolaevsk in May 1920, they massacred thousands, supposedly in revenge for the murder of some Japanese soldiers. After Cossacks entered Khabarovsk under the notorious ataman Ivan Kalmykov, they carried out an orgy of murder and theft and mounted a reign of terror. Eleven Austrian musicians who were performing in the town were murdered. The story goes that Kalmykov declared: 'That music is awful. I order these players to be shot' – although it may be that his order was actually a punishment for the musicians giving lodgings to a Bolshevik for the night. Their bodies, half-naked, were left on the ground for several days.[28] Anyone with associations with the other side was particularly vulnerable. As one report put it tersely: 'Today [1920] we received a report that the unhappy wives of officers who had not been able to get out of Chita, were tortured.'[29]

Life in the White capital was a nightmare. Omsk suffered economic and social collapse. As refugees and injured soldiers flooded into the town its population soared from 300,000 to somewhere between half a million and a million. The majority of refugees were women and children; a local Omsk newspaper noted that many died of hunger, cold and disease before even reaching the town; those that did get there often found themselves without shelter. In January 1919, refugees from Ufa were not even allowed to disembark at Omsk station but were sent further east, to an uncertain fate.[30] White soldiers in Omsk were left to fend for themselves on the streets and inevitably spread disease. 'The dead contaminated the living and Omsk became a city of the living dead,' commented a contemporary.[31] The administration was quite unable to provide basic services for the inhabitants and was in any event hopelessly corrupt.

The Whites initially had control of at least some of the tsarist gold supplies in Kazan in European Russia, but this did not prevent the collapse of the currency in White Siberia. The Omsk government introduced its own rouble, known variously as the Omsk, the Kolchak, the Siberian and the 'yellow' rouble, but did not attempt to adhere to the gold standard. This new rouble promptly collapsed in value and inflation soared. The currency situation was further destabilised by the deliberate flooding of the town by the Bolsheviks with Bolshevik and tsarist roubles. At one stage there were six different currencies in use in the town, the most reliable of which was the US dollar.

Inflation and the disruption to communications meant that goods became prohibitively expensive or simply unobtainable. Prices doubled for soap, tripled for boots, and vastly increased for cloth and coffee. People could live without coffee, but by 1919 there were no candles and no fuel. Disturbances were relatively few, simply because people were too busy just surviving. After the Kolchak coup, a Bolshevik-inspired railway strike took place but it was ruthlessly crushed. A combination of unemployment, the influx of refugees, and a lack of basic government and supplies inevitably led to a breakdown in law and order and an increase in crime – theft in particular.

A few people in Omsk prospered, and the image of officers and their hangers-on partying and flaunting their wealth proved very harmful to the White cause. One contemporary commented on the 'extravagant sums derived from unknown sources spent on luxuries and absurdities' while workers starved and soldiers lay untended in hospitals. But in hopelessly over-crowded Omsk even the wealthy found themselves crammed into hotel rooms; some lived in crowded railway wagons on specially constructed sidings outside the railway station.[32] Some of their conspicuous consumption could be inter-preted as displaying an 'eat, drink and be merry' attitude to their world as it collapsed around them.

In terms of physical conditions, White Vladivostok in the Far East was spared some of the extremes of Omsk. It suffered the same currency madness, however. Tsarist money, Kolchak money and Soviet money were all in circu-lation. Eleonora Prey commented from Vladivostok that the currency situa-tion deteriorated all the time and that Omsk banknotes were worse than original tsarist ones, 'which led to great confusion'.[33] As in Omsk, US dollars were most sought after. At the very end, the Provisional Amur (Priamur) Government had its own currency called 'Romanovskis'; the towns of Chita and Khabarovsk also had their own currencies (there is an excellent collec-tion of the various notes in circulation during the Civil War in the Khabarovsk Regional Museum).[34] As in Omsk, there was a vast increase in the price of goods. In the period 1914–19 as a whole, the price of potatoes in Vladivostok rose by 45 times, milk rose by 28 times, eggs by 35 times and grain by 17 times.[35] These were not luxuries but basic foodstuffs.

Although Vladivostok was not fought over by different armies, life in the city was violent. Troops put down strikes in the town brutally, including one by the Union of Music Hall Workers, Cinema Usherettes and Stagehands.[36] When the Japanese took over the town they attacked the Korean quarter, slaughtered and beat the residents, and set fire to the school. Three hundred Koreans were massacred.[37] There was only ever a sullen acceptance of the Japanese presence, a situation that was not helped by the complete lack of sensitivity to local feelings on the part of the Japanese troops, who paraded down the main streets and hung flags from all the main buildings. No wonder there was no resistance when the Bolsheviks entered the town in 1922; they at least were Russian.

In the countryside, there was little enthusiasm for either army. Peasants resisted conscription of their sons and fathers for the Whites and Reds alike. All armies claimed to be fighting for the people but peasants were not so foolish as to be convinced that any cause was worth the loss of their lives. As one put it: 'One is a People's Army and the other is also a People's Army, and they fight each other! Oh Lord, we can't begin to make it out. Is it perchance the end of the world?'[38]

The Bolsheviks were not popular because they had seized grain and other foodstuffs in areas under their control in 1918. Richer peasants were more hostile to Bolsheviks than were poorer peasants, but rich and poor alike resented grain seizure by Bolshevik urban detachments and soldiers. Ultimately, economic differences between peasants were less important than their shared hostility to 'outsiders'. The Whites were not able to offer peasants a more attractive land policy or to gain their support by other means. Kolchak was too dependent on support from the right and from Cossack warlords to make the simple promise to give peasants ownership of the land they farmed without any payment. In November 1919, a White report on the 'mood of the peasants' noted that 'many are completely indifferent' to the question of who should win the war and just wanted it to end.[39]

Peasants were victims of atrocities at the hands of both Reds and Whites. It was the atrocities of the latter which were initially highlighted in the records of the Soviet Union, but examples of 'Red Terror' are now beginning to emerge. Reds targeted anyone who could be seen as bourgeois or as a representative of the old, tsarist order. This included not only generals and nobles but also minor officials in the countryside. A few examples illustrate how individuals became caught up in the conflict simply as a result of being in the wrong place at the wrong time. In the Eniseisk region in 1918:

The elderly policeman Daniil Panchuk was caught in a fight with Bolshevik bands in the village of Stepnyi Badchei in October 1918 and was killed . . . . [That] left his wife, son and daughter who had been in his care without any belongings . . . . the young policeman Vasilii Mikhailovich Karachev was shot by the Bolsheviks in the village of Tasevsk. He left a wife and three children.[40]

In Nikolaevsk, a gang under a local Bolshevik partisan leader massacred all the Japanese residents.

The peasants suffered far more at the hands of the Whites, not simply because the Whites were physically present in Siberia for longer than the Reds but because their troops were less disciplined. One estimate is that some 33,000 peasants were executed by the White armies.[41] In one incident reported in 1920 in the Altai region 12 'bandits' were shot by Whites but many of those bandits were peasants and it was noted that 'executions for crimes in the villages among peasants produced an ugly mood'.[42] The violence of the Cossack warlords was particularly senseless and brutal. When ataman Ivan Krasilnikov arrived in the Eniseisk region: 'The Whites . . . had burned the country and had killed much of the population. Many of the villages were ploughed up, leaving nothing to indicate there has once been a prosperous settlement on the spot.'[43]

Partisan movements in Siberia, which may have involved up to 175,000 people, including many peasants and non-Russians, might be both anti-Red and anti-White. Partisans could fight simply to acquire a few, rather pathetic basic necessities. In October 1919, partisans captured the village of Bolshoi Mamyr in the Irkutsk region and 'in the battle took prisoners and many boots, and provisions'.[44] Other peasant partisan groups could take on regular forces, Red or White. One group in Irkutsk district numbered 150 men bearing 60 rifles between them. There were some 600 peasant disturbances in the Novoudinskii region alone in 1920 in eastern Siberia.

Could, and should, events in Siberia have altered the outcome of the Civil War and, as a result, altered the course of Russian history? Some military and tactical errors were made: Kolchak's choice of leaders was sometimes poor; coordination with other theatres of conflict was weak; discipline was not maintained, particularly in retreat. All of these factors, however, were indicative of deeper flaws within White Siberia. The reality was that the Whites were never able to develop a coherent or attractive vision of a new Russian empire. Their only cause was a loathing of the Bolsheviks, but this could not be translated into a realistic alternative to their rule. Within Siberia, there were too many conflicting interests for Kolchak to put together a programme that could appeal to all, or really any, of the social and ethnic groups. Put another way, he simply could not inspire enough people to die for him and his government to overthrow the Bolsheviks.

I was surprised on a recent visit to Irkutsk to find a statute of Kolchak there, looking across to the river Angara where his corpse was unceremoniously dumped. Kolchak had done little for the people of Irkutsk, who were in any event in the sphere of influence of the Cossacks. In Omsk, the idea of erecting a statue to Kolchak remains controversial. While the debate continues, a 'Kolchak Irish pub' has opened – money can always be made, even from the most unworthy of subjects.

CHAPTER FOURTEEN

Collectivisation and the Camps

THE YOUNG Soviet state went to war on its enemies. In the process, those who were designated as 'enemies of the people' were demonised and dehumanised. The first victims were the relatively prosperous peasants, known as kulaks (or 'fists'). In all, over a million peasant families (some 5–6 million people) were 'dekulakised', that is, had their possessions seized, were expelled from their homes, deported to remote parts of the country, sent to labour camps or simply executed and, as a result, were eliminated as a social group. The state in effect conducted a civil war against all the peasantry by forced collectivisation. This was followed by an attack on all those who were perceived to be hostile to the new regime. By the 1930s, some 300,000 people were in corrective labour camps, known as Gulags. Over the next two decades the number of inmates increased massively – not only peasants who resisted collectivisation but anyone convicted of anti-state or counter-revolutionary activity as well as common criminals could be sent to them. At their peak, in 1942–3 during the Second World War there were some 4 million people in labour camps and prisons in the Soviet Union.[1] But far more people passed through the camps – perhaps some 18 million between the late 1920s and the 1950s.

Siberia was at the centre of this human tragedy. Many prosperous Siberian peasants were defined as kulaks; in addition, some 2 million peasants were deported from European Russia to Siberia and Kazakhstan. Particular groups in Siberia were targeted for collectivisation and then persecuted – these included shamans and members of religious sects. There were camps all over the Soviet Union, but those in the far north and north-east of Siberia were particularly notorious and feared.

The young Soviet state inherited a situation where the destruction and loss of manpower during the Civil War had already had a devastating effect on Siberian agriculture. Tomsk province in 1920 was said to be 'in a situation of total ruin . . . . the majority of farmers did not have either a horse, or a harness or machinery or fodder, or work hands.'[2] A report in 1920 stated that the Ostiaks (Khanty) were 'completely destitute' and 'lack both outer and inner garments . . . and footwear.'[3] People in the towns starved: a report from Tomsk in May 1920 stated that prices had rocketed and that the hunger there was so great that people had committed suicide, while on the streets people were 'dragging themselves from weakness and hardly able to move their limbs'. The following month there was no bread at all in Irkutsk and such 'terrible hunger' that children were dying in the streets.[4]

The Bolsheviks exacerbated the situation by sending in detachments to seize food and by trying to force a 'levelling' by redistributing livestock among peasants. This, combined with poor harvests, led to severe disorder as well as distress. Bands of impoverished peasants and deserters terrorised the local population. In one village in Tiumen, in western Siberia, a gang killed ten peasants, injured another ten and stole 100 horses.[5] In Tobolsk, some 30,000 desperate peasants invaded the town, with the result that thousands were killed on both sides of the ensuing violence.[6] Peasants starved to death. One later recalled: 'During the night the people of the village would go to the cemetery and dig up these bodies and eat them. The people were so hungry they resorted to cannibalism.'[7] The distress was even worse in Ukraine and European Russia, to the point that starving peasants there fled to Siberia: 'Sometimes refugees would come into the village for something to eat or drink. Some of them could hardly speak, and several fell and died on the porches of the houses they had approached.'[8]

The desperate situation was only alleviated by the introduction of the New Economic Policy in 1921, which allowed the peasants to keep and trade their surplus grain. In the years 1924 to 1926, Siberia recovered, perhaps to a greater extent than the rest of the country. The population on the land increased, in part as a result of further migration from European Russia. Siberian peasants and villages bought more agricultural machinery than peasants elsewhere in the country. The grain surpluses in Siberia rose massively, and peasants prospered. Those in Sibiria, recognised the change in their circumstances. One said: 'in 1926, 1927 and 1928 we had so much grain, so much bread, that we did not know what to do with it.'[9]

This recovery, however, disguised some fundamental weaknesses in Siberian agriculture, as more and more grain was demanded to feed the inhabitants of the new cities. Most Siberian villages, as we have seen, used the long-term fallow system, whereby land was exhausted by grain production and then left fallow as pasture land for between 5 and 16 years to recover. This was not an efficient method of grain production, and was only possible because of the abundance of land in Siberia and because the pasture land was used for the lucrative dairy industry. The extent of village lands, and the distances between the strips, also meant that Siberian villages relied more on agricultural machinery and needed more horses than did villages in European Russian villages. As a result, after an initial boom there was a dip in productivity as the land became exhausted and the dairy and livestock industries were neglected. Increased affluence and population growth also led to a rise in consumption in the countryside just at the time when more grain and other foodstuffs were needed for a larger urban population. The increase in agricultural equipment had motivated more Siberian peasants to join cooperatives, but this did not, as the Bolsheviks had hoped, naturally encourage socialisation of agriculture because it was the richest peasants who purchased machinery and joined the co-operatives.

This was the background to the crisis in 1927 when grain production fell by 30 per cent in the country as a whole, but by 50 per cent in Siberia.[10] There were some harvest failures in key regions of Siberia that year, and rising peasant consumption also led to a reduction in grain available for export. The situation was also exacerbated by the short-sightedness of government policy. Grain prices were low and peasants could make bigger profits by selling dairy products or, indeed, by selling off part of their dairy herds since prices for meat were very high. Manufactured goods were not being produced quickly enough because factories had not recovered from the Civil War so peasants were reluctant to sell their grain when they were unable to purchase agricultural machinery in return.

I have presented this crisis as an *economic* crisis. Stalin, however, and many other Bolsheviks, particularly in Moscow – far away from events on the ground – saw it as an *ideological* crisis, brought about by deliberate acts of sabotage on the part of wealthy Siberian peasants and by the feebleness of the response of local Bolshevik officials. Stalin became more convinced of this view during a tour of Siberia in 1928 and was determined that the 'kulaks' had to be broken. In order to do this, however, local Bolsheviks first had to determine just who the kulaks were, and divide them into categories according to their culpability as 'exploiters'. Although presented with some appearance of methodological rigour, the reality was that the categorisation was completely arbitrary, at odds with the nature of commercial relationships within the village, and ultimately destructive, not only to individual peasants but to the whole peasant community.

Bolshevik officials defined as kulaks those who 'exploited' the labour of other peasants, owned machinery or were simply richer than the rest, and sought them out as enemies of the state who were deliberately undermining the state as well as harming other peasants. This definition, however, ignored the reality of life in villages, where wealthier peasants provided work and hired out their machinery, so that what the authorities defined as 'exploitation' might equally have been described as providing help and mutual assistance. A poor female peasant who had fought with the Red Army asked: 'Why should we reveal the rich, when the rich help us? If the state helps us, then let us bring them the rich.'[11] Wealth was relative and the measures employed had to be seen in context: larger households had more horses and dairy farmers had more cows – but they were not necessarily individually richer as a result. What was a kulak? A list of kulaks in the Barnaul region in 1927 included a certain Rukavkin who owned 157 acres of land, 10 horses, 8 cows and 70 sheep, but also a peasant called Rybakov who owned far less – 27 acres of land, 3 horses and 2 cows.[12] 'If we are kulaks, then all Siberia is kulak,' stated a peasant tersely, a Red Army veteran.[13]

The first attack on those defined as kulaks saw the seizure of their goods, forced grain collection and substantial fines for hoarding grain. In 1929, there were some 3,000 arrests of kulaks in Siberia and about 8,000 farms had property sequestered.[14] This affected, however, only a small proportion of households. Many richer peasants simply fled, which in turn led to the economic collapse of villages. One village, Solonovka, lost 127 of its 548 families between May 1929 and February 1930.[15] In consequence, the extent of land sown by wealthy peasants in Siberia dropped sharply.

The dekulakisation policy required the cooperation of those who were defined as poor peasants in identifying and denouncing their richer neighbours. Peasants were fully aware of who owned what and might resent richer neighbours and relish the opportunity to settle old scores. There were many examples of 'kulaks' being beaten up and their goods pillaged. Some villages carried out grotesque carnivalesque public humiliations of rich peasants, when they were chased through the village naked or tarred and feathered. Such rituals had their roots in local tradition, in the sense that peasants in the past had been publicly shamed in a similar manner by the village as a punishment for unacceptable behaviour, but the fresh addition of Bolshevik slogans could make the occasion totally absurd. In one Siberian village peasants were marched through the village with black banners round their necks reading: 'We are friends of Chamberlain.' Such phrases, referring to the British Prime Minister Neville Chamberlain, perhaps implying disloyalty to the Soviet state, meant nothing to peasants.[16]

Many poor peasants supported their richer fellow peasants against the 'outsiders', the local Bolshevik officials. Peasants instinctively distrusted the state and believed, not without reason, that they would be targeted next. Local officials had to induce some poorer peasants to attack their neighbours by small gifts of tobacco or other goods. All this indicated that local officials were at odds with the peasant community, but rather than recognise the reality on the ground, the authorities in Moscow blamed the kulaks for the disorder and intensified action against them. Some 1,500–2,000 peasants were arrested in Siberia every week in 1930.[17] Around 60,000 households in Siberia were 'dekulakised', a euphemism for destroyed, and 300,000 Siberian kulak families were foribly moved from their homes in 1930–2. Local officials were given 'targets' of numbers of kulaks of various categories to exile.

Kulaks from European Russia were deported to Siberia. In 1929, 213,000 kulaks arrived;[18] in the period 1930–1, some 400,000 kulaks were resettled there.[19] These peasants – from within Siberia and from European Russia – were resettled in particularly remote areas, as exiled convicts had been in the nineteenth century. They were supposed to be supplied with grain and basic equipment, again as earlier exiles had been, but in practice often no provision was made for them at all. During the tsarist period the exiles had been convicted of crimes or found guilty of poor behaviour or were members of dissident religious sects: in 1930–2, wealthy peasants were condemned simply for meeting an arbitrary definition of wealth or of exploitation. A kulak was always a kulak and could not be rehabilitated or change status. Doctors and local people were often forbidden to help such 'enemies of the people'. Nor could their immediate families be anything other than kulaks too, that is, associated with their crimes. In March 1930, a group of alleged kulaks were forced to leave a village in Novosibirsk province during a blizzard. It was recalled afterwards that 'on some sledges lay three to four children of kulaks frozen to death'.[20] The language used – 'enemies', 'exploiters', 'parasites', 'manipulators' – is significant and similar to the terms used later for prisoners in the Gulags.

The horror of the fate which met many kulaks can be seen in this description by someone who was 11 years old at the time:

My father, Petr Averianov, was arrested at night in April, 1932, and taken to who knows where. Afterwards they arrested my mother, Varvara, in May on the night before Easter and threw us seven children, including me, out of the house. They sat us four older children on two horses, tied up with the reins so we wouldn't run away, and put the three smaller ones to bed with no clothing. They took us to Atiashevo station .... The next day they brought railroad cars and loaded us in, a few families in each car, and locked us in again. There was no bathroom. The men used their knives to make a hole and [everyone] did their business there without any sense of shame. People became crazed .... I don't remember how many days we travelled. Several people in our car starved to death. We got to Tomsk and they unloaded us, a few families. They pulled a few corpses – children, old men, and young people – out of the car. From Tomsk, they took us to a pier, loaded us onto a barge, and we sailed up the Chulym River. I don't remember how long we travelled. They unloaded us onto a pier, and we walked three kilometres to the village of Pesochnoe in Bogatovsk Region. Two of the children in our family, Nastia and Vania, died on the way there. They abandoned us there, 'Live as you like!'[21]

The resistance by poor peasants to the initial attack on the kulaks convinced Stalin that not only did the kulaks have to be eliminated as a class but that all other peasants had to be forced into collective farms. This was in effect a declaration of war on *all* the peasantry and not simply its wealthier members. Dekulakisation and forced collectivisation went hand in hand. Villages were transformed into collectives with extraordinary speed. By the end of 1930, about 50 per cent of Siberian peasants were in collective farms, a much more rapid change than across the country as a whole.[22] There were mass disturbances across Siberia against collectivisation, often led by the women in the village. Peasants slaughtered their animals rather than allowing them to be collectivised. One peasant village killed all its pigs because it did not want 'socialised pigs'. Many, however, reluctantly joined collectives out of fear that they would suffer the same fate as kulaks.

Forced collectivisation did not only affect Russian settlers in Siberia. Indigenous people were also moved to collective farms. Non-nomadic peoples – such as Buriats, Bashkirs and Tatars – were the first to be collectivised, in a process similar to that experienced by Russian peasants. Indigenous people had been prey to violence at the hands of new settlers from the first appearance of Russians in Siberia, and had had their lands seized and their economic activities disrupted, but they had never experienced such a brutal assault on their way of life as they did now. Collectivisation was met with resistance and, as in Russian villages, it was often the women who were most hostile. In the Altai region between 1929 and 1932, over half the cattle were destroyed by farmers in protest at being forced into collective farms. In Iakutia, slaughter of cattle, arson and sabotage took place on a large scale in resistance to collectivisation.[23]

Many non-agricultural indigenous people in Siberia were also collectivised, despite the fact the state often had little or no understanding of their economic activities or economic relationships. Fishermen in the Amur region, on the north-eastern coast on Kamchatka peninsula and Sakhalin Island were forced into fishing collectives. Reindeer hunters were particularly targeted, with the owners of large herds being designated 'kulaks' and having their herds confiscated and all herders being forced into collectives. Reindeer herds were massively depleted as a result.

Collectivisation also served to crush religious sects, which had existed in Siberia since the seventeenth century. Many of the 'spirit-wrestlers' had left Russia at the end of the nineteenth century but those who remained were now forced into collective farms and their separate villages were destroyed. Five out of ten spirit-wrestler villages in the Amur region were abandoned in the period 1926–32.[24] The 'milk-drinkers' and 'self-castrators' almost died out after collectivisation (high-profile self-castrators were executed or sent to camps after a show trial in Moscow in 1929). The early Soviet state was able to do what the tsarist system had never achieved, despite devoting considerable resources to punishing and supervising sectarians – it almost eliminated these dissident religious sects.

Many Old Believers saw collectivisation in particular, and the Soviet state in general, as 'evil' and 'godless'. An Old Believer, E. T. Fefelov, reminded his congregation that 'before the end of the world the Antichrist will bring torment' and linked this with the newly established collective farms. An Old Believer priest, L. S. Talovsky, spoke of the 'persecution of the faithful' which would happen before the end of the world and warned that that time had now come. Others referred to 'godless communists' and to the presence of the Antichrist on collective farms. Some Old Believers were categorised as kulaks and had their property confiscated. The rest were forced into collective farms, and many of their leaders and priests were arrested, or escaped into exile.[25]

The collective farms – arbitrarily created, poorly equipped, deprived of many of their most productive members – often collapsed. There was famine throughout the country in 1932–3. The experience of one village illustrates the widespread trauma of this period. Aleksandrovka in the Altai region comprised 160 Russian and Belarusian families in 1916. In 1928, it faced an economic crisis after poor harvests. As a result, the richest peasants in the village had their possessions and land seized. Then a collective farm was set up in 1930, although this met with little enthusiasm among the villagers, irrespective of their wealth. Indeed, the peasants met in an assembly and resolved that 'the poor [peasants] did not see an advantage in collectivisation'. Women, as in other villages, showed themselves particularly hostile to the collective farm but the whole process of collectivisation of agriculture was described as a 'shock' for the peasants. Poor peasants complained that the state determined their activities and their work norms but failed to provide them with enough grain to live. A local Bolshevik official noted that the 'mood of peasants without grain towards Soviet power was passive and even hostile'. The harvest failed in 1932–3 and 'many peasants died of starvation in Aleksandrovka'. Peasants ate grass. Further famines occurred in 1935 and 1936, and the population of the village dropped from over 1,000 in 1926 to 672 in 1940, as peasants died or fled to the towns.[26]

The peasants had been defeated by the state. The wealthiest layer had been eliminated, or 'liquidated' in the language of the time. Others had been forced into collective farms, and their agricultural practices and way of life destroyed. Some left for towns; others became brigands. The majority did what peasants have always done best – they engaged in passive resistance. In an Ostiak (Khanty) village in Tomsk province in 1930, residents noted that 'young people do not want to work' and that 'some of the people do not work at all'.[27] The tragedy for the Siberian countryside, and for Russia generally, was that agriculturally rich land was wasted and the peasants who had worked it most productively were crushed. There was at best sullen acceptance of the collective farm but no incentives or enthusiasm to improve agricultural production.

In the 1920s, intellectuals were also exiled to Siberia. R. K. Belsky, from Odessa, was sent to Narym, where he worked as a teacher, and then to Novosibirsk (former Novo-Nikolaevsk), where he worked in a financial organisation. The Leningrad jurist and journalist A. M. Volkenshtein was exiled to Novosibirsk where he worked in a cinema studio. Exiled engineers were employed in newly built Siberian factories.[28] Former Whites and exiles were categorised as 'people without rights', and as many as 166,000 such people were living in Siberia in 1929.[29] They were not yet, however, in camps.

Originally camps had been set up by the Soviet state as 'rehabilitation' and 'corrective' centres: doing hard labour for the state would reform inmates into good citizens. Indeed, early corrective labour experiments such as the building of the White Sea canal, linking Leningrad with the White Sea, were presented as positive initiatives, despite the terrible death rates and sufferings of those who laboured under appalling conditions on such projects. In the same way, camps in Siberia were originally intended to use human endeavour to open up the great resources of the remote regions of the north and the north-east, and were originally a central part of Soviet economic planning. The corrective, and the economic, potential of the early camps was set aside, however, as the number of inmates increased massively from 1937 onwards. Millions of people were sentenced to the camps and the Gulags became a 'system' in which people were starved or worked to death. The economic absurdity of the camps soon became clear; slave labour was unproductive and the cost of maintaining the system outweighed the value of the goods and resources produced. Camps were intended to punish, if not to murder, the 'enemies of the people', not to reform and rehabilitate them. In the process, prisoners were deliberately dehumanised. Stalin referred to them as 'filth' and 'vermin'.[30]

Gulags were set up all over Russia and there were large and particularly fearsome camps in Siberia. Siblag, in western Siberia, was one of the largest. BAMlag was set up to build a new railway line from Baikal to the Amur region; some 180,000 prisoners were sent there between 1933 and 1936. There was a lack of proper planning and equipment, so tens of thousands of these prisoners, many of them already sick and weak, were left on minimum rations to

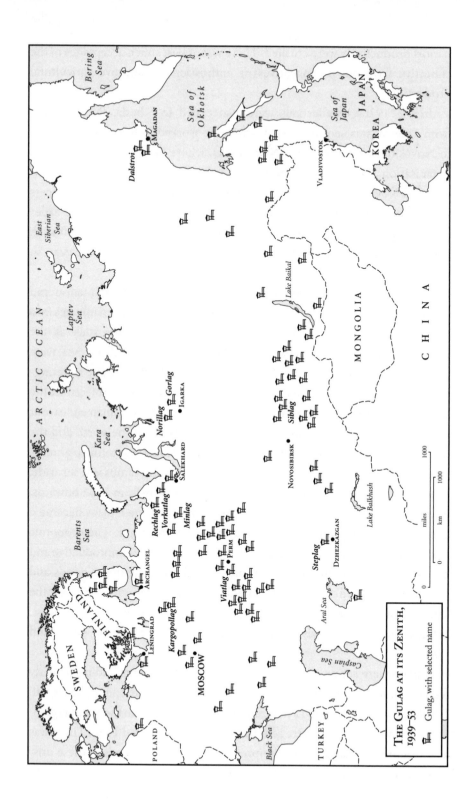

THE GULAG AT ITS ZENITH,
1939–53

⚒ Gulag, with selected name

starve to death before construction work even started. The most notorious camps, however, were in the Kolyma region, in the remote north-east of Siberia. Temperatures fell to minus 45 degrees Celsius and lower in the winter. Men, and also women, weakened by disease and poor nutrition, worked 12-hour shifts in the gold mines, chopping down trees or constructing highways with ineffective equipment, inadequate clothing, poor medical provision and no concern for their safety. The death rates in all the camps were appallingly high – a quarter of all prisoners died during the war years – but the rates were highest in Kolyma.

In the nineteenth century, convicts had been expected to walk across Siberia, at least until the construction of the Trans-Siberian railway. In the Soviet period, they were transported to the camps in Siberia by train, and then by boat from Vladivostok to Magadan, but the conditions of travel were, if anything, worse than they had been a century previously. Prisoners were packed into prison wagons (known, ironically, as 'Stolypin' wagons) or cattle trucks, with no medical care, no sanitation, and little food and water. Many died en route. The boat journey from Vladivostok was particularly horrific: prisoners were kept below deck and had food and water simply thrown down to them; criminality, including rape, was common. Many prisoners died before even reaching the camps: only some 10,000 of the first 16,000 prisoners sent to Kolyma arrived.

The camps included a large number of peasants. These might be sentenced for any activity regarded as hostile to the collective farm and, by extension, to the state. That could include 'theft' of a few rotting potatoes or grain that had been left in the fields. A member of a collective farm in Siberia recalled: 'Every person that was arrested, who I remember, was poor . . . . They disappeared suddenly and at night; it was usually at night.' Her own father was arrested in 1937 and never seen again.[31]

In the 1940s, the number of political prisoners in the camps rose sharply to some 30–40 per cent of all inmates, and by the time the 'system' was ended in the 1950s they were in the majority. 'Politicals' included not only intellectuals, but also anyone who had done, written or said – or was *accused* of doing, writing or saying – anything that could be construed as hostile to the state or counter-revolutionary. Anyone with a foreign name or foreign connections, anyone in a Communist Party office or state institution who may at any time have expressed doubts about Party policy, anyone who could be seen in any way as having sympathised with the Whites or foreign powers, anyone associated with someone who had been arrested, the families of prisoners ... all were vulnerable. Old scores were settled and people denounced others in order to save themselves.

Family members left behind might be ostracised. Galina Sheludchenko discovered what it meant to be related to an 'enemy of the people' when her father, a school director in Eniseisk, was arrested: 'My mother was sacked. I stopped playing with children .... They were forbidden by their parents. Everyone was afraid. Almost every day someone was arrested.'[32] The atmosphere became so threatening and anxieties were so heightened that some people found it almost a relief to be arrested. This was truly an Orwellian war by the state on its own people in which 'all those who are not for us are against us'.

The impact on intellectuals, and the arbitrariness of the 'system', can be illustrated with examples of arrests in Siberia. In 1937 and 1938, some 150 members of higher-educational establishments in Tomsk were arrested. P. M. Iukhnev, a scholar of the economy, history and geography of the Altai region, was arrested because he had served in the White administration during the Civil War; A. I. Miliutin, the librarian of Tomsk University, was arrested for having books 'that should not be preserved'; Professor V. P. Chekhov, a geneticist, was arrested along with 20 associates – all but one were shot in 1937; Professor M. V. Krupenin spent ten years in prison for allegedly supporting an anti-Soviet theory on the future of schools. In 1935, the director of the Tomsk Industrial Institute, A. M. Kashkin, gave a speech in which he said that 'we now are beginning more and more to restrict the places in the Institute where class enemies secretly and quietly endeavour to work'. He was then himself arrested in 1936 and accused of organising a Trotskyist group along with other members of the Institute. S. P. Fridolin, also a member of the Institute, was accused of being a counter-revolutionary after a colleague read an article in the newspaper about the German occupation of Ukraine in 1918 and pointed out that Fridolin had worked in Kiev at the time when Ukraine had been 'sold off'. He was then attacked because one of his books on the milk industry and the crossbreeding of cattle was considered to contradict Party directives. A special assembly of the Institute condemned him as an enemy of the people and he was sacked.[33]

All intellectuals were targeted, whatever their occupation. An exhibition I saw in 2013 about archivists in the Khabarovsk regional archive ended with a poignant note in the last cabinet stating that four members of the archive were accused of destroying documents, Trotskyism and anti-Soviet activities, and arrested in the late 1930s. According to this note, one was shot, the fate of another is unknown, that is, he almost certainly perished as well. Almost all the members of the Oriental Institute in Vladivostok were arrested, imprisoned or shot.

Priests of the Orthodox Church and other denominations were sent to camps. This included Old Believers and members of other religious sects in Siberia. Shamans and shamanism were targeted in the 1920s and 1930s. Only a few shamans escaped the camps, although legends grew up about those who avoided this fate. A not untypical one related to a shaman named Chodok in the far east who was arrested: 'They enter his tent and tell him to get dressed. Chodok puts his fur coat on and says he is ready to go. They leave the camp and walk for some time. Look! The shaman's coat walks empty!'[34]

The children of 'enemies of the people' suffered particularly badly if both parents were arrested or if they were born in the camps. Orphanages were set up for them, but many did not survive the ordeal. In western Siberia, a report on such orphanages commented that in the town of Narym

> there is no fat or meat; there is not enough grain. In this connection, mass infection of children with tuberculosis and malaria have been observed in some orphanages. Thus in the Poludenovsk orphanage of the Kolpashevsk district, out of 108 children only one is healthy; in the Shirokovskii-Karagosoksk district, out of 134 children: 69 have tuberculosis and 46 have malaria.[35]

The sheer number of prisoners, drawn from all walks of life, meant that Siberians, like other Russians, could not have been unaware of the Gulags. Everyone knew somebody who had been arrested or who had simply 'disappeared'. One former inmate of the Gulags, who had been interrogated in the Vladivostok prison, commented: 'Everyone in Vladivostok knew this sinister building' despite the fact that 'cries and moans were muffled by the trams clattering along their rails'.[36]

Train carriages transporting prisoners were sealed. When they were not actually on the move, captives were kept in large transit camps, cut off from neighbouring towns by high walls and barbed wire. Large groups of prisoners, however, had to move through Siberia and the numbers meant their presence could not be hidden from town inhabitants. So many prisoners passed through Siberian towns that they could be regarded with indifference.[37] Perhaps people simply did not want to admit to themselves what they knew was happening around them. Nevertheless, some compassion could be shown to prisoners. In Petropavlovsk, on Sakhalin Island, local people threw bread and potatoes to prisoners (as they had done to Dostoevsky's convoy in the nineteenth century). In Magadan, a town created for the Gulag, and the last stop before the Kolyma camps, local people knew all too well what the camps were like because many had served out a sentence there. One former prisoner recalled:

> People going to work would stop, their faces expressing compassion. Magadan's population is the whole flower of Russia's exile community; these were people who had been let out of the camps but who had no right of return to the 'mainland'. And so they knew well what was awaiting us.[38]

In the tsarist period, exiles and convicts had been sentenced to hard labour in mines but they had worked alongside free labourers, and most tsarist exiles were settled in villages where they lived alongside free settlers and, in time, became integrated into that community. Exile was a punishment but was also seen as an opportunity to populate Siberia to the ultimate benefit of all its inhabitants, free and unfree, even if, as we have seen, this often did not work well in practice. Soviet 'enemies of the people', however, were intended to be kept away from the local population. Camps were run entirely on slave labour, and were located in underpopulated areas, well away from existing settlements. Very few prisoners escaped from the camps in Kolyma, simply because they were so remote and the terrain and climate were so hostile. If prisoners did escape, they were usually re-captured. It was said in Sakha (Iakutia) that the local children used to cry out 'There's a herring coming' on sighting a stranger as they were rewarded with flour, tea, cloth or herrings for handing in prisoners.[39]

Nevertheless, there was some contact between prisoners and local people. A recent study has challenged the view that the camps were completely isolated from the rest of Soviet society, showing that prisoners worked in factories and as labourers in towns in western Siberia, that some convoys moved around without guards, and that the camps could be of some economic benefit to the local population, to the extent that some prisoners became involved in the black market.[40] Prisoners from the camps worked on the BAM railway and helped to build new Soviet cities and towns, including Magadan, alongside free labour.

When prisoners were finally released from the camps after serving their sentence, they could be restricted to residence in Siberian towns and not allowed to return to European Russia, depending on their offence. In effect, they were in internal exile, as so many exiles had been in the eighteenth and nineteenth centuries. Even after the camps closed in the 1950s, thousands of prisoners were left in Magadan. This created a strange society, mixing free people – officials, settlers – with the unfree, both prisoners passing through and former prisoners settled in the town. The groups were kept apart; the public baths were reserved on alternate days for town inhabitants and prisoners.[41]

After Eugenia Ginzburg was released from the camps she had to live in Magadan and worked in a kindergarten there for the children of prisoners. There was also a kindergarten for the children of officials, which was filled with 'spruce little boys and girls', but Ginzburg's kindergarten by contrast was for 'thirty-eight neurotics, some high-strung and over-excitable, others subdued and silent'. Of these children, 'some were painfully thin and pale, with blue rings about their eyes; others had grown disproportionately fat from a diet too rich in carbohydrates'. She came across the woman who had been the chief of her camp, who now worked as a doctor in Magadan hospital:

> she would greet us [Ginzburg and her husband] amiably and pass some remark such as 'I see there is a good film on today in the Gorniak Cinema . . .'. It was difficult to believe that only a few years before she had exercised the power of life and death.[42]

The peak of the camp system lasted from 1937 to the death of Stalin in 1953, but even after his date denunciations and persecution continued. The life of a young lecturer in Tomsk, Erik Iudin, was destroyed in the late 1950s after he was reported by a student for alleged falsities in his lecture on Marxism-Leninism; it was also claimed that he had referred to religion as a form of 'public consciousness' in a lecture on historical materialism. As a result, he was accused of being an 'apologist' for religion and of stating his 'own points of view' in these lectures. Furthermore, it was claimed that he listened to the BBC and Voice of America. Iudin was sacked from the university and expelled from the Communist Party. Even after that, the young man was not left alone by his enemies, who used his letters to his father as evidence against him and accused him of further 'anti-Party' activities. Iudin was condemned as an 'enemy of the Party' and as 'anti-Soviet' in 1957 and sentenced to ten years in prison. He was 27. He served three years in a camp, and was afterwards employed in Moscow as a worker and then a teacher. His health and spirit broken, he died aged 46. He was rehabilitated in the 1980s.[43]

It was this deliberate attempt to crush the spirit of a whole generation – be they peasants or intellectuals – that was the most poisonous legacy of the camps. As Ginzburg recalled from Magadan:

> Those who were waiting for transport back to the mainland [that is, Russia outside Kolyma] took their stand on the despairing formula: 'What will be, will be! I'll get to see my family, and after that . . .'. Those who remained behind did their utmost to find themselves an opening in manual labour or some sort of craft. Hardly anyone, except the doctors, worked at or even wanted to work at his old profession. The animal hatred of the authorities for the intelligentsia was all too familiar from our experience of our years in camp. The thing to do was to be a tailor, a cobbler, a cabinet maker, a laundress – to crawl into some quiet, warm nook, so that it would never occur to anyone that once upon a time you read seditious literature.[44]

Giuzel Galieva was the daughter of academics. Her father was the Tatar writer Gumer Galir, who spent ten years in a camp in Norilsk in northern Siberia; her mother spent five years in Siblag corrective labour camp. Giuzel and her sister were placed in an orphanage as children of 'enemies of the people'. She recalled that after her mother, a graduate of the Financial-Economic Institute, was released she 'would get work but be fired very often . . . . We didn't have anything to eat at all.' Galieva was refused entry to the chemistry faculty at the university in Kazan 'as they could not admit children of "enemies of the people"' in case they were sent to a chemical factory where they might 'organise an explosion'. With typical arbitrariness, she was admitted to the physics and mathematics department instead. She later reflected bitterly on her experiences:

> Everyone has his own fate . . . . They took us to the children's home. That is, they tore us away, they took both parents, both Mama and Papa . . . . There are those whose fathers were shot right away. But again, they stayed with

their mama. [But] the most awful consequence, the very biggest tragedy for our country, is that the very smartest people died . . . . And what writers died! And as far as scholars go, there's just nothing to say. They destroyed our national intelligentsia so that they could bring us down to the lowest common denominator. Well, again, the best people died. So I think that is the greatest sorrow. Because the worst remain.[45]

As we have seen, Siberia had been at the heart of the exile system throughout the tsarist period, but the sheer scale of human misery in these decades had never been experienced or witnessed before. One Gulag survivor was haunted by the abandoned and starving peasant children he had seen in the 1930s in Blagoveshchensk, on the river Amur:

They were lying under market stalls and on the sidewalks. Alive but no longer able to move, they were being eaten alive by flies and worms. This was such a terrible sight that even though more than half a century has passed, I can still see it as if it were today.[46]

What Soviet citizens emerged from this nightmare? This is the subject of the next chapter.

CHAPTER FIFTEEN

The New Soviet Citizen

I visited my daughter in the city – it's amazing: you have the Angara and the forest right there, and toilet-bath. You don't have to come out on the street for a year if you don't want to. There's a faucet, like that one on the samovar, and you turn it on and water comes put; one has cold, the other hot. And you don't have to throw logs on the stove, it has a faucet you turn and the heat comes. Cook and fry. There's so much – it spoils a woman! And the bread doesn't come from your stove, no, it comes from the store . . . . What's even stranger is that the bath and toilet are in the same corner, just the way heathens have, by the kitchen. That's wrong. You sit, you worry, and tremble that they don't hear you at the table. And the bath . . . . But they splash in it and climb out wet. And so you'll live like a lady, Natasha, lying around; everything is in the house, you won't have to lift a finger.

In Valentin Rasputin's 1979 novel *Farewell to Matyora*, one old woman thus describes to another, 'either in comfort or mockery', the delights of urban living when she is faced with moving to a town apartment from her Siberian village which is about to be flooded in a dam project on the river Angara. Rasputin's novels are a critique of the destruction of old communities, and old ways of life, in the Soviet period, and he struck a chord with many readers. 'Living among strangers!' was the response of the old woman. 'How can you transplant an old tree?'[1]

In fact, as we have seen, vast numbers of people had moved within and across Siberia in the late nineteenth and early twentieth centuries – seeking a better life, displaced by civil war, transported as kulaks or as 'enemies of the people'. Moreover, from the 1930s, there was a massive industrialisation of the USSR, and of Siberia in particular, attracting migrants from the country-side and European Russia to expanded and entirely new cities. In the short term the Second World War saw a drop in the population of Siberia, as so many men were lost,[2] but thousands of factories moved to the east during the war, bringing migrants with them, and the exploitation of coal, gas, oil and other natural resources meant the momentum of industrialisation and population movement continued through the 1950s and 1960s.

The population of Siberia including the Far East (Siberia was divided and re-divided in the 1920s and 1930s but was broadly divided into three regions: Western Siberia, Eastern Siberia and the Far East) increased at a greater rate than in European Russia. It rose from some 12.6 million in 1926 to 16.5 million in 1939 and 22.4 million in 1959, reaching some 32 million people by 1989.[3] Industrialisation and modernisation, however, did not simply create new urban residents; they were also supposed to civilise individuals and whole groups of society, in effect to create a new 'Soviet citizen'. This was true of *all* citizens of the USSR, after the elimination of the old dominant social groups – aristocrats, bureaucrats, capitalists, intelligentsia or wealthy peasants. Old differences were supposed to disappear in a new, equal, homogeneous and classless society. In a Siberian context, this affected not only people living in the new cities and in villages but also nomadic indigenous peoples, whose way of life was changed forever.

The opening up of the vast coal, nickel, oil and gas reserves of Siberia transformed the landscape and population. By the 1980s, Siberia had become the source of more than 80 per cent of the Soviet Union's oil resources and 90 per cent of its gas.[4] Whole new cities were founded and the population of existing cities massively increased, with enormous suburbs stretching far into the forest and the tundra. The Kuznetsk basin (known by the abbreviation of Kuzbass) in the south-west of Siberia became one of the largest coal-mining areas in the world, covering some 27,000 acres and resulting in the construction of vast new urban conurbations. The town of Leninsk-Kuznetskii, for example, grew from 26,000 people in 1926 to 128,000 in 1972. In the far east, the new town of Komsomolsk-on-Amur was founded in the 1930s. It became an important ship-building and industrial centre, and a city of 300,000 inhabitants by 1942. In the far north, new towns were established to exploit natural resources, and became the centres of the Gulag system in those regions. Norilsk, founded officially in 1935 as the northernmost city in the world to mine the largest nickel deposits in the world, and Magadan, founded in 1929 in the far north-east, both grew into towns with over 150,000 inhabitants. Well-established towns also expanded massively: Novosibirsk, Omsk and Barnaul doubled their populations between 1939 and 1960. Novosibirsk and Omsk now have populations of around 1.5 million.

This was the period of giant projects, when it looked as if the Soviet Union, and its people, could achieve great feats which would be the envy of the Western, capitalist, world. Many of these great projects were in Siberia. The town of Bratsk grew by 3.6 times between 1959 and 1970 because of the great dam project there which attracted thousands of workers, engineers and technicians.[5] When it came online in the early 1960s, the Bratsk hydroelectric plant had an output of over 4,000 megawatts. The dam was followed by even more ambitious projects in Krasnoiarsk and Saianogorsk. This was also the time when Soviet scientists in Novosibirsk believed they could create new forms of science to transform the economic life of the country by, among other things, reversing the flow of the great Siberian rivers. And it was when it was believed that vast uncultivated lands could be transformed into a giant 'breadbasket'. In the 1950s, the so-called 'Virgin Lands' policy was supposed to use advanced technology and agricultural science, as well as sheer manpower, to cultivate huge empty lands in Kazakhstan, the Volga region and western Siberia so that the USSR would become a great grain-producing country to rival the United States and Canada. People took genuine pride in the scientific and technological achievements of the Soviet state, whether it was building massive dams in Siberia or sending the first man into space. 'We were proud to be Russians,' recalled one Siberian villager. 'We were proud when we heard that Iurii Gagarin had been launched into space successfully .... We were also proud of the Soviet Union's military achievements.'[6]

A new railway line, the Baikal-Amur Mainline (BAM), was constructed north of the Trans-Siberian line to open up resources in the north and east of Siberia. It was 2,687 miles (4,299 kilometres) long, and finally comprised 21 tunnels and over 4,000 bridges. Built over the permafrost, it was famously described by President Leonid Brezhnev as 'the construction project of the century'. The industrial belts along the line of the Trans-Siberian and the new BAM railways became heavily populated and urbanised. In all, some 500,000 people settled in the 'BAM zone' in the far east.

The new railways moved goods and people across Siberia, and more roads were constructed, but it was air travel which transformed communications within Siberia. An airport opened in Ulan-Ude (formerly Verkhneudinsk) in 1926. Further airports were opened in Irkutsk in 1928, in Novosibirsk, Tomsk and Novokuznetsk (in the Kuzbass coal area) in 1932, and in Norilsk in 1941. By 1951, the number of air passengers for the whole of Siberia (including the far east) was recorded at almost 336,000; that number had risen to almost 9 million by 1970 and to over 19 million by 1980.[7] Prices of air tickets were kept artificially low to enable people to travel, and ensured that links between Siberia and the heartland of European Russia were easier to maintain. It was not only the main air routes linking Siberia with big cities in European Russia which were important. Local lines and small airports made it possible for people in smaller settlements to reach Siberian cities, and opened up the north, which had never been, and could never have been, reached by railways. I met people from Siberia in the 1970s, when I was a student in Leningrad, who saw their first aeroplane before they ever set eyes on a train. The appearance of an aeroplane in the sky would remind people in the remotest areas that their lives were no longer untouched by the modern world.

Soviet propaganda of the time portrayed migration to Siberia, and in particular to the far east, as a 'noble' undertaking, helping to unlock the wealth of the remotest parts of the country and to bolster the thinly-populated borders with China. Moving there was an expression of patriotism, duty, personal self-sacrifice to a higher cause and a 'boundless sacred love for their mighty socialist Motherland'. Similar sentiments were employed to encourage young people to migrate to the Virgin Lands in northern Kazakhstan and western Siberia, and, in the 1930s, young Jews to settle in a new Jewish Autonomous Region (Birobidzhan) on the river Amur on the border with China. The newly populated lands were to be a battleground – against foreign imperialists, against the climate and the hostile terrain. Popular cinema of the 1930s glorified the conquest of new lands and the taming of nature by young, idealistic workers, peasants and specialists. Special ceremonies and festivals were put on to greet the new arrivals.

As in the tsarist period, most of the new settlers were male, so creating a fresh gender imbalance in Siberia. In February 1937, Valentina Khetagurova, a very photogenic, committed and energetic officer's wife who had settled in the far east, appealed in the Komsomol (or Soviet Youth League) paper: 'Girls! Come to the Far East!' Over 20,000 young women responded to her call to join her in this 'marvellous land' over the next two years.[8] Khetagurova's sentiments were not so different from those expressed in the 1850s about the wonderful prospects in the east even if they now sound naive, if not rather comical:

> I am from the Union's heart – from a flowering capital
> I bring to the Far East my greetings
> Let my song run across the eastern sky
> Carried by the storm of spring, our victory song
> I am just like all of them, those tens of fervent
> Young women of our great Motherland
> We will work diligently with a happy tune –
> We are full of health, energy and strength!
> And there are not a few who hurry to the Far East
> Pedagogues, poets, actors, doctors:
> We want the country to blossom everywhere
> So that it bubbles with joy, like a mountain brook.[9]

A special pavilion was erected for these women outside Khabarovsk cathedral, where they could dance and meet young men – again, not so very different from Governor-General Muravev in the late nineteenth century dispatching young women from bars in Irkutsk to the Amur region to provide brides for settlers, or attempts in the mid-seventeenth century to settle women in Siberia forcibly.

The idealism of the 150,000 young members of the Komsomol from western cities who volunteered to work on the BAM or to build Komsomolsk-on-Amur was real. 'We want to be useful .... We chose your new city of youth,' wrote a young couple from Kazan who wanted to move to Komsomolsk.[10] Shock workers in the Kuznetsk coal fields, such as P. K. Samarin, a bricklayer, who set a record laying 17,000 bricks in a single shift, or Demidenko, a peasant and former Red Army soldier, who worked for 24 hours without a break in temperatures of minus 45 degrees Celsius,[11] genuinely believed that they were making a heroic contribution to the industrial power of the state. The words of one young woman as she set off for the far east – 'I am going to do a great deed. They wait for me! Just think how great that is!'[12] – could only have come from the heart. Some of the 300,000 young Komsomol members who left their home in the summer of 1954 to open up the Virgin Lands did so out of patriotism and a belief that they were going to transform their world. 'We went there "to feed the country", one farmer recollected with some bitterness many years later, when the young idealists' achievements seemed to have been forgotten or dismissed.[13] The young Jewish settlers in Birobidzhan believed they were creating a new homeland, a new 'Soviet Zion', where Jewish culture could flourish. They may have been inspired by the state film *The Seekers of Happiness*, which told the story of a Jewish family who escaped the Great Depression to make a new life for themselves in the Soviet far east.

The reality was often very different, of course. Young Komsomol workers found themselves totally unprepared for the working conditions on the BAM, which included inadequate equipment and supplies and slipshod organisation. It was not, in fact, so different from the problems associated with the construction of the Trans-Siberian railway, albeit in even more hostile terrain and climatic conditions. Furthermore, this had never been a purely idealistic enterprise: early workers on the line had been prisoners in the Gulag, in the notorious BAMlag. As many as 150,000 German and Japanese prisoners of war died there during construction in the 1940s, and in the 1970s volunteers worked alongside Chinese and Korean labourers. The town of Komsomolsk-on-Amur was named after the Komsomol members who helped to construct it in the 1930s, but slave labour from local camps was also used. Some of the new towns which sprung up in the north and opened up new resources such as oil, gas, timber and aluminium – Norilsk, Vorkuta and Magadan among them – were in fact largely built by slave labour.

Many of the people who were driven by idealism to move to remote parts of Siberia on these great schemes became personally disappointed with their lives, or suffered a worse fate. Some young women who sought a new life in the far east found professional and personal fulfilment and happiness, but others were shocked by the poor living and working conditions they encountered. In 1989, Magadan town council commissioned a bust of Eduard Berzin because he had helped to build the town – he was a director of a gold mine, but was arrested in 1937 and shot the following year.[14] Jewish intellectuals were purged in the 1930s, including many from the Autonomous Region. In any event, Soviet policy towards the creation of a Jewish homeland changed with the outbreak of the Second World War and the establishment of the state of Israel. The region is today overwhelmingly non-Jewish (some 92 per cent of the population).

Many people migrated to Siberia for economic and personal reasons as much as from ideological or idealistic motives – better job prospects, the

promise of higher salaries, to escape difficult family circumstances or simply
for a bit of adventure and to break the monotony and restrictions of life in the
towns and villages of European Russia. At a time when it was very difficult to
move from one's town or village of birth without permission, and when there
were desperate housing shortages in European Russia, Siberia offered a rare
opportunity for self-betterment and to start a new life.

The varied motivations of new settlers can be seen in the memoirs of
one small settlement: Kysyl-Syr. This is a village some 30 miles (some 50 kilometres) from Iakutsk, where exploration for natural gas took place in the 1960s
and 1970s and which had grown to a population of some 7,000 people by 1989.
The first new arrivals found almost nothing there – some wooden barrack-like
buildings and almost no facilities. A recent publication[15] includes some
touching accounts of early life in the village which demonstrate the varied
reasons why people came and then stayed in such a northern wilderness (of
course, the voices of those who left as soon as they could are not recorded).
The accounts by residents ring true, and the photographs in the volume show
simple pleasures – a picnic in the forest, a wedding, a fishing trip, a primary-
school concert, the staff standing proudly in front of a newly built hospital, a
party to mark a Soviet national holiday. Many people found professional satisfaction and personal happiness in this remote spot, and that was true not only
of the geologists and engineers who came but also of the teachers, medical
workers and others who were needed to make the new settlement function.

Aleksei Vatunsky, a drilling technician, stated: 'although I don't consider
myself a hero, I am proud that my work for the good of the homeland has not
vanished'. Aleksandr Faflei, a geophysicist, said: 'after my studies I only
wanted to work in Iakutsk – [it was] far away, unknown'. Vladimir Beliaev
recalled the hard work and terrible cold but noted that they had 'good provisions'. Vera Beliaeva, a medical worker from Saratov on the river Volga, said:
'It seemed to me that there was real life . . . . the north gave us a lot that was
good.' There were few material goods but there were 'good people'. Beliaeva
found employment in the hospital and met her future husband in Kysyl-Syr.
Nadezhda Potanina, a driller, came at first with her husband in 1960. In 1965,
she left after the difficult birth of her daughter, but returned after her husband
persuaded her with the words: 'we haven't a place of our own to live in, the
work is not easy, but all the same it's good in the north!' He also reminded her
that the people are different, 'good, open'. What was more, it was 'boring'
where she was. She returned and worked in the local shop. Some women

came to escape unhappiness. Nelli Cherdantseva, a doctor in Ukraine, recalled: 'I left my husband . . . we lived badly and he crushed me.' She found the life hard when she arrived but then: 'I loved it – the people, the nature.' 'Why did I go to Kysyl-Syr?' asked Ionna Pinkevicha from Stavropol in Ukraine; 'like many, I followed my husband'. She became a manager of the kindergarten.

Young people could have fun in this new environment; there were dances and parties and freedom from parental control. Alli Rafikova had attended a prestigious music school attached to the Hermitage in Leningrad. She followed her husband to Kysyl-Syr, but arriving in 1968 she found only two buildings had been erected. When, however, she saw their allotted 'space' in one of the buildings she discovered to her joy that someone had bought a piano for her.

Life was very hard in many Soviet Siberian towns, especially in the early years. Idealistic plans were developed in the 1930s to provide living spaces for 'new Soviet citizens' – whole cities constructed of glass and concrete, with communal services and ample recreation space – but they were never realised in practice because of the costs involved. The speed with which towns were constructed or extended was also in part to blame, as were poor planning, the practice of cutting costs wherever possible and some frankly odd ideas about the future living habits of the new Soviet citizen. In Magnitogorsk, at the southern end of the Urals, which expanded massively in the 1930s from having been a fort on the Orenburg line to a city of over 400,000 with the largest steel and iron works in the country, the first housing blocks obliged families to share bathrooms and did not include kitchens as the planners had assumed people would use public canteens. The streets had not been paved so it was almost impossible in spring and autumn to move about in the thick mud.[16] Infectious diseases were common and death rates from tuberculosis, bronchitis and typhoid were high. Drunkenness and hooliganism were common. In the years after the Civil War and after the Second World War, gangs of orphaned children roamed the streets, begging and carrying out petty thefts.

The description below was made just before Second World War by a eulogist of Soviet Russia whose enthusiasm nevertheless flagged when it came to Siberia:

The cities of Siberia were frightening . . . . True, there were the usual Parks of Culture and Rest, the concert-halls, the dancing-floors in these Siberian cities, but they lacked the atmosphere of spontaneous gaiety prevalent in the cities of European Russia – or even the cities of the Urals. Life here was a fierce stern business which left little time for light relaxation. When the Siberians danced they did so with the same dogged thoroughness which characterised their work, when they listened to music they preferred sombre tunes to joyous ones, when they visited the theatre they demanded tragedy instead of comedy.[17]

The Second World War years were particularly harsh as productivity in the countryside was hit by the conscription of so many men and foodstuffs were diverted to the front. One memoirist from Krasnoiarsk recalled in 1944 that her teacher died of hunger.[18]

The rapid industrialisation of the Soviet Union resulted in a desperate housing shortage and many families having to live in communal flats with shared kitchens and bathrooms. In the late 1950s, the shortage was addressed by Khrushchev with the introduction of a massive urban housing programme which was far greater in scale than any programme in post-war western Europe.[19] Miles of identical five-storey blocks (popularly known as *Khrushchevki*) were constructed on the outskirts of all Soviet towns. The aim was not only to house the masses but also to assert the equality of all citizens and to reject the grandiose style and exclusivity of the blocks which had been built for the elite in the Stalin period. The programme also presented a new image of the Soviet Union – dynamic and capable of transforming and modernising people's lives on a massive scale. Siberian towns shared in this development. Few concessions were made to the extreme climatic conditions, although construction costs were higher in places such as Magadan and Norilsk, but then few concessions had been made in the eighteenth and nineteenth centuries when classical buildings were built in the style of European Russia in the centres of towns like Tomsk and Irkutsk.

What was life like in the new urban suburbs, popularly known as 'sleeping regions'? The experience in Siberia was the same as in other towns in the Soviet Union which grew rapidly. Buildings were put up hastily and standards of construction were often poor; plumbing and wiring were often unreliable; lifts frequently broke down; double windows (essential in the winter) were fitted badly. The planning process regularly neglected to provide for basic local services, and residents often had to travel long distances to kindergartens, schools, doctors and shops, as well as to work in factories or offices. Certainly to an outsider like myself in the 1970s, the distribution of shops on the ground floor of the blocks seemed completely random. On the other hand, for many people the new flats offered a far better quality of life than the crowded communal flats or barracks of the 1930s, and most people seized the opportunity to have a place of their own, with a separate bathroom and kitchen.

The new flats did achieve a certain level of equality: doctors, academics, and office and factory workers lived in the same blocks. There were no exclusively 'middle-class' or 'upwardly mobile' areas in the new Soviet cities, in Siberia or in other areas of the Soviet Union. At the same time, the new developments rejected earlier Soviet notions that the family might disappear under socialism: flats reasserted the importance of the family unit as they were designed for family occupation, and there was almost no provision for single people, for childless married couples, or for elderly couples or single pensioners. At the same time, the pressures increased on family life because most women worked but still had to find childcare, and it was difficult and time-consuming to acquire the basic necessities such as food and clothing. As a result, people had fewer children and it was common for grandmothers to live with their offspring and take on many of the household chores. Ironically, Soviet society ushered in a return to a more traditional family unit in which three generations often lived and worked together under the same roof.[20] Indeed, it could be said that the very speed of urbanisation in Soviet Russia ensured that residents recently arrived from the country retained some of the social relationships and communal attitudes of the village.[21]

Life in some Siberian towns remained – and remains – unpleasant by any standards, and were some of the worst in the Soviet Union. Norilsk, the great nickel-mining centre in the far north, is an extreme example: temperatures can fall as low as minus 50 degrees Celsius in the winter; there are snow storms for some 110–30 days a year; it is dark for almost six months of the year. In 2007, it was listed as one of the most polluted places on earth: berries and mushrooms found in a 30-mile (48-kilometre) radius from the town are toxic. Mining conditions in Norilsk were, and remain, dangerous. One might ask why anyone would volunteer to live there – indeed, the population dropped from a high of 183,000 in 1985 to 131,900 in 2005. Professionals and workers could only be attracted to Norilsk in the Soviet period by the promise of higher pay and better living conditions than they were entitled to in European Russian cities.

Pollution was appalling in many of the new steel and coal towns. In Kuzbass, the coal dust poisoned miners and other citizens alike and lung-cancer rates were a third higher than in other Russian industrial cities. The Kemerovo factories in western Siberia pumped out such high levels of sulphur dioxide, sulphuric acid and nitrous oxide that the population now suffers disproportionately from kidney disease and chronic bronchitis, and children have a high rate of mental disabilities.[22]

Conditions in the new towns in Siberia remained poor in the 1960s and 1970s in comparison with older, more established towns. Accommodation and transport were often poor, and there were fewer resources such as kindergartens and medical facilities. The quality of life in the new town of Saianogorsk, for example, remained lower than that in the more established cities of Novosibirsk or Krasnoiarsk in the same region. Families in Saianogorsk had less living space, and even in the 1970s some 20 per cent of the population lived in communal flats. The number of household goods in the shops increased in the 1950s and 1960s but residents in Saianogorsk still had fewer domestic conveniences – washing machines, vacuum cleaners, televisions. The population of the town was young, which put pressure on pre-school places. Residents were more likely to come from unstable families and to be divorced or separated themselves. Perhaps because of the grim living conditions, more residents in Saianogorsk than in Krasnoiarsk wanted to go into higher education and stayed on at school after the age of 16. The main leisure activity in Saianogorsk was reading.[23] Similar points could be made about other new towns – there was such a shortage of pre-school places in Kiselevsk, in the Kuzbass region, in the 1980s that it was claimed that 1,200 mothers were not able to work.[24] In Magadan, the young workers were called 'fliers' as they could not settle there. The town had the highest divorce rate in the country.[25]

This is not to say that life in all the new Siberian towns, or for that matter in other Soviet towns, was one of endless misery. Social life for young people often revolved around the cinema, and the number of cinemas and theatres increased rapidly in the years after the Second World War. National holidays were an opportunity for parties, dances and social gatherings, as well as providing a day off work. People I spoke to in Siberia who had been brought up in the 1950s and 1960s remembered their childhoods with pleasure, including family picnics in the summer, mushroom and berry gathering in the autumn, winter sports and family celebrations. Part of this fondness stems from the fact that there was a conscious ethos of 'doing everything for the children' in the Soviet Union, which provokes nostalgia today:[26] more toys were produced; children's theatres and puppet theatres were opened in major Siberian towns; there were special TV programmes for children ('Good night, little ones'); the pioneer groups provided social activities and summer camps. Small luxuries also made life bearable – Soviet champagne, perfume, sweets (the Vladivostok sweet factory over-fulfilled its plan and produced 32 types of caramel),[27] holidays far away from Siberia on the Black Sea. After the turbulence and shock of the Civil War, dekulakisation, arbitrary arrests, and the losses and hardships of the Second World War, the importance of this 'normalisation' of life should not be underestimated.

A fair and equal society could easily take on a monotonous uniformity: the blocks of houses were identical; 'norms' for living space were determined by central government; the layouts of the new flats followed set patterns; there was little choice over household goods including electrical goods, furniture, kitchenware and even wallpaper; there were limited varieties of shoes and clothing available; towns suffered the same shortages of foodstuffs; shops and restaurants looked identical in all towns; the same slogans festooned the walls of buildings and streets; Soviet festivals were celebrated everywhere and in much the same way; people went to work on the same style of buses or trams and paid the same fares; cinemas showed the same films. Small differences took on a disproportionate interest or value in this environment, particularly family heirlooms, such as furniture or pieces of china, or gifts from abroad – clothing, books, records, gadgets, bottles of coke. The extent of uniformity should not be exaggerated, however. Despite living in the same blocks, the professional and middle classes had different lifestyles, interests, and social and cultural attitudes from factory workers. Siberia was no different in this respect from the rest of the Soviet Union.

Schools, higher-education and technical institutions gave young people greater opportunities for professional training. The number of schools and teachers in Siberia increased significantly from the 1930s to the 1960s and illiteracy was almost eradicated, at least among the young. Universities and institutions of higher education expanded rapidly and were opened in all major Siberian cities in the Soviet period. In the decade between 1965 and 1975, the number of students in Siberia rose from 31,700 to 51,000.[28] At the same time, the education system became 'Sovietised', that is, secular and homogeneous. In the 1930s, schools that taught in European languages other than Russian were closed down. The ethnic composition of Siberia had always been diverse; in 1922, for example, there were 130 German schools in Siberia. In 1935, 21 teachers in German schools were declared 'class enemies'; in 1938, 87 German, one Korean and two Estonian schools were closed in the Altai region, affecting over 6,000 pupils and 169 teachers.[29]

Most significantly for Siberia, an 'academy town' was constructed in Novosibirsk in the 1950s.[30] At one level, Akademgorodok was simply an attempt to decentralise scientific activities, which had been concentrated in Moscow, and create a regional hub for research. At another level, however, it represented a much more ambitious project and was an attempt to overcome the traditional barriers between different scientific disciplines – between chemistry, physics, mathematics, biology – and between pure science and developments in applied science and industry. At its most utopian, the scheme envisaged the creation of a new 'science' and a new scientific community that would explore new areas of research and in turn help to bring about a new, rational society which would not only compete with the West but would supersede it. The new scientific researchers brought enormous energy and talent to the project. They opened up whole new areas of research in subjects such as physics and were confident that they could change nature.

Part of the early success of Akademgorodok arose from imaginative planning. The new 'science park' was designed to allow academics to communicate ideas more easily by building laboratories in close proximity to each other and by making sure that there were opportunities for scientists to meet and share ideas. The quality of housing, and the quality of life in general, was much higher for scientists than for ordinary Soviet citizens in other towns. Furthermore, life was simply freer in Akademgorodok – people could talk more freely, scientific papers on challenging subjects, including the environmental damage caused by rapid industrialisation, could be published. The academic press in Novosibirsk was under fewer constraints than the press in Moscow.

In time, however, the academic work in Akademgorodok became stifled. Rigid central planning and shortages of essential, but very expensive, equipment meant that areas of research fell behind the West. More curbs on freedom of expression, particularly after the uprising in Czechoslovakia in 1968, hit academic expression. The focus shifted from creating a new scientific society to a more prosaic concentration on economic development to benefit local industry. Nevertheless, Akademgorodok managed to retain some independence of thought. Academics from Akademgorodok were in the forefront when it came to raising environmental issues in Siberia, and in 1983 its academics wrote a report that was critical of the state of the economy and that laid the foundations for Mikhail Gorbachev's subsequent reforms.[31] There is a genuine pride in Siberia in the existence and achievements of Akademgorodok – several people said to me when I visited Novosibirsk in 1991 that its independence of thinking had its roots in Siberian history, not least the lack of serfdom and the pioneering activities of the seventeenth and eighteenth centuries.

The urban population of Siberia grew far more quickly than the rural population.[32] In the tsarist period, the boundaries separating towns and villages were often difficult to define but village and urban life became more differentiated in the Soviet period, a process which, as we have seen, started with the construction of the Trans-Siberian railway at the end of the nineteenth century but which increased rapidly as a result of mass urbanisation. Not only did its urban/rural balance shift, so too did the population's ethnic and gender composition. The Siberian urban population became more Russian, as Russian, and to a lesser extent Ukrainians and Belarusian, migrants moved into Siberian cities; as a result, the proportion of indigenous people in Siberia fell, even though their overall numbers increased. Russians were even more dominant in industrial and urban occupations. In 1963, only 10 per cent of industrial and transport workers in Iakutia were Iakuts.[33] The majority of migrants were young and male. Siberia, as we have seen, had always suffered from a shortage of female settlers – whether it was free settlers in the seventeenth and eighteenth centuries, or forced settlers in the nineteenth-century exile system – but the Soviet period reinforced this imbalance, which was further exacerbated by the urban/rural divide.

The urban population in Siberia grew in part because people left the countryside. In the period 1959–70, approximately 3.3 million inhabitants left Siberian villages for towns, a shift that was greater in Siberia than in European Russia.[34] This was only in part compensated for by the movement of some peasants from European Russia to Siberia. The region which had been primarily rural before the twentieth century, had become an urbanised society.

The traditional way of life and traditional social relationships within the village had been shattered by dekulakisation. The Second World War then brought further hardship. Nail Baugutdinov recalled the sufferings of those years in his 'obscure Siberian village'. His father was at the front, and he recalls: 'I never saw mother eat during the war years.' Life was dominated by constant hunger; there weren't even any potatoes to eat. He and his siblings did not have boots, so they were unable to go to school in the next village because they could not walk through the snowdrifts to get there.[35] Kira Koroleva was nine years old when the Second World War broke out. Her village lost 'fathers, brothers and sons', women and children worked in the fields and, in her words, 'there were many hungry people'. She remembered scouring the fields for potatoes and returning empty-handed.[36] The war also took its toll in the village of Izmaelovka: 'within a short period of time, Izmaelovka had lost most of its men'. Women and children worked in the fields and 'only a few men returned home'.[37] In the novel *Live and Remember*, Valentin Rasputin puts these words into the mouth of Nadya, a young peasant war widow, as she reflects on her life as other women's husbands come home from the fighting:

> 'And my parasite couldn't stay alive? What are you staring at? Isn't it true, then? He made all these children . . . and died a hero's death. And what am I supposed to do with his hero's death now? Feed them with it or what?' Nadya nodded in the direction of her house, where her three children lived, and cried, smearing the tears over her dusty face. 'Who'll take me now with all that baggage? And I'm only twenty-seven. Twenty-seven – and my life is over. It's all gone forever.'

After the war, many of the younger and more ambitious peasants left for the cities. Poor schooling in the villages, where few graduates wanted to work as teachers, meant that opportunities were very limited and it was hard to escape. Vera Cherniaeva worked in the 'Path to Socialism' collective in Tomsk province as a milkmaid. Her family left the village for the town, but when her father failed to find work the family had to return to the village, even poorer than before. They had 'no cow, or any other livestock, or grain, or potatoes'. She did not attend school in the village, but by chance went to live with a relative in the town and was educated there.[38] 'I loved to study and had hoped one day to attend a university in a large city such as Moscow,' recalled another milkmaid, Mariia Murzina. But the family was too poor to send her to school and she was sent to look after the cows from the age of 11.[39]

Life got a bit easier in the villages in the 1950s and 1960s. There were more goods in the shops, and better transport links to the cities. Village club houses showed films and provided a space for social events, which was important as traditional Church-related ceremonies declined. Religious belief remained stronger in the countryside than the towns, particularly among women and the elderly. Church services were never abolished completely but the number of active churches declined in the 1960s.[40] Collective farms suffered from a lack of incentives and opportunities for advancement within the village, where there were clear status and salary differentials, according to occupation. At the top were the tractor drivers, and in particular their team leader; at the bottom were the general labourers. It was hard, however, for the commune to discipline idle or drunken workers and very difficult to sack anyone. Young men had to leave the village for military service and many never returned. The reality was that the brightest and best left for the cities.

The Virgin Lands policy (which mainly applied in north Kazakhstan but also included land in western Siberia) introduced by Nikita Khrushchev in the 1950s was, however, supposed to transform the cultivation of the fields, and the lives of new settlers, in the way that new industries were transforming the cities. In all, some 28–30 million hectares of new land were devoted to grain, in an attempt to alleviate the USSR's dependence on imports from the USA. The vast enterprise involved enormous state investment in agricultural machinery and seed and the movement of tens of thousands of new settlers. The first promising harvests in the late 1950s were followed by failure in the early 1960s: poor and unrepaired machinery, the lack of fertiliser and, above all, drought and soil erosion prevented the expected mass cultivation of grain.[41]

Conditions in the new settlements in the Virgin Lands were as poor as in many of the new towns in Siberia. New settlers arrived to find themselves housed in barracks, or even tents, with little heating, no privacy and poor food which included almost no fresh fruit (in canteens, where little was served except *kasha*, semolina or buckwheat porridge). Most of those who arrived were young and single; as in Kysyl-Syr, some of them found the experience liberating, enjoyed themselves at dances, parties and cinema showings, and made new friends, even if their elation was tempered by violent clashes between different ethnic groups in the new villages, including Kazakhs, Russians from Harbin (in China) and deported Germans and Chechens. It was hard, however, for anyone to settle permanently as there was a dearth of proper housing, kindergartens and even basic medical facilities.[42] It is no surprise that many young people, including the most skilled, left the Virgin Lands when they could and returned to European Russia. By the time Khrushchev fell from power, in 1964, the Virgin Lands project had clearly failed.

The indigenous peoples of Siberia had their lives changed forever by the industrialising, urbanising, collectivising, modernising and secularising policies of the Soviet state. In the first instance, the state had given the various peoples of Siberia a degree of independence, and set up autonomous regions not only for larger groups such as Buriats and Iakuts but also for smaller ethnic groups.[43] This was soon followed, however, as we saw in the last chapter, by an assault on the way of life of nomadic peoples and their forced integration into Soviet life. In this respect, indigenous people were being treated like any other group in Soviet society, where diversity and anything else which could be deemed to be 'anti-Soviet' were crushed. There was, however, an additional element in the Soviet policy towards indigenous people in the assumption that 'Sovietisation' went hand in hand with 'modernisation' and 'civilisation'. These were people who had to be removed forcibly from backwardness and superstition and raised to the level of Soviet citizens through education and forced changes in their way of life. In effect, it was made a 'crime' to be backward. In the process, indigenous people had to be made to work, live and think differently.

The growing physical presence of Russians in this period overwhelmed the indigenous population. Those who lived alongside the new BAM route found new settlements of Russian workers occupying their land and disrupting their agriculture. New industrial towns in the north, such as Norilsk, destroyed their native habitat. Ulan-Ude in Buriat territory became a largely Russian city as industry expanded and migrants flooded in: the town grew from 26,000 people in 1926 to 174,000 in 1959 and to over 250,000 by the 1970s. The Kolyma region in the far north-east was opened up as a penal colony by the prisoners in the Gulag system and Magadan became a town for Soviet officials and released prisoners. It is noticeable that, in the account by the residents of Kysyl-Syr cited above, no mention was made of the local Iakut population – this was now an almost entirely Russian/Ukrainian settlement. Kulaks and others who had been exiled to 'remote parts' of Siberia in the 1930s were given land previously occupied by nomadic peoples. Indigenous people who settled in the new towns were few among many Russians.

It was important for the state to create homogeneous Soviet citizens, and this required the eradication of 'differences'. Children of indigenous people were sent to boarding schools in Russian towns and were taught by Russian teachers using Russian textbooks. They often forgot their native languages, as well as their local customs, diet, dress and traditional skills as trappers and hunters. The secular thrust of Soviet education turned many young people away from the beliefs of their parents, whether shamanistic, Muslim or Buddhist (or Christian for that matter). Native languages were re-written using Western scripts – Latin at first but Cyrillic from 1937. In any event these languages could not counter the dominance of Russian, which was a prerequisite for any professional job. The few indigenous people who were trained in Leningrad at the Institute of Native Peoples, or in higher-education institutes in Siberian cities, often lost touch with their roots and became Russified or, more properly speaking, Sovietised, in the process. They also died for the Soviet Union. The village of Diarkhan in the Sakha republic (formerly Iakutia), which had been formed as a collective farm in 1929–34, sent 99 men to fight in the Second World War; 59 of them never returned.

To an extent, changes to the way of life of indigenous people were an inevitable consequence of urbanisation and modernisation, and the opening up of opportunities and new forms of communication, some of which would have happened under any ideological or economic system. Young indigenous men conscripted into the army, for example, saw life outside their community. New habits and interests were spread by better communications with the outside world. Factory-made clothes and goods in the shops replaced home-woven cloth and traditional domestic items. Russian food and drink became more common. Soviet cultural institutions – cinema, classical ballet, theatrical performances – established themselves in major Siberian towns, and indigenous costumes and folk dances could all too easily be reduced in status to lower forms of culture, appealing to less sophisticated villagers and tourists.

To some extent, the economic policies of the state kept indigenous people artificially in the countryside, by supporting collective farms which were unproductive and providing links by air and road which were also uneconomic. Diarkhan, for example, was obliged to grow grain, even though it did not flourish in the climatic conditions. The village was kept alive artificially by subsidies until the collapse of the USSR.[44]

There was also, however, a vicious assault on the way of life and beliefs of indigenous people in the name of progress. Shamans were targeted in particular; many were persecuted and arrested. Soviet cinema portrayed shamanism as evil and backward – in the film *Samoed Boy* in 1928, a boy escapes the clutches of an evil shaman and becomes a new Soviet man. In principle, shamanism was eradicated, and it is certainly the case that better medical provision diminished the shaman's role and undermined the popularity of traditional healing. Nevertheless, belief in shamans and their magical powers persisted. In the village of Diarkhan, the shaman was still active in the 1950s.

It was only possible to undermine shamanism and other rituals associated with, for example, hunting by deliberately undermining the economic life of the indigenous population. As we saw in the last chapter, nomads, hunters, reindeer herders and fishermen were forced into collective farms. Categorising wealthier hunters and fishermen as kulaks ignored traditional economic and social relationships.

As a Soviet teacher in Chukotka remarked without any irony: 'the Chukchi language still does not have words to express certain socioeconomic phenomena. For example, there is no word for "struggle" in its class meaning.'[45] Nevertheless, smashing traditional relationships and the leading clan families had broken traditional social relationships within communities and destroyed kinship groups and traditional values. A study of Buriat village life in the 1960s and 1970s demonstrated that in most respects the Buriat village had become a Russian village. The traditional layout inside houses was still, however, maintained and kinship groups still helped to preserve a combined family contribution to the management of family plots and privately owned livestock. Culturally, a syncretistic process had taken place by which Buddhist and traditional festivals merged. The traditional Buriat spring festival celebrating physical prowess had become a secular day of sport which also celebrated the foundation of the Buriat republic. Other festivals and rituals – honouring ancestors, sacrifices for spirits, wedding and funeral customs, divination, spells – were kept separate and private. Buriat rituals certainly survived into the 1960s, although it is hard to know how far this reflected the continuation of genuine beliefs and how far it was simply an excuse, as some young men said, to dress up in traditional clothes and enjoy oneself 'in a Buriat way'.[46]

Was a new Soviet citizen created in these years? At least some of the scientists in Akademgorodok and the young men and women who went to work in the remote parts of Siberia thought they were creating something new and exciting based on different ideas and values. Siberia changed more than many other parts of the Soviet Union as a result of rapid industrialisation and the exploitation of its natural resources. Some of these changes came about through Soviet ideology, but others were the inevitable result of modernisation, urbanisation and new forms of media and communications. Siberia experienced a fresh wave of migration as new opportunities for work opened up in new towns. Siberian society became more urbanised, more secular and better educated. Urban society became less differentiated – between the lifestyles of people in different occupations and backgrounds, between Russians and non-Russians, and between Christians and non-Christians. The pattern was, however, different in the countryside. Collectivisation had broken traditional agricultural practices and the traditional village way of life but the countryside lagged behind the towns in modernisation and in the opportunities offered to young people. As differentiation decreased within towns, it increased between town and village, and the traditional way of life of indigenous people was destroyed without them becoming fully integrated into Soviet society.

By the 1980s, the country's economy had stagnated and its social and political problems were being exposed in the freer media. The Soviet Union was formally dissolved in December 1991 as its economy disintegrated and its political system lost credibility. Problems had been evident in Siberia in the previous four decades: poor housing in towns, industrial pollution, stagnating agriculture. How well were Siberian citizens equipped to face the new challenges of a post-communist Russia?

CHAPTER SIXTEEN

The New Siberia

Torn from the land.
Contaminated by vodka and wine.
Corrupted.
Severed from the root that binds a people to its land.[1]

These are the Khanty (Ostiak) writer Eremei Aipin's reflections on the destruction of the way of life of his people. It was not only indigenous people who blamed Moscow for all their ills in post-Soviet Russia. 'The Centre betrayed us – let's save ourselves' was the headline in a Khabarovsk newspaper in 1990.[2] The economic and social trauma of the 1990s and the challenges of the twenty-first century not only changed the lives of the approximately 30 million people who lived in Siberia but also affected the way they thought about Siberia and its future.

The economic collapse in the post-Soviet 1990s had a dramatic impact on Siberia. Centres of industry – coal, steel, armaments – suffered as trade contracted and factories closed. Unemployment soared as internal trade fell apart, prices rose faster than wages, the rouble collapsed and savings became worthless. Soviet planning had created uneconomic units – from the vast towns in the frozen north to the artificially constructed collectives – and many of these imploded when subsidies from the centre were reduced or ceased altogether. The population of Siberia and the far east fell from a high of 32 million at the end of the Soviet period to some 30 million.[3] For example, the population of Magadan in the far north-east halved. Some towns and settlements in the far north were simply abandoned because the cost of continuing to supply goods and heat buildings was too high to sustain. A BBC programme, 'The World's Most Dangerous Roads', broadcast in August 2010, showed a completely deserted town on the road between Iakutsk and Magadan. (Settlements have disappeared before – we saw in Chapter 3 that the same fate befell the town of Mangazeia in the late seventeenth century.) The Pacific Fleet was neglected in the far east and Vladivostok declined, while the weakness of the infrastructure in Siberia was exposed: the costs associated with, and poor construction of, the BAM resulted in capacity declining by half between 1990 and 1997.[4]

Mortality rates in the towns went up as medical services contracted and standards of heath and diet declined. Goods disappeared from the shelves of shops and people were forced to rely on relations in the country for basic foodstuffs, which was particularly difficult in Siberian towns that lacked a productive agricultural hinterland. I can recall entering a large supermarket in Irkutsk in 1991 – the shelves were completely empty apart from a few tins of fish and jars of Bulgarian fruit juice. It was a frightening experience, followed by a worse one at Irkutsk airport where no planes were flying because there was no fuel. This was a country in economic meltdown.

The economic crisis came as a great psychological shock to the people of Siberia. In Kysyl-Syr, described in the previous chapter, a telegram in 1994 tersely announced that the exploitation of natural gas at the site would cease: 1,400 people suddenly lost their jobs. The residents suffered from a loss of income and a lack of supplies in the local store, and a lack of security for their future – the Russian government reneged on its promise to house those who had worked there for over 15 years in any town of their choice in the country. Moreover, this experience shattered the idealism of those who thought they were making a genuine and serious contribution to the future of the country by their pioneering work in a remote corner of Siberia. 'People hoped it was some sort of mistake because their work and they themselves were still needed by the state,' wistfully commented Valentina Diakonova, a geophysicist who had lived in Kysyl-Syr since 1972.[5]

In the country, people had their own vegetable plots and access to the produce of the collective farms, but they still suffered as a result of the economic instability and many looked back on the past nostalgically:

Suddenly the consumer goods disappeared from the stores. The shelves in the store in Izmaelovka and in the stores of Magnitogorsk became empty

.... It became difficult to find a staple product such as cereal .... In 1992 our paper money lost almost all its value. Who could have predicted that the price of products would rise so high? ... We were accustomed to great difficulties in Izmaelovka, but we had never suffered from the terrible effects of an unstable economy. Many of us agreed that living under the old economic system had been better. Under the new system we felt lost. The shock was so severe that it affected our health. The changes were particularly hard on the men in the village. The changes drove them to drinking. I think they turned to vodka because they lost hope for gaining a better life.[6]

The young and able left for the towns, leaving the elderly behind. Many villages reverted to subsistence farming.

Indigenous people had been forced into collectives and were obliged to follow instructions from the centre on the organisation of their agriculture, fishing or reindeer herding. In the 1990s, much of this artificial economy collapsed. The village of Diarkhan in the Sakha republic (Iakutia), for example, reverted to a subsistence economy after subsidies ended for uneconomic grain and dairy farming. Broken machinery was left to rust and the villagers went back to using horses and farming by hand.[7] The ending of uneconomic flights and bus services from the village to the town pushed Diarkhan back into the isolation it had experienced before the Revolutions. Hunting peoples, like the Chukchis and Koriaks, also reverted to a subsistence economy in the 1990s.[8] Children of Aipin's clan had not become oilmen or geologists because they had not acquired sufficient education to achieve professional status. They remained in the least skilled occupations and many young men died from alcohol abuse or in fights: 'The clan died from a sense of hopelessness, a sense of doom.'[9]

Siberia suffered badly in the 1990s, perhaps more so than most other territories of the former USSR, but it also held the key to national recovery after 2000. As is often quoted, particularly by those who live there, Siberia holds 80 per cent of the oil, 85 per cent of the natural gas and 80 per cent of the coal of the Russian Federation. Oil and gas have been central to the post-Soviet revival.[10] It is the revenues from Siberian oil and natural gas which have enabled the country to invest in restructuring its economy and modernising its infrastructure. This policy has given rise to a number of questions about the future: for instance, to what extent does the very richness of Siberian resources cause an imbalance in the economy, as the oil and energy sector

now predominate to the detriment of other industries? There are also questions about the future sustainability of this model: the resources are not infi-
nite and they are in locations which are expensive to exploit and maintain.
Already the resources of western Siberia are declining and those of more
remote eastern Siberia need to be developed to replace them. The oil industry
is not labour-intensive, a fact which has led to a drop in the urban, industrial
population in southern Siberia, which is the centre of the declining coal and
steel industries. The Russian government, and those who live in Siberia, are
concerned about this loss of population, which could create a political
problem if an 'empty east' faces a resurgent China on its borders. Finally, there
are questions about the environmental costs of this policy, to which I shall
return.

As well as its natural resources, Siberia also has access to the markets of
the Far East, in particular Japan and China, through Vladivostok and the
towns along its enormous border with China. Anyone visiting Vladivostok
cannot fail to notice that almost all the cars are Japanese. There is a recognition that Siberia now needs to look outwards, having artificially had its
economy focused internally in the Soviet period. There is also a recognition
that Siberia needs significant investment in its communications and infrastructure. As one speaker commented at the Baikal Economic Forum in
2002, looking back to the great projects of the past (admittedly without
considering the economic and human costs of such projects):

> When the Trans-Siberian railway was built, it cost one billion gold roubles.
> It also cost a huge amount of money to build the Norilsk nickel plant and
> the Baikal-Amur railway. Developing the region further would require new
> investment. The problem is we've forgotten how to attract investment over
> the last decade and now we have to learn how to do it again.[11]

Clearly more investment is needed in infrastructure, as anyone who
has travelled on the roads and railways or has experienced the limited
facilities of Siberian regional airports will testify. There is, nonetheless,
already an air of dynamism in many Siberian cities. Trade has increased since
2000 in the eastern cities and construction is booming. This confidence
is illustrated by the building of a completely new university campus for
the new Far Eastern Federal University outside Vladivostok, intended
specifically to open up new opportunities for Russia to become a leader in

technical and national development. In 2004, the *Russia Journal* featured the headline 'Krasnoiarsk Krai Set to Transform Siberia'. 'Today's Siberia is a vast expanse of land endowed with human and natural resources,' it continued; Krasnoiarsk is a 'gem of Russian Siberia'. 'Gem' might be newspaper hyperbole but to the outside observer towns such as Krasnoiarsk certainly do not seem depressed.

The indigenous peoples of Siberia suffered disproportionately as their economy collapsed. The only exception was in remote Chukotka, where Roman Abramovich was governor from 2002 to 2008 and is said to have spent millions of his own fortune on improving the infrastructure. For example, Amguema, a village of 600 Chukchis, was transformed by his generosity, with the construction of new homes, a guesthouse and a new boarding school. 'Thank you for everything you have done for us,' gushed a middle-aged nurse, Olga Kymytyul, as she greeted the governor. He even made sure the salaries of public sector workers were paid on time. 'It's a Revolution!' enthused a local Amguema official.[12]

The post-Soviet transition has come at a high human cost. This is true for the whole of Russia, but Siberia has experienced particular problems. There are significant health problems in Siberia, not least because 75–80 per cent of the adult population of Siberia smoke, compared with some 40 per cent in the rest of Russia. The *Moscow Times* in 2009 noted that TB and AIDS were a particular problem in the region. The city of Irkutsk had the highest number of officially registered cases of AIDS in the country, three times more than Moscow. Infant mortality is high, particularly in the remote Altai and Tuva regions and among indigenous peoples generally in Siberia. Life expectancy is low throughout Russia but lower in Siberia than the average for the Russian Federation as a whole: 59 for men and 73 for women (compared with 64 for men and 76 for women in the Federation overall).

The reduction in size of the Pacific Fleet and the army on the border with China has had a particular impact on life in towns which had previously housed large numbers of naval and military personnel. An article in the *Moscow Times* on 7 December 2012 entitled 'Far Eastern Towns in Race to Disappear' featured Iasnaia, in the Chita region, which had become a ghost town after the departure of the army in 2011. Derelict buildings were being dismantled by locals who were selling bricks for 60 copecks each. 'We are like *** in the eyes of the administration,' commented one resident, aged 63, who had moved to Siberia 34 years earlier to work on the BAM line, perhaps as one of those young and idealistic Komsomol members who believed they were striving for the greater good of the country and now felt abandoned by the new regime.

Some of the recent social and political concerns raised in the local and national press could as easily have been written about Siberia in the eighteenth or nineteenth centuries, or during the traumatic decades of the early twentieth century. As the grip of the state weakened, particularly in the more distant regions, so organised crime networks grew and violent crime increased. Vladivostok acquired the reputation of being the crime capital of the East, not least because it was the hub for importing and smuggling goods from Japan for the Russian market. Social problems such as alcoholism and family breakdown increased with economic instability. Residents of Irkutsk commented to me during my visit in 2009 about the high levels of alcoholism and crime in their city. A report in August 2011 in a local paper, *All the News,* featured concerns about caring for orphans in Tomsk so that they were 'not left on streets'. Local papers report on the failings and corruption of officials in Vladivostok and elsewhere. Such problems are not unique to Siberia, or to Russia, or to the twenty-first century for that matter, but perhaps it is felt there more acutely as there is a suspicion that local officials can act with impunity as they are so far from Moscow's reach and have their own local power base, in some cases supported by the mafia. Finally, the concerns expressed today about the migration of Chinese and Korean workers echo the concerns expressed at the end of the nineteenth century about the 'Yellow Peril'. In September 2011, an article in the Khabarovsk business paper *The Golden Horn* expressed fears about the illegal migration of Chinese workers. Certainly, many Chinese and Korean migrants can be seen on construction sites and in markets in Siberian cities, giving rise to resentment, hostility and fear.[13]

Some of these problems have been exacerbated in Siberia because it has a high concentration of new towns and large industrial complexes and was a major base for the armed forces, with the result that there have been significant economic adjustments and hardships in the most recent period. Others simply arose from Siberia's geographical position – its distance from Moscow, its long border with China and its ports in the east. The displacement of population into and within Siberia in the twentieth century had been massive. That included free settlers (from peasants in the early twentieth century to young men and women in the 1930s to the 1950s), forced deportees (convicts, kulaks, 'enemies of the people') and people forced away from their traditional way of life into collectives. Perhaps it was harder for people here to adjust to the new environment after the collapse of the Soviet Union than for people in the more settled communities in European Russia.

It is significant that not only Orthodoxy but also new religious movements have particularly flourished in Siberia. There has been a considerable increase in the number of Orthodox churches, including reconstruction of cathedrals which had been destroyed, restoration of churches which had been neglected or put to other uses, and the construction of entirely new cathedrals (for instance, in Khabarovsk on a hill overlooking the river Amur – and the Chinese frontier). Churches had simply not been built in the new Siberian towns but that omission is now being rectified. Photographs of Norilsk on the town's website feature the new church as well as ugly, jerry-built Soviet apartment blocks and the overwhelming nickel factory complex. In 2010, the *Vladivostok Times* reported that a new cathedral was to be built; in April 2011, the governor and his family led the religious procession at Easter as their tsarist predecessors had done.

There has been an even greater increase in practising Baptists, Jehovah's Witnesses and Seventh-Day Adventists. In 2001, there were 251 non-Orthodox churches in the Khabarovsk region alone.[14] More extreme sects have also taken root in Siberia, including followers of Burkhanism – a mixture of shamanism, Buddhism and Christianity – in the Altai. Vissarion (real name Sergei Torop), who claims to be a reincarnation of Christ, has established his 'Church of the Last Testament' in a settlement of some 4,000 people in a remote corner of Krasnoiarsk province. They live abstemiously without alcohol or tobacco and, like Old Believers and other sects before them in Siberia, await the end of the world.

Furthermore, the state has been unable to overcome a centuries-long sense of alienation in the peasantry. These contemporary sentiments from a peasant in the village of Izmaelovka could equally have been expressed by a state peasant in the eighteenth or nineteenth centuries, or a newly collectivised peasant in the 1920s or 1930s:

We in the villages were forced to give to the State what we produced. The State took from us much of our wool and much of everything else we produced. The State gave us little in return for our hard labour, and now it seems the State has forgotten about us. The State only remembers us when it needs our produce or when it needs our young boys for military service. We give birth to our sons, we nurse them, we raise them and we teach them, and then the State takes them from us to fight its wars.[15]

It is the combination of two perceptions – that the wealth of natural resources in Siberia is propping up the national economy and that the people have suffered disproportionately from the pain of economic transition but are being ignored – that drives local resentment against the centre. The feeling of detachment from life in European Russia is also fuelled by the sharp increase in the cost of internal flights so that Moscow has become prohibitively expensive to reach and less attractive than tourist destinations in East Asia. A particular focus of this resentment is the environmental damage done to Siberia by the exploitation of natural resources in the Soviet period. This is particularly felt in the regions in the far north and north-east by indigenous people who have seen their grazing grounds for reindeer destroyed and their rivers polluted by oil and gas firms. As Aipin put it: 'What's more valuable, an extra ton of oil or the fate of a human being? A ton of oil or the fate of an entire people? Can this barbarity be stopped?'[16]

The hostility is increased by the 'Russianness' of the newcomers – European Russian or international firms – who are seen to be riding roughshod over local concerns in order to extract the maximum profit. In the Khanty-Mansi (Ostiak) region in western Siberia, local activists have attempted to protect their interests but have found themselves powerless to stop further destruction of their lands by oil and gas companies, a destruction which has included the violation of their sacred lands.[17] Evenki (Tungus) living along the route of the Eastern-Siberian Pacific Ocean oil pipeline have voiced their concerns about the impact on their fishing and grazing, and have complained that it crosses their cemeteries. The oil company Transneft invited members of the public to express their concerns, but many Evenki could not afford to undertake the journey to the company offices and, in any event, assumed they would be ignored. 'No one will listen to us,' said one; 'they decided this long ago, without us . . . . who is going to ask us?' said another.[18] It has been difficult for grassroots movements to challenge government policy. To be effective, movements need international support and funding, and much of that has been concentrated on saving endangered species, such as the Amur leopard and Siberian tiger, rather than highlighting local environmental concerns.[19]

The campaign to protect Lake Baikal from pollution has brought together activists from a broader section of the Russian community. The main focus of their protest is the giant Baikal paper and cellulose plane, established in the 1950s, but it extends to a more general desire to preserve the lake with its unique fauna and wildlife. The cellulose plant was closed in 2008, primarily because it was no longer profitable, but reopened in 2010, with assurances from Vladimir Putin about pollution controls. The *Moscow Times* reported in August 2013 that the plant would finally close in November of that year, with the loss of 800 jobs. Transneft has agreed to divert the route of the Siberian East Pacific Ocean pipeline away from Lake Baikal and other nature reserves.

Resentment against the despoliation of Siberia is driving a new regionalist movement. There are similarities between this and the regionalists in the late nineteenth century. There has been a revival of interest in the concept of Siberia as a 'colony' which was asserted so strongly by Nikolai Iadrintsev in the 1880s. There is the same resentment that the 'centre' exploits the land and people of Siberia and gives little back. A separate Siberian literature has also emerged in recent years. Some authors depict Siberia, and Siberians, as freer and less corrupt than their European counterparts, a theme which would be familiar to eighteenth- and nineteenth-century Russian and European commentators on Siberia. The new literature is also closely bound up with environmental concerns and the need to resist further destruction of Siberia's land and the way of life of its people. There has been an attempt to create a 'Siberian' language – essentially a reconstruction of north Russian dialects used by free settlers in the seventeenth and eighteenth centuries.

How strong is this movement and what does it want to achieve? In October 2010, Paul Goble, in a piece entitled 'Window on Eurasia: Siberian Nationalists Appeal to the World', reported in his blog *Window on Eurasia* that Siberian nationalists wanted a new, separate, nation.[20] He saw a clear link between the movement and environmental damage and also a resentment against the exploitation of Siberia by Moscow. In an earlier post in the same month, Goble drew attention to an article in the *Kyiv Post* that claimed that in the 2010 census people were not allowed to describe themselves as 'Siberians'. Despite this, and despite one census-taker allegedly stating that 'there is no such nationality', some 6,000 respondents entered themselves as 'Siberians'. Six thousand is a tiny number in a region of 30 million, but Goble also cited an article in *Komsomolskaia Pravda* in May 2011 which claimed that one-third

of people living in Siberia identified themselves as 'Siberians' and saw themselves as separate from Russia. People can have multiple identities, of course
– seeing themselves as belonging to their region, to Siberia and to Russia
simultaneously – but the driving force behind this identification was the
perception that Moscow was stealing Siberia's wealth while neighbouring
China was becoming ever more prosperous.

The possibility of a strong Siberian separatist movement is lessened by
several factors. First, the coherence of the whole region has been weakened
by the administrative restructuring in 2000 which divided the region into
three separate areas: Western Siberia (but excluding some historically western
Siberian regions which are now under the administration of the Ural region),
Eastern Siberia and the Far East. The newly defined Far East now comprises
not only the Amur region but also the Sakha republic (Iakutia) and the far
north-east (which had been administratively part of eastern Siberia in the
nineteenth century) and Kamchatka, and is now acquiring a distinct identity.
It is the smallest region in terms of population (some 6.7 million) but includes
some of the richest deposits of oil and gas and, most importantly, is orien-
tating itself towards the east through its ports, such as Vladivostok. The
awareness that the Far East has different needs and aspirations from the rest
of historic Siberia weakens the case for a separate but unified Siberia.

Second, the existence of conflicting proponents of Siberian separateness
reduces the cohesion of the movement. One group, Siberian Freedom, is
based in Tomsk; another, the National Alternative of Siberia, is based in
Irkutsk. The inability of different groups within Siberia to coordinate and
agree on policies was one of the weaknesses of the resistance to the Bolsheviks
in the Civil War. The same is true today – there is no accepted main party or
leader.

Third, there is a natural tendency to resent Moscow, and Muscovites,
which is not exclusive to Siberia (or to Russia, for that matter, when it comes
to attitudes to a country's capital and its inhabitants) and which makes it
more difficult to portray Siberia as a special case. As one person, born and
brought up in Siberia but now living in Moscow, said to me: 'Siberians, like all
provincials, love to criticise the centre; they accuse the authorities of a
commercial attitude to the region. They think that the richness of their
natural resources makes the region self-sufficient.'

A final weakness is the nature of Siberia itself, which I hope has emerged
from this study. The historically mixed ethnic composition of Siberia has

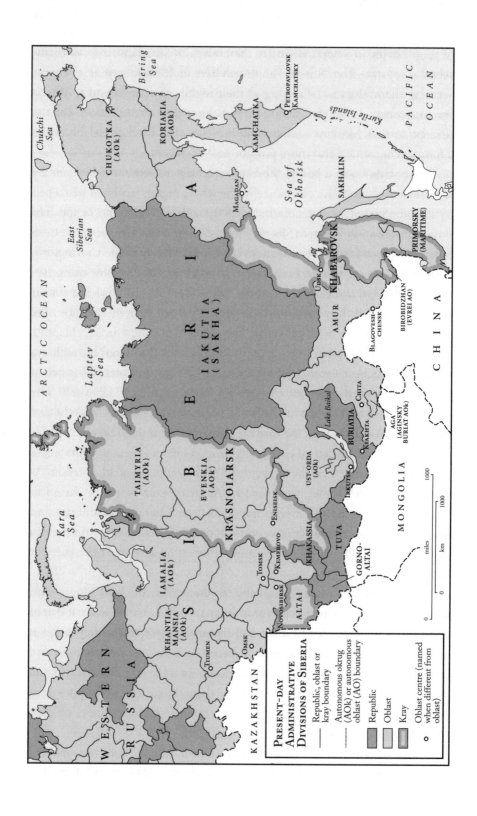

PRESENT-DAY
ADMINISTRATIVE
DIVISIONS OF SIBERIA

—— Republic, oblast or
    kray boundary

---- Autonomous okrug
    (AOk) or autonomous
    oblast (AO) boundary

Republic

Oblast

Kray

○ Oblast centre (named
    when different from
    oblast)

become something to celebrate in terms of Siberian distinctiveness; the regional historical museum in Omsk, for example, has an interesting display about the dress and lifestyles of the non-Russian peoples in its region. Siberia was, however, primarily a land of colonists – either free or unfree – but these colonists were ethnically predominantly Russian and if they were not Russian they were more likely to be east Slav (Ukrainian or Belarusian). Furthermore, the indigenous Siberians became more and more of a minority as more settlers arrived and this process intensified in the twentieth century: ethnic Russians now make up 84 per cent of the population. The influence of indigenous culture on the new settlers was always limited – be it in diet, lifestyle, economic activity or spiritual beliefs – and has diminished over time. It is significant that when a new language was constructed to assert Siberian separateness, it was derived from north Russian – it was simply not practical, or deemed appropriate, to choose between the many indigenous languages of Siberia.

Even in the pre-Revolutionary period, it was hard to define a separate 'Siberian culture' – not simply because so many cultural activities were imported from European Russia but also because many religious, social and ethnic groups formed their own, separate identities in Siberia. Culture, architecture, diet, habits, language, fashions, laws, ideology, technology, ideas – all have spread from the west to the east. In the twentieth century, the 'Sovietisation' of society led to an even greater homogeneity in lifestyles, education and cultural pastimes.

Siberian development has, however, moved at a different pace from that in European Russia, as we have seen: at some points it was backward compared with European Russia; at other points it led the way. In the seventeenth century, and in many ways until the late nineteenth century, Siberia lagged behind European Russia in economic development. Siberian administration was even more corrupt and incompetent than in European Russia; Siberian towns were cultural and economic backwaters; Siberian villages were slow to adopt new agricultural methods; life in remote forts remained harsh and precarious. Even in this period, however, some adventurous and dedicated individuals had unique achievements to their name of which Siberians today are rightly proud – these include the intrepid Cossacks and explorers who from the late sixteenth century opened up new lands, and who reached the coast of North America, and the Decembrists and other notable exiles who made important educational and cultural contributions. The construction of the Trans-Siberian railway transformed the economic, social and cultural life of Siberia in the late nineteenth and early twentieth centuries so that it became one of the most, if not *the* most, dynamic regions of the Russian empire.

This favoured position was shattered by the Civil War and then by the annihilation of not only individuals but also whole groups of people during the period of dekulakisation, collectivisation and the Gulags. Siberia was at the centre of the rapid industrialisation of the Soviet Union; though it suffered acutely from the economic collapse of the USSR in the 1990s, it is key to the revival of the Russian economy today. There has always been an awareness of the richness, or at least potential richness, of Siberia, despite its forbidding climate and remoteness – from the fur trade in the seventeenth century, to the unrealised hopes of the opening up of the Amur and North American coast in the nineteenth century, to the exploitation of its oil and gas resources in the twentieth and twentieth-first centuries.

It is understandable that many people in Siberia think that their develop-ment has been distinct and that their economic, and even their political, future lies in a different direction from the rest of Russia. Finally, there is a sense today, as in earlier centuries, that Siberia and its people are different. There was a strong sense of Siberia as a land of 'freedom' for hunters and Cossacks in the seventeenth century, peasants escaping serfdom in the eight-eenth century, peasant settlers in the early twentieth century, young women seeking adventure in the 1930s and scientists in Iakutia or Akademgorodok in the 1960s, and that sentiment is still expressed by people in Siberia today. There is also an awareness that Siberia has been a terrible place of punish-ment, suffering and imprisonment – for Old Believers and members of other religious sects, political opponents of the tsar, revolutionaries, convicts, kulaks, Whites and various other 'enemies of the people'. The region is only just coming to terms with the importance of memorialising its many victims by establishing regional museums of oppression, often in old KGB headquar-ters, as with the small but moving museum in Tomsk, and by setting up memorials to those who died in this period at the sites of Gulags or in major towns.

Moscow has always been a long way away, even in the eras of railway and aeroplanes, and Siberia and Russian Siberians have always had other, non-European neighbours. And there is still the uniqueness of the sheer vastness of Siberia and the beauty of its untamed forests and mountains and the size and power of its great rivers. 'Siberians' regard themselves as having special characteristics – 'trustworthy', 'reserved', 'quieter' are characteristic words used by people I have met – traits deriving not only from having to live in and adapt to a hostile and remote land but also from having come to love that land.

What else can explain the fascination of Siberia to both Russians and foreigners like myself? As Valentin Rasputin put it:

And why at the merest mention of the word *Siberia* do people living farthest from it . . . who have never made it to Siberia, involuntarily perk up and pay attention: what's it like there, in Siberia? What is it in them that responds to this word? Which is it – joy or sorrow, hope or disappointment, expectation or compassion? What has Siberia's all-pervasive vitality breathed into them? Don't they, with their vague notions and feelings, believe that we may commit errors in remaking nature anywhere we please, only not in Siberia? . . . We have only one Siberia . . . . It is an exception in being a wilderness preserved intact until recent times, one currently experiencing the immense, unprecedented influence of our economic activity. Here the human race is now being tested to see what it has become in the present and what can be expected of it in the future.

Isn't this still another reason why people are drawn here, to feel in themselves the boundary between the temporal and the eternal, the inconstant and the true, the ruined and the preserved?[21]

Notes

Introduction

1. *Istoricheskaia entsiklopediia Sibiri*, vol. 2, pp. 434–41. I have found different estimates of the size of the population of Siberia today, ranging from 30 to 40 million. Part of this variation arises from the contemporary geographical definition of Siberia, and whether it includes the far east and the historically Siberian provinces which are now administratively part of the Ural region. An estimate of 32 million is for all the lands east of the Urals and including what is now the administrative territory of the Far East, is given in the *Historical Encyclopaedia* based on statistics in 1989, but before the results of the 2010 census have been made public.
2. The best accounts in English are Lincoln, *The Conquest of a Continent: Siberia and the Russians*; Wood, *Russia's Frozen Frontier: A History of Siberia and the Russian Far East 1581–1991*; Forsyth, *A History of the Peoples of Siberia: Russia's North Asian Colony, 1581–1990*; Slezkine, *Arctic Mirrors: Russia and the Small Peoples of the North*.
3. Hartley, 'Gizhiga: Military Presence and Social Encounters in Russia's Wild East'.
4. Used mainly in my forthcoming article 'Education in the East: The Omsk Asiatic School'.

Chapter One: Cossacks and Conquest

1. Armstrong, *Yermak's Campaign in Siberia*, pp. 71–2.
2. Vvedenskii, *Dom Stroganovykh v XVI–XVII vekakh*, p. 75.
3. Fisher, *The Russian Fur Trade*, p. 25.
4. Lantzeff, Pierce, *Eastward to Empire*, p. 87.
5. Armstrong, *Yermak's Campaign in Siberia*, pp. 12, 208.
6. Ibid., p. 137.
7. Ibid., pp. 160–5.
8. Fisher, *The Russian Fur Trade*, p. 26.
9. Armstrong, *Yermak's Campaign in Siberia*, p. 140.
10. Ibid., p. 46.
11. Ibid., p. 216.
12. Ibid., pp. 13–17.
13. Bassin, *Imperial Visions*, pp. 62–3.
14. Collins, 'Plans for Railway Development in Siberia, 1857–1890', pp. 149–85.
15. *Krest'ianstvo Sibiri v epokhu feodalizma*, pp. 366–7.
16. Lantzeff, Pierce, *Eastward to Empire*, p. 120.
17. Fisher, *The Russian Fur Trade*, p. 43.
18. Dmytryshyn, *Russia's Conquest of Siberia*, vol. 1, p. 137.

19. Fisher, *The Voyage of Semen Dezhnev in 1648*, pp. 58–9, 61, 62.
20. Ibid., pp. 93–4.
21. Avvakum, *The Life of the Archpriest Avvakum*, p. 73.
22. Aleksandrov, *Rossiia na dal'ne-vostochnykh rubezhakh*, pp. 37–8.

Chapter Two: Land, Indigenous Peoples and Communications

1. Armstrong, *Yermak's Campaign in Siberia*, p. 54.
2. This section is drawn from Forsyth, *A History of the Peoples of Siberia*.
3. Forsyth, 'The Siberian Native People before and after the Russian Conquest', pp. 69–71.
4. Martin, *Treasure of the Land of Darkness*, p. 80.
5. Georgi, *Russia*, vol. 1, p. 178.
6. Ibid., p. 132.
7. Lesseps, *Travels in Kamtschatka during the Years 1787 and 1785*, p. 95.
8. *Etnografiia russkogo krest'ianstva Sibiri XVI–seredina XIX vv.*, pp. 79–80.
9. Tomsk, GATO, f. 3, op. 20, d. 20, on the settlement of peasants, 1858.
10. Safronov, *Russkie krest'iane v Iakutii*, p. 48.
11. *Krest'ianstvo Sibiri v epokhu feodalizma*, p. 132.
12. Lantzeff, *Siberia in the Seventeenth Century*, p. 159.
13. Golder, *Bering's Voyages*, vol. 1, pp. 11–17, 20.
14. Smith, *The First Kamchatka Expedition of Vitus Bering*, pp. 61, 89.
15. Bol'shakov, *Ocherki istorii rechnogo transporta Sibiri XIX vek*, p. 16.
16. Gibson, *Imperial Russia in Frontier America*, p. 61.
17. Quoted in Gentes, *Exile to Siberia 1590–1822*, p. 200.
18. Marsden, *On Sledge and Horseback to Outcast Siberian Lepers*, pp. 18–21.

Chapter Three: Traders and Tribute-Takers

1. Fisher, *The Russian Fur Trade*, pp. 158–63.
2. Ibid., p. 97.
3. The figure given was 50,000 *chetverti* of grain. This is a dry measure of grain, one *chetvert'* being the equivalent of approximately 288 English pounds, but there were many deviations from this, so it is impossible to be accurate about these figures.
4. Shunkov, *Ocherki po istorii zemledeliia Sibiri (XVII vek)*, p. 308.
5. Zalkind, *Prisoedinenie Buriatii k Rossii*, p. 191.
6. Boulay, *Travels through Spitzbergen, Siberia, Russia Etc*, p. 36.
7. Foust, *Rhubarb: The Wondrous Drug*, pp. 49–50.
8. Downs, 'Trade and Empire', p. 126.
9. Kotilaine, *Russia's Foreign Trade and Economic Expansion in the Seventeenth Century*, pp. 98, 194.
10. Baron, 'Thrust and Parry: Anglo-Russian Relations in the Muscovite North', pp. 19–40.
11. This section is drawn from Downs, 'Trade and Empire', pp. 217–66.
12. Ibid., p. 294.
13. Ibid., p. 283.
14. Kopylov, 'Tamozhennaia politika v Sibiri v XVII v.', pp. 332, 334.
15. Downs, 'Trade and Empire', p. 256.
16. Ides, *Three Years Travels from Moscow Over-land to China*, p. 22.
17. *Polnoe sobranie zakonov*, no. 1590, vol. 3, p. 329, 23 June 1697.
18. Lantzeff, *Siberia in the Seventeenth Century*, p. 70.
19. Fisher, *The Russian Fur Trade*, p. 56.
20. Dmytryshyn, *Russia's Conquest of Siberia*, vol. 1, p. 44.
21. *Polnoe sobranie zakonov*, no. 1526, vol. 3, pp. 215–16, 26 December 1695.
22. Zalkind, *Prisoedinenie Buriatii k Rossii*, pp. 27–8.
23. Pavlov, *Promyshlovaia kolonizatsiia Sibiri v XVII v.*, p. 12.
24. Kivelson, 'Claiming Siberia', p. 31.

25. Pavlov, *Promyshlovaia kolonizatsiia Sibiri v XVII v.*, p. 13.
26. Ibid., pp. 107–8.
27. Zalkind, *Prisoedinenie Buriatii k Rossii*, pp. 24, 30.
28. Quoted in *Sibirskie pereseleniia*, vol. 3, *Osvoenie Verkhnego Priirtysh'ia*, pp. 20–1.
29. Aleksandrov, *Russkoe naselenie Sibiri*, p. 23.
30. *Sibirskie pereseleniia*, vol. 3, *Osvoenie Verkhnego Priirtysh'ia*, pp. 34, 36.
31. Moscow, RGADA, f. 214, op. 5, d. 927, Siberian Office, case concerning a Kirghiz attack.
32. Downs, 'Trade and Empire', p. 107.
33. Ibid., pp. 261–2.

Chapter Four: Early Settlers

1. Aleksandrov, *Russkoe naselenie Sibiri*, pp. 53, 98.
2. Puzanov, *Voennye faktory russkoi kolonizatsii zapadnoi Sibiri*, p. 125.
3. Lantzeff, *Siberia in the Seventeenth Century*, p. 69.
4. Nikitin, *Sluzhilye liudi v zapadnoi Sibiri XVII veka*, p. 102.
5. Ibid., pp. 131–2.
6. Liutsidarskaia, *Starozhily Sibiri*, p. 57.
7. Ibid., pp. 77, 87, 91.
8. Safronov, *Russkie na severo-vostoke Azii*, p. 172.
9. Preobrazhenskii, *Ural i zapadnaia Sibir' v kontse XVI–nachale XVIII veka*, p. 67.
10. Shorokhov, *Korporativno-votchinoe zemlevladenie i monastyrskie krest'iane v Sibiri*, pp. 32–3.
11. Ibid., p. 45.
12. Gentes, *Exile to Siberia 1590–1822*, p. 35.
13. Ryan, *The Bathhouse at Midnight*, p. 83.
14. Bushkovitch, *Religion and Society in Russia*, p. 135.
15. Avvakum, *The Life of the Archpriest Avvakum*, p. 69.
16. Gentes, *Exile to Siberia*, p. 52.
17. Safronov, *Krest'ianskaia kolonizatsiia basseinov Leny i Ilima*, pp. 47, 60, 63–4.
18. Aleksandrov, *Rossiia na dal'nevostochnykh rubezhakh*, p. 46.
19. Safronov, *Krest'ianskaia kolonizatsiia basseinov Leny i Ilima*, pp. 47, 53.
20. Safronov, *Russkie na severo-vostoke Azii*, p. 64.
21. Ivanov, *Sotsial'no-ekonomicheskie otnosheniia v Iakutii*, p. 93.
22. Sofroneev, *Iakuty v pervoi polovine XVIII veka*, p. 119.
23. Downs, 'Trade and Empire', p. 127.
24. Ivanov, *Sotsial'no-ekonomicheskie otnosheniia v Iakutii*, p. 97.
25. Collins, 'Sexual Imbalance in Frontier Communities', p. 165.
26. Aleksandrov, *Russkoe naselenie Sibiri*, p. 126.
27. Gentes, '"Licentious Girls"', p. 8.
28. Aleksandrov, *Russkoe naselenie Sibiri*, p. 126.
29. Gentes, '"Licentious Girls"', p. 6.
30. Forsyth, *A History of the Peoples of Siberia*, p. 67.
31. Discussed in more detail in Hartley, 'Slaves and Spouses'.

Chapter Five: Life in a Siberian Village

1. Moon, *The Russian Peasantry*, p. 99.
2. Khudiakov, *Agrarnaia politika tsarizma v Sibiri v poreformennyi period*, p. 176.
3. *Krest'ianstvo Sibiri v epokhu feodalizma*, pp. 130, 132.
4. Krasnoiarsk, GAKO, f. 592, op. 1, d. 216, l. 99, Krasnoiarsk Clerical Board papers.
5. Ibid., l. 244.
6. Ibid., l. 17.
7. Bykonia, *Zaselenie russkimi prieniseiskogo kraia v XVII v.*, p. 104.
8. Golikova, Minenko, Poborezhnikov, *Gornozavodskie tsentry i agrarnaia sreda v Rossii*.
9. Tomsk, GATO, f. 264, op. 1, d. 6, l. 125, Kolyvan' Clerical Board papers.

10. Moscow, RGADA, f. 298, op. 1, d. 33, Chancellery of the Siberian Factories papers.
11. Ibid., d. 17.
12. Mamsik, *Krest'ianskoe dvizhenie v Sibiri*, p. 87.
13. Irkutsk, GAIO, f. 534, op. 1, d. 1, ll. 5, 13, Office of the Balagan Department (Buriats).
14. *Istoriia Sibiri v sostave feodal'noi Rossii*, vol. 2, p. 288.
15. Krasnoiarsk, GAKO, f. 592, op. 1, d. 216, l. 254ob., Krasnoiarsk Clerical Board papers.
16. Tomsk, GATO, f. 3, op. 2, d. 782, Tomsk Provincial Board papers, 1857.
17. Ibid., f. 264, op. 1, d. 6, ll. 137, 555, Kolyvan' Clerical Board papers.
18. Watrous, *John Ledyard's Journey through Russia and Siberia*, pp. 60, 61, 65.
19. Parkinson, *A Tour of Russia, Siberia, and the Crimea*, pp. 122-3.
20. Coxe, *Travels into Poland, Russia*, vol. 2, p. 21.
21. Gromyko, *Trudovye traditsii russkikh krest'ian Sibiri*, p. 254.
22. Parkinson, *A Tour of Russia, Siberia, and the Crimea*, p. 133.
23. Crull, *The Ancient and Present State of Muscovy*, vol. 1, p. 163.
24. Quoted in Moon, *The Russian Peasantry*, pp. 299-300.
25. Shelegina, *Ocherki material'noi kul'tury russkikh krest'ian zapadnoi Sibiri*, p. 320.
26. Parkinson, *A Tour of Russia, Siberia, and the Crimea*, p.152.
27. Tomsk, GATO, f. 264, op. 1, d. 6, l. 3, Kolyvan' Clerical Board papers.
28. Ibid.
29. Minenko, *Russkaia krest'ianskaia sem'ia*, p. 155.
30. Anon., *A New and Exact Description of Muscovy*, p. 9.
31. Minenko, 'K izucheniiu semeinoi etiki Sibirskogo krest'ianstva', pp. 79-80.
32. Minenko, 'The Living Past', p. 167.
33. Minenko, *Russkaia krest'ianskaia sem'ia*, pp. 288-9.
34. Hartley, 'The Russian Recruit'.
35. Minenko, 'Obshchinnyi skhod v zapadnoi Sibiri', pp. 3-48.

Chapter Six: Life in a Siberian Town

1. Speranskii, *Pis'ma k docheri*, p. 101.
2. Watrous, *John Ledyard's Journey through Russia and Siberia*, pp. 72-3.
3. Christie, *The Benthams in Russia, 1780-1791*, p. 239.
4. Hartley, *A Social History of the Russian Empire*, pp. 19-24.
5. *Istoriia Sibiri*, vol. 2, p. 415.
6. Cochrane, *Narrative of a Pedestrian Journey through Russia and Siberian Tartary*, pp. 134, 141.
7. Ivonin, *Goroda zapadnoi Sibiri*, p. 65.
8. *Istoriia Sibiri*, vol. 2, p. 274.
9. Müller, *Conquest of Siberia*, pp. 48, 52.
10. Ibid., pp. 408, 257.
11. Wikipedia entry for Irbit Fair (last modified in March 2013).
12. Ibid., p. 237.
13. Omsk, GAOO, f. 3, op. 1, d. 901, Main Administration of Western Siberia papers, 1829-30.
14. *Gorod u Krasnogo Iaga*, pp. 121-2.
15. Gromyko, *Zapadnaia Sibir' v XVIII v.*, pp. 69, 70, 79.
16. Emel'ianov, *Gorod Tomsk v feodal'nuiu epokhu*, p. 32.
17. *Istoriia Sibiri*, vol. 2, pp. 260-2.
18. *Gorod u Krasnogo Iaga*, pp. 224-35.
19. Goncharov, *Gorodskaia sem'ia Sibiri*, p. 105.
20. Tikhonov, 'Sibirskie evrei, ikh prava i nuzhdy', p. 279.
21. Now called Kuibyshev, but not to be confused with the town of Samara which was also renamed Kuibyshev in the Soviet period.
22. Goncharov, *Ocherki istorii evreiskikh obshchin zapadnoi Sibiri*.
23. Cochrane, *Narrative of a Pedestrian Journey through Russia and Siberian Tartary*, p. 516.
24. Rabstevich, 'Sotsial'nyi sostav organov gorodskogo samoupravleniia zapadnoi Sibiri', pp. 80-96.

25. Akishin, *Rossiiskii absoliutizm: Upravlenie Sibiri XVIII veka*, p. 314.
26. Zol'nikova, *Sibirskaia Prikhodskaia obshchina*, p. 90.
27. Chappe d'Auteroche, *A Journey into Siberia*, pp. 301, 303–4.
28. Ivonin, *Goroda zapadnoi Sibiri*, p. 35.
29. Iushovskii, *Eskiz siuzheta (40 etiudov o 400-letnem Tomske)*, p. 203.
30. Skubnevskii, Goncharov, *Goroda zapadnoi Sibiri*, p. 139.
31. Watrous, *John Ledyard's Journey through Russia and Siberia*, p. 157.
32. Boiko, Sitnikova, *Sibirskoe kupechestvo*, p. 26.
33. Tol', 'Vospominaniia o vostochnoi Sibiri', p. 920.
34. Wenyon, *Four Thousand Miles across Siberia on the Great Post-Road*, pp. 89–90.
35. Wilmot, Wilmot, *The Russian Journals*, p. 86.
36. Boiko, *Kupechestvo zapadnoi Sibiri*, p. 165.
37. Lind, 'The First Pianist in Okhotsk', pp. 55, 58.
38. Komleva, 'Vliianie kupechestva prieniseiskikh gorodov na gorodskuiu sredu', pp. 28–9.
39. Stites, *Serfdom, Society and the Arts*, p. 110.
40. Parkinson, *A Tour of Russia, Siberia and Crimea*, p. 140.
41. Cochrane, *Narrative of a Pedestrian Journey through Russia and Siberian Tartary*, pp. 116, 169.
42. Speranskii, *Pis'ma k docheri*, p. 108.
43. Stites, *Serfdom, Society and the Arts*, p. 255.
44. Ibid., p. 167.
45. Nozrin, 'Kul'turnaia zhizn' goroda Kainska v XIX–nachale XX vv.', pp. 160–77.
46. *Istoriia Sibiri*, vol. 2, pp. 164–5.
47. Kopylov, *Kul'tura russkogo naseleniia Sibiri v XVII–XVIII vv.*, p. 62.
48. Sofronov, *Tri veka Sibirskogo missionerstva*, vol. 1, p. 32.
49. Ibid., p. 325.
50. *Iz istorii Omska (1716–1917 gg.)*, p. 100.
51. See my forthcoming article, 'Education in the East: the Omsk Asiatic School', based on material on the Omsk Oblast State Archive.
52. Skubnevskii, Goncharov, 'Siberian Merchants', p. 29.
53. *Istoriia Sibiri*, vol. 2, p. 328.
54. Malysheva, 'Iz istorii formirovaniia pedagogicheskikh kadrov grazhdanskikh shkol gorodov zapadnoi Sibiri', pp. 189–211.
55. Serebrennikov, 'Materialy dlia istorii razvitiia prosveshcheniia v Sibiri', p. 139.
56. Tomsk, GATO, f. 3, op. 1, d. 157, Tomsk Provincial Board papers.
57. Omsk, GAOO, f. 3, op. 1, d. 1563. ll. 4, 16–16ob, Main Administration of Western Siberia, material on Siberia in 1812.
58. Shakherov, *Goroda vostochnoi Sibiri v XVII–pervoi polovine XIX vv.*, p. 143.

Chapter Seven: Life in a Remote Siberian Garrison

1. Pushkin, *The Complete Prose Tales of Alexander Sergeyevitch Pushkin*, pp. 355–6.
2. Moscow, RGADA, f. 24, op. 1, d. 65, Siberian Office, report from Gustav Shtrandman from Omsk fortress, 1791.
3. Kul'sharipov, *Politika tsarizma v Bashkortostane 1775–1800 gg.*, pp. 38, 88.
4. *Polnoe sobranie zakonov*, no. 16085, vol. 22, pp. 236–7, 13 October 1784.
5. *Polnoe sobranie zakonov, knigi shtatov*, no. 25091, vol. 43, 2, p. 412, 9 April 1812.
6. See Hartley, 'Gizhiga: Military Presence and Social Encounters in Russia's Wild East', pp. 665–84.
7. Shakhovskoi, 'Mnenie o sposobakh prodovol'stviia zhitelei Okhotskago i Gizhiginskago uezdov', p. 290.
8. Dobell, *Travels in Kamchatka and Siberia*, vol. 1, p. 157.
9. Moscow, RGVIA, f. 14808, op. 1, d. 47, ll. 179ob-80, Gizhiga fort, out-book, 1773; Moscow, RGADA, f. 1096, op. 1, d. 56, ll. 125–32ob, Gizhiga fort, in-book, 1809.
10. Herzen, *My Past and Thoughts*, p. 22.
11. Moscow, RGVIA, f. 14808, op. 1, d. 7, ll. 143–6, Gizhiga fort, correspondence with Kamchatka, 1778.

12. Nedbai, *Istoriia Sibirskogo kazach'ego voiska*, vol. 1, p. 204.
13. Moscow, RGADA, f. 1096, op. 1, d. 56, ll. 125, 126ob, 130, Gizhiga fort, in-book, 1809.
14. Moscow, RGVIA, f. 14808, op. 1, d. 10. l. 58, Gizhiga fort, reports on soldiers and Cossacks, 1762.
15. Kul'sharipov, *Politika tsarizma v Bashkortostane*, p. 84.
16. Moscow, RGVIA, f. 14808, op. 1, d. 71, ll. 112ob, 278, 249ob, Gizhiga fort, various papers, 1778.
17. Ibid., d. 47, ll. 40ob, 88, 213–15, Gizhiga fort, out-book, 1773.
18. Ibid., d. 44, Gizhiga fort, decrees.
19. 'Opis' 1000 del kazach'iago otdela', p. 139.
20. Moscow, RGADA, f. 1096, op. 1, d. 39, Gizhiga fort, case of Kuznetsov.
21. Cochrane, *Narrative of a Pedestrian Journey through Russia and Siberian Tartary*, p. 170.
22. Moscow, RGVIA, f. 14808, op. 1, d. 169, ll. 36–8, 181, Gizhiga fort, records of the Gizhiga Lower Rasprava.
23. Edinburgh, National Library of Scotland, MS 8985, Scottish Missionary Society, p. 32.
24. See Hartley, *Russia 1762–1825: Military Power, the State and the People*, pp. 39–43.
25. Moscow, RGADA, f. 1096, op. 1, d. 51, ll. 182–6, Gizhiga fort, Cossack papers.
26. Ibid., d. 56, ll. 125–32ob, Gizhiga fort, in-book, 1809.
27. Cochrane, *Narrative of a Pedestrian Journey*, p. 169; Dobell, *Travels in Kamchatka and Siberia*, vol. 1, p. 152.
28. Minenko, *Istoriia kazachestva aziatskoi Rossii*, vol. 1, p. 165.
29. Moscow, RGVIA, f. 14808, op. 1, d. 47, ll. 186–6ob, 225ob, 236, Gizhiga fort, out-book, 1773.
30. Ibid., d. 71, ll. 8–9ob, 127–9, Gizhiga fort, various papers 1778.
31. Vagin, *Istoricheskie svedeniia o deiatel'nosti Grafa M. M. Speranskogo v Sibiri*, vol. 2, pp. 419–20; Gibson, *Feeding the Fur Trade*, p. 52.
32. Vagin, *Istoricheskie svedeniia o deiatel'nosti Grafa M. M. Speranskogo v Sibiri*, vol. 2, p. 29,
33. Hartley, 'Gizhiga: Military Presence and Social Encounters in Russia's Wild East', pp. 683–4.

Chapter Eight: Governing and the Governed

1. Wilmot, M. Wilmot, C. *The Russian Journals*, p. 308.
2. Moscow, RGVIA, f. 14808, op. 1, d. 13, Gizhiga fort papers.
3. *Istoricheskaia entsiklopediia Sibiri*, vol. 2, p. 435.
4. Moscow, RGADA, f. 20, op. 1, d. 304, l. 9ob, recruit levy papers from Irkutsk and Kolyvan', 1789–91.
5. Rafienko, *Problemy istorii upravleniia i kul'tury Sibiri*, p. 75.
6. *Polnoe sobranie zakonov*, no. 6407, vol. 9, pp. 131–2, 21 May 1733.
7. *Polnoe sobranie zakonov*, no. 7009, vol. 9, pp. 876–8, 9 July 1736.
8. *Polnoe sobranie zakonov*, no. 9210, vol. 12, pp. 452–3, 24 September 1745.
9. Moscow, RGADA, f. 214, op. 5, d. 632, Siberian Office, case of the 'white' Kalmyks.
10. Sofroneev, *Iakuty v pervoi polovine XVIII veka*, p. 56.
11. Damashek, *Iasachnaia politika tsarizma v Sibiri*, pp. 22–3.
12. Minanko, 'The Living Past', p. 163.
13. Moscow, RGADA, f. 214, op. 5, d. 2627, Siberian Office, case of Dioltovskii.
14. Bykonia, *Russkoe nepodatnoe naselenie vostochnoi Sibiri v XVIII–XIX vv.*, p. 126.
15. Minenko, 'Obshchinnyi skhod v zapadnoi Sibiri', p. 12.
16. Bykonia, *Russkoe nepodatnoe naselenie vostochnoi Sibiri*, p. 72.
17. *Polnoe sobranie zakonov*, no. 3284, vol. 5, pp. 616–17, 18 January 1719; no. 3292, vol. 5, pp. 622–3, 31 January 1719.
18. Korb, *Diary of an Austrian Secretary of Legation at the Court of Czar Peter the Great*, vol. 1, pp. 68–9.
19. Nikitin, *Sluzhilye liudi v zapadnoi Sibiri XVII veka*, pp. 60–1.
20. Bykonia, *Russkoe nepodatnoe naselenie vostochnoi Sibiri*, p. 143.
21. Ibid., p. 71.
22. Givens, *Servitors or Seigneurs*, p. 411.

23. Moscow, RGADA, f. 16, op. 1, d. 386, ll. 222, 252, Cabinet Office, report on resolved and unresolved cases.
24. Moscow, RGADA, f. 259, op. 1, d. 4222, ll. 498–511, 735–9, papers of the First Department of the Senate.
25. Akishin, *Rossiiskii absoliutizm*, pp. 324–33.
26. Bykonia, *Russkoe nepodatnoe naselenie vostochnoi Sibiri*, p. 125.
27. Ibid., p. 128.
28. Akishin, *Rossiiskii absoliutizm*, pp. 270, 336, 352.
29. Ibid., pp. 344, 345, 356, 358–9.
30. Watrous, *John Ledyard's Journey through Russia and Siberia*, p. 146.
31. Raeff, *Siberia and the Reforms of 1822*, p. 40.
32. Ibid., p. 8.
33. Raeff, *Michael Speransky*, p. 254.
34. Omsk, GAOO, f. 3, op. 1, d. 202, 512, 514, 736, Main Administration of Western Siberia papers. See my 'Slaves and Spouses: Russian Settlers and Non-Russians in Siberia' for a more detailed analysis of these cases.
35. Mamsik, *Krest'ianskoe dvizhenie v Sibiri*, p. 77.
36. Quoted in Rogachevskii, 'The Representation of Bribery', p. 115.
37. Gogol, *Plays and Petersburg Tales*, p. 254.

Chapter Nine: Exiles and Convicts

1. Ryan, *The Bathhouse at Midnight*, p. 240.
2. Poshchevskaia, *Revoliutsionery-raznochhintsy v zapadno-sibirskom izgnanii*, p. 36.
3. Wood, 'Russia's "Wild East": Exile, Vagrancy and Crime in Nineteenth-Century Siberia', p. 118.
4. Watrous, *John Ledyard's Journey through Russia and Siberia*, p. 152.
5. Dolgikh, 'Ssylka krest'ian na poselenie v Sibir'.
6. Moscow, RGADA, f. 214, op. 5, d. 2439, Siberian Office, list of convicts at Tomsk, 1736.
7. Gentes, *Exile, Murder and Madness in Siberia*, p. 46.
8. *Sbornik starinnykh bumag, khraniashchikhsia v muzee P. I. Shchukina*, vol. 8, pp. 354–6.
9. Gentes, *Exile, Murder and Madness*, p. 29.
10. Parkinson, *A Tour of Russia, Siberia and the Crimea*, p. 120.
11. Ivonin, *Gorodovoe kazachestvo zapadnoi Sibiri*, p. 40.
12. Gentes, *Exile to Siberia*, p.119.
13. Assonov, *V tylu armii. Kaluzhskaia guberniia v 1812 god*, p. 39.
14. Bessonov, Milovidov, 'Voennoplennye poliaki', p. 181.
15. Sirotkin, 'Sud'ba plennykh soldat i ofitserov Velikoi Armii', p. 257.
16. Tomsk, GATO, f. op. 4, d. 6, Tomsk Provincial Board papers, report on prisoners of war, 1824.
17. Gentes, *Exile, Murder and Madness*, p. 132.
18. Gentes, 'Siberian Exiles and the 1863 Polish Insurrectionists'.
19. Omsk, GAOO, f. 3, op. 4, d. 6330, Main Administration of Western Siberia papers.
20. Ibid., d. 6923.
21. Latimer, *Dr Baedeker and his Apostolic Work in Russia*, p. 121.
22. Ostrovskii, 'Pol'skie predprinimateli v Sibiri na rubezhe XIX–XX vekov', pp. 12–17.
23. *Uchastniki Pol'skogo Vosstaniia 1860–1863 gg.*, p. 26.
24. Irkutsk, GAIO, f. 24, op. 3, d. 90, l. 101, Provincial Board, papers on state convicts.
25. *Uchastniki Pol'skogo Vosstaniia 1860–1863 gg.*, p. 25.
26. Sutherland, *The Princess of Siberia*, pp. 162–3.
27. Gentes, *Exile to Siberia*, p. 125.
28. Tomsk, GATO, f. 127, op. 1, d. 1083, Tomsk Town Duma papers.
29. Irkutsk, GAIO, f. 24, op. 3, d. 90, Provincial Board, papers on state convicts.
30. Ibid.
31. Tal'skaia, 'Bor'ba administratsii s vlianiem Dekabristov v zapadnoi Sibiri', p. 83.
32. Gentes, *Exile, Murder and Madness*, p. 34.

33. Koleskinov, 'Ssylka i zaselenie Sibiri', pp. 48–9.
34. Gentes, *Exile, Murder and Madness*, pp. 165–6.
35. Wood, *Russia's Frozen Frontier*, p. 130.
36. Gentes, *Exile, Murder and Madness*, pp. 165–6.
37. Ibid., pp. 167–8.
38. Dostoevsky, *Memoirs from the House of the Dead*, p. 97.
39. Gentes, *Exile to Siberia*, p. 162.
40. Gentes, *Exile, Murder and Madness*, p. 47.
41. Wood, 'Vagrancy and Violent Crime in Siberia', p. 293.
42. Wenyon, *Four Thousand Miles across Siberia on the Great Post-Road*, p. 203.
43. Thorvaldsen, 'Swedes in Siberia Diaspora', pp. 53–5.
44. Kopylov, Malysheva, 'Dekabristy i prosveshchenie Sibiri v pervoi polovine XIX v.', pp. 104–5.
45. Shatrova, *Dekabristy i Sibir'*, p. 151.
46. Bakhaev, *Obshchestvenno-prosvetitel'skaia i kraevedcheskaia deiatel'nost' Dekabristov v Buriatii*, p. 72.
47. Fomenkova, 'Pol'skie revoliutsionery XIX v. na Viatskoi zemle', pp. 183–4.
48. Gentes, *Exile, Murder and Madness*, p. 140.
49. Dulov, *Petrashevtsy v Sibiri*, pp. 238–40.
50. Kennan, *Siberia and the Exile System*, p. 92.
51. Lincoln, *The Conquest of a Continent*, p. 220.
52. Azadovskii, *Stranitsy istorii Dekabrizma*, p. 81.
53. Shteingel', *Sochineniia i pis'ma*, vol. 1, p. 269.
54. Fedorov, *Memuary Dekabristov: Severnoe obshchestvo*, p. 139.
55. Bassin, 'Inventing Siberia', p. 776.
56. Gentes, *Exile, Murder and Madness*, p. 89.

Chapter Ten: Religion and Popular Beliefs

1. *Kodinskii (Kondinskii) Sviato-Troitskii monastyr'*, pp. 47–8, 82.
2. *Polnoe sobranie zakonov*, no. 7836, vol. 10, pp. 806–7, 15 June 1739.
3. Zol'nikova, *Sibirskaia prikhodskaia obshchina*, p. 173.
4. Quoted in Bulygin, 'Nekotorye voprosy kul'tury pripisnoi derevni Kolyvan'-Voskresenskikh gornykh zavodov XVII v.', p. 74.
5. Mukhortova, 'Problema material'nogo obespecheniia gorodskogo dukhovenstva Sibiri', p. 85.
6. Watrous, *John Ledyard's Journey through Russia and Siberia*, p. 156.
7. Il'in, 'Vzaimootnosheniia gosudarstvennoi vlasti i ofitsial'noi tserkvi so staroverami na Altae', pp. 43–8.
8. *Polnoe sobranie zakonov*, no. 10138, vol. 13, pp. 890–1, 4 October 1753.
9. Quoted in Crummey, *The Old Believers and the World of the Antichrist*, pp. 191–2.
10. Zol'nikova, *Sibirskaia prikhodskaia obshchina*, p. 176.
11. Boiko, Sitnikova, *Sibirskoe kupechestvo i formirovanie arkhitekturnogo oblika goroda Tomska*, p. 108.
12. Tomsk, GATO, f. 3, op. 19, d. 515, Tomsk Provincial Board papers, 1854–7.
13. Safronov, *Russkie krest'iane v Iakutii*, p. 128.
14. Robson, *Old Believers in Modern Russia*, pp. 23–4.
15. Omsk, GAOO, f. 2, op. 1, d. 356, Governor-General of Siberia papers, 1819.
16. Bolonev, *Staroobriadtsy Zabaikal'ia*, p. 55.
17. Tomsk, GATO, f. 3, op. 11, d. 726, Tomsk Provincial Board papers, 1858–9.
18. Bolonev, *Staroobriadtsy Zabaikal'ia*, p. 61.
19. Cottrell, *Recollections of Siberia in the Years 1840 and 1841*, pp. 284–5.
20. Tomsk, GATO, f. 3, op. 11, d. 726, ll. 12–13, Tomsk Provincial Board papers, 1858–9.
21. Krasnoiarsk, GAKO, f. 812, op. 1, d. 64, Tobol'sk Clerical Board papers.
22. Omsk, GAOO, f. 3, d. 295, ll., 6, 9ob, 14ob, 28–30, 66–7, 84, Governor General of Siberia papers.
23. Gentes, *Exile, Murder and Madness*, p. 42.

24. Safronov, *Russkie krest'iane v Iakutii*, pp. 108–9, 113–14, 125.
25. Quoted in Engelstein, *Castration and the Heavenly Kingdom*, p. 126.
26. Khodarkovsky, 'The Conversion of Non-Christians in Early Modern Russia', pp. 115–43.
27. Sofronov, *Khristianizatsiia Tobol'skogo severa*, pp. 47–8.
28. Quoted in Slezkine, *Arctic Mirrors*, p. 49.
29. Sofronov, *Khristianizatsiia Tobol'skogo severa*, p. 50.
30. Damashek, 'Russkaia tserkov' i narody Sibiri v pervoi polovine XIX veka', pp. 41–2.
31. Schorkowitz, 'The Orthodox Church, Lamanism, and Shamanism among the Buriats and Kalmyks', pp. 203–5.
32. Sofronov, *Tri veka Sibirskogo missionerstva*, vol. 1, p. 81.
33. Frost, *Bering: The Russian Discovery of America*, p. 44.
34. Putilov, 'Letopis' Usinskoi missii', pp. 458, 461.
35. Safronov, *Krest'ianskaia kolonizatsiia basseinov Leny i Ilima*, pp. 178–9.
36. Damashek, 'Russkaia tserkov' i narody Sibiri v pervoi polovine XIX veka', p. 44.
37. Shorokhov, 'Uzniki Sibirskikh monastyrei v XVIII veke', p. 298.
38. Quoted in Slezkine, *Arctic Mirrors*, p. 51.
39. Watrous, *John Ledyard's Journey through Russia and Siberia*, p. 152.
40. Krasnoiarsk, GAKO, f. 592, op. 2, d. 21, ll. 97–100, Krasnoiarsk Clerical Board papers.
41. See Hartley, 'Slaves and Spouses: Russian Settlers and Non-Russians in Siberia'.
42. Krasnoiarsk, GAKO, f. 812, op. 1, d. 147, case about the conversion of 43 pagans, 1800.
43. *Istoriia Sibiri*, vol. 2, p. 288.
44. 'Iz putevykh zapisok pravoslavnogo missionera', pp. 54–7.
45. Chikachev, *Russkie na Indigirke*, pp. 130, 137.
46. Jordan, *Material Culture and Sacred Landscape: The Anthropology of the Siberian Khanty*, p. 222.
47. Balzer, *The Tenacity of Ethnicity*, pp. 69–70.
48. Ryan, *The Bathhouse at Midnight*, p. 194.
49. Lipinskaia, *Starozhily i pereselentsy*, pp. 187–9.
50. Mironova-Shapovalova, 'Paskhal'nye obriady i obriadovoi fol'klor staroobriadtsev Zabaikal'ia', pp. 498–507.
51. Ryan, *The Bathhouse at Midnight*, p. 49.
52. Ibid., p. 47.
53. Paderin, 'Zapiski Sibiriakov', p. 936.
54. Ryan, *The Bathhouse at Midnight*, p. 75.
55. Gromyko, *Trudovye traditsii russkikh krest'ian Sibiri*, pp. 332–3.
56. Ryan, *The Bathhouse at Midnight*, p. 197.
57. Ibid., pp. 45, 46, 47, 100, 103.
58. Minenko, *Russkaia krest'ianskaia sem'ia v zapadnoi Sibiri*, p. 130.
59. Minenko, 'The Living Past', p. 185.
60. Ryan, *The Bathhouse at Midnight*, pp. 419, 422.
61. Lesseps, *Travels in Kamtschatka during the Years 1787 and 1788*, vol. 1, pp. 306–7.
62. Ryan, *The Bathhouse at Midnight*, p. 30.
63. Balzer, *The Tenacity of Ethnicity*, pp. 64–5.

Chapter Eleven: Explorers and Imperialists

1. Bassin, *Imperial Visions*, p. 53.
2. Polevoi, 'The Discovery of Russian America', p. 21.
3. Golder, *Bering's Voyages*, vol. 1, pp. 275–6, 279.
4. Stewart, 'Discovering a Continent: Early Explorers in Siberia', p. 212.
5. Black, 'Opening Up Siberia: Russia's Window on the East', p. 63.
6. Quoted in Slezkine, *Arctic Mirrors*, p. 56.
7. Quoted in Lincoln, *The Conquest of a Continent*, p. 119.
8. *Steller's History of Kamchatka*, pp. 218, 220, 222, 227.
9. Stewart, 'Discovering a Continent: Early Explorers in Siberia', pp. 220–1.
10. Quoted in Beer, 'The Exile, the Patron and the Pardon', p. 24.

11. Gibson, *Russian California*, forthcoming, doc. no. 189.
12. Gibson, *Imperial Russia in Frontier America*, p. 21.
13. Quoted in Slezkine, *Arctic Mirrors*, p. 42.
14. Divin, *The Great Russian Navigator A. I. Chicherin*, p. 114.
15. Ides, *Three Years Travels from Moscow Over-land to Siberia*, pp. 19–20, 29.
16. Postnikov, 'Geographic Explorations of Russian Orthodox Church Missionaries', pp. 271–2.
17. Hartley, 'The Russian Empire: Military Encounters and National Identity', pp. 218–34.
18. *12 soldatskikh pesen*, p. 12.
19. Bassin, *Imperial Visions*, p. 52.
20. Ibid., p. 54.
21. Ibid., p. 158.
22. Ibid., p. 198.
23. Ibid., p. 244.
24. Gibson, 'Russian Expansion in Siberia and America: Critical Contrast', p. 38.
25. Gibson, *Imperial Russia in Frontier America*, p. 26.
26. Ibid.
27. Gibson, 'Russian Dependence upon the Natives of Alaska', p. 99.
28. Gibson, *Imperial Russia in Frontier America*, p. 37.
29. Gibson, 'The Sale of Russian America to the United States', pp. 271–94.

Chapter Twelve: Railways and Change

1. Seebohm, *The Birds of Siberia*, vol. 2, *The Enisei*, p. 480.
2. *Istoriia Sibiri*, vol. 3, p. 180.
3. Norman, *All the Russians*, p. 153.
4. Collins, 'Plans for Railway Development in Siberia, 1857–1890', pp. 149–85.
5. Quoted, in the original French, in ibid, p. 158.
6. Marks, *Road to Power: The Trans-Siberian Railroad*, on which this section is based.
7. *Revoliutsionnoe dvizhenie v Zaibaikal'e 1905–1907 gg.*, p. 115.
8. Marks, *Road to Power: The Trans-Siberian Railroad*, pp. 200–6.
9. Belous, 'O roli Iaponskikh pereselentsev v razvitii ekonomiki Priamur'ia', p. 42.
10. Prei, *Pis'ma iz Vladivostoka 1894–1930*, p. 312.
11. Ibid., pp. 312, 320.
12. Datsyshen, 'Japanese Deportees and Prisoners of War in Siberia, 1904–05', pp. 233–4.
13. Fraser, *The Real Siberia*, p. 194.
14. Datsushen, *Kitaitsy v Sibiri v XVII–XX vv.*, pp. 48–52.
15. Norman, *All the Russians*, p. 149.
16. Stephan, *The Russian Far East*, pp. 72–3.
17. Khabarovsk, GAKhK, И-282, op. 1, d. 1, ll. 263, 275ob, 289–93, Administration of the Ussuri State Railway; Borzunov, *Proletariat*, p. 127.
18. Tomsk, GATO, f. 3, op. 6, d. 63, Tomsk Provincial Board, papers on the supervision of Chinese and other foreigners.
19. Safronov, *Stolypinskaia agrarnaia reforma i ee vliianie na khoziaistvennoe razvitie vostochnoi Sibiri*, pp. 96–7, 101–3.
20. *Krest'ianstvo Sibiri v epokhu kapitalizma*, pp. 16–18.
21. Davletbaev, *Krest'ianskaia reforma 1861 v Bashkirii*, pp. 75, 76, 81.
22. Tomsk, GATO, f. 3, op. 48, d. 2, Tomsk Provincial Board papers, on peasant affairs, 1867.
23. Poppe, 'The Economic and Cultural Development of Siberia', p. 144.
24. Jefferson, *Roughing It in Siberia with Some Account of the Trans-Siberian Railway*, pp. 21, 25.
25. Meakin, *A Ribbon of Iron*, p. 110.
26. Coquin, *La Sibérie*, pp. 411–20.
27. Volgine, 'Entrepreneurship and the Siberian Peasant Commune', p. 36.
28. Tomsk, GATO, f. 3, op. 44, d. 92, Tomsk Provincial Board papers, on peasant affairs, 1889–90.
29. *Nemtsy v Sibiri*, pp. 30, 76.
30. *Massovye agrarnye pereseleniia*, p. 80.

31. Macey, ' "A Wager on History": The Stolypin Agrarian Reforms as Process'.
32. *Istoricheskaia entsiklopediia Sibiri*, vol. 3, pp. 190–1.
33. Pallot, *Land Reform in Russia 1906–1917*, p. 137.
34. Goryushkin, 'The Economic Development of Siberia in the Late Nineteenth and Early Twentieth Centuries', p. 14.
35. *Massovye agrarnye pereseleniia na vostok Rossii*, pp. 41, 47.
36. Asal'khanov, *Sel'skoe khoziaistvo Sibiri kontsa XIX–nachala XX v.*, p. 49.
37. Fraser, *The Real Siberia*, pp. viii, 28.
38. Goryushkin, 'The Economic Development of Siberia in the Late Nineteenth and Early Twentieth Centuries', p. 17.
39. *Istoriia Sibiri*, vol. 3, pp. 325, 322.
40. Mukhin, *Rabochie Sibiri v epokhu kapitalizma*, p. 131.
41. Norman, *All the Russias*, p. 144.
42. Poppe, 'The Economic and Cultural Development of Siberia', p. 148.
43. Meakin, *A Ribbon of Iron*, p. 128.
44. Skubnevskii, *Urbanizationnye protsessy v Sibiri*, pp. 89–90.
45. Jefferson, *Roughing It in Siberia, with Some Account of the Trans-Siberian Railway*, p. 52.
46. Skubnevskii, Goncharov, *Goroda zapadnoi Sibiri*, pp. 99, 101.
47. Goncharov, *Ocherki istorii evreiskikh obshchin zapadnoi Sibiri*, p. 36.
48. Serebrennikov, 'Materialy dlia istorii goroda Tomska', pp. 102–9.
49. Litovtsyn, 'Zhizn' sibirskikh gorodov', pp. 25–31.
50. *Istoriia obshchestvennogo samoupravleniia v Sibiri*, p. 246.
51. Boiko, Sitnikova, *Sibirskoe kupechestvo i formirovanie arkhitekturnogo oblika goroda Tomska*, p. 53.
52. Serebrennikov, 'Gramotnost'' v Sibiri po perepisi 28 ianvaria 1897 goda', pp. 15–19.
53. Nozrin, 'Predstavleniia krest'ian Sibiri v nachale XX v.', pp. 74–5.
54. Lapshov, 'Narodnoe obrazovanie v Sibiri', pp. 30–6.
55. *Iz istorii Omska*, pp. 189, 190–1.
56. *Materialy po istorii Vladivostoka*, vol. 1, p. 161.
57. Skubnevskii, Goncharov, 'Siberian Merchants in the Latter Half of the 19th Century', p. 37.
58. Roshchevskaia, *Revoliutsionery-raznochintsy v zapadnosibirskom izgnanii*, p. 109.
59. Zinov'ev, 'Ob Oktiabr'skikh sobytiiakh 1905 g. v Tomske', pp. 80–93.
60. *Istoriia kul'tury dal'nego vostoka Rossii (XIX v.–1917 g.)*, pp. 122, 146, 156.
61. Khabarovsk, GAKhK, И-2, op. 1, d. 7, Priamur Branch of the Imperial Geographical Society, list of activities for 1898.
62. Ibid., d. 1, ll. 64–5, 302, 362–3, Priamur Branch of the Imperial Geographical Society, papers 1894–7.
63. Ibid., l. 64ob.
64. Tomsk, GATO, f. 3, op. 2, d. 6271, Tomsk Provincial Board papers, information on cultural institutions.
65. *Istoriia kul'tury dal'nego vostoka Rossii (XIX v.–1917 g.)*, pp. 105–6.
66. Mukhin, *Rabochie Sibiri v epokhu kapitalizma*, p. 139.
67. *Iz istorii Omska*, p. 150.
68. Borzunov, *Proletariat Sibiri i Dal'nego Vostoka nakanune pervoi russkoi revoliutsii*, p. 22.
69. Khabarovsk, GAKhK, И-282, op. 1, d. 1, l. 177ob, Administration of the Ussuri State Railway, 1895–7.
70. Khobta, *Stroitel'stvo Transsiba*, p. 158.
71. *Istoriia Sibiri*, vol. 3, p. 177.
72. Belimov, *Zheleznodorozhnyi proletariat Sibiri v revoliutsii 1905–1907 gg.*, pp. 59–65.
73. Baindin, 'Vliianie politicheskikh ssyl'nykh na soldatskie massy v Sibiri v gody pervoi rossiiskoi revoliutsii', p. 95.
74. Kudrizhinskii, 'Vladivostok v 1905 g. Iz nabliudenii ochevidtsa', pp. 45, 49.
75. Melancon, 'The Ninth Circle: The Lena Goldfield Workers and the Massacre of 4 April 1912', pp. 766–95.

76. Pereira, 'Regional Consciousness in Siberia before and after October 1917', p. 112.
77. Watrous, 'The Regionalist Conception of Siberia, 1860 to 1920', pp. 113–32.
78. Turner, *A Record of Travel, Climbing and Exploration*, p. 28.

Chapter Thirteen: Wars and Revolutions

1. Stone, *The Eastern Front, 1914–17*, p. 213.
2. Reitsh, *Russia's Peasants in Revolution and Civil War*, p. 46.
3. Eremin, *Tomskaia guberniia kak tylovoi raion Rossii v gody Pervoi Mirovoi Voiny*, pp. 53, 97–8, 111.
4. Prei, *Pis'ma iz Vladivostoka*, p. 342.
5. *Tomskie eparkhial'nyia vedomosti*, vol. 2, 1915, pp. 48–53.
6. Eremin, *Tomskaia guberniia kak tylovoi raion Rossii v gody Pervoi Mirovoi Voiny*, p. 260.
7. Ibid., pp. 15, 53.
8. Gatrell, *Russia's First World War: A Social and Economic History*, p. 173.
9. Kokoulin, *Povsednevnaia zhizn' gorozhan Sibiri v voenno-revoliutsionnye gody*, pp. 13, 43–5.
10. *Ocherki istorii Chukotki s drevneishikh vremen do nashikh dnei*, p. 147.
11. Pereira, *White Siberia: The Politics of Civil War*, pp. 29–81.
12. *Bol'sheviki zapadnoi Sibiri v bor'be za sotsialisticheskuiu revoliutsiu*, p. 19.
13. Zinov'ev, 'Sotsial'no-politicheskii oblik Sibirskogo otriada rabochego klassa Rossii nakanune revoliutsii 1917 gg.', p. 16.
14. Safronov, *Oktiabr' v Sibiri*, p. 431.
15. Zykova, Iakimova, 'Obshchestvenno-politicheskaia zhizn' Sibirskogo krest'ianstva v 1917 g.', p. 24.
16. *Grazhdanskaia voina na dal'nem vostoke (1918–1922): Vospominaniia veteranov*, pp. 86–91.
17. Prei, *Pis'ma iz Vladivostoka*, p. 349.
18. Smith, *Captives of Revolution*, p. 125.
19. *Bol'sheviki zapadnoi Sibiri*, p. 282.
20. Varneck, 'Siberian Native Peoples after the February Revolution', pp. 70–88.
21. *Organizatsiia samoupravleniia v Tobol'skoi gubernii*, p. 295.
22. Kennan, *Siberia and the Exile System*, vol. 1, pp. 140–1.
23. Smith, *Captives of Revolution*, p. 128.
24. Ibid., pp. 173–5.
25. Mawdsley, *The Russian Civil War*, p. 146.
26. Smith, *Vladivostok under Red and White Rule*, p. 153.
27. Bisher, *White Terror*, p. 126.
28. Ibid., pp. 100–1.
29. Balmasov, *Krasnyi terror na vostoke Rossii*, p. 264.
30. Kokoulin, *Povsednevnaia zhizn'*, pp. 170–1.
31. Smele, *Civil War in Siberia*, p. 367.
32. Ibid., pp. 363, 367.
33. Prei, *Pis'ma iz Vladivostoka*, p. 355.
34. Tsipkin, *Antibol'shevistskie rezhimy na dal'nem vostoke Rossii v period grazhdanskoi voiny*, p. 103.
35. Vasilevskii, *Zaobaikal'skoe kazach'e voisko v gody revoliutsii i grazhdanskoi voiny*, p. 135.
36. Smele, *Civil War in Siberia*, pp. 350, 356, 369, 370.
37. Smith, *Vladivostok under Red and White Rule*, p. 41.
38. Pereira, *White Siberia: The Politics of Civil War*, p. 70.
39. *Poslednie dni Kolchakovshchiny*, p. 402.
40. Balmasov, *Krasnyi terror na vostoke Rossii*, p. 254.
41. Smele, *Civil War in Siberia*, p. 386.
42. Shishkin, *Sibirskaia Vandeia: Vooruzhennoe soprotivlenie kommunisticheskomu rezhimu*, pp. 290, 293.
43. Smele, *Civil War in Siberia*, p. 387.
44. *Bor'ba za vlast' sovetov v Irkutskoi gubernii*, p. 97.

Chapter Fourteen: Collectivisation and the Camps

1. Appelbaum, *Gulag: A History*, p. 103, from which much of the material here on Gulags is drawn.
2. Shishkov, *Sotsialisticheskoe stroitel'stvo v Sibirskoi derevne*, p. 86.
3. Forsyth, *A History of the Peoples of Siberia*, p. 242.
4. Kokoulin, *Povsednevnaia zhizn' gorozhan Sibiri v voenno-revoliutsionnye gody*, pp. 265–6.
5. *Za sovety bez kommunistov: Krest'ianskoe vosstanie v Tiumenskoi gubernii*, p. 154.
6. Hughes, *Stalin, Siberia and the Crisis of the New Economic Policy*; I have relied on this work for many points in this chapter.
7. *The Women of Izmaelovka*, p. 56.
8. Ibid., p. 16.
9. Hughes, *Stalin, Siberia and the Crisis of the New Economic Policy*, p. 24.
10. Ibid., p. 104.
11. Quoted in ibid., pp. 101–2.
12. Gushchin, 'Raskulachivanie' v Sibiri, pp. 36–7.
13. Quoted in Viola, *Peasant Rebels under Stalin*, p. 96.
14. Hughes, *Stalinism in a Russian Province*, pp. 104, 125, on which much of this section is based.
15. Viola, *Peasant Rebels under Stalin*, p. 82.
16. Hughes, *Stalinism in a Russian Province*, pp. 46–7.
17. *Stalinskii terror v Sibiri 1928–1941*, p. 39.
18. Ibid., p. 151.
19. Gushchin, *Naselenie Sibiri v XX veke*, p. 42.
20. Hughes, *Stalinism in a Russian Province*, pp. 199, 202, 42.
21. Frierson, Vielensky, *Children of the Gulag*, p. 104.
22. Makarov, *Vlast' i obshchestvo v Sibiri: 1927–1933 gg.*, p. 104.
23. Forsyth, *A History of the Peoples of Siberia*, pp. 301, 316.
24. Lane, *Christian Religion in the Soviet Union*, pp. 95, 97–9.
25. Kupriianova, *Staroobriadtsy Altaia v pervoi treti XX veka*, pp. 144–55.
26. Il'inykh, 'Sibirskaia derevniia v period kollektivizatsii', pp. 142–55.
27. *Istoriia Iugry v dokumentakh iz Tomska*, pp. 197, 199.
28. *Marginaly v Sotsiume. Marginaly kak Sotsium. Sibir'*, pp. 18–21.
29. Krasil'nikov, 'Marginal'nye gruppy v Sibiri: ikh sotsio-kul'turnye kharakteristiki v 20–30-e gody', p. 88.
30. Appelbaum, *Gulag: A History*, pp. 104, 112.
31. *The Women of Izmaelovka*, pp. 42–3.
32. *Detstvo, opalennoe voinoi*, pp. 64–5.
33. Klikushin, 'Letopis' arestov: Nauchnaia intelligentsiia Sibiri v gody Stalinskikh repressii', pp. 96–119.
34. Quoted in Ssorin-Chaikov, *The Social Life of the State in Subarctic Siberia*, p. 91.
35. Frierson, Vilensky, *Children of the Gulag*, p. 115.
36. Solzhenitsyn, *Voices from the Gulag*, p. 177.
37. Appelbaum, *Gulag: A History*, p. 161.
38. Quoted in ibid., p. 205.
39. Reid, *The Shaman's Coat: A Native History of Siberia*, p. 188.
40. Bell, 'Was the Gulag an Archipelago?'.
41. Lipper, *Eleven Years in Soviet Prison Camps*, p. 97.
42. Ginzburg, *Within the Whirlwind*, pp. 215, 135.
43. *Tomskie zamorozki Khrushchevskoi ottepeli*.
44. Ginzburg, *Within the Whirlwind*, p. 228.
45. Gheith, Jolluck, *Gulag Voices: Oral Histories of Soviet Incarceration and Exile*, pp. 138, 140, 142.
46. Solzhenitsyn, *Voices from the Gulag*, p. 173.

Chapter Fifteen: The New Soviet Citizen

1. Rasputin, *Farewell to Matyora*, p. 11.
2. Tkacheva, *Dal'nevostochnoe obshchestvo v gody Velikoi Otechestvennoi Voiny*, p. 113.

3. *Istoricheskaia entsiklopediia Sibiri*, vol. 2, pp. 439–40.
4. See figures in Wood, *Russia's Frozen Frontier*, pp. 204, 226.
5. Kuksanova, *Sotsial'no-bytovaia infrastruktura Sibiri*, p. 53.
6. *The Women of Izmaelovka*, p. 57.
7. *Istoricheskaia entsiklopediia Sibiri*, vol. 1, pp. 15–16
8. Shulman, '"Those Who Hurry to the Far East"', pp. 197–8.
9. Quoted in ibid., p. 213.
10. Geldern, Stites, *Mass Culture in Soviet Russia*, p. 255
11. *Istoriia industrializatsii zapadnoi Sibiri*, pp. 180–1.
12. Shulman, '"Those Who Hurry to the Far East"', p. 221.
13. Pohl, *The Virgin Lands between Memory and Forgetting*, p. 201.
14. Raizman, *Ocherki istorii severo-vostoka Rossii v period massovykh repressii*, p. 25.
15. *Est' takoi poselok Kysyl-Syr'*.
16. Fitzpatrick, *Everyday Stalinism*, pp. 47–53.
17. Bigland, *The Key to the Russian Door*, p. 172.
18. *Detstvo, opalennoe voinoi*, p. 120.
19. Best described by Smith, *Property of Communists*.
20. Lovell, 'Soviet Russia's Older Generation', p. 281.
21. Hosking, *The Awakening of the Soviet Union*, p. 28.
22. Lincoln, *The Conquest of a Continent*, pp. 402–3.
23. Kutsev, *Novye goroda*, p. 97.
24. Kuksanova, *Sotsial'no-bytovaia infrastruktura Sibiri*, p. 141.
25. Kerblay, *Modern Soviet Society*, pp. 119, 123.
26. Kelly, '"Good Night, Little Ones": Children in the "Last Soviet Generation"'.
27. *Materialy po istorii Vladivostoka*, vol. 2, p. 136.
28. *Istoricheskaia entsiklopediia Sibiri*, vol. 3, p. 361.
29. Cherkaz'ianova, *Shkol'noe obrazovanie rossiiskikh nemtsev*, pp. 181, 251, 256.
30. Josephson, *New Atlantis Revisited: Akademgorodok, the Siberian City of Science*, on which this section is based.
31. Hosking, *The Awakening of the Soviet Union*, pp. 45, 52.
32. Moskovskii, Usupov, *Formirovanie gorodskogo naseleniia Sibiri*, pp. 30–1.
33. Kerblay, *Modern Soviet Society*, p. 43.
34. Ibid., p. 17.
35. *Detstvo, opalennoe voinoi*, pp. 87–110.
36. Ibid., pp. 224–6.
37. *The Women of Izmaelovka*, pp. 47, 51.
38. *Tomskie zhenshchiny XX vek*, pp, 121–5
39. *The Women of Izmaelovka*, p. 67.
40. Davis, *A Long Walk to Church*, pp. 33, 44, 54.
41. McCauley, *Khrushchev and the Development of Soviet Agriculture: The Virgin Lands Programme*.
42. Pohl, *The Virgin Lands between Memory and Forgetting*.
43. Forsyth, *A History of the Peoples of the Siberia*, pp. 283–7, on which this section is largely based.
44. Jordan, Jordan-Bychkov, *Siberian Village: Land and Life in the Sakha Republic*.
45. Quoted in Slezkine, *Arctic Mirrors*, p. 242.
46. Humphrey, *Karl Marx Collective*, p. 410.

Chapter Sixteen: The New Siberia

1. Yeremei Aipin, 'And So Dies my Clan', in *The Way of Kinship: An Anthology of Native Siberian Literature*, p. 58.
2. Stephan, *The Russian Far East: A History*, p. 199.
3. Websites give the population of Siberia and the Far East today around 40 million. A figure of 32 million is based on the 1989 census and includes historic Siberia, including the current administrative regions of the Far East and also the Tiumen region which is now part of the Urals administration.

4. Bradshaw, *The Russian Far East and Pacific Asia: Unfulfilled Potential*, p. 81.
5. *Est' takoi poselok Kysyl-Syr'*, p. 620.
6. *The Women of Izmaelovka*, p. 103.
7. Jordan, Jordan-Bychkov, *Siberian Village: Land and Life in the Sakha Republic*.
8. Rethmann, *Tundra Passages: History and Gender in the Russian Far East*.
9. Aipin, 'And So Dies my Clan', p. 56.
10. Hill, 'Siberia: Russia's Economic Heartland and Daunting Dilemma', pp. 324–31, on whose analysis this paragraph is based.
11. Quoted in *The Russian Journal*, no. 436, 13 September 2002.
12. 'Roman Abramovich: Engineer, Billionaire and Governor of Chukotka Region', www.engology.com/eng5abramovich.htm.
13. Alexseev, 'Chinese Migration in the Russian Far East: Security Threats and Incentives for Co-operation in Primorskii Krai', pp. 319–30.
14. *Religiia i vlast' na dal'nem vostoka Rossii*, p. 364.
15. *The Women of Izmaelovka*, p. 10.
16. Aipin, 'And So Dies my Clan', p. 63.
17. Stewart, 'The Khanty: Oil, Gas and the Environment', pp. 25–34.
18. Fondahl, Sirina, 'Rights and Risks: Evenki Concerns Regarding the Proposed Eastern Siberia-Pacific Ocean Pipeline', pp. 115–38.
19. Henry, *Red to Green: Environmental Activity on Post-Soviet Russia*, p. 141.
20. I should like to thank Edward Lucas, of the *Economist* magazine, for drawing my attention to this website.
21. Rasputin, 'Your Siberia and Mine', in *Siberia on Fire*, p. 179.

Bibliography

Unpublished Primary Sources

Edinburgh: National Library of Scotland

MS 8985, Scottish Missionary Society papers.

Irkutsk: Gosudarstvennyi arkhiv Irkutskoi oblasti (GAIO)

Fond 24, opis' 3, delo 90, papers on state convicts.
Fond 534, opis' 1, delo 1, Office of the Balagan Department (Buriats) papers.

Khabarovsk: Gosudarstvennyi arkhiv Khabarovskogo kraia (GAKhK)

Fond И-2, opis' 1, delo 1, delo 1A, delo 7, papers of the Priamur section of the Imperial Russian Geographical Society.
Fond И-282, opis' 1, delo 1, Administration of the Ussuri State Railways papers, 1899.

Krasnoiarsk: Gosudarstvennyi arkhiv Krasnoiarskoi oblasti (GAKO)

Fond 592: opis' 1, delo 216; opis' 2, delo 21, Krasnoiarsk Clerical Board papers.
Fond 812: opis' 1, delo 64, delo 147, Tobol'sk Clerical Board papers.

Moscow: Rossiiskii gosudarstvennyi arkhiv drevnikh aktov (RGADA)

Fond 16, opis' 1, delo 386, Cabinet Office papers.
Fond 20, opis' 1, delo 304, recruit levy papers.
Fond 24, opis' 1, delo 65, papers of the Siberian Office.
Fond 214, opis' 5, delo 632, delo 927, delo 1413, delo 2439, delo 2627, papers of the Siberian Office.
Fond 259, opis' 1, delo 4222, First Department of the Senate papers.
Fond 298, opis' 1, delo 17, delo 33, papers of the Chancellery of the Siberian factories.
Fond 1096, opis' 1, delo 39, delo 51, delo 56, Gizhiga fort papers.

Moscow: Rossiiskii gosudarstvennyi voenno-istoricheskii arkhiv (RGVIA)

Fond 14808, opis' 1, delo 7, delo 10, delo 13, delo 44, delo 47, delo 71, delo 169, Gizhiga fort papers.

Omsk: Gosudarstvennyi arkhiv Omskoi oblasti (GAOO)

Fond 2, opis' 1, delo 194, delo 356, Governor-General of Siberia papers.
Fond 3, opis' 1, delo 202, delo 295, delo 356, delo 512, delo 514, delo 736, delo 557, delo 901, delo 1563; opis' 4, delo 6330, delo 6923, Main Administration of Western Siberia papers.

Tomsk: Gosudarstvennyi arkhiv Tomskoi oblasti (GATO)

Fond 1, opis' 1, delo 173, Tomsk Criminal Court papers.
Fond 3, opis' 1, delo 157; opis' 2, delo 782; opis' 2, delo 6271; opis' 4, delo 6; opis' 6, delo 63; opis' 11, delo 726; opis' 19, delo 515; opis' 20, delo 20; opis' 44, delo 92; opis' 48, delo 2, Tomsk Provincial Board papers.
Fond 104, opis' 1, delo 51, Tomsk Town Police Board papers.
Fond 127, opis' 1, delo 1083, Tomsk Town Duma papers.
Fond 264, opis' 1, delo 6, Kolyvan' Clerical Board papers.

Published Primary Sources

12 soldatskikh pesen, St Petersburg, 1898.
Anon. *A New and Exact Description of Moscovy*, London, 1698.
Armstrong, T. (ed.) *Yermak's Campaign in Siberia*, London, 1975.
Assonov, V. I. *V tylu armii. Kaluzhskaia guberniia v 1812 god*, Kaluga, 1912.
Avvakum. *The Life of the Archpriest Avvakum* [by himself], transl. J. Harris, H. Mirrlees, London, 1963.
Azadovskii, M. K. *Stranitsy istorii Dekabrizma*, Irkutsk, 1991.
Balmasov, S. S. *Krasnyi terror na vostoke Rossii v 1918–1922 gg.*, Moscow, 2006.
Bigland, E. *The Key to the Russian Door*, London, 1942.
Bol'sheviki zapadnoi Sibiri v bor'be za sotsialisticheskuiu revoliutsiu, Novosibirsk, 1957.
Bor'ba za vlast' sovetov v Irkutskoi gubernii (1918–1920 gg.). Sbornik dokumentov, Irkutsk, 1959.
Boulay, J. de. *Travels through Spitzbergen, Siberia, Russia Etc*, n.p., n.d. [1820].
Chappe d'Auteroche, J. B. *A Journey into Siberia*, London, 1770.
Cochrane, J. D. *Narrative of a Pedestrian Journey through Russia and Siberian Tartary*, London, 1824.
Cottrell, C. H. *Recollections of Siberia in the Years 1840 and 1841*, London, 1842.
Coxe, W. *Travels into Poland, Russia, the Krimea, the Caucasus and Georgia*, 2 vols, London, 1825.
Crull, J. *The Ancient and Present State of Muscovy*, London, 1698.
Detstvo, opalennoe voinoi, ed. G. N. Ermolina et al., Krasnoiarsk, 2011.
Dmytryshyn, B. (ed.). *Russia's Conquest of Siberia: Three Centuries of Russian Eastward Expansion, 1558–1700*, vol. 1, Portland, OH, 1985.
Dobell, P. *Travels in Kamchatka and Siberia, with a Narrative of a Resident in China*, vol. 1, London, 1830.
Dostoevsky, F. *Memoirs from the House of the Dead*, transl. J. Coulson, Oxford, 2008.
Downs, E. M. 'Trade and Empire: Merchant Networks, Frontier Commerce and the State in Western Siberia, 1644–1728', PhD thesis, Stanford, CA, 2007.
Est' takoi poselok Kysyl-Syr', Iakutsk, 2006.
Fedorov, V. A. *Memuary Dekabristov: Severnoe obshchestvo*, Moscow, 1981.
Fisher, R. H. (ed.). *The Voyage of Semen Dezhnev in 1648*, London, 1981.
Fraser, J. F. *The Real Siberia*, London, 1902.
Frierson, C. A., Vilensky, S. S. *Children of the Gulag*, New Haven, CT, London, 2010.
Geldern, J. von, Stites, R. (eds). *Mass Culture in Soviet Russia*, Bloomington, IN, 1995.
Georgi, J. G. *Russia: or A Compleat Historical Account of All the Nations Which Compose That Empire*, vol. 1, London, 1780.
Gheith, J. M., Jolluck, K. R. *Gulag Voices: Oral Histories of Soviet Incarceration and Exile*, Basingstoke, 2011.
Gibson, J. R. *Russian California*, 2 vols, Hakluyt Society, London, forthcoming.
Ginzburg, E. *Within the Whirlwind*, London, 1979.
Givens, R. D. *Servitors or Seigneurs: The Nobility and the Eighteenth-Century Russian State*, PhD, University of California, Berkeley, 1975.

Gogol, N. *Plays and Petersburg Tales*, transl. C. English, Oxford, 1995.

Golder, F. A. (ed.). *Bering's Voyages*, 2 vols, New York, 1922.

Gorod u Krasnogo Iaga: Dokumenty i materialy po istorii Krasnoiarska XVII–XVIII vv., Krasnoiarsk, 1981.

Grazhdanskaia voina na dal'nem vostoke (1918–1922): Vospominaniia veteranov, Moscow, 1973.

Herzen, A. *My Past and Thoughts: The Memoirs of Alexander Herzen*, transl. C. Garnett, London, 1968.

Ides, E. Y. *Three Years Travels from Moscow Over-land to China*, London, 1706.

Istoriia industrializatsii zapadnoi Sibiri (1926–1941 gg.), Novosibirsk, 1967.

Istoriia Iugry v dokumentakh iz Tomska, Tomsk, 2009.

Iz istorii Omska (1716–1917 gg.): Ocherki, dokumenty, materialy, Omsk, 1967.

'Iz putevykh zapisok pravoslavnogo missionera', *Dukhovnaia beseda*, 1858, no. 27, vol. 3, pp. 39–66.

Jefferson, R. L. *Roughing It in Siberia with Some Account of the Trans-Siberian Railway*, London, 1897.

Kennan G. *Siberia and the Exile System*, New York, 1891.

Kodinskii (Kondinskii) Sviato-Troitskii monastyr' v 1-oi polovine XVIII veka, Tiumen', 2003.

Kollektivizatsiia sibirskoi derevni ianvar'–mai 1930 g., Novosibirsk, 2009.

Korb, J.-G. *Diary of an Austrian Secretary of Legation at the Court of Czar Peter the Great*, vol. 1, London, 1863.

Krasheninnikov, S. P. *Explorations of Kamchatka, 1735–1741*, transl. E. A. P. Crownhart-Vaughan, Portland, OH, 1972.

Kudrizhinskii, M. A. 'Vladivostok v 1905 g. Iz nabliudenii ochedvidtsa', *Minuvshie gody*, 1908, 4, pp. 17–55.

Latimer, R. S. *Dr Baedeker and his Apostolic Work in Russia*, London, 1907.

Lesseps, J.-B.-B., Baron de. *Travels in Kamtschatka during the Years 1787 and 1788*, London, 1790.

Lipper, E. *Eleven Years in Soviet Prison Camps*, London, 1971.

Marsden, K. *On Sledge and Horseback to Outcast Siberian Lepers*, London, 1891.

Massovye agrarnye pereseleniia na vostok Rossii, Novosibirsk, 2010.

Materialy po istorii Vladivostoka, 2 vols, Vladivostok, 1960.

Meakin, A. M. B. *A Ribbon of Iron*, London, 1901.

Müller, G. F. *Conquest of Siberia and the History of the Transactions, Wars and Commerce etc. Carried On between Russia and China*, London, 1842.

Nemtsy v Sibiri: Sbornik dokumentov i materialov po istorii nemtsev v Sibiri. 1895–1917, ed. P. P. Vibe, Omsk, 1999.

Norman, H. *All the Russians*, London, 1902.

'Opis' 1000 del Kazach'iago otdela', *Trudy Orenburgskoi uchenoi arkhivnoi komissii*, 24, 1913.

Organizatsiia samoupravleniia v Tobol'skoi gubernii (vtoraia polovina XIX–nachalo XX vv.), Tiumen', 1995.

Parkinson, J. *A Tour of Russia, Siberia, and the Crimea 1792–1794*, London, 1971.

Paderin, A. 'Zapiski Sibiriaka', *Istoricheskii vestnik*, vol. 78, no. 9, 1898, pp. 925–37.

Polnoe sobranie zakonov Rossiiskoi imperii, series 1 and 2, St Petersburg, 1830, 1881.

Poslednie dni Kolchakovshchiny, Moscow and Leningrad, 1926.

Prei [Prey], E. L. *Pis'ma iz Vladivostoka 1894–1930*, Vladivostok, 2011.

Pushkin, A. S. *The Complete Prose Tales of Alexander Sergeyevich Pushkin*, transl. G. R. Aitkin, London, 1978.

Putilov, N. 'Letopis' Usinskoi missii', *Sibirskii arkhiv*, 1914, nos 7–8, pp. 324–52.

Rasputin, V. *Farewell to Matyora*, transl. A. W. Bouis, Evanston, IL, 1991.

Rasputin, V. *Siberia on Fire: Stories and Essays by Valentin Rasputin*, transl. G. Mikkelson, M. Winchell, De Kalb, IL, 1989.

Revoliutsionnoe dvizhenie v Zabaikal'e 1905–1907 gg., Chita, 1955.

Safronov, S. A. *Stolypinskaia agrarnaia reforma i ee vliianie na khoziaistvennoe razvitie vostochnoi Sibiri v 1906–1917 gg.*, Krasnoiarsk, 2006.

Sbornik starinnykh bumag, khraniashchikhsia v muzee P. I. Shchukina, vol. 8, Moscow, 1901.

Seebohm, H. *The Birds of Siberia*, vol. 2, *The Enisei*, London, 1901.

Shakovsko, A. 'Mnenie o sposobakh prodovol'stviia zhitelei Okhotskago i Gizhiginskago uezdov', *Severnyi arkhiv*, 1823, no. 4, pp. 45–52.

Shteingel', V. I. *Sochineniia i pis'ma*, vol. 1, Irkutsk, 1985.

Sibirskie pereseleniia, vol. 3, *Osvoenie Verkhnego Priirtysh'ia vo vtoroi polovine XVII–nachale XX vv.*, Novosibirsk, 2010.

Solzhenitsyn, A. (ed.). *Voices from the Gulag*, Evanston, IL, 2010.

Speranskii, M. M. *Pis'ma k docheri*, Novosibirsk, 2002.

Steller's History of Kamchatka, transl. M. Engle, K. Willmore, Fairbanks, AK, 2000.

Tol', F. G. 'Vospominaniia o vostochnoi Sibiri', *Vek*, 1861, no. 30, pp. 919–24, no. 32, pp. 977–81, no. 34, pp. 1025–31.

Tomskie zamorozki Khrushchevskoi ottepeli (sbornik dokumentov i materialov), Tomsk, 2010.

Tomskie zhenshchiny XX vek. Sbornik dokumentov i materialy, Tomsk, 2003.

Turner, S. *A Record of Travel, Climbing and Exploration*, London, 1905.

Watrous, S. D. (ed.). *John Ledyard's Journey through Russia and Siberia 1787–1788*, Madison, MI, London, 1966.

The Way of Kinship: An Anthropology of Native Siberian Literature, transl. A. Vaschenko, C. C. Smith, Minneapolis, WI, London, 2010.

Wenyon, C. *Four Thousand Miles across Siberia on the Great Post-Road*, London, 1909.

Wilmot, M. and Wilmot, C. *The Russian Journals of Martha and Catherine Wilmot*, London, 1934.

The Women of Izmaelovka: A Soviet Collective Farm in Siberia, transl. A. Vinogradov, A. Pleysier, Lanham, MD, 2007.

Za sovety bez kommunistov: Krest'ianskoe vosstanie v Tiumenskoi gubernii. Sbornik dokumentov, Novosibirsk, 2000.

Secondary Sources

Akimov, Iu. G. *Severnaia Amerika i Sibir' v kontse XVI–seredine XVIII v. Ocherk sravnitel'noi istorii kolonizatsii*, St Petersburg, 2010.

Akishin, M. O. *Politicheskoe gosudarstvo i Sibirskoe obshchestvo epokha Petra Velikago*, Novosibirsk, 1998.

Akishin, M. O. *Rossiiskii absoliutizm: Upravlenie Sibiri XVIII veka*, Novosibirsk, 2003.

Aleksandrov, V. A. *Rossiia na dal'nevostochnykh rubezhakh (vtoraia polovina XVII v.)*, Khabarovsk, 1984.

Aleksandrov, V. A. *Russkoe naselenie Sibiri XVII–nachala XVIII v. (Eniseiskii krai)*, Moscow, 1964.

Alexeev, A. 'Chinese Migration in the Russian Far East: Security Threats and Incentives for Co-operation in Priamurskii Krai', in J. Thornton, C. E. Ziegler (eds), *Russia's Far East: A Region at Risk*, Seattle, WA, London, 2002, pp. 319–30.

Anan'ev, D. A. et al. (eds). *'Novye zemli' i osvoenie Sibiri v XVII -XIX vv. Ocherki istorii i istoriografii*, Novosibirsk, 2006.

Anan'ev, D. A. *Voevodskoe upravlenie Sibiri v XVIII veke*, Novosibirsk, 2005.

Appelbaum, A. *Gulag: A History*, London, 2003.

Asal'khanov, I. A. *Sel'skoe khoziaistvo Sibiri kontsa XIX–nachala XX vv.*, Novosibirsk, 1975.

Baindin, V. I. 'Vliianie politicheskikh ssyl'nykh na soldatskie massy v Sibiri v gody pervoi rossiiskoi revoliutsii', in *Politicheskaia ssylka i revoliutsionnoe dvizhenie v Rossii konets XIX–nachalo XX v.*, Novosibirsk, 1988, pp. 89–98.

Bakhaev, V. P. *Obshchestvenno-prosvetitel'skaia i kraevedcheskaia deiatel'nost' Dekabristov v Buriatii*, Novosibirsk, 1980.

Balzer, M. M. (ed.). *Russian Traditional Culture: Religion, Gender, and Customary Law*, New York, London, 1992.

Balzer, M. M. *The Tenacity of Ethnicity: A Siberian Saga in Global Perspective*, Princeton, NJ, 1999.

Baron, S. H. 'Thrust and Parry: Anglo-Russian Relations in the Muscovite North', *Oxford Slavonic Papers*, 21, 1988, pp. 19–40.

Bassin, M. *Imperial Visions: Nationalist Imagination and Geographical Expansion in the Russian Far East, 1840–1865*, Cambridge, 1999.

Bassin, M. 'Inventing Siberia: Visions of the Russian East in the Early Nineteenth Century', *American Historical Review*, 96, 1991, pp. 763–94.

Bawden, C. R. *Shamans, Lamas and Evangelicals: The English Missionaries in Siberia*, London, 1985.

Beer, D. 'The Exile, the Patron, and the Pardon: The Voyage of the *Dawn* (1877) and the Politics of Punishment in the Age of Nationalism and Empire', *Kritika*, 14, 2013, pp. 5–30.

Belimov, I. T. *Zheleznodorozhnyi proletariat Sibiri v revoliutsii 1905–1907 gg.*, Novosibirsk, 1967.

Bell, W. T. 'Was the Gulag an Archipelago? De-convoyed Prisons and Porous Borders in the Maps of Western Siberia', *Russian Review*, 72, 2013, pp. 116–41.

Belous, B. S. 'O roli iaponskikh pereselentsev v razvitii ekonomiki Priamur'ia vo vtoroi polovine XIX v.', in *Tret'ie gorodikovskoe chtenie*, Khabarovsk, 2001, pp. 40–3.

Berdnikov, L. P., Lonina, S. L. *Ot denezhnoi kladovoi do Ministerstva Finansov*, Krasnoiarsk, 2009.

Bessonov, V. A., Milovidov, B. P. 'Voennoplennye poliaki 1812–1814', in *Epokha 1812 goda: Issledovaniia. Istochniki. Istoriografiia*, 7, Moscow, 2008, pp. 134–88.

Bisher, J. *White Terror: Cossack Warlords of the Trans-Siberian*, London and New York, 2005.

Black, J. L. 'Opening Up Siberia: Russia's Window on the East', in Wood, *The History of Siberia*, pp. 57–68.

Boiko, V. P. *Kupechestvo zapadnoi Sibiri v kontse XVIII–XIX vv.*, Tomsk, 2009.

Boiko, V. P., Sitnikova, E. V. *Sibirskoe kupechestvo i formirovanie arkhitekturnogo oblika goroda Tomska v XIX–nachala XX vv.*, Tomsk, 2008.

Bolonev, F. F. *Staroobriadtsy zabaikal'ia XVIII–XX vv.*, Novosibirsk, 1994.

Bol'shakov, V. N. *Ocherki istorii rechnogo transporta Sibiri XIX vek*, Novosibirsk, 1991.

Borzunov, V. F. *Proletariat Sibiri i Dal'nego Vostoka nakanune pervoi russkoi revoliutsii*, Moscow, 1965.

Bradshaw, M. J. *The Russian Far East and Pacific Asia: Unfulfilled Potential*, Richmond, Surrey, 2001.

Brefogle, N. B., Shrader, A. M., Sunderland, W. (eds). *Peopling the Periphery: Borderland, Colonization in Eurasian History*, London, 2009.

Bulygin, Iu. S. 'Nekotorye voprosy kul'tury pripisnoi derevni Kolyvan'-Voskresenskikh gornykh zavodov XVII v.', in *Krest'ianstvo Sibiri XVIII–nachala XX vv.*, Novosibirsk, 1975, pp. 64–74.

Bushkovitch, P. *Religion and Society in Russia: The Sixteenth and Seventeenth Centuries*, New York and Oxford, 1992.

Bykonia, G. F. *Russkoe nepodatnoe naselenie vostochnoi Sibiri v XVIII–XIX vv. Formirovanie voenno-biurokraticheskogo dvorianstva*, Krasnoiarsk, 1985.

Bykonia, G. F. *Zaselenie russkimi prieniseiskogo kraia v XVII v.*, Novosibirsk, 1981.

Byt i iskusstvo russkogo naseleniia vostochnoi Sibiri, vol. 2, Zaibaikal'e, Novosibirsk, 1975.

Castells, M., Kiselyova, E. 'Russian Federalism and Siberian Regionalism, 1990–2000', *City*, 4, 2000, pp. 175–98.

Cherkaz'ianova, I. V. *Shkol'noe obrazovanie rossiiskikh nemtsev*, St Petersburg, 2004.

Chikachev, A. G. *Russkie na Indigirke*, Novosibirsk, 1990.

Christie, I. R. *The Benthams in Russia, 1780–1791*, Oxford, 1993.

Collins, D. N. 'Plans for Railway Development in Siberia, 1857–1890: An Aspect of Tsarist Colonialism?', *Sibérie II, questions sibériennes*, Paris, 1995, pp. 149–61.

Collins, D. N. 'Sexual Imbalance in Frontier Communities: Siberia and the New France', *Sibirica*, 3, 2003, pp. 162–85.

Coquin, F.-X. *La Sibérie: Peuplement et immigration paysanne au XIXe siècle*, Paris, 1969.

Crews, R. D. *For Prophet and Tsar: Islam and Empire in Russia and Central Asia*, London, 2006.

Crummey, R. O. *The Old Believers and the World of the Antichrist: The Vyg Community and the Russian State 1694–1855*, Madison, MI, London, 1970.

Damashek, L. M. *Iasachnaia politika tsarizma v Sibiri v XIX–nachale XX veka*, Irkutsk, 1983.

Damashek, L. M. 'Russkaia tserkov' i narody Sibiri v pervoi polovine XIX veka', in *Sotsial'no-ekonomicheskoe razvitie Sibiri XIX–XX vv.*, Irkutsk, 1976, pp. 39–45.

Datsushen, V. G. *Kitaitsy v Sibiri v XVII–XX vv.: Problema migratsii i adaptatsii*, Krasnoiarsk, 2008.

Datsyshen [Datsushen], V. G. 'Japanese Deportees and Prisoners of War in Siberia, 1904–05', in J. W. M. Chapman, I. Chihara, *Rethinking the Russo-Japanese War, 1904–05*, vol. 2, Folkestone, Kent, 2007, pp. 232–40.

Davis, N. *A Long Walk to Church: A Contemporary History of Russian Orthodoxy*, Boulder, OH, 1995.

Davletbaev, B. S. *Krest'ianskaia reforma 1861 v Bashkirii*, Moscow, 1983.

Diment, G., Slezkine Y. (eds). *Between Heaven and Hell: The Myth of Siberia in Russian Culture*, New York, 1993.

Divin, V. A. *The Great Russian Navigator A. I. Chicherin*, transl. R. H. Fisher, Fairbanks, AK, 1993.

Dmitr'ev, A. V. *Voiska 'novogo stroia' v Sibiri vo vtoroi polovine XVII veka*, Novosibirsk, 2008.

Dmitr'ev-Mamonov, A. I. *Dekabristy v zapadnoi Sibiri: Istoricheskii ocherk*, St Petersburg, 1905.

Dolgikh, A. 'Ssylka krest'ian na poselenie v Sibir' po vole pomeshchikov v zakonodatel'stve Rossiiskoi imperii', *Rossiiskaia istoriia*, 3, 2013, pp. 74–84.

Dulov, A. V. *Petrashevtsy v Sibiri*, Irkutsk, 1996.

Dunaevskii, V. A. 'Otechestvennaia voina 1812 g. i Sibir'', *Voprosy istorii*, 1983, no. 8, pp. 98–102.

Emel'ianov, H. F. *Gorod Tomsk v feodal'nuiu epokhu*, Tomsk, 1984.

Engelstein, L. *Castration and the Heavenly Kingdom: A Russian Folktale*, Ithaca, NY, London, 1999.

Eremin, I. A. *Tomskaia guberniia kak tylovoi raion Rossii v gody Pervoi Mirovoi Voiny (1914–1918 gg.)*, Barnaul, 2005.

Etkind, A. *Internal Colonization: Russia's Imperial Experience*, Cambridge, 2011.

Etnografiia russkogo krest'ianstva Sibiri XVII–seredina XIX vv., Moscow, 1981.

Fisher, R. H. *The Russian Fur Trade, 1500–1700*, Berkeley, CA, 1943.

Fitzpatrick, S. *Everyday Stalinism*, Oxford, 1999.

Fomenkova, V. M. 'Pol'skie revoliutsionery XIX v. na Viatskoi zemle', in *Politicheskaia ssylka i revoliutsionnoe dvizhenie v Rossii konets XIX–nachalo XX v.*, Novosibirsk, 1988, pp. 180–8.

Fondahl, G., Sirina, A. 'Rights and Risks: Evenki Concerns Regarding the Proposed Eastern Siberia-Pacific Ocean Pipeline', *Sibirica*, 5, 2006, pp. 115–38.

Forsyth, J. *A History of the Peoples of Siberia: Russia's North Asian Colony, 1581–1990*, Cambridge, New York, 1992.

Forsyth, J. 'The Siberian Native People before and after the Russian Conquest', in Wood (ed.), *The History of Siberia*, pp. 69–91.

Foust, C. M. *Rhubarb: The Wondrous Drug*, Princeton, NJ, 1992.

Frost, O. *Bering: The Russian Discovery of America*, New York, London, 2004.

Gatrell, P. *Russia's First World War: A Social and Economic History*, Harlow, 2005.

Gentes, A. A. *Exile, Murder and Madness in Siberia, 1823–1861*, Basingstoke, 2010.

Gentes, A. A. *Exile to Siberia, 1590–1822*, Basingstoke, 2008.

Gentes, A. A. '"Licentious Girls" and Frontier Domestication: Women and Siberian Exile from the Late 16th Century to the Early 19th', *Sibirica*, 3, 2003, pp. 3–20.

Gentes, A. A. 'Siberian Exiles and the 1863 Polish Insurrectionists according to Russian Sources', *Jahrbücher für Geschichte Osteuropas*, 51, 2003, pp. 197–217.

Gentes, A. A. 'Towards a Demography of Children in the Tsarist Siberian Exile System', *Sibirica*, 5, 2006, pp. 1–23.

Geraci, R. P., Khodarkovsky, M. (eds). *Of Religion and Empire: Missions, Conversions, and Tolerance in Tsarist Russia*, Ithaca, NY, 2001.

Gibson, J. R. *Feeding the Fur Trade: Provisionment of the Okhotsk Seaboard and Kamchatka Peninsula 1639–1856*, Madison, MI, 1969.

Gibson, J. R. *Imperial Russia in Frontier America: The Changing Geography of Supply of Russian America, 1784–1867*, New York, 1976.

Gibson, J. R. 'Russian Dependence upon the Natives of Alaska', in Starr, *Russia's American Colony*, pp. 77–104.

Gibson, J. R. 'Russian Expansion in Siberia and America: Critical Contrast', in Starr, *Russia's American Colony*, pp. 32–42.

Gibson, J. R. 'Russian Occupation of the Far East 1639–1750', *Canadian Slavonic Papers*, 12, 1970, pp. 60–78.

Gibson, J. R., 'The Sale of Russian America to the United States', in Starr, *Russia's American Colony*, pp. 271–94.

Golikova, S. V., Minenko, N. A., Poborezhnikov, I. V. *Gornozavodskie tsentry i agrarnaia sreda v Rossii: Vzaimodeistviia i protivorechiia*, Moscow, 2000.

Goncharov, Iu. M. *Gorodskaia sem'ia Sibiri vtoroi poloviny XIX–nachalo XX vv.*, Barnaul, 2002.

Goncharov, Iu. M. *Ocherki istorii evreiskikh obshchin zapadnoi Sibiri (XIX–nachalo XX vv.)*, Barnaul, 2005.

Goncharov, Iu. M. *Zhenshchiny Sibiri XIX–nachalo XX vv.*, Barnaul, 2008.

Goryushkin, L. M. 'The Economic Development of Siberia in the Late Nineteenth and Early Twentieth Centuries', *Sibirica*, 2, 2002, pp. 12–20.

Gromyko, M. M. *Trudovye traditsii russkikh krest'ian Sibiri (XVII–pervaia polovina XIX vv.)*, Novosibirsk, 1975.

Gromyko, M. M. *Zapadnaia Sibir' v XVIII v. Russkoe naselenie i zemledel'cheskoe osvoenie*, Novosibirsk, 1965.

Gushchin, N. Ia. *Naselenie Sibiri v XX veke*, Novosibirsk, 1995.

Gushchin, N. Ia. *'Raskulachivanie' v Sibiri (1928–1934)*, Novosibirsk, 1996.

Hartley, J. M. 'Education in the East: The Omsk Asiatic School', forthcoming.

Hartley, J. M. 'Gizhiga: Military Presence and Social Encounters in Russia's Wild East', *Slavonic and East European Review*, 86, 2008, pp. 665–84.

Hartley, J. M. 'Napoleonic Prisoners in Russia', in N. Iu. Erpyleva, M. E. Gashi-Butler (eds), *Forging a Common Legal Destiny: Liber Amicorum in Honour of William E. Butler*, London, 2005, pp. 714–26.

Hartley, J. M. *Russia 1762–1825: Military Power, the State and the People*, Westport, CT, London, 2008.

Hartley, J. M. 'The Russian Empire: Military Encounters and National Identity', in R. Bessel, N. Guyatt, J. Redall (eds), *War, Empire and Slavery, 1770–1830*, Basingstoke, 2010, pp. 218–34.

Hartley, J. M. 'The Russian Recruit', in J. Klein, S. Dixon, M. Franje (eds), *Reflections on Russia in the Eighteenth Century*, Cologne, 2001, pp. 32–42.

Hartley, J. M. 'Slaves and Spouses: Russian Settlers and Non-Russians in Siberia', forthcoming.

Hartley, J. M. *A Social History of the Russian Empire, 1650–1825*, Harlow, 1999.

Haywood, A. J. *Siberia: A Cultural History*, Oxford, 2010.

Henry, L. A. *Red to Green: Environmental Activity on Post-Soviet Russia*, Ithaca, NY, London, 2010.

Hill, F. 'Siberia: Russia's Economic Heartland and Daunting Dilemma', *Current History*, October 2004, pp. 324–31.

Hindley, H. S. 'Defending the Periphery: Tsarist Management of Buriat Buddhism', *Russian Review*, 69, 2010, pp. 231–50.

Hosking, G. *The Awakening of the Soviet Union*, London, 1990.

Hosking, G. *Beyond Soviet Realism: Soviet Fiction since Ivan Denisovich*, London, Toronto, New York, Sydney, 1980.

Hughes, J. *Stalin, Siberia and the Crisis of the New Economic Policy*, Cambridge, 1991.

Hughes, J. *Stalinism in a Russian Province: A Study of Collectivization and Dekulakization in Siberia*, Basingstoke, 1996.

Humphrey, C. *Karl Marx Collective: Economy, Society and Religion in a Siberian Collective Farm*, Cambridge, 1983.

Iadrintsev, N. M. *Sibir' kak koloniia*, St Petersburg, 1882.

Il'in, V. I. 'Vzaimootnosheniia gosudarstvennoi vlasti i ofitsial'noi tserkvi so staroverami na Altae v XVII–nachale XX vv.', in *Staroobriadchestvo: Istoriia, kul'tura, sovremennost'*, Moscow, 2003, pp. 43–8.

Il'inykh, V. A. 'Sibirskaia derevniia v period kollektivizatsii (poselok Aleksandrovka Zav'ialovskogo raiona Altaiskogo kraia)', in *Gosudarstvo i obshchestvo Sibiri XVII–XX vekov*, Novosibirsk, 2008, pp. 181–92.

Istoricheskaia entsiklopediia Sibiri, 3 vols, Novosibirsk, 2010.

Istoriia Buriat-Mongol'skoi ASSR, vol. 1, Ulan-Ude, 1954.

Istoriia kul'tury dal'nego vostoka Rossii (XIX v.–1917 g.), Vladivostok, 1991.

Istoriia obshchestvennogo samoupravleniia v Sibiri vtoroi poloviny XIX–nachala XX veka, Novosibirsk, 2006.

Istoriia Sibiri, vol. 2, *Sibir' v sostave feodal'noi Rossii*, Leningrad, 1968.

Istoriia Sibiri, vol. 3, *Sibir' v epokhu kapitalizma*, Leningrad, 1968.

Iushovskii, V. *Eskiz siuzheta (40 etiudov o 400–letnem Tomske)*, Tomsk, 2003.

Ivanov, V. F. *Sotsial'no-ekonomicheskie otnosheniia v Iakutii konets XVII–nachalo XIX vv.*, Novosibirsk, 1992.

Ivonin, A. V. *Goroda zapadnoi Sibiri v poslednei chetverti XVIII–nachale 60-kh. XIX vv.*, Barnaul, 2009.

Ivonin, A. V. *Gorodovoe kazachestvo zapadnoi Sibiri v XVIII–pervoi chetverti XIX vv.*, Barnaul, 1996.

Jordan, B. B., Jordan-Bychkov, T. G. *Siberian Village: Land and Life in the Sakha Republic*, Minneapolis, MI, 2001.

Jordan, P. *Material Culture and Sacred Landscape: The Anthropology of the Siberian Khanty*, New York, Oxford, 2003.

Josephson, P. R. *New Atlantis Revisited: Akademgorodok, the Siberian City of Science*, Princeton, CA, 1997.

Kaufman, A. A. *Krest'ianskaia obshchina v Sibiri: Po mestnym issledovaniiam 1886–1892 gg.*, reprint, Moscow, 2012.

Kelly, C. ' "Good Night, Little Ones": Children in the "Last Soviet Generation"', in S. Lovell (ed.), *Generations in Twentieth-Century Europe*, Basingstoke, 2007, pp. 165–89.

Kerblay, B. *Modern Soviet Society*, London, 1983.

Khobta, A. *Stroitel'stvo Transsiba: Ocherki istorii (konets XIX–nachalo XX vv.)*, Irkutsk, 2010.

Khodarkovsky, M. 'The Conversion of Non-Christians in Early Modern Russia', in Geraci, Khodarkovaky, *Of Religion and Empire: Missions*, pp. 115–43.

Khudiakov, V. N. *Agrarnaia politika tsarizma v Sibiri v poreformennyi period*, Tomsk, 1986.

Kivelson, V. 'Claiming Siberia: Colonial Possession and Property Holding in the Seventeenth and Early Eighteenth Centuries', in Brefogle, *Peopling the Russian Periphery*, pp. 21–41.

Klikushin, M. V. 'Letopis' arestov: Nauchnaia intelligentsiia Sibiri v gody Stalinskikh repressii', in *Diskriminatsiia intelligentsii v posle-revoliutsionnoi Sibiri (1920–30-e gg.)*, Novosibirsk, 1994, pp. 96–110.

Kokoulin, V. G. *Povsednevnaia zhizn' gorozhan Sibiri v voenno-revoliutsionnye gody (iiul' 1914–mart 1921 g.)*, Novosibirsk, 2013.

Kolesnikov, A. D. 'Ssylka i zaselenie Sibiri', in *Ssylka i katorga v Sibiri (XVIII–nachalo XX vv.)*, Novosibirsk, 1975, pp. 38–58.

Komleva, E. V. 'Vliianie kupechestva prieniseiskikh gorodov na gorodskuiu sredu (pervaia polovina XIX v.)', in *Goroda Sibiri XVII–nachala XX vv.*, vol. 2, Barnaul, 2004, pp. 21–32.

Kopylov, A. N. *Kul'tura russkogo naseleniia Sibiri v XVII–XVIII vv.*, Novosibirsk, 1968.

Kopylov, A. N. *Russkie na Enisee v XVII v.*, Novosibirsk, 1965.

Kopylov, A. N. 'Tamozhennaia politika v Sibiri v XVII v.', in *Russkoe gosudarstvo v XVII veke: Sbornik statei*, Moscow, 1961, pp. 330–70.

Kopylov, A. N., Malysheva, M. P., 'Dekabristy i prosveshchenie Sibiri v pervoi polovine XIX v.', in Shatrova, *Dekabristy i Sibir'*, Novosibirsk, 1977, pp. 98–107.

Kotilaine, J. *Russia's Foreign Trade and Economic Expansion in the Seventeenth Century: Windows on the World*, Leiden, 2005.

Krasil'nikov, S. A. 'Marginal'nye gruppy v Sibiri: ikh sotsio-kul'turnye kharakteristiki v 20–30-e gody', in *Sibirskaia provintsiia i tsentr: Kul'turnoe vzaimodeistvie v XX veke*, Novosibirsk, 1997, pp. 87–108.

Krasil'nikov, S. A. (ed.). *Massovye agrarnye pereseleniia na vostok Rossii (konets XIX–seredina XX vv.)*, Novosibirsk, 2010.

Krest'ianstvo Sibiri v epokhu feodalizma, Novosibirsk, 1982.

Krest'ianstvo Sibiri v epokhu kapitalizma, Novosibirsk, 1983.

Kuksanova, N. V. *Sotsial'no-bytovaia infrastruktura Sibiri (1956–1980-e gg.)*, Novosibirsk, 1993.

Kul'sharipov, M. M. *Politika tsarizma v Bashkortostane 1775–1800 gg.*, Ufa, 2003.

Kupriianov, A. I., *Russkii gorod v pervoi polovine XIX veka*, Moscow, 1995.

Kupriianova, I. V. *Staroobriadtsy Altaia v pervoi treti XX veka*, Barnaul, 2010.

Kutsev, G. F. *Novye goroda*, Moscow, 1982.

Lane, C. *Christian Religion in the Soviet Union: A Sociological Study*, London, 1979.

Lantzeff, G. V. *Siberia in the Seventeenth Century: A Study of Colonial Administration*, Berkeley, CA, 1943.

Lantzeff, G. V., Pierce, R. A. *Eastward to Empire: Exploration and Conquest on the Russian Open Frontier to 1750*, Montreal, London, 1973.

Lapshov, I. 'Narodnoe obrazovanie v Sibiri', *Sibirskie voprosy*, 1911, nos 28–9, pp. 30–8.

Lincoln, W. B. *The Conquest of a Continent: Siberia and the Russians*, London, 1994.

Lind, N. O. 'The First Pianist in Okhotsk: New Information on Anna Christina Bering', in *Under Vitus Bering's Command: New Perspectives on the Russian Kamchatka Expedition*, Aarhus, 2003, pp. 51–62.

Lipinskaia V. A. *Starozhily i pereselentsy: Russkie na Altae XVIII–nachalo XX vv.*, Moscow, 1966.

Litovtsyn, 'Zhizn' sibirskikh gorodov', *Sibirskie voprosy*, 44, 1909, pp. 25–31.

Liutsidarskaia, A. A. *Starozhily Sibiri: istoriko-etnograficheskie ocherki XVII–nachalo XVIII v.*, Novosibirsk, 1992.

Lovell, S. 'Soviet Russia's Older Generation', in S. Lovell (ed.), *Generations in Twentieth-Century Europe*, Basingstoke, 2007, pp. 205–26.

McCauley, M. *Khrushchev and the Development of Soviet Agriculture: The Virgin Lands Programme*, London, 1978.

Macey, D. A. J. '"A Wager on History": The Stolypin Agrarian Reforms as Process', in J. Pallot, (ed.), *Transforming Peasants: Society, State and the Peasantry, 1871–1930*, Basingstoke, 1998, pp. 149–73.

Makarov, A. A. *Vlast' i obshchestvo v Sibiri: 1928–1933*, Abakan, 2010.

Malysheva, M. N. 'Iz istorii formirovaniia pedagogicheskikh kadrov grazhdanskikh shkol gorodov zapadnoi Sibiri v kontse XVIII–pervoi polovine XIX v.', in *Goroda Sibiri (epokha feodalizma i kapitalizma)*, Novosibirsk, 1978, pp. 189–211.

Mamsik, T. S. *Krest'ianskoe dvizhenie v Sibiri: Vtoraia chetvert' XIX veka*, Novosibirsk, 1987.

Marginaly v sotsiume. Marginaly kak sotsium. Sibir' (1920–1930-e gody), Novosibirsk, 2004.

Marks, S. M. *Road to Power: The Trans-Siberian Railroad and the Colonization of Asian Russia 1850–1917*, London, Ithaca, NY, New York, 1991.

Martin, J. *Treasure of the Land of Darkness: The Fur Trade and its Significance for Medieval Russia*, Cambridge, 1986.

Martin, V. *Law and Custom in the Steppe: The Kazakhs of the Middle Horde and Russian Colonisation in the Nineteenth Century*, London, 2001.

Matkhanova, N. P. *Vysshaia administratsiia vostochnoi Sibiri v seredine XIX veka*, Novosibirsk, 2002.

Mawdsley, E. *The Russian Civil War*, London, 1987.

Melancon, M. 'The Ninth Circle: The Lena Goldfield Workers and the Massacre of 4 April 1912', *Slavic Review*, 53, 1994, pp. 766–95.

Milovidov, 'Voennoplennie poliaki v Sibiri v 1813–14', in *Otechestvennaia voina 1812 goda: Istochniki. Pamiatniki. Problemy*, Mozhaisk, 2009, pp. 325–59.

Minenko, N. A. *Istoriia kazachestva aziatskoi Rossii*, vol. 1, Ekaterinburg, 1995.

Minenko, N. A. 'K izucheniiu semeinoi etiki Sibirskogo krest'ianstva vtoroi poloviny XVIII v.', in *Krest'ianstvo Sibiri XVIII–nachala XX vv.: Klassovaia bor'ba, obshchestvennoe soznanie i kul'tura*, Novosibirsk, 1975, pp. 75–84.

Minenko, N. A. *Kul'tura russkikh krest'ian zaural'ia XVII–pervaia polovia XIX vv.*, Moscow, 1991.

Minenko, N. A. 'The Living Past: Daily Life and Holidays of the Siberian Village in the Eighteenth and First Half of the Nineteenth Centuries', in Balzer, *Russian Traditional Culture*, pp. 159–224.

Minenko N. A. 'Obshchinyi skhod v zapadnoi Sibiri XVIII–pervoi poloviny XIX vv.', in *Obshchestvennyi byt i kul'tura russkogo naseleniia Sibiri*, Novosibirsk, 1983, pp. 3–48.

Minenko, N. A. *Russkaia krest'ianskaia sem'ia v zapadnoi Sibiri (XVIII–pervoi polovine XIX vv.)*, Novosibirsk, 1979.

Mironova-Shapovalova, N. A. 'Paskhal'nye obriady i obriadovoi fol'klor staroobriadtsev Zabaikal'ia (semeiskikh)', in *Staroobriadchestvo, istoriia, kul'tura, sovremennost'*, Moscow, 2002, pp. 498–507.

Moon, D. *The Russian Peasantry 1600–1930: The World the Peasants Made*, London, New York, 1999.

Moskovskii, A. S., Usupov, V. A. *Formirovanie gorodskogo naseleniia Sibiri (1926–1939)*, Moscow, 1984.

Mukhin, A. A. *Rabochie Sibiri v epokhu kapitalizma (1861–1917 gg.)*, Moscow, 1979.

Mukhortova, N. A. 'Problema material'nogo obespecheniia gorodskogo dukhovenstva Sibiri', in *Voprosy sotsial'no politicheskoi istorii Sibiri (XVIII–XX veka)*, Novosibirsk, 1997, pp. 82–98.

Narodonaselenie Sibiri: Strategii i praktiki mezhkul'turnoi kommunikatsii (XVII–nachalo XX veka). Sbornik statei, Novosibirsk, 2008.

Nedbai, Iu. G. *Istoriia Sibirskogo kazach'ego voiska*, Omsk, 2001.

Nikitin, N. I. *Sluzhilye liudi v zapadnoi Sibiri XVII veka*, Novosibirsk, 1988.

Nikulin, P. F. *Ekonomicheskii stroi krest'ianskogo khoziaistva zapadnoi Sibiri nachala XX v.*, Tomsk, 2009.

Nozrin, G. A, 'Kul'turnaia zhizn' goroda Kainska v XIX–nachale XX vv.', in *Goroda Sibiri*, vol. 2, Barnaul, 2004, pp. 160–77.

Nozrin, G. A. 'Predstavleniia krest'ian Sibiri v nachale XX v. O reorganizatsii obrazovaniia v strane', in *Kul'turnyi obrazovatel'nyi i dukhovnyi potentsial Sibiri*, Novosibirsk, 1997, pp. 74–92.

Ocherki istorii Chukotki s drevneishikh vremen do nashikh dnei, Novosibirsk, 1974.

Ostrovskii, L. K. 'Pol'skie predprinimateli v Sibiri na rubezhe XIX–XX vekov', in *Gosudarstvo i obshchestvo Sibiri XVII–XX vekov*, Novosibirsk, 2008, pp. 12–17.

Pallot, J. *Land Reform in Russia 1906–1917*, Oxford, 1999.

Pavlov, P. N. *Promyshlovaia kolonizatsii Sibiri v XVII v.*, Krasnoiarsk, 1974.

Pereira, N. G. O. 'Regional Consciousness in Siberia before and after October 1917', *Canadian Slavonic Studies*, 30, 1988, pp. 112–33.

Pereira, N. G. O. *White Siberia: The Politics of Civil War*, Montreal, London, Buffalo, NY, 1996.

Pohl, M. *The Virgin Lands between Memory and Forgetting: People and Transformation in the Soviet Union 1954–60*, PhD thesis, University of Indiana (reprint edition), 1999.

Polevoi, B. P. 'The Discovery of Russian America', in Starr, *Russia's American Colony*, pp. 13–31.

Poppe, N. 'The Economic and Cultural Development of Siberia in the Late Nineteenth and Early Twentieth Centuries', in G. Katkov, ed., *Russia Enters the Twentieth Century 1894–1917*, London, 1971, pp. 138–51.

Poshchevskaia, L. P. *Revoliutsionery-raznochintsy v zapadno-sibirskom izgnanii*, Leningrad, 1983.

Postnikov, A. V. 'Geographical Explorations of Russian Orthodox Church Missionaries in the Russian America', *Archives internationales d'histoire des sciences*, 58, 2008, pp. 271–300.

Preobrazhenskii, A. A. *Ural i zapadnaia Sibir' v kontse XVI–nachale XVIII veka*, Moscow, 1972.

Pundani, V. V. *Gosudarstvennaia derevnia zapadnoi Sibiri vo vtoroi polovine XVIII–pervoi polovine XIX v.*, Cheliabinsk, 1984.

Puzanov, V. D. *Voennye faktory russkoi kolonizatsii zapadnoi Sibiri konets XVI–XVII v.*, St Petersburg, 2010.

Rabstevich, V. V. 'Sotsial'nyi sostav organov gorodskogo samoupravleniia zapadnoi Sibiri v 80-kh gg. XVIII–pervoi chetverti XIX v.', in *Istoriia gorodov Sibiri dosovetskogo perioda (XVII–nachalo XX vv.)*, Novosibirsk, 1977, pp. 80–96.

Raeff, M. *Michael Speransky: Statesman of Imperial Russia, 1772–1839*, The Hague, 1958.

Raeff, M. *Siberia and the Reforms of 1822*, Seattle, WA, 1956.

Rafienko, L. S. *Problemy istorii upravleniia i kul'tury Sibiri XVIII–XIX vv.*, Novosibirsk, 2006.

Raizman, D. I. *Ocherki istorii severo-vostoka Rossii v period massovykh repressii (30–50-e XX v.)*, Magadan, 2006.

Reid, A. *The Shaman's Coat: A Native History of Siberia*, New York, 2002.

Reitsh, A. B. *Russia's Peasants in Revolution and Civil War*, Cambridge, 2008.

Religiia i vlast' na dal'nem vostoka Rossii, Khabarovsk, 2001.

Remenev, A. 'Siberia and the Russian Far East in the Imperial Geography of Power', in J. Burbank, M. von Hagen, A. Remenev (eds), *Russian Empire: Space, People, Power 1700–1930*, Bloomington and Indianapolis, 2007, pp. 425–54.

Rethmann, P. *Tundra Passages: History and Gender in the Russian Far East*, University Park, PA, 2001.

Revoliutsionnoe dvizhenie v Sibiri i na dal'nem vostoke, Tomsk, 1965.

Robson, R. R. *Old Believers in Modern Russia*, Dekalb, IL, 1995.

Rogachevskii, A. 'The Representation of Bribery in Nineteenth-Century Russian Literature', in S. Lovell, A. Ledeneva, A. Rogachevskii (eds), *Bribery and Blat in Russia: Negotiating Reciprocity from the Middle Ages to the 1990s*, Basingstoke, 2000, pp. 114–40.

Rol' gosudarstsva v osvoenii Sibiri i verkhnego Priirtysh'ia v XVII–XX vv., Novosibirsk, 2009.

Romanova, V. V. *Evrei na dal'nem vostoke Rossii II pol. XIV v.–I chet. XX v.*, Khabarovsk, 2000.

Roshchevskaia, L. P. *Revoliutsionery-raznochintsy v zapadnosibirskom izgnanii*, Leningrad, 1983.

Russkie starozhily i pereselentsy Sibiri v istoriko-etnograficheskikh issledovaniiakh, Novosibirsk, 2002.

Ryan and W. F. *The Bathhouse at Midnight: An Historical Survey of Magic and Divination in Russia*, Stroud and University Park, PA, 1999.

Safronov, F. G. *Dekabristy v Iakutskoi ssylke*, Iakutsk, 1975.

Safronov, F. G. *Krest'ianskaia kolonizatsiia basseinov Leny i Ilima v XVII veke*, Iakutsk, 1956.

Safronov, F. G. *Russkie krest'iane v Iakutii (XVII–nachalo XX vv.)*, Iakutsk, 1981.

Safronov, F. G. *Russkie na severo-vostoke Azii*, Moscow, 1978.

Safronov, S. A. *Oktiabr' v Sibiri*, Krasnoiarsk, 1962.

Schorkowitz, D. 'The Orthodox Church, Lamanism and Shamanism among the Buriats and Kalmyks, 1825–1925', in Geraci, Khodarkovsky, *Of Religion and Empire*, pp. 201–25.

Schrader, A. M. 'Unruly Felons and Civilizing Wives: Cultivating Marriage in the Siberian Exile System, 1822–60', *Slavic Review*, 66, 2007, pp. 230–56.

Serebrennikov, A. M. 'Gramotnost'' v Sibiri po perepisi 28 ianvaria 1897 goda', *Sibirskie voprosy*, 17, 1907, pp. 15–22.

Serebrennikov, A. M. 'Materialy dlia istorii goroda Tomska', *Sibirskie voprosy*, 1903, no. 6, pp. 59–63, no. 7, pp. 102–9.

Serebrennikov, A. M. 'Materialy dlia istorii razvitiia prosveshcheniia v Sibiri', *Sibirskii nabliudatel'*, 1903, no. 9, pp. 120–5, 138–47.

Shakherov, V. P. *Goroda vostochnoi Sibiri v XVII–pervoi polovine XIX vv. Ocherki sotsial'no-ekonomicheskoi i kul'turnoi zhizni*, Irkutsk, 2001.

Shatrova, G. P. *Dekabristy i Sibir'*, Tomsk, 1962.

Shelegina, O. N. 'Material'naia kul'tura russkogo naseleniia Sibiri v XVIII–XIX vv.: Traditsii i novatsii', in *Ot srednevekov'ia k novomu vremeni etnosotsial'nye protsessy v Sibiri XVII–nachala XX vv. Sbornik nauchnykh trudov*, Novosibirsk, 2005, pp. 313–30.

Shelegina, O. N. *Ocherki material'noi kul'tury russkikh krest'ian zapadnoi Sibiri (XVIII–pervaia polovina XIX vv.)*, Novosibirsk, 1998.

Shishkin, V. I. *Sibirskaia Vandeia: Vooruzhennoe soprotivlenie kommunisticheskomu rezhimu v 1920 godu*, Novosibirsk, 1997.

Shishkov, V. I. *Sotsialisticheskoe stroitel'stvo v Sibirskoi derevne nov. 1919–mart 1921 gg.*, Novosibirsk, 1985.

Shorokhov, L. P. *Korporativno-votchinnoe zemlevladenie i monastyrskie krest'iane v Sibiri v XVII–XVIII vekakh*, Krasnoiarsk, 1983.

Shorokhov, L. P. 'Uzniki Sibirskikh monastyrei v XVIII veke', in *Ssylka: Obshchestvenno-politicheskaia zhizn' v Sibiri*, Novosibirsk, 1978, pp. 294–307.

Shulman, '"Those Who Hurry to the Far East": Readers, Dreamers and Volunteers', in Brefogle, *Peopling the Periphery*, pp. 213–35.

Shunkov, V. I. *Ocherki po istorii zemledeliia Sibiri (XVII vek)*, Moscow, 1956.

Sibir' v Otechestvennoi Voine 1812 goda, Omsk, 2011.

Sibir' v Sostave Rossiiskoi Imperii, Moscow, 2007.

Sirotkin, V. G. 'Sud'ba plennykh soldat i ofitserov Velikoi Armii v Rossii posle Borodinskogo srazheniia', in *Otechestvennaia voina*, Borodino, 2000, pp. 246–66.

Skrynnikov, R. G. *Sibirskaia ekspeditsiia Ermaka*, Novosibirsk, 1982.

Skubnevskii, V. A. *Urbanizatsionnye protsessy v Sibiri vtoroi poloviny XIX–nachale XX vv.*, Barnaul, 2010.

Skubnevskii, V. A., Goncharov, Iu. M. *Goroda zapadnoi Sibiri vo vtoroi polovine XIX–nachale XX v.*, Barnaul, 2003.

Skubnevskii, V. A., Goncharov, Iu. M. 'Siberian Merchants in the Latter Half of the 19th Century', *Sibirica*, 2, 2002, pp. 21–42.

Slezkine, Y. *Arctic Mirrors: Russia and the Small Peoples of the North*, Ithaca, NY, London, 1994.

Slovtsov, P. A. *Istoriia Sibiri ot Ermaka do Ekateriny II*, Moscow, reprint 2006.

Smele, J. D. *Civil War in Siberia: The Anti-Bolshevik Government of Kolchak*, Cambridge, 1996.

Smith. C. F. *Vladivostok under Red and White Rule: Revolution and Counter-Revolution in the Russian East, 1920–1922*, Seattle, WA, London, 1975.

Smith, J. L. *The First Kamchatka Expedition of Vitus Bering, 1725–1730*, Anchorage, AK, 2002.

Smith, M. B. *Property of Communists: The Urban Housing Program from Stalin to Khrushchev*, DeKalb, IL, 2010.

Smith, S. B. *Captives of Revolution: The Socialist Revolutionaries and the Bolshevik Dictatorship, 1918–1923*, Pittsburgh, PA, 2011.

Sofroneev, P. S. *Iakuty v pervoi polovine XVIII veka*, Iakutsk, 1972.

Sofronov, V. Iu. *Khristianizatsiia Tobol'skogo severa*, Tobol'sk, 2007.

Sofronov, V. Iu. *Tri veka Sibirskogo missionerstva*, vol. 1, Tobol'sk, 2005.

Sokolovskii, I. R. '*Sluzhilye 'inozemtsy' v Sibiri XVII veka (Tomsk, Eniseisk, Krasnoiarsk)*, Novosibirsk, 2004.

Ssorin-Chaikov, N. V. *The Social Life of the State in Subarctic Siberia*, Stanford, CA, 2003.

Stalinskii terror v Sibiri 1928–1941, Novosibirsk, 1997.

Starr S. F. (ed.). *Russia's American Colony*, Durham, NC, 1987.

Stephan, J. J. *The Russian Far East: A History*, Stanford, CA, 1966.

Stewart, J. M. 'Discovering a Continent: Early Explorers in Siberia', in *Sibérie II, questions sibériennes*, Paris, 1995, pp. 211–23.

Stewart, J. M. 'The Khanty: Oil, Gas and the Environment', *Sibirica*, 1, 1995, pp. 25–34.

Stites, R. *Serfdom, Society and the Arts in Imperial Russia: The Pleasure and the Power*, New Haven, CT, London, 2005.

Stone, N. *The Eastern Front, 1914–17*, London, 1975.

Sutherland, C. *The Princess of Siberia*, London, 1985.

Tal'skaia, O. S. 'Bor'ba administratsii s vlianiem Dekabristov v zapadnoi Sibiri', in L. M. Goriushkin (ed.), *Ssylka i katorga v Sibiri*, Novosibirsk, 1975, pp. 75–93.

Tal'skaia, O. S. 'Ssyl'nye Dekabristy na gosudarstvennoi sluzhbe v Sibiri', in *Ssylka i obshshestvenno-politicheskaia zhizn' v Sibiri (XVIII–nachalo XX vv.)*, Novosibirsk, 1978, pp. 231–54.

Teriushkov, 'Revoliutsionnoe dvizhenie uchashchikhsia vostochnoi Sibiri v gody pervoi russkoi revoliutsii', in *Predposylki Oktiabrskoi Revoliutsii v Sibiri*, Novosibirsk, 1964, pp. 166–84.

Thorvaldsen, G. 'Swedes in Siberia Diaspora', *Sibirica*, 7, 2008, pp. 47–66.

Tikhonov, T. I. 'Sibirskie evrei, ikh prava i nuzhdy', *Sibirskie voprosy*, 1, 1905, pp. 278–85.

Tkacheva G. A. *Dal'nevostochnoe obshchestvo v gody Velikoi Otechestvennoi Voiny (1941–45)*, Vladivostok, 2010.

Treadgold, D. W. *The Great Siberian Migration: Government and Peasant Resettlement from Emancipation to the First World War*, Princeton, NJ, 1957.

Tsipkin, Iu. N. *Antibol'shevistskie rezhimy na dal'nem vostoke Rossii v period Grazhdanskoi Voiny (1917–1922 gg.)*, Khabarovsk, 2003.

Uchastniki Pol'skogo vosstaniia 1860–1863 gg. v Tobol'skoi ssylke, Tiumen', 1963.

Vagin, V. *Istoricheskie svedeniia o deiatel'nosti Grafa M. M. Speranskogo v Sibiri s 1819 po 1822 god*, vol. 2, St Petersburg, 1872.

Varneck E. 'Siberian Native People after the February Revolution', *Slavic Review*, 21, 1943, pp. 70–88.

Vasilevskii, V. I. *Zaibaikal'skoe kazach'e voiska v gody revoliutsionoi i grazhdanskoi voiny*, Chita, 2007.

Viola, L. *Peasant Rebels under Stalin: Collectivisation and the Culture of Peasant Resistance*, Oxford, 1996.

Vitebsky, P. *The Reindeer People: Living with Animals and Spirits in Siberia*, Boston, MA, New York, 2005.

Volgine, I. V. 'Entrepreneurship and the Siberian Peasant Commune in Late Imperial Russia', in D. J. O'Brien, S. K. Wagren (eds), *Rural Reform in Post-Soviet Russia*, Baltimore, MD, London, 2002, pp. 23–41.

Vvedenskii, A. A. *Dom Stroganovykh v XVI–XVII vekakh*, Moscow, 1962.

Watrous, D. 'The Regionalist Conception of Siberia, 1860–1920', in Diment, Slezkine, *Between Heaven and Hell*, pp. 113–32.

Wood, A. (ed.). *The History of Siberia: From Russian Conquest to Revolution*, London, 1991.

Wood, A. *Russia's Frozen Frontier: A History of Siberia and the Russian Far East, 1581–1991*, London and New York, 2011.

Wood, A. 'Russia's "Wild East": Exile, Vagrancy and Crime in Nineteenth-Century Siberia', in Wood, *The History of Siberia*, pp. 117–38.

Wood, A. *Siberia: Problems and Prospects for Regional Development*, London, New York, Sydney, 1987.

Wood, A. 'Vagrancy and Violent Crime in Siberia: Problems of the Tsarist Exile System', in *Sibérie II, questions sibériennes*, Paris, 1995, pp. 283–93.

Zalkind, E. M. *Prisoedinenie Buriatii k Rossii*, Ulan-Ude, 1958.

Zhenshchina v istorii Urala i Sibiri XVIII–nachale XX v., Ekaterinburg, 2007.

Zheravina, A. N. *Ocherki po istorii propisnykh krest'ian kabinetskogo khoziaistva v Sibiri*, Tomsk, 1985.

Zinov'ev, V. P. 'Ob Oktiabr'skikh sobytiiakh 1905 g. v Tomske', in *Revoliutsiia 1905–1907: Godov i obshchestvennoe dvizhenie v Sibiri i na dal'nem vostoke*, Omsk, 1995, pp. 80–93.

Zinov'ev, V. P. 'Sotsial'no-politicheskii oblik Sibirskogo otriada rabochego klassa Rossii nakanune revoliutsii 1917 gg.', in *Iz istorii sotsial'noi i obshchestvenno-politicheskoi zhizni Sovetskoi Sibiri*, Tomsk, 1992, pp. 13–18.

Zol'nikova, N. D. *Sibirskaia prikhodskaia obshchina v XVIII veke*, Novosibirsk, 1990.

Zuev, A. C. *Prisoedinenie Chukotki k Rossii (vtoraia polovina XVII–XVIII vek)*, Novosibirsk, 2009.

Zykova, V. G., Iakimova, T. V. 'Obshchestvenno-politicheskaia zhizn' Sibirskogo krest'ianstva v 1917 g.', in *Iz istorii sotsial'noi i obshchestvenno-politicheskoi zhizn' Sovetskoi Sibiri*, Tomsk, 1992, pp. 24–45.

Index